This Noble Harbour

A History of the Cromarty Firth

(Photo: *The Scotsman*)

Dr Marinell Ash (1941–1988) was born in California and studied at the universities of California at Santa Barbara, St Andrews and Newcastle upon Tyne. A lecturer in Scottish History at St Andrews University from 1967 to 1972 and producer in the education department of BBC Scotland from 1972 to 1983, she created in 1983 the first public history agency in Scotland, Historical Services (Scotland). She was active in many scholarly organisations including the Society of Antiquaries of Scotland, the Royal Historical Society, the Scottish History Society and the Conference of Scottish Medieval Research, and through her publications, broadcasts and teaching aids encouraged many others in Scottish and North American studies.

This Noble Harbour

A History of the Cromarty Firth

MARINELL ASH

Edited by
JAMES MACAULAY and MARGARET A. MACKAY

CROMARTY FIRTH PORT AUTHORITY, INVERGORDON
IN ASSOCIATION WITH
JOHN DONALD PUBLISHERS LTD, EDINBURGH

ISBN 0 859763 196

A catalogue record for this book is available
from the British Library.

Typeset by Pioneer Associates, Perthshire
Printed and bound in Great Britain by
J. W. Arrowsmith Ltd., Bristol

IN MEMORIAM
MARINELL ASH
1941–1988

By the same author
The Strange Death of Scottish History

Foreword

It was in late 1984 that Cromarty Firth Port Authority first conceived the idea of commissioning a book to draw together the disparate strands of the history of the Firth and its surrounding communities. From the very start the brief was wide and included the geological, social, economic and maritime development of the area. After one or two false starts in the search for a writer, Dr D Stevenson, Director of the Centre for Scottish Studies at Aberdeen University, suggested Dr Marinell Ash, whom he described as 'that rare creature, a free-lance historian with excellent qualifications and wide experience'. Dr Ash responded to our initial enquiry with the vigour and enthusiasm which we were to learn were her special hallmark and by May 1985 agreement had been reached on the scope and methodology of the work. The remainder of 1985 was taken up with the completion of other works in progress by Dr Ash and her endeavours in respect of this book started in earnest in 1986.

Chapter by chapter the drafts arrived until, in March 1987, we heard the dreaded news that Marinell, as we by then knew her, had cancer. The next few months were a terrible battle for Marinell, fighting the effects of chemotherapy, surgery and then radiotherapy. Throughout she remained cheerful and determined — after the radiotherapy commenced she wrote to us 'just so long as it does not involve losing my hair again I really don't mind; it's just begun to grow and I look like a middle-aged skinhead.' Our boat crew have a happy memory of her at this time, when she visited the port and asked to see the entrance of the Firth from seaward 'just to get the feel of it'. They set out in the launch in a stiff breeze to find a high sea running outside the Sutors. The crew tentatively suggested that she might wish to turn back but she would have none of it and, with headscarf tying down a slightly awry wig, she revelled in the wind and the pitching and heaving of the small boat. No ivory towers for Marinell, her history was real and alive and colourful and filled with a relived experience that brought understanding, as well as fact, to her work.

Marinell's long illness, as is so often the case, had its periods of remission when hope was rekindled and she would work on revisions and corrections of this book and other assignments, but sadly she died on 20 December 1988.

There can be no more fitting memorial to Marinell Ash than the completion and publication of this work. We in the Port Authority are proud to have been associated with it and I would wish to thank the literary executors, Dr James

Macaulay and Dr Margaret A. Mackay, for their invaluable assistance and advice.

In closing I would remind the reader that Dr Ash was a professional historian and, as such, held independent views arrived at through her own researches. From the beginning it was explicitly understood that she, and through her the literary executors, had editorial control of the book. The development of Easter Ross over the last twenty-five years has not been without controversy and the views expressed in this respect are those of the author and do not necessarily reflect those of the Port Authority or of the individuals who have been members of the Authority since its inception in 1974.

Duncan J. McPherson
Invergordon, 1991

Preface

The tasks which fell to us as editors, tinged with sadness, for they arose from the early death of a friend, we took on readily for reasons of that friendship. Many people helped to lighten our work and to them we owe particular thanks.

Mr and Mrs Philip Durham of Scotsburn and Mr and Mrs Arthur Munro Ferguson of Novar and Raith provided generous hospitality and much besides. Miss Catherine Cruft, National Monuments Record of Scotland; Mrs Rosemary Mackenzie, Tain; Dr Rosalind K. Marshall, Scottish National Portrait Gallery; and Ms Joyce M. Swinburne, Invergordon Heritage Association, assisted with illustrations as did Mrs George Chamier, Achindunie; Mrs Margaret Gourgey, Invergordon; Graham Watson, Ross and Cromarty District Council; the staff at the Dingwall Museum; and Mrs V. Carvalho, Mackintosh School of Architecture, Glasgow. R. W. Munro, Edinburgh; Ian Mowat, Hull; and David Alston, Cromarty, advised on matters in the text; Ian Campbell gave permission for lines from his song, 'The Gulls o' Invergordon' to be included in Chapter 9. Joanna Bruning and Jane Ryder gave strong support throughout, and this we received as well from Mr John R. Dunthorne, Secretary to the Cromarty Firth Port Authority. Helpful advice came at all times from the staff of John Donald Publishers Ltd.

With the generosity which typified her, Marinell Ash acknowledged in relevant footnotes and elsewhere her debt to many of those who provided her with information or assisted in other ways, but there are others who have made a contribution to this study who are not known to us. We hope that those whose names do not appear individually will understand the circumstances and will accept the warm gratitude which we extend to all who have been involved in this project.

This Noble Harbour is the result of work which Marinell had largely completed at the time of her death. It does not incorporate the findings of research in publications which have appeared since, such as Eric Richards and Monica Clough, *Cromartie: Highland Life 1650–1914* (Aberdeen, 1989) and Leah Leneman, *Fit for heroes?: Land settlement in Scotland after World War I* (Aberdeen, 1989), both certain to be of interest to readers of this book.

James Macaulay and Margaret A. Mackay
Glasgow and Edinburgh, 1991

Photographic Acknowledgements

The following sources of illustrations are acknowledged:

Figs. 1, 7, 8, 15, 18, 29, 32, 34: The Royal Commission on the Ancient and Historical Monuments of Scotland.

Figs. 2, 3, 11, 13, 14, 17, 19, 22 to 28, 30, 31, 36: Dr James Macaulay.

Figs. 4, 5, 16, 59 to 62: Tain Museum.

Fig 6: The National Library of Scotland.

Fig 10: The Scottish Record Office, RHP 45193.

Fig 12: Dr Marinell Ash.

Figs. 20, 35, 38, 40, 42 to 44, 46 to 53, 55 to 57, 63, 64: Invergordon Heritage Association.

Fig 33: Dr Margaret A. Mackay.

Figs. 37, 41, 58: University of St Andrews, Valentine Collection.

Fig 45: The British Library.

Fig 54: The Imperial War Museum.

Figs. 65 to 72: The Cromarty Firth Port Authority and D.G.S. Films Ltd.

The illustration on the front cover is from a painting entitled *Cromarty Bay, from the East. (Cromarty-shire)* by T. Allom, engraved by S. Fisher and reproduced by courtesy of the British National Oil Corporation, 150 St Vincent Street, Glasgow G2 5LJ.

Contents

page

Foreword — vii
Preface — ix
Acknowledgements — x
Abbreviations — xii

1. 'A portion of the geologic day' — 1
2. 'Polish'd with art and agriculture' — 20
3. 'Learned and full of Faith' — 42
4. 'Any man offering . . . to inclose . . . shall be preferred' — 70
5. 'No longer an independent peasantry' — 106
6. 'Cromarty a sort of depôt for the whole' — 143
7. 'This noble harbour' — 175
8. 'The war was a very peculiar thing' — 210
9. 'A kind o' perpetual Hogmanay' — 247

Bibliography — 274
Index — 299

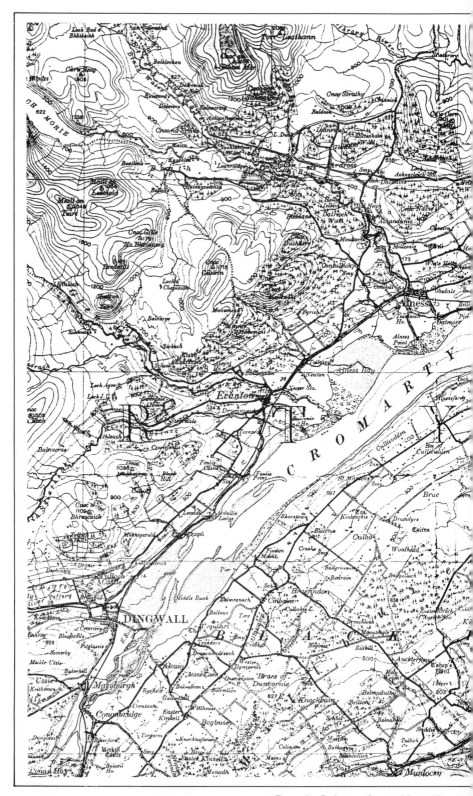

(*From the Ordnance Survey Map of Scotland*

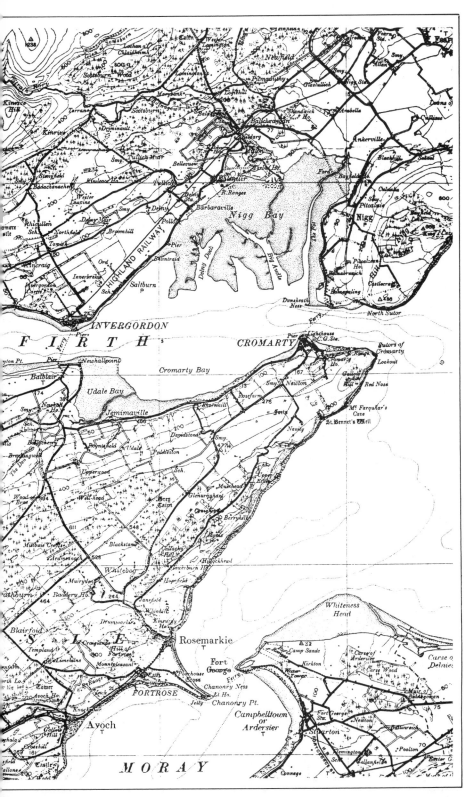

(912. Scale of 2 miles to 1 inch)

Abbreviations

CM	*Celtic Monthly*
Firthlands	J. R. Baldwin (ed.), *Firthlands of Ross and Sutherland*, Edinburgh, 1986.
NLS	National Library of Scotland
NSA	*New Statistical Account of Scotland*
OSA	*Old Statistical Account of Scotland*
PP	*Parliamentary Papers*
R C Book	D. Omand (ed.), *The Ross and Cromarty Book*, Golspie, 1984.
RPC	*Register of the Privy Council of Scotland*
SHR	*Scottish Historical Review*
SHS	*Scottish History Society*
SRO	Scottish Record Office
SS	*Scottish Studies*
TGSI	*Transactions of the Gaelic Society of Inverness*
THASS	*Transactions of the Highland and Agricultural Society of Scotland*
TISSFC	*Transactions of the Inverness Scientific Society and Field Club*

1

'A portion of the geologic day'

One hundred and fifty years ago a lone figure could be seen exploring the headland of the South Sutor and the shores of the Cromarty and Moray Firths. The man was a local stonemason named Hugh Miller, born in 1802 in the ancient burgh of Cromarty. He grew up in a small, traditional community that retained many ancient beliefs in the supernatural and unchancy beings such as brownies and fairies. Some of the stories Hugh Miller heard as a child explained how the landscape itself was created by a race of giants. They were credited with dropping huge stones about the countryside. One woman giant had dropped stones from her creel and formed the Highland mountains that rose at the head of the Cromarty Firth to the west.[1] The Sutors themselves were said to be two giants who had been turned to stone for their wrongdoings and made to stand perpetual guard over the Firth and its lands; another version claimed that two gigantic shoemakers had used the two hills at the entrance to the firth as workbenches — hence their name, The Sutors (shoemakers).

As a boy Hugh Miller relished these stories, but as he grew up he became equally fascinated by the history of the countryside as revealed in its geology and it was from his wanderings in the fields and on the seashores of the Cromarty Firth that the geological history of the area was first established. The Sutors are the oldest features of the landscape, not the workbenches of giant shoemakers but the upthrust of rocks that had been changed by intense geological pressures from soft sandstone into harder sandstone (moine psammite). Trapped against the South Sutor were tilted layers of softer sandstone, the successive beds of long-vanished seas that had once covered the entire area of the Cromarty Firth.

When Hugh Miller had first been apprenticed to the trade of stonemason about 1820 he had worked in a quarry on the south shore of the Cromarty Firth. There he noticed sandstone blocks that still showed the sandy ripples of this ancient seabed on their surface. Later, in the sandstone layers of the walls of Eathie Den to the southwest of Cromarty, he found evidence of the teeming life of this vanished sea in the fossilised remains of millions of increasingly sophisticated marine animals preserved forever in the walls of this narrow, stream-cut valley. He recalled: 'It was the wonders of . . . Eathie . . . that first gave direction and aim to my curiosity.'[2]

Hugh Miller may have established the outlines of the geological history of the Cromarty Firth, but not even he could imagine how immensely old was this part of Scotland. The western part of the old county of Ross along the

Atlantic seaboard and the Hebrides is made up of the oldest of European
rocks — Lewisian gneiss — dating back nearly 3,000 million years in some
areas. The Cromarty Firth itself is somewhat younger: the two Sutors that
guard the Firth are part of an ancient mountain range created between 1,200
and 800 million years ago, during the same cataclysmic period that created
the parallel fault line of the Great Glen, as well as others that run through the
Cromarty Firth. One fault runs through Nigg Bay to the south of Udale Bay,
while the west or Strathglass Fault runs from Dingwall to Tain. Over the
millennia this mountain range was slowly eroded, and particles of soil were
carried east and deposited in the warm and shallow inland sea of which Hugh
Miller found such abundant evidence. Much of this sediment was stained by
iron ore, thus giving it its characteristic colour and name: the 'Old Red
Sandstone' is between 400 and 350 million years old and forms the basic
geology of the region.

The creation of the present-day landscape began about 70 million years
ago, when the climate of Scotland was humid and tropical. The runoff from
frequent warm rains cut the routes of the river valleys of modern Scotland.
Then huge glaciers — some of them nearly two and a half thousand feet thick
— scoured the land during the last European ice age. The weight of the
glaciers pressed the land down, creating drowned river valleys, including that
of the Cromarty Firth. The grinding action of the moving glaciers rounded the
shapes of the hills. Because the Sutors were composed of harder rock they
were more resistant than the surrounding sandstone, although at some point a
glacier cut through this high stone barrier and created the narrow entrance to
the Firth.[3]

Between 13,000 and 10,000 years ago the ice finally retreated, leaving
behind, in outline, the landscape of the present day. Gradually, as the weight
of the glaciers melted away, the land rose, creating the numerous raised
beaches found around the Firth. Initially, the land was barren of plant life but
slowly grasses, shrubs and small trees such as birches, appeared. About 7,000
years ago the land was covered by extensive forests composed of pine, oak,
elm, alder and ash and in these woods there were elk and deer, bear and
wolves.

Against the long geological history, man was a newcomer, as Hugh Miller
well knew: '. . . human history [forms] but a portion of the geologic day that is
passing over us, [it does] not extend into the *yesterday* of the globe, far less
touch the myriads of ages spread out beyond.'[4] The human history of the
Cromarty Firth region began with the arrival of Mesolithic (Middle Stone
Age) people. They came in the same manner as thousands of others have
continued to arrive down to the present day, as seafarers perhaps travelling in
hollowed-out log canoes.

With primitive stone tools the first arrivals hunted animals for food and
clothing. These nomadic hunters may have been responsible for establishing
the basic transport system of the Firth that would survive into modern times:

the ferry crossings and the track over Nigg Sands between Pitcalnie Brae and Meddat. One of their seasonal migration routes was the ancient track from Sutherland into Ross that forded the Oykel and passed to the west of Struie over the high land between the Dornoch and Cromarty Firths, following roughly the course of the modern A836 until it turned south west to Novar, Drummond and Foulis. This track continued up the tidal valley of Strathpeffer to Fodderty where the burn was fordable. From thence the track passed below the steep hill of Coll an Righe and, following the later line of Dingwall's High Street, led to the ferry crossing opposite Alcaig in the parish of Urquhart. This track would form the basis of several later communication routes, roads, bridges, ferries, railroads, as well as determining the layout of the medieval town of Dingwall.[5]

The first people to leave evidence of their way of life in the area came after these original navigators, nomadic Stone Age hunter-gatherers whose piles of fish bones and shells (called 'middens') are located along the raised beaches of the Firth, such as those below Castlecraig and near Ankerville in the parish of Nigg.[6]

About 3500 BC new arrivals came, driven from their homes on the Continent of Europe by pressure on land. These people were the region's first farmers, using their polished stone tools to fell trees to clear fields and to build their huts and pens for animals. Eventually, they merged with the existing population and created permanent settlements. These neolithic farmers raised barley and oats, sheep, cattle and swine, and were also skilled weavers and potters. This more settled way of living allowed for a complex social and religious system, indicated by the huge chambered tombs built by the whole community to hold groups of important burials. It has been estimated that some of these tombs went on being used and added to for as long as twenty-two centuries. Such structures suggest a society based on large, extended families, perhaps an early system of clan groupings. The chambered tombs of the Cromarty Firth region, such as the line of tombs on the higher land to the north of the modern Alness-Tain road, at Stittenham and Scotsburn Wood, looking out over the Firth, display an eye for landscape.

Technological change is one of the continuing themes of the history of the Cromarty Firth. The first and, until the twentieth century, perhaps the most important of these changes occurred *c.* 2500 BC when copper working and bronze making were introduced from the continent into Scotland as the beginning of 'The Bronze Age'. At first this fundamental change seems to have had little effect on the everyday lives of the people, although the possession of metal tools, weapons and ornaments was of great significance to small and elite groups within society. The Bronze Age may have been a time of increasing social stratification among those who worked the land, those who fought, and those responsible for the religious life of the people. Certainly the possession of metal, and the knowledge of how to make it and shape it, conferred power and prestige. Warriors decked themselves in golden *lunulae* (necklets), brooches and armlets with golden decorations on their spears and swords. The blades of the swords themselves were first made of copper and later of bronze.

Increasingly, people came to have specialised roles within society. The Bronze Age was the period of the first widespread trading contacts between the Firth and the continent of Europe and there needed to be men to produce the raw materials and finished products for this trade, and sailors and navigators to carry the goods. It was perhaps during this period that the Cromarty Firth first began to build up its continental trading links; certainly by classical times the Firth was known to mariners as a place of safe refuge.[7]

About 3,000 years ago, towards the end of the Bronze Age, there was a marked deterioration in climate and people moved their homes and fields further up the hillsides, away from the increasingly boggy flat lands along the shore. In some cases they abandoned agriculture altogether and became pastoralists. The wood and stone huts they built within encircling walls are the earliest surviving domestic buildings around the Cromarty Firth. These late Bronze Age settlements can still be seen in the huts and field system in Kinrive Wood on the north side of the Firth, and the scattered groups of buildings and enclosures on the old common land of Cromarty.

The Bronze Age also brought changes in religious beliefs. The Stone Age cairn burial which depended on the whole community for its creation and maintenance was abandoned in favour of individual graves, stone lined cists, in which the body was placed along with earthenware pots ('beakers') to hold food and, often, jewellery and weapons for use in the afterlife. Communal religion was now centred on a number of new types of structures: cup and ring marked stones, henges and standing stones. The purpose of the enigmatic Bronze Age cup and ring marked stones is difficult to determine. Both the 'henge monuments' (large circular areas marked out by ditches) and standing stones may have had some astronomical function, indicating that the religion of the Bronze Age was tied to agriculture and the passing seasons and that there existed a priestly caste with some knowledge of geometry and simple astronomy.

In addition to these religious structures the people of the Cromarty Firth were now also required to help build large, defensive duns and promontory forts. These may date, in some cases, from the end of the Bronze Age but come into their own as the characteristic buildings of the Scottish Iron Age of the first millennium BC. They are connected with the arrival from the continent of a new people, the Celts, who appear in Scotland in the seventh century BC. The Celts may have come as refugees in small scattered groups but gradually there was assimilation with the indigenous people. They were horsemen and iron-makers, and their abilities as warriors and craftsmen helped to transform Scotland.

Celtic Iron Age society was organised on a tribal basis, with all its members claiming kinship with each other and their chief. By the time Ptolemy compiled his geography (*c*. 140 AD) the Cromarty Firth area was apparently shared between two tribes: the Decantae (east from the Beauly River) and the Smertae, centred on the Dornoch Firth (although some interpretations of Ptolemy's map show the Cromarty area inhabited only by the Decantae). Thus, already in the centuries before the Roman penetration of Scotland in the second and third centuries AD, the territorial and tribal subdivisions of Scotland were established. These areas were based in part on geography; the name Ross means a promontory and probably originally applied to Tarbat Ness. However, such regions as Ross were also associated with groups of people who often took their names from an area, or gave their name to a region. Traditionally, the seven ancient divisions of Scotland were said to have been the kingdoms (with subordinate kingdoms attached to them) of seven brothers who gave their names to the lands they ruled: Angus with the Mearns, Atholl with Gowrie, Strathearn with Menteith, Fife with Forthriff, Mar with Buchan, Moray with Ross, and Caithness. The area around the Cromarty Firth was, therefore, known from a very early period as 'Ross' and it was linked tribally and politically with the area of Moray, a linkage that was to survive well into modern times. For example, during the period of agricultural change in the eighteenth and nineteenth centuries many of the improving farmers (and ideas) came from Moray.[8]

For the Celts warfare was a way of life. Their forts were huge structures, often placed on strategic hills and headlands and surrounded by extensive walls and ditches. The Cromarty Firth contains some notable examples of these huge fortifications such as the promontory fort of Castledownie overlooking Eathie Burn, Easter Rarichie on the northeastern slope of the North Sutor, Carn Mor at Culbokie and the incomplete fort at Cnoc an Duin north west of Scotsburn. There is one known example of a broch in the area, the large doublewalled structure surrounded by ramparts and ditches near Scotsburn House. Some archaeologists have argued that these mysterious round towers were built as defensive lookouts at the time of the Roman invasions, but it now appears that some of them, at least, were built earlier than the first and second centuries AD.

Brochs are usually associated with the first people of the Cromarty Firth for whom a name has survived — the Picts. Little is known of this Celtic-speaking people's language or social organisation, although it seems possible that they were an aristocratic elite, ruling an earlier and subordinate people. The Picts have left abundant evidence of their early settlement in the characteristic place-name element 'pit', meaning a portion or share of land and found in such places as Pitcalnie and Pitmaduthy.

By the sixth century AD the Picts were divided into two powerful kingdoms, or confederations of tribes, occupying almost all of the eastern part of Scotland. Brude, the powerful King of the Northern Picts in the second half of the sixth century, may have had his seat on Craig Phadrig in Inverness.

For some years Irish settlers (the *Scotti* or Scots) had been establishing themselves in the south and west of Scotland. In Irish society the organisation of the church was based on the clan: it was said in Ireland that 'a tribe was no tribe which did not possess three things — a lord, a bard, and a church'.[9] The Celtic church was a decentralised one, based on the tribal monastery. The clan chief and the local priest or abbot were usually of the same family. Both the chiefs and, eventually, the priests and abbots held their positions hereditarily, hence the later common Gaelic surnames, MacTaggart (son of the priest) and MacNab (son of the abbot). Much stress was placed on long missionary journeys to convert the heathen. St Columba (521–97) was born in Ireland and founded several monasteries there before coming to Iona in 563. Columba's monastery at Iona was meant to be not only a religious centre for these Scots, but also a centre for missionary trips to the pagan Picts of the east.

Despite Columba's well-known journey to King Brude at Inverness, the first missionary known to have penetrated the area around the Cromarty Firth was Columba's kinsman Moluoc, Abbot of Lismore in Loch Linnhe and a follower of St Brendan the Voyager, who established a monastery at Rosemarkie in 592. Another kinsman of Columba was Earnan, who also may have travelled to the Black Isle where Killearnan (the church of Earnan) commemorates his name.[10] These Celtic missionaries often founded their new churches on pagan holy places.[11] Indeed, at several places around the Cromarty Firth churches and chapels were established in association with pagan standing stones as at the chapel at Ardross. Another example may be the Pictish Thief's Stone (*Clach a'Mheirlich*) to the west of Rosskeen churchyard (Invergordon), perhaps first raised to mark the boundary of some pagan sanctuary — the stone's markings do not include Christian symbols — and still the subject of stories about its supernatural powers.[12] A similar process occurred at Nigg, whose Gaelic name ('the notch') probably refers to the V-shaped promontory between two streams on which the church is located.[13] A Bronze Age standing stone that once stood in the churchyard indicates that this place had been holy for centuries before the coming of Christianity. Nigg's early importance as a Christian centre is indicated by the survival of the Nigg stone (Fig. 1), dated *c.* 800 and one of the masterpieces of Pictish art. At the apex two bearded priests with books in their hands lean forward in adoration of a chalice; beneath them is a magnificent rectangular cross surrounded by foliage bosses. On the other side of the cross slab are the figures of David and Daniel killing the lion while at the bottom a group of Pictish nobles rides out with their hunting dogs.[14]

The Pictish tribal group at Nigg may have accepted Christianity early and erected the stone as a visible sign of their new faith. Perhaps they showed their devotion to the newly-established church by endowing it with gifts such as the fine chalice shown on the top of the Nigg stone. Other gifts to the Celtic church have left their mark on the landscape to the present day. On the north eastern slopes of the North Sutor is the placename, *Loch na h-Annaid* (Annat), meaning a church containing a relic of its founder: the church is lost, the

1. The Nigg stone.

founder unknown, but the name attached to the lands with which the church was endowed still remains. A similar name is 'Navity' (the church lands) south west of Cromarty; the site still has the remains of three ancient chapels and a holy well. As late as the seventeenth century it was believed that at the end of the world the people of Cromarty would be gathered on the moor of Navity for the Last Judgement.

Throughout the whole Cromarty Firth region there are similar chapel sites, perhaps originally the cells of hermits and often associated with holy wells, to which generations of people were drawn by their power to cure. Long after the original purpose of many of these early Christian sites has been forgotten they still exercise an influence on the life and thought of the people of the region.

There are other survivals of the Celtic church. At Urquhart at the southwestern end of the Firth it is still possible to see, amidst the later gravestones, the outline of a curving wall, part of the outer rampart of earth and stone that probably surrounded the small enclosed yard of a Celtic church. Urquhart is one of the traditional sites for the martyrdom of St Maelrubha, the founder of the great monastery of Applecross on the western coast of Scotland.[15] In fact Maelrubha seems to have died safe in bed at Applecross in 722. Nevertheless, Urquhart was undoubtedly an important Celtic church.[16]

Early in the eighth century the Pictish King Nechtan ordered that the churches in his kingdom should all conform to Roman usages in such matters as recognising Papal authority and calculating the date of Easter. This shift in religious orientation is indicated by the presence of churches dedicated to St Peter as at Rosemarkie, where the dedication is shared with Boniface (or Curitan) who was King Nechtan's agent in enforcing this change. It is likely that Curitan himself was also active elsewhere around the Cromarty Firth for a small enclosure to the north of Assynt House still bears the name *Cladh Churidan*. Later King Nechtan himself retired into religion, living for part of the time as a hermit, perhaps in the cave on the seaward face of the North Sutor that is still called the King's Cave. Nearby runs *Cadha Neachdain* (Nechtan's path).[17]

The conversion of the Picts to Christianity was not complete until perhaps the ninth century. The process was part conversion and part assimilation, for Columba and his successors were followed to the east by Gaelic-speaking Scottish settlers. While the intrusion of these alien people from the west must have caused tensions, Scottish immigration seems to have been largely a peaceful process involving the settlement of farmers and craftsmen. Evidence for the nature of Scottish settlement is found in such place names as Balnagown (the smith's farm), Balnacraig (rock farm) or Balliskilly in Resolis which may mean 'the farm of the storyteller' — perhaps the local tribal bard. By the tenth century the Pictish language had been replaced by Scottish Gaelic, which remained the language of most of the Cromarty Firth for over a thousand years. Even today the great majority of farm names and the names for natural features (ben, loch, strath) are of Gaelic origin.

The beginning of Viking raids in the eighth century initiated three hundred years of radical change, culminating in the absorption of Ross into the medieval kingdom of Scotland. Although the Vikings came first as raiders, there is ample evidence that soon they began to settle and farm — a sprinkling of Scandinavian names around the Cromarty Firth includes not only features of the landscape that sea-voyagers would note (Shandwick=sandy bay) but also farm names (Cadboll=Cat farmstead; Braelangwell=hill of the long field). Dingwall itself at the head of the Firth was the seat of a Viking court, or *ting*.[18]

The lands north of the Moray Firth were of major importance to the Scandinavian Earls of Orkney for they gave access to the Great Glen portage route across Scotland that led to the Viking-controlled Hebrides. For several centuries, then, the Cromarty Firth region was a kind of buffer zone between the earldom to the north and the power of the Mormaers ('great lords') of Moray and, later, the Kings of Scots in the south.

The first Viking attempt to control the area came in the ninth century when the armies of Earl Sigurd 'The Mighty' laid waste Moray and Ross. Earl Sigurd is said to have built a castle in Moray, perhaps at Burghead, but the conquest of these lands was short-lived. According to the *Orkneyingasaga*, Earl Sigurd died after tying the severed head of a defeated native earl, Maelbrighte, to his saddle bow. The earl's protruding tooth cut into Sigurd's leg and he died of blood poisoning. He was buried in an earthen mound on the River Oykel in the southernmost part of his earldom (Sigurd's Howe: modern Cyderhall) looking south towards the lands of Ross and Moray which he had tried to conquer.

A century later the Scandinavian earls turned their attention south again; this time they were faced by the powerful Scottish Mormaers of Moray, overlords of both Moray and Ross. Another Earl Sigurd may have briefly extended his control south to the Moray Firth, but it was his son, Thorfinn 'The Mighty' (*c*. 1030–*c*. 1065) who was able to incorporate the lands north of the Moray Firth into his domain. At some time early in the reign of Thorfinn the fleets of the Earl and Mormaer (who was probably Macbeth himself) landed and met in a battle at Tarbat Ness. The battle was commemorated in suitably heroic verse in the *Orkneyingasaga*:

> A keen sword at Tarbatness
> Reddened the wolf's fare.
> The young Prince wielded it —
> It was a Monday.
> Their swords sang there,
> South of Oykel.
> There fought with Scotland's king
> Our valiant lord.

Earl Thorfinn was victorious over the Mormaer and for the rest of his long life controlled both Ross and Moray. It may have been during this period that the 'Ting' was established that gave Dingwall its name.

When Earl Thorfinn died it was said 'many realms that the Earl had subdued fell away and men sought protection for themselves under the hereditary chiefs in the realm.' Ross was undoubtedly one of these realms, and by the early twelfth century at least, its hereditary chiefs were the MacHeth Earls of Ross. These Earls were descended from the Mormaers of Moray, and as such, were of the family of Macbeth, King of Scots (*c.* 1005–1057) who was also 'Thane of Cromarty and Mormaer of Ross'.[19] After Macbeth's murder in 1057 by King Malcolm III 'Canmore', his claim to the Scottish throne was maintained by his Macbeth descendants who led successive rebellions throughout the twelfth century (often now in alliance with the Scandinavian earls of Orkney) against the Kings of Scots, the descendants of King Malcolm and Queen Margaret.

Matters came to a head in the reign of Malcolm's great grandson, William the Lion (1165–1214). In the early 1170s a major rebellion had broken out in the north, led by Earl Harald Maddadson and Malcolm MacHeth. In 1179 the king marched north as far as Inverness and was able to assert control over Moray. Ross proved more difficult, but it was probably soon after this campaign that the two royal strongholds of Redcastle (*Etherdouer*) in the Black Isle, and Dunskeath, on the North Sutor, were built.[20] Both of these were originally wooden structures set within an outer defensive work of ditches. The wooden tower at Dunskeath, and the stone one that succeeded it, have both disappeared, but the outer trenches can still be seen on the high ground overlooking the entrance to the Cromarty Firth.

Castles were keys to the assertion of royal authority over this difficult and distant region. Dunskeath's prime strategic position on the North Sutor was recognised when the site was partially built over by the twentieth century naval defences. The castle of Dunskeath not only controlled access to the Cromarty Firth and overlooked wide stretches of the Moray Firth but could also be used as a centre for royal administration. It may not have been too long before a similar wooden royal castle was built on an artificially constructed 'motte hill' across the channel in Cromarty.

King William's campaign of 1179 did not end problems in the north. There was a further royal campaign in 1187 and another in Caithness in 1197, at the end of which Harald Maddadson and his son, Thorfinn, were sent in chains by King William to Roxburgh castle. Following Harold's release, however, there was further trouble in the north, culminating in the mutilation of the bishop of Caithness. King William ordered the blinding and castration of Thorfinn, so that he could not succeed to the title of Earl. Nevertheless, there was yet another rising in 1211 and the aged King marched north one last time. Redcastle and Dunskeath were rebuilt, although one of them was later taken by the rebel army before its leader was betrayed and executed in 1212.[21]

It was King William's son, Alexander II, 'the little red fox', who would finally solve the problem of the north and bring Ross firmly into his kingdom. In 1215, a year after he became king, rebellion broke out again. It was put down by a man from the west, Farquhar MacTaggart, a descendant of the hereditary abbots of the monastery of Applecross. He sent the heads of the rebellion's leaders to the King and was knighted for his efforts.

With the help of such loyal allies as MacTaggart, the King could now think of the pacification of Ross. The key to this was the settlement of feudal landowners, men who held their land from the King and who owed him service for it. Not all the new 'feudal families' were alien incomers; the Munros, for example, made a successful transition from Celtic chiefs to feudal lords. Nevertheless, twelfth century Scotland was a country for younger sons and ambitious men, many of them of Anglo-French origin, who were attracted north by the chance of land and advancement. Several of the families settled in Ross by King William were from this group; for example, the Bissets, originally from France, became lords of The Aird (including the royal stronghold of Redcastle). Another Anglo-Norman family was that of *Monte Alto* (Mowat) who were followers of the Comyn Earls of Buchan, hereditary sheriffs of Dingwall.[22] Through the help of the Comyns, the Mowats became lords of Cromarty and probably Dunskeath as well by the middle of the thirteenth century. These feudal tenants usually held their lands in return for carrying out certain duties or exercising specific offices: the Mowats apparently held theirs for exercising the office of sheriff (the king's local legal and tax-gathering representative) in Cromarty.

Despite these changes, the lives of the ordinary people of the Cromarty Firth region went on much as before. The seasons and the crops came and went. There were years of plenty and years of famine, just as there had always been. But some changes did come with the introduction of feudalism. Legally, men and women and children were now bound to the land and to their masters as nefys (serfs). A certain number of days every year had to be given to the lord's service, and rent (usually in kind) was owed to him. All tenants would be thirled to the lord's mill — bound to take their grain there for grinding and to pay the appropriate dues. Some tenants would also be required to provide military service, usually as part of a local defence force.

Such service was needed for in 1228 there was again trouble in the north. The Lord of Abertarff, another incomer who had been settled in the north by the king, was burned to death in his wooden castle by disaffected locals who may have claimed to be acting on behalf of the MacHeths. The King came north in 1230 and held his Christmas court in Elgin. It was time to end the MacHeth problem for good and all. King Alexander decided to create a new Earl of Ross and chose Sir Farquhar MacTaggart, who had shown his loyalty to the crown in such active and bloodstained ways. The pacification of the north could now be completed by this new royal deputy.[23]

One method of settling an area and improving economy was the founding

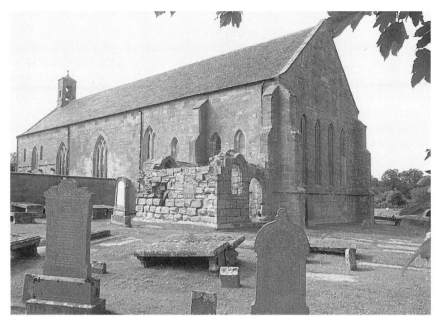

2. Fearn abbey.

of monasteries. Monks were the agricultural improvers of the Middle Ages. Not only did they clear land and farm it, they also experimented with improved plants and livestock. Even before he became Earl of Ross Farquhar MacTaggart had brought canons (priests who lived by a monastic rule) from Whithorn in Galloway to Fearn on the south shore of the Dornoch Firth. About 1238, however, he moved the monastery to 'New' Fearn (Fig. 2) in the parish of Tarbat, where amongst other things the canons began the centuries' long process of draining the plain of Nigg.[24] Perhaps because of their French background the Bisset lords of The Aird looked to the austere French Valliscaulian order when planning their monastic foundation. These Cistercian monks specialised in opening up wilderness areas and turning them into places of beauty. In 1230 a group of French monks arrived and established a monastery on Bisset land, at the place they called Beauly (Beaulieu: beautiful place).

Monasteries were perhaps the most visible manifestations of medieval religious life, but there is other evidence that the church touched the lives of all the people. By the twelfth century the Cromarty Firth was part of the medieval diocese of Ross, with the seat of its bishop at Fortrose on the south side of the Black Isle.[25] Thirteen parishes ringed the Firth — Nigg, Logie Easter, Kilmuir Easter, Rosskeen, Alness (Fig. 3), Kiltearn, Lemlair, Dingwall, Urquhart, Logie Wester, St Martins (Cullicudden, later Resolis), Kirkmichael and Cromarty. The centre of each parish was its church, served by a priest

3. Alness old parish church.

responsible for carrying out Christian services for the people — masses, baptism, confession, marriage and funerals. In return the people were expected to support the priest by the payment of teinds (tithes). By the thirteenth century, however, these revenues were being diverted from the parish priest to pay the salaries of the officers of the cathedral church, leaving a stipendiary chaplain in charge of the parish. This system of diverting revenues — known as 'appropriation' — became a major grievance. These chaplains were often ill-qualified and their poverty made them avaricious. Sometimes they would charge for their services and the collection of 'mort pennies' (payment for burial), for example, came to be deeply resented by the people.

Despite such abuses, however, religion was as important in the lives of the people as it had been to their prehistoric ancestors. Religious faith was expressed in such things as devotion to the cult of saints. Ross was fortunate in having its own particular saint, Duthac, who was born at Tain early in the eleventh century and was educated there before going to Ireland for further study. The rest of his life was shared between the two countries. His reputation for personal sanctity grew quickly and he was said to be able to work great miracles. Many people came to seek his advice and experience his spiritual power. Duthac became a major figure in the church in Ireland and Scotland, so that at the time of his death and burial at Armagh in 1065 he was called 'Chief confessor of Erin and Alba'.

Such was Duthac's prestige that his birthplace at Tain quickly became an important religious centre (Fig. 4), its boundaries marked by four sanctuary crosses. In 1253 the saint's remains were returned to Tain and the shrine became a major place of pilgrimage (Fig. 5), attracting not only local people but the great, including King James IV, who was especially devoted to the cult of St Duthac.[26]

A major force in drawing medieval Ross into the mainstream of Scottish life was the creation of towns. There was no tradition of organised town life in Scotland until the reign of King David I (1124–53) when new towns, called royal burghs, began to be founded by the king, who would issue a royal charter setting out the new town's rights and privileges. In addition to creating a self-governing civic corporation, the royal charter granted to the burgesses a monopoly of trade in the town and surrounding area. The burgh also had the privilege of holding markets and courts to deal with problems of lawlessness within the town boundaries. In some cases the burgh also became the centre of a sheriffdom.

Despite the long tradition that Tain was granted its liberties by Malcolm Canmore in the late eleventh century, it does not seem to have become a burgh until several centuries later.[27] The first burgh of the region was Dingwall, created by King Alexander II in 1227 in the final stages of his long campaign to bring Ross under royal control. Dingwall was also the seat of a sheriff, whose centre of authority was the royal castle built on a small promontory overlooking the crossing of the River Peffery; it was important enough to be shown on Matthew Paris' early thirteenth century map of Scotland.[28]

The connection between the sheriff and the burgh was just as close in Cromarty, the other local royal burgh founded in the thirteenth century. It is not known exactly when the town was founded, for no charter has survived, but it seems likely that it was later than Dingwall, perhaps following the creation of Farquhar MacTaggart as Earl of Ross. Cromarty's two provosts (aldermen) first appear in the returns made by the Mowat sheriff of Cromarty to the royal exchequer in 1264–6, in the reign of King Alexander III.[29]

By the early fourteenth century both burghs, and their sheriffdoms, had been granted by King Robert I (the Bruce) to the Earls of Ross, a sign of how much this king depended on the loyalty of local magnates in resettling his kingdom after the wars with England in the late thirteenth and early fourteenth century.[30] The Earls of Ross had, in fact, supported John Balliol as King of Scots, and after he was deposed had taken an oath of loyalty to King Edward I and acted as the English king's Wardens north of the Spey. In 1306 the Earl violated the sanctuary of Tain and captured Bruce's wife and daughter, who had taken refuge there following King Robert's defeat at the battle of Methven. Despite the fact that the Earl of Ross had handed his queen and her daughter over to English imprisonment, Bruce and the Earl were reconciled in the following year and the Earl's son married the king's sister. The Earl fought at Bannockburn, doubtless with many local footsoldiers in his train, and until his death in 1322 remained a faithful supporter of King Robert. Two years

4. Tain church.

before, in 1320, he had been one of the barons to affix his seal to the Declaration of Arbroath, the letter sent to the Pope in support of Robert the Bruce.

By the thirteenth century the area around the Cromarty Firth became at last part of the kingdom of Scotland. However, the basic population of the region did not change, nor did its language and culture. The greatest family of the region, the Earls of Ross, were of ancient Celtic stock. Much of their power and authority was based on ties of kinship and loyalty that were far older than the introduction of feudalism and royal authority; and it was the ties of kinship that outlived the Earldom itself, through the development of the Clan Ross. Following a series of family alliances the title of Earl of Ross passed to the Lords of the Isles and, after the forfeiture of the Earldom of Ross in 1476, to the Crown of Scotland. The Ross clan derived from a younger son of the Earls who had been granted the lands of Rarichie by his father in the 1330s. By the early fifteenth century this family was settled on the lands of Balnagown and through its descent from the male line of Farquhar MacTaggart the family of Ross of Balnagown became recognised heads of the Ross clan.[31]

Membership in a clan was based on real or imagined kinship and an implied common origin. By the fifteenth century at least this was often expressed in the use of a common surname, in this case the regional title, 'Ross'. At least one other local family related to the Rosses also bore the name of their

5. The interior of Tain church.

original lands, Urquhart. In the second quarter of the fourteenth century the Earl of Ross gave the lordship of Cromarty to Adam Urquhart, 'my attendant and kinsman', in return for the payment of one penny each year at the market cross of the burgh and service in the King's army.

Clans could also have dependent but unrelated families of different names, called septs. In the case of the Rosses, these dependent families included MacCulloch, Denoon, Corbett, Dunbar and Vass (Vaux). Clan ties were expressed by loyalty and service, particularly in the clan feuds that punctuated so much of Highland history in the fifteenth and sixteenth centuries such as the endemic raiding between Rosses and the Mackays of Strathnaver and the systematic herschip (wasting) of the Urquhart lands of Cromarty by the Roses of Kilravock from across the Moray Firth in the late fifteenth century.

The other important local family who first appears in the medieval period is Munro of Foulis.[32] The antecedents of this family are obscure, although they claimed descent from an Irish chief, Donald, who gave his name to Ferindonald, the Munro lands on the northwestern shore of the Cromarty Firth. It may be that the family originally came from Moray. The Munros first appear in the Black Isle, but by the middle of the fourteenth century they had been granted Ferindonald by the Earl of Ross. From this centre the family spread; younger sons took up surrounding estates, thus creating the various cadet branches of the clan.

From the clans of the Cromarty Firth, Rosses, Munros, Mackenzies, and others, have come soldiers, explorers, doctors, lawyers, saints and sinners, who have spread local names around the world: for example, from this part of Scotland have come at least one President of the United States and a Prime

Minister of New Zealand. The clansmen and women of the region are a reminder that the history of this area is not just about the different peoples who have come to live here over thousands of years, but also about the people of the Firth who have gone out into the wider world. The Cromarty Firth has always been not just *portus salutis* — a safe port of arrival — but a port of departure, as well.

NOTES

1. H. Miller, *Scenes and Legends of the North of Scotland*, Edinburgh, 1885, p. 14.

2. *Ibid.*, p. 171.

3. For the geology of the Cromarty Firth see C. Gillen, 'The physical background', in D. Omand (ed.), *The Ross and Cromarty Book*, Golspie, 1984, and the same author's 'Geology and landscape in Easter Ross and Sutherland', in J. R. Baldwin (ed.), *Firthlands of Ross and Sutherland*, Edinburgh, 1986, pp/ 1–22.

4. H. Miller, *My Schools and Schoolmasters*, London, n.d., p. 469.

5. R. Bain, *History of the Ancient Province of Ross from the Earliest to the Present Time*, Dingwall, 1899, pp. 9–11.

6. For the early archaeology of the Cromarty Firth region see R. Gourlay, 'The ancient past', in *RC Book*, pp. 99–125. The following account is based on this article and the listing of sites given in the Royal Commission on the Ancient and Historical Monuments of Scotland, Society of Antiquaries of Scotland Archaeological Field Survey, 'The Black Isle' (October, 1979) and 'Easter Ross' (February, 1979).

7. It is a common claim that the Latin name for the Firth, *Portus Salutis*, was first applied to the Cromarty Firth by the third century AD Greek geographer, Ptolemy. Although he does name local tribes on his map, the only geographical names he gives are for the Moray Firth and Tarbat Ness (*Ripa Alta*). See I. A. Richmond, *Roman and Native in North Britain*, Edinburgh, 1958, pp. 141, 134. The earliest use of *Portus Salutis* I have been able to trace occurs in the fourteenth century Scottish chronicle of John of Fordoun who is apparently Latinising an English term, 'Zikersound' (Safe sound), that dates back at least to Geoffrey of Monmouth in the thirteenth century, and continued to be the common name for the Firth throughout the middle ages. See, for example, John Major's *History of Greater Britain* (1521): 'Scotland possesses a great many harbours of which Cromarty at the mouth of the Northern River [the Moray Firth] is held to be the safest — and by reason of its good anchorage is called by sailors Sykkersand, that is 'safe port'.

8. I. Mowat, 'Moray Firth Province', *Firthlands*, pp. 69–87.

9. W. J. Watson, 'The Celtic church in Ross', *TISSFC*, vol. 6 (1899–1906), p. 4.

10. There may have been, in fact, an earlier missionary penetration from Whithorn in Galloway, founded by St Ninian, *c.* 400. The late W. Douglas Simpson argued that the saint — or his successors — had made such journeys and, although this thesis is no longer accepted in detail, R. G. Cant says that '. . . there is good reason to believe that a strong Christian presence linked with Whithorn, by way of Strathclyde, eastern Pictland and northern Ireland, existed in the far north before St Columba established his much publicised centre at Iona, in the late sixth century'. ('The medieval church in the north', *Firthlands*, p. 47). The ancient ruined church of Nonikil is dedicated to St

Ninian, and his association with St Martin of Tours may be reflected in St Martin's church in the Black Isle.

11. D. Wilson, *Archaeology and Prehistoric Annals of Scotland*, Edinburgh, 1851, p. 110.

12. Gourlay, 'Ancient Past', *RC Book*, pp. 117–19.

13. *Origines Parochiales Scotiae*, Edinburgh, 1850–55, vol. 2, Part 2, p. 454; W. J. Watson, *The Placenames of Ross and Cromarty*, Inverness, 1904, p. 50.

14. It has recently been suggested that these stones were raised to mark tribal boundaries and record dynastic marriages; see A. Jackson, *The Symbol Stones of Scotland*, Stromness, 1984.

15. Anderson, A. O., *Early Sources of Scottish History*, Edinburgh, 1922, vol. 1, p. 220, note.

16. Watson, 'Celtic church', p. 10.

17. *Ibid.*, pp. 11–13.

18. Much of the following discussion of the Viking period around the Cromarty Firth is based on B. E. Crawford, 'The making of a frontier, the Firthlands from the ninth to the twelfth centuries', *Firthlands*, pp. 33–40.

19. Andrew of Wyntoun, *The Orygynale Cronykil of Scotland*, ed. D. Laing, Edinburgh, 1872, vol. 1, p. 128. It seems likely that it is at least from Macbeth's period that the extent of the 'shire of Cromarty' was established. It included the entire parish of Cromarty and the neighbouring parish of Kirkmichael (with the exception of Easter Balblair, the ferry point, and possibly Kirkmichael itself), along with the farm of Easter St Martins in the parish of Cullicudden (Resolis). Cromartyshire was ten miles at its greatest length and had an average width of one and three quarter miles; its total extent was seventeen and a half square miles.

20. W. M. Mackenzie, 'The old sheriffdom of Cromarty', reprinted from *The Northern Chronicle*, Inverness, 1922, pp. 10–11; see also *Regesta Regum Scottorum*, vol. 2 (Acts of William the Lion), ed. G. W. S. Barrow, Edinburgh, 1971, p. 11.

21. See A. A. M. Duncan, *The Making of the Kingdom*, Edinburgh, 1975, p. 194ff.

22. Mackenzie, 'Sheriffdom', pp. 13–14; *Exchequer Rolls of Scotland*, Edinburgh, 1878, vol. 1, p. 19.

23. Duncan, *Making of the Kingdom*, p. 529.

24. I. B. Cowan and D. E. Easson, *Medieval Religious Houses: Scotland*, 2nd edn, London, 1976, pp. 101–2.

25. For the medieval diocese of Ross, see R. G. Cant in *Firthlands*.

26. For the cult of St Duthac, see R. W. and J. Munro, *Tain Through the Centuries*, Tain, 1966, p. 9ff. and J. Durkan, 'The sanctuary and college of Tain', *Innes Review*, vol. 13 (1962), pp. 147–156.

27. *Ibid.*, pp. 12–13.

28. Duncan, *Making of the Kingdom*, pp. 596–7.

29. Mackenzie, 'Sheriffdom', suggests that the creation of the burgh of Cromarty occurred at the same time as the creation of the sheriffdom; p. 15.

30. For the medieval earldom of Ross, see J. Munro, 'The clan period', *RC Book*, p. 127ff, and the same author's 'The earldom of Ross and the Lordship of the Isles', *Firthlands*, pp. 59–67.

31. Much of this discussion of the Rosses is based on D. Mackinnon, *The Clan Ross*, Edinburgh, 1957.

32. This discussion of the early Munro history owes much to C. I. Fraser, *The Clan Munro*, Edinburgh and London, 1954, and R. W. Munro, *The Munro Tree (1734)*, Edinburgh, 1978.

2

'Polish'd with art and agriculture'

In the middle of the seventeenth century Richard Franck, who had been in the Cromwellian army of occupation in Scotland, returned to make a pleasure tour of the country. His account of the journey, *Northern Memoirs calculated for the meridian of Scotland writ in the year 1658*, provides the first word picture of the Firth.[1] Some things Franck describes are unfamiliar and long vanished, such as 'Miltown, a castle opposite to Cromerty [*sic*]', soon to be converted into the first modern house in the region by Mackenzie of Tarbat and renamed 'New Tarbat'. Other sights survived to modern times, such as the 'rugged ferry' of Inverbreakie [Invergordon] which ceased running only when the Cromarty Firth bridge opened in 1979.

Above all Franck was impressed by the Firth's unique position as a fertile area within sight of the Highlands: 'It is a pleasant part of the country I confess, though methinks it stands almost out of the world. These Highlands, to my thinking, but represent a part of creation left undrest . . .' On the favoured 'fertile shores of Cromerty' Franck saw wasted potential:

> Because their shores are uncapable of freezing, for no snow lies here, though bordering almost on the frigid zone, nor does ice incrustate the earth near the shores, and this is the reason the shores are enriched with fertility, were but the people polish'd with art and agriculture; for were it so, I should then conclude them blest with a delightful prospect.

Franck's book caught the Cromarty Firth at one of the turning points of its history, between the old past, symbolised by an age-old and inefficient system of agriculture and the old Munro castle of Miltown, and the beginning of changes that over the next century would fill out the familiar physical outlines of the Firth with new fields, houses, roads and harbours.

The seventeenth century landscape of the Cromarty Firth region was open, unenclosed, and aside from a few scattered stands of ancient forest there were scarcely any mature trees, although some tree planting was beginning to take place. There were few bridges and no roads, only the ancient tracks following their courses laid down in prehistoric times. The population was tiny and thinly spread; the population density of seventeenth century Scotland has been estimated at 11 people per square kilometre, compared with 27 for Ireland and between 30 and 40 for England.[2]

At the beginning of the century Dingwall and Tain had populations of a few hundred; the events of the century did not deal kindly with them, and their populations probably fell. Tain was a small huddle of thatched houses (only the very wealthy could afford new-fangled Caithness slates on their roofs), clustered round about the ruinous church, council chamber and the tolbooth steeple. It was claimed that by midcentury there had been only three merchants in Tain whose stock had exceeded £1,000 (Scots) and that they had been forced to give up trade.[3] By the time of the Restoration in 1660 things had improved slightly, for the trade stent rolls of the town in the late 1650s and early 1660s list 34 farmers, 4 maltmen, 1 messenger, 4 weavers, 15 merchants, 2 skinners, 2 dyers, 9 shoemakers, 5 tailors, 1 customs officer, 1 saddler, 4 masons, 1 wright, 1 brewer, 1 peat caster, 1 smith, 4 postmen, 1 snuff miller, 1 goldsmith, 1 coppersmith, 2 peddlers and a 'burne wyffe' (washerwoman).[4] The largest town in the region was Cromarty. By the end of the seventeenth century there were perhaps 1,400 people living there, while the Black Isle had a total population of perhaps 3,000.[5] Nevertheless, by the end of the century Tain's share of taxes to the Convention of Royal Burghs was half what it had been forty years before, and in 1685 Cromarty was expunged from the roll of royal burghs because, it was said, of its poverty.[6]

As Richard Franck remarked, the Cromarty Firth region was potentially one of the richest agricultural areas in Scotland, but its farming methods were primitive. Matters were made worse by a long-term deterioration in the climate in the seventeenth century that led to short summers and failed harvests. Famine was a regular occurrence throughout the period, most notably in 1594, 1598, 1623, 1634–6 and then, after a long period of relative plenty, there came the disastrous series of harvest failures in the late 1690s, known as 'King William's Ill Years'.

Yet this difficult period between the Reformation in 1560 and the Union with England in 1707 was one of crucial importance in the region. It was a period in which the old order fell apart and a new one began to emerge. The varying fortunes of the major families of the region are a barometer of change. The nature of the clan system meant that the history of the great families determined, in large measure, the lives of their followers. Ordinary clan members might be obliged to follow their leaders without question but within the upper ranks of the clan rights and obligations were, increasingly, put into written bonds or agreements. One such was the 1559 agreement between Abbot Nicholas Ross and Alexander Ross of Balnagown, one of the more violent and unreliable Highland chiefs of the period. He had long been notorious, terrorising the countryside with an eighteen pound cannon and a private army. Balnagown saw the Reformation as a further opportunity to extend his power and did not scruple about the means. Even while Nicholas Ross was south in Edinburgh to attend the Reformation Parliament, Alexander had intimidated three of the monks of Fearn into assigning him some of the abbey lands.[7]

Controlling such Highland chieftains had been a perpetual problem for the medieval kings of Scots, and it continued to be for the regents who governed in the name of the infant king, King James VI, born in 1566. Eventually Alexander Ross went too far. A feud with the family of Innes of Plaids over rent ended with Balnagown capturing Innes, who was induced to resign the lands.[8] Ross signalled his victory by dismantling the Innes castle of Cadboll and imprisoning the unfortunate laird. As a result he was summoned to Edinburgh by the Regent Morton to answer for his crimes before Parliament.[9] At first Ross refused to come, but apparently thought better of his resistance when he was declared an outlaw. In March 1573 he came to Edinburgh and was sentenced to a period in Tantallon Castle that did nothing to mend his character. Although he was only released on a promise to rebuild Cadboll Castle, he had repudiated this undertaking within a year of his return to the north.[10]

By now Alexander Ross had gone too far even for his own clansmen, who were alarmed that his activities might destroy the whole clan. In August 1577 Alexander's son, along with Thomas Ross, commendator of Fearn, and other 'kin and friends', wrote a letter to him reminding him of the house of Balnagown's 'immaculate' behaviour in favour of 'the prince and autorities, quhill now of lait they see ane appeirrance of ane fall and utter wrak to cum upon the said hous and tinsal of the riggs [loss of the lands] without provision be found . . .'[11] They desired the laird to fix a meeting with them where the dangers they foresaw could be discussed and dealt with. This seems, briefly, to have restricted Balnagown's activities, but by the early 1580s he was up to his old tricks again. This time Thomas Ross complained to the Privy Council in Edinburgh of Alexander's 'barbarous cruelties, injureis [sic] and intolerable oppressions and bludeshed . . . committed not only on his own tenants but upon others, seizing them and threatening so that many honest householders have been compelled to leave their houses and beg their meat.'[12]

Within a few years the young King James VI was beginning to grapple effectively with Highland lawlessness. Distance was one problem; as late as the end of the eighteenth century letters took a fortnight to travel between Tain and Edinburgh and back. Armies, assuming they could be raised, took much longer to move. In 1587, therefore, James established the device of the 'general band' as a means of controlling the Highlands, making the chief responsible for the good behaviour of his clan and tenants and for paying cash sureties that were forfeit if the system broke down. General bands were created at Balnagown, Foulis and within the sheriffdom of Cromarty. The Highlands did not become law-abiding overnight but the 'general band' was a milestone in the extension of control by the crown over a region it considered distant and difficult.

Some of James's other Highland policies were less successful. His attempt to plant Lowland protestants in Lewis (which he later extended to Ulster) was a disastrous failure. There is some evidence that the king attempted something similar in the Cromarty Firth. Until the end of the last century a tradition persisted in Cromarty that the King had induced three Fife families to settle in the town for the purpose of developing the fisheries by granting them the mussel beds of the lower reaches of the Firth.[13]

Such infusions of law-abiding Lowlanders into the region had little influence on Ross of Balnagown. Even by the standards of the time he and his family stood out; they were not just violent, but violent with a kind of wilful madness. The same streak is found in Alexander's son George who, despite being educated at St Andrews and having had to control his father's excesses during his lifetime, behaved little better when in 1592 he finally succeeded the reprobate Alexander. His methods of dealing with people who crossed him could be just as brutal and arbitrary. In 1600 John Ross, rector of Logie, who had loaned the impecunious laird six hundred merks, had his house at Strathcarron broken into by Balnagown and eighty of his followers 'all armed with . . . jacks, steill bonnettis, hagbuttis, culverings, bowis, swordes and utheris wapponis.' They injured John Ross's servants, destroyed his salted salmon, and stole eight stones of cheese, four stones of butter and two mares in foal in addition to killing four cows and four sheep.[14]

Alexander's daughter Katherine was cut from the same cloth. In 1577 she was at the centre of one of the most notorious of Scottish witchcraft cases. Belief in magic and the existence of supernatural powers and beings, such as elves and fairies, was ancient. Witches or wise women had long had a place in Scottish society. Witchcraft itself was only declared a crime in an act of the Scottish Parliament of 1563. The witches in the Foulis case were not the creatures that appear in the later, more lurid, instances of witchcraft, abandoned beings who had sold their souls to the devil and participated in the black mass, but they were nevertheless sinister individuals who were prepared to use their real or imagined powers for evil. The details of the case come from the depositions made by those accomplices of Lady Foulis who were condemned to death and who were thus perhaps anxious to cast as much blame on their erstwhile employer as possible. Nevertheless the outlines of the case are clear.[15]

Relations between the Munro and Ross families had always been at least outwardly cordial; given Alexander Ross's character it was as well to have him on one's side. In 1563 this state of cautious friendship was sealed by the marriage of Robert Munro, laird of Foulis, and Alexander's daughter, Katherine, who became his second wife. Munro's heir, Robert younger of Foulis, was the son of his first marriage. But as Katherine's own son, George Munro, grew up she became ambitious for him to succeed. A further element was added when her brother, George, who was married to Marian Campbell of Cawdor, fell in love with Robert Munro the younger's wife, Marjory Mackenzie of Kintail. The chance to see her son succeed to Foulis, and her brother marry the widow of Foulis the younger, appealed to Katherine. By 1576 she was thinking of means to achieve her ambitions.

At midsummer that year Lady Foulis asked Agnes Roy to go to the hills to ask the 'little folk' if the heir of Foulis and her sister-in-law, Lady Balnagown, should die. Apparently the answer was unsatisfactory for Lady Foulis then took more active means to secure her ends. At Easter time in the following year she was alleged to have received a 'box of witchcraft' at Foulis. But despite this supernatural aid, her first attempt at actual murder involved straightforward poisoning, using the good offices of William McGillivray, whom she sent to the local gypsies 'to haif knawledge of thame how to poysoun the young Laird of Fowles and the young Lady Balnagoune.' Apparently acting on what the gypsies had said, Lady Foulis sent McGillivray to Elgin where he bought eight shillings worth of rat poison.

The history of the botched attempts to kill the younger Foulis and Lady Balnagown would have an air of black comedy about them except for their deadly consequences. The 'pig of poysoun' she sent to her stepson by the hand of her old nurse broke, and when the nurse accidentally drank some of the contents, she died. Lady Foulis was somewhat more successful with the poison she sent to the hunting lodge at Ardmore, where Lady Ross and a party of friends were staying. This was served up in the kidneys of a deer killed by the hunting party and produced 'vomit and vexation [for the] young Lady Balnagown and her cumpany, of the quhilk poysoun, the young lady Balnagown contractit deadlie seiknes, quharin sho remanis yet [1590].'[16]

In addition to these direct attempts at murder, Lady Foulis and her accomplices also practised what is today known as sympathetic magic: the making of images of the intended victims and the symbolic injuring of them. On two occasions in early June 1577 Lady Foulis and her witches made images in butter and in clay of Robert Munro and Lady Balnagown and fired at them with elf-arrow bolts (neolithic arrowheads that were thought to be of supernatural origin and power). The bolts failed to hit, and the victims failed to die.

Lady Foulis did little more to achieve her ends until October, when once again she had a long meeting with William McGillivray. By this time action was being taken against the witches for, considering the number of people involved with Lady Foulis, her designs must have been an open and notorious secret. In January 1577 a letter, a Commission of Justice, had been sent from Edinburgh appointing a number of local lairds, including Walter Urquhart, sheriff of Cromarty, and Robert Munro of Foulis to act as justices and to apprehend, imprison and try a number of witches. Three are named, two women who are known to have consorted with Lady Foulis, and 'Kennoth, alias Kennoch Owir' who has passed into local legend as the Brahan Seer.[17] Nothing was done until late October when another letter of Commission was sent from Edinburgh. The Commission probably arrived soon after Lady Foulis had recommenced her murderous activities. At the witching time of All Hallows (1 November) Katherine Munro and two accomplices made two further clay images of their intended victims and shot an elf-bolt at them. This time they planned to take the additional precaution of depositing one image at Ardmore and the other at the bridgend of the Stank [marsh or sluggish stream] of Foulis, where the action of the water would achieve the dissolution of the clay, just as Katherine hoped for the dissolution of Lady Balnagown and young Foulis. Within days of this final action her husband, Robert Munro, and the Sheriff of Cromarty finally moved to deal with the named parties and 'all other men and women using and exercising the diabolical, iniquitous and odious crimes of the art of magic, sorcery and incantation.' The witches, or at least some of them, were brought to trial and several were burned, perhaps including Coinneach Odhar who according to tradition was executed in a burning tar barrel at Chanonry. Lady Foulis only escaped prosecution by going before two notaries and swearing that the charges against her were slanderous, and immediately fleeing on horseback to her maternal homeland of Caithness, where she remained for nine months before her husband could be persuaded to take her back.

But the most extraordinary part of the case was yet to come. In 1588 Robert Munro of Foulis died (only a few months after Robert the younger) and was succeeded by his second son, Hector, who moved quickly to bring his step-mother to trial. Katherine Ross was imprisoned in 1589 and tried in July 1590. By then Katherine had a case of her own to bring, against Hector, for using witchcraft to cure himself and his elder brother and bringing about the death of her son, George Munro, who had sickened and died between April and July 1590. The two trials were both conducted on the same day and, not surprisingly, both the accused were acquitted.[18]

The remarkable thing, however, is that the case ever came to trial at all, both in 1577 and thirteen years later. In 1577 the Sheriff of Cromarty and Robert Munro of Foulis had probably only dared to move against Katherine and her accomplices because her terrible father was, momentarily at least, under the restraint of his son and fellow clansmen. The case brought by Hector Munro a dozen years later looks like the result of long years of waiting for revenge upon his step-mother, even though he must have known that he could not hope to obtain a conviction. Perhaps the final element that led Hector to take action was the visit of King James himself to Chanonry and Cromarty in July 1589, where he enjoyed himself seeing the countryside and hunting. The King's interest in witchcraft was already well established, and he certainly knew of the Foulis case.[19] By the following year he would be active himself in the persecution of the North Berwick witches supposed to have summoned up adverse winds against the fleet bringing his bride, Anne of Denmark, to Scotland.

Katherine's countersuit was not only defensive; it was also the result of immediate grief for the death of the son for whom in 1577 she had been ambitious enough to commit murder. Katherine's charges were the final vindictive throw of a terrible, and remarkable, woman.

The Foulis trial, although its details are unique, fits well into the general history of Scottish witchcraft. It took place at the beginning of the period of the first of the great witch scares in Scotland in 1590–1. Throughout the following century there were to be periodic outbreaks of witch panic and trials. With the exception of the panic of 1649, when no witch trials are recorded in the region, the rise and fall of prosecutions in the Cromarty Firth area tended to follow the national pattern.[20] There were outbreaks in the late 1620s and early 1630s, and again in 1662–3 (when three witches were tried at Scatwell and two at Cromarty), and again in the mid-1670s and the late 1690s. The fate of the vast majority of local witches is not known, although a few were given non-capital sentences. The only ones known to have suffered burning were those involved in the Foulis case. By the second half of the seventeenth century increasing doubts were being expressed about the methods of torture used to obtain confessions and 'proof' as well as the diabolical nature of witchcraft itself. Amongst those who were strongly critical of the use of torture to obtain convictions in witchcraft cases was the Lord Advocate, George Mackenzie of Rosehaugh. Nevertheless, as late as 1698 the presbytery of Tain was much concerned with rooting out 'spells, charms and other practice of witchcraft.'[21]

It may have been as a result of this that a number of witches were brought before the bailie of Fortrose for examination in 1699. Amongst the accused was Margaret Kyle, the wife of David Stewart, in Balmaduthy (now Belmadathy). The charge grew out of an argument Margaret had had with a neighbour, Katherine Davidson, when their stock became mixed up together. Margaret had threatened Katherine 'that she should have neither sock nor coulter going upon the ground, and that thereafter she lost ane ox that fell and brake his bones.'[22] It is easy to see from this example why the bulk of witchcraft accusations sprang from arguments between neighbours and, more often than not, were focussed upon women with sharp tongues, who may or may not have had special powers.

This appears to have been the last witchcraft case in the region to have come before a properly constituted court for hearing. Its result is unknown. By now the courts were more usually concerned with those who attacked suspected witches than with witchcraft itself. In 1737 the presbytery of Tain moved to deal with people who cut suspected witches on the forehead as a countercharm. At a meeting at Cromarty the presbytery ordered all ministers within its jurisdiction to instruct their people against such evil practices.[23]

Nevertheless, as late as 1750, a particularly horrible case of this counter magic emerged in Rosskeen, where a number of Munro tacksmen from Alness and Rosskeen used the cover of darkness to break into two houses occupied by Frasers in Obsdale. They dragged the inhabitants from their beds, cut their foreheads with swords, and then took away squares of cloth cut from their victims' shirts to take away their magical powers. Only a servant girl escaped by having the presence of mind to call out, 'I'm a Munro.' The terrified victims were called before the kirk session and, slowly, the sorry story came out. The case was remitted to the presbytery in Tain where the tacksmen were ordered to be publicly rebuked before the congregations of Rosskeen and Alness.[24]

The Obsdale incident shows that, even as the official attitude towards witchcraft relaxed, the belief in it throughout the countryside remained strong and elements of these beliefs survive to the present day. Hugh Miller, for all his scientific rationalism, never completely overcame the childhood beliefs in spells, witches and ghosts; indeed, the tension between the scientific and superstitious halves of his intellect may have contributed to his mental breakdown and suicide in 1856. The witch craze of the seventeenth century was but one symptom of a profoundly disturbed society. It was inevitable that many would look to find the source of their ills in supernatural powers and seek to find scapegoats. Thus the seventeenth century peaks of the Scottish witch craze coincide with periods of plague or famine, or with political change and warfare.

The clans of the Cromarty Firth were also affected by these periods of instability. By the early seventeenth century the chief's traditional right to raise military levies was being slowly transformed into the 'clan regiment' as something more professional and organised, not to say entrepreneurial. Some of these 'clan regiments' were large. The funeral of Lord Lovat in the early 1630s was said to have been attended by nine hundred Mackenzies, a thousand Rosses and hundreds of Munros.[25] Some chiefs were using clansmen as the basis of mercenary regiments. A company under Robert Monro, the younger brother of Monro of Obsdale, sailed from Cromarty on Wednesday 10 October 1626 for Lugstad on the Elbe where it joined a regiment raised by Sir Donald Mackay of Strathnaver fighting for the King of Denmark and later Gustavus Adolphus, King of Sweden.[26] Soon they were joined by other Munros, led by the chief himself with a number of followers, including his castle porter. Over the next few years regular recruiting went on throughout the Cromarty Firth. It was claimed that by 1631 the Scots Brigade consisted of 13,000 men of whom three generals, eight colonels, five lieutenant colonels, eleven majors and over thirty captains were Munros. This army fought its way from Sweden to the shores of the Adriatic, 'and, had our Master of worthy memory lived, we had crossed the Alps into Italie, and saluted the Pope within Rome.'[27]

Aside from the raising of 'clan regiments' there were other changes taking place in the clan system as well. By the end of the middle ages the traditional rights of the chief had been supplemented by a legal structure, granting him extensive rights over his followers, including in some cases that of hearing criminal cases usually reserved to the crown such as murder and arson. Below these regality courts were baron courts associated with the administration of the chief's estates and dealing with more mundane matters, such as boundary disputes and settling agricultural rents and practices, such as preventing the cutting of young trees and too many peats.

But the overriding change that determined the political course of the next century and a half was the Reformation of 1560. Its most immediate effect around the Cromarty Firth was the scramble for church lands, which began even before the Reformation, by important local families. The practical consequences of this change can be seen in the careers of the two local lairds who voted for the abolition of the Mass and papal authority in the Reformation Parliament: Nicholas Ross, abbot of Fearn and Provost of Tain, and Robert Munro of Foulis.

Ross, the son of a priest and the father himself of four hopeful sons, saw the decline of the old church as a means of advancing his own career and establishing a family dynasty. He had been legitimated on royal authority in 1543, and obtained the same privilege for his sons in the following year. Then he set about acquiring land and building up a complex network of alliances and obligations that made him one of the most powerful men in the region in the years leading up to 1560. In 1559 he entered into the agreement with his even more ruthless kinsman, Alexander Ross of Balnagown, who promised 'to mantene and defend ye said Nicholas . . . contrar all mortal . . . I sall use the councell of the said Nicholas in all effars perteyning to my hous, kyn and freynds induring my lyfetyme.'[28]

Nicholas used this promised protection when, before he set out for the Edinburgh Parliament in 1560, he transferred a number of relics from Tain to Balnagown for safekeeping, including 'ane hede of silver callit sanct Duthois hede, his chast blede [chest bone] in gold and his ferthyr [portable shrine] in silver gylt with gold.'[29] The relics that had been at the centre of Tain's centuries-old pilgrimage trade were never returned, and their fate is unknown.

Although organised monastic life ended with the Reformation the holding of hereditary church offices did not. Nicholas remained abbot of Fearn, only resigning in 1567 when he was succeeded in office by his son. By now, of course, such offices were scarcely spiritual ones: hereditary abbots (or commendators) were, in effect, landlords of the secularised lands that had once belonged to the religious house.

Something similar was going on further to the west. Between 1541 and 1558 Robert Munro of Foulis was granted the church lands of Lemlair, Pellaig, Wester Glens and Boath by the bishop of Ross, and at the beginning of 1560 he obtained the lands of Kiltearn from the vicar general of the pre-Reformation diocese.[30] Munro held these lands in return for a stipulated rent to be paid to the relevant church authority. After the Reformation these rents continued to be paid, but by holding such lands lairds were able to direct church affairs closely on their estates. Where the laird was a supporter of the Reformation it took effect quickly. Thus, the first reformed minister of Kiltearn was Foulis' kinsman, Donald Munro, Dean of the Isles in the pre-Reformation church, who appears as reformed 'Superintendent' of Ross in 1563.

With the possible exception of the Urquharts of Cromarty, all the local families benefitted from the land rush after the abolition of the old church. Immediately after the Reformation Henry Sinclair, Bishop of Ross, who as president of the College of Justice spent most of his time in Edinburgh, complained that his castle in Chanonry had been seized by Highland ruffians for nine months. When Sinclair was succeeded by John Leslie in 1567 the new bishop gave a charter for his lands — including the castle — to a cousin, who then sold it to Mackenzie of Kintail. The stage was set for a long and unseemly wrangle over Chanonry castle between the new owner and the bailie of the bishop's lands, Munro of Newmore, who had been appointed to this office by the regent of the baby King James VI. The feud lasted for three years and occasionally erupted into violence, before being won by Mackenzie forces who had captured and held the steeple of the cathedral.[31]

By the early seventeenth century, however, some local chiefs were in financial difficulties. After the death of George Ross in 1615 the creditors moved in on 'the distrest house of Balnagown' and desperate shifts had to be made to stave off the sale of the entire estate.[32] The estate of Robert Dubh, the 'Black Baron' of Foulis, had been mortgaged to his uncle, Lord Lovat, by 1617, and in 1626 he took service on the continent in an attempt to revive his fortunes after having been, in the somewhat indulgent words of his cousin, Colonel Robert Munro, 'a little prodigall in his spending [and] having engaged his revenues for some years to pay his creditors . . .'[33]

The Black Baron died in Germany of 'a languishing Feaver' from a foot wound received in battle in 1633, and his successor, his brother Hector, after returning briefly to Scotland also died on the continent in 1635. On the whole, however, the Munro lairds were successful in retaining control of their estates. The military abilities of the returning Munro soldiers, and the family's largely presbyterian sympathies, were important elements in preserving the Munro heritage during a difficult period. Colonel Robert Munro returned in 1642 to lead a Scottish covenanting army in Ireland before being captured and spending some time in the Tower of London. At the Restoration Sir George Munro of Newmore and Culcairn was appointed military commander-in-chief in Scotland. Sir John Munro of Foulis, nicknamed 'the presbyterian mortarpiece' for his long and costly adherence to that church during the period of episcopacy, eventually reaped the reward of his constancy when in 1689 he was one of the representatives who offered the Scottish crown to William and Mary.[34]

Other families, such as the Urquharts of Cromarty, were destroyed by the civil war, their fate having been sealed by their unwavering support for the crown. Sir Thomas Urquhart (Fig. 6) is one of the most remarkable figures in seventeenth century Scotland, the fantastical representative of a family whose pretensions had long outrun their means. After a brief and ineffectual royalist campaign in Aberdeenshire in 1638 young Thomas went south with other Royalists to the court of Charles I, and began his literary career with a collection of epigrams designed to ensure his reputation as a Cavalier wit.

Thomas Urquhart was knighted by the King in 1641, and succeeded his father in the following year to what he called 'ane crazed estate.' He came to Cromarty and made some attempt to put his affairs in order before returning south and taking up again his career as courtier and writer: this time he produced *The Trissotetras*, a work on trigonometry. By 1645 he was back

6. Sir Thomas Urquhart of Cromarty.

again in Cromarty, surrounded by creditors and Covenanters, but taking little active part in the growing political crisis. It was only after Charles I's execution in January 1649 that he joined with a group of royalist lairds that was defeated at Balvenie.

King Charles's namesake and heir crossed to Scotland, accepted the Covenant, and was crowned at Scone on New Year's Day 1651. A new

Scottish army was raised to take the new king's cause into England. It included Sir Thomas and David Ross of Balnagown, who had by now changed sides three times. Ross fitted out a company of clansmen and marched south; Sir Thomas, apparently, took only himself and a chest of his precious manuscripts that were lost in the rout at Worcester in which large numbers of Ross clansmen were killed. Both Balnagown and Urquhart were taken prisoner. Ross would die in prison, but for Sir Thomas imprisonment was a liberation of his literary talents. During his time in the Tower of London he produced the family genealogy that traced the Urquharts back to Adam and Eve, as well as *The Jewel* and *The Logopandecteision*. Urquhart hoped that these strange, encyclopaedic works, and the first two books of his remarkable English translation of Rabelais's *Gargantua and Pantagruel* that were published in 1653, would secure his release and revive his fortunes. He was only successful in the first objective, for by the mid 1650s he had been freed and was living in Holland.

According to tradition, Sir Thomas Urquhart died in a fit of laughter upon hearing of the restoration of King Charles II in 1660. Certainly, by August of that year Sir Thomas's brother, Sir Alexander Urquhart, was petitioning, unsuccessfully, for a commission as hereditary sheriff of Cromarty, apparently as Sir Thomas's heir. In fact, from 1650 onwards Sir Thomas's lands had been slowly dissipated and although Alexander was able to retain some rights, the bulk of the lands had passed into the hands of a Covenanting cousin, John Urquhart of Craigstoun. In 1661 the barony and sheriffdom of Cromarty were made over entirely to Craigstoun who, with King Charles restored to his throne, immediately changed sides, and became a Royalist, a supporter of episcopacy, and a friend of Middleton, Charles II's Scottish governor.

But even this *volte face* could not preserve the estates in the family. Craigstoun, who inherited the family instability, was in constant financial difficulties and in 1678 he committed suicide by disembowelling himself at a dinner party. His heir, Jonathan, was dissolute, feckless and no match for the rising power of Sir George Mackenzie, who had been casting covetous eyes on the estate for some time. In 1684 the latter was able to buy the lands and sheriffdom of Cromarty at a judicial sale.[35]

Of all the families to benefit from the changes brought by the Reformation and the civil war, perhaps the most important, and successful, were the Mackenzies. They were relative newcomers to the extreme fringes of Easter Ross, although they had been established in Strathpeffer and the western part of the county from at least the fourteenth century. The rise of the family of Mackenzie of Seaforth dates from the forfeiture of the Lords of the Isles in the late fifteenth century, when they were able to exploit the power vacuum left in the west to their own advantage. The power of the clan grew through the establishment of a large number of cadet branches in the sixteenth and seventeenth centuries.

Among the Mackenzies two branches that were to be of particular consequence in the Cromarty Firth area were Tarbat and Rosehaugh, and their rise shows a family moving from a traditional Celtic and Highland past to positions of power and influence in Edinburgh and London. By the early seventeenth century the Seaforth heir was a minor and the affairs of the family were in the capable hands of Sir Rorie Mackenzie, Tutor of Kintail, who built Castle Leod in Strathpeffer (Figs 7, 8). He not only discharged his duties towards his young nephew; he also created his own family dynasty through the purchase of lands in the eastern part of the county of Ross, largely at the expense of one of the family's traditional adversaries, the Munros. In 1623 Sir Rorie bought a wide stretch of lands between Tarrell and Tarbat Ness from George Munro of Meikle Tarrel for 110,000 merks,[36] and in 1656 his grandson, Sir George Mackenzie of Tarbat purchased another old Munro estate, Milntoun [modern Milton], from Sir John Innes, changing the castle's name to New Tarbat and making it his family's main northern residence. From this compact land base in Easter Ross Mackenzie of Tarbat extended his power and influence. The family's rise in fortune was marked by the creation of the viscountcy of Tarbat in 1685 and the earldom of Cromartie, conferred by a grateful Queen Anne for Tarbat's loyalty and service to the crown, in 1703 (Fig. 9).

The other important local Mackenzie family, that of Rosehaugh, sprang from another Sir George Mackenzie whose father, the laird of Lochslin, was trained as a lawyer. After the Restoration his gifts, and support for the royal house, led to a rapid rise in the legal hierarchy and he was able to purchase the estate of Rosehaugh in the Black Isle in 1668–9. In 1677 Sir George Mackenzie became Lord Advocate, and his prosecutions of the Covenanters earned him his common nickname, 'Bloody Mackenzie'. Yet there was another, much more attractive, side to Sir George Mackenzie. He was, unlike so many public figures of the period, constant in his political beliefs and support of the Stuart dynasty, and a charming and witty speaker who also possessed considerable literary gifts. In 1661 he had written the first Scottish novel, *Aretina*, and towards the end of his life founded the Advocates' Library in Edinburgh (now the National Library of Scotland). His last act before going into exile after the deposition of King James VII was to write a Latin oration for the opening of the library.

As relative newcomers to Easter Ross the Mackenzies perhaps depended less on the ties of kinship and the personal loyalty of local followers and clansmen than did the older established families of the region. For the Mackenzie cousins the ties that mattered were those of loyalty between branches of the family, and the loyalties of their political allies, clients and lawyers in Edinburgh and London.

While the first half of the century had still belonged to the 'old families' of Munro, Ross and, to a lesser extent, Urquhart, the rise of the Mackenzies, especially the Earls of Cromartie, dominates the history of the region in the later seventeenth century. Clan alliances and clan feuds continued to be

7. Castle Leod.

important factors in life around the Firth until well into the seventeenth century, when to a certain extent they were overtaken by the fullscale conflict of the Civil Wars. Yet even then the choice of sides was often determined as much on the basis of family loyalties and antagonisms as political or religious beliefs. Although there was frequent changing of sides it is possible to say that, on the whole, the Rosses and Munros supported the rights of the presbyterian church and parliament against the royalist and episcopalian Mackenzies and Urquharts.

Because of the political allegiances of the major families, the Cromarty Firth region played its part in the conflicts of the mid-seventeenth century and, so far as the ordinary people were concerned, this usually meant the menfolk following their chiefs to war. Immediately after the National Covenant had been drawn up in 1638, lairds such as Balnagown and Foulis were ordered to call up their levies: four hundred men from the presbyteries of Inverness, Dingwall, Chanonry and Tain were ordered to meet at Elgin.[37] These local militias were supplemented by the trained mercenaries who returned from their service on the continent. Until the English occupation of Scotland in 1651, when garrisons were placed at Inverness, Cromarty and Brahan, these local levies for military service were a regular occurrence and they resumed again in the 1660s, on a much more organised basis. In 1664, for example, the magistrates of Tain were ordered by the Privy Council in

33

8. The entrance to Castle Leod.

Edinburgh to draw up a list of able-bodied seamen and fishermen living within
their bounds, for possible service in the navy.[38] In the 1670s and 80s regular
recruiting in the Highlands began, supplemented by the fixed levies raised and
equipped by landlords. In 1680, for example, George Paterson of Seafield,
lieutenant of a local regiment of foot, acknowledged the arrival of David Ross
of Balnagown's eight 'sufficient soldiers which is his full proportione.'[39] Not
only were men called away to fight, the land itself was fought over and sacked
by passing armies. Troops were quartered in local communities and forced
levies raised to feed and clothe them. Quartering was unpopular and could
have dire economic consequences. In 1690 the tenants and heritors of
Pitmaduthy made a claim against the government for damage sustained when
soldiers from Castle Leod were quartered on them.[40]

9. Sir George Mackenzie, 1st Viscount Tarbat and Earl of Cromartie.

The effect of war on the small, isolated agricultural communities of the Cromarty Firth must have been terrible. Men left to fight and some of them never returned. For a society in which life and labour was based on the family unit, the consequences of being without an able bodied man, or becoming an orphan or widow, could be stark. There is evidence of this in a sad entry in the minutes of the Dingwall Presbytery records. In 1666 the case of Janet Neinan of Kiltearn came before the fathers and elders. Her husband had been captured at the Battle of Worcester fifteen years before and transported to Barbados. She had learned that he had married there and now she wished to be free to marry again.[41]

Even with the Restoration and the end of fighting, there is evidence that the long years of conflict had left their unsettling marks on local society. In 1682, part of the general instructions sent out by the Commissioners of Justiciary in Ross and Cromarty to parish constables included orders to seize, in addition to ordinary lawbreakers, '. . . all persons travelling and carrying firearms seven miles from their ordinary homes and seize all wanting [not having] passes, all night walkers, sturdie beggars, Egyptians [gypsies] . . .'[42]

Yet, despite the dislocation brought by the civil wars, there were at the same time signs of improvement. Even as the wars raged some landlords were looking to the future. One of these was the ever-hopeful Sir Thomas Urquhart, who, in characteristic style, wrote of his plans in his *Logopandecteision*, in 1653:

> I have, or at least had, before I was sequestered, a certain harbour or bay in goodness equal to the best in the world, adjacent to a place which is the head town of the Shire . . . This harbour, in all the Latine maps of Scotland is called *Portus salutis*; by reason that ten thousand ships together may within it ride in the greatest tempest that is as in a calm; by vertue of which conveniency, some exceeding rich men, of five or six several nations, masters of ships and merchant adventurers, promised to bring their best vessels and stocks for trading with them and dwell in that my little town with me . . .
>
> By which means, the foresaid town of Cromarty, for so it is called, in a very short space, would have easily become the richest of any within threescore miles thereof.

Alas, as with so many of Sir Thomas's schemes, this one too was destined to come to nothing, but he deserves to be remembered as the first in a long line of planners and dreamers who have foretold fantastic futures for the Cromarty Firth. It was not to be the ancient family of Urquhart of Cromarty that was to achieve Sir Thomas's dream of:

> Keeping at work many hundreds of persons in divers kindes of manufactures; brought from beyond sea the skillfull'st artificers could be hired for money, to instruct the natives in all manner of honest trades . . . induced masters of husbandry to reside amongst my tenants, for teaching them the most profitable way . . . of digging, ditching, hedging, dunging, sowing, harrowing, grubbing, reaping, threshing, killing, milling, baking, brewing, batling of pasture ground, mowing, feeding of herds, flocks, horse and cattel; making good use of the excresence of all these; improving their herbages, dayries, mellificiaries fruitages; setting up the most expedient agricolary instruments of wains, carts, slades, with their several devices of wheels and axle-trees, plows and harrows of divers sorts, feezes, winders, pullies, and all other manner of engines fit for easing the toyl and furthering the work . . .

Ironically, it was the man who supplanted Sir Thomas's family who began to make these dreams come true, not out of the idealism that Sir Thomas professed, but from the most hard-headed of motives: George Mackenzie of Tarbat was building a powerful family dynasty and supporting an active public career and both these strenuous activities required money. The most immediate consequence of Mackenzie's takeover of Cromarty was that he was able to combine the estate and the Urquharts' hereditary sheriffdom with his own scattered holdings, to create a new county, Cromarty, which remained separate until the nineteenth century.

George Mackenzie, first Earl of Cromartie, was the region's first improver and the changes he brought though they did not solve his perpetual cash problems set the area on its modern course.[43] Cromarty's thriving trade had declined badly during the wars. In 1655 an English Customs officer sent north by the Cromwellian government to advise on Scottish Customs described Cromarty as a 'little toune in a bottome, with one of the delicatist harbours reputed in all of Europe . . . [but] nothing [exciseable] comes more than a little salt to serve the countrey.'[44] By the 1660s this picture of an underutilised port, with no export trade, was changing. Bere and other cereals were being exported in large quantities in the 1660s, and from the time Lord Tarbat became the baron he executed regular agreements with Leith merchants and Edinburgh brewers for the sale of his crops and fish, which were shipped south in specially chartered vessels. The town's change from being a royal burgh to a burgh of barony may, in fact, have been a sign of success rather than a symbol of decline. It was certainly so for Lord Tarbat, since by converting it to a 'burgh of barony' he brought the economic life of the town entirely under his control, and avoided having to pay a number of onerous dues. Cromarty was Lord Tarbat's access to the world, and it was the world's point of access to the Firth; a small southern foothold on the edge of the Highlands. Thus, by the end of the seventeenth century the burgh was essentially English-speaking while Gaelic remained the language of the other parishes around the Firth.[45]

Over the door of Royston, his Edinburgh house, Sir George Mackenzie of Tarbat had had carved an elegant Latin motto which translated said:

> Riches unemployed are of no use/but made to circulate they are of much good . . .

Another means of employing his riches was to stimulate local trade, and so, in addition to Cromarty, Tarbat founded several other burghs of barony, local communities on his estates to whom he gave the right to hold weekly markets. These new burghs included Tarbat (1678), and 'Castlehaven' [Portmahomack] (1678) where Lord Tarbat was building a harbour in the closing years of the seventeenth century. The small community at Milton, next to New Tarbat house, was raised to the status of a burgh of regality; even today the small eighteenth century cross in the middle of the green is a reminder of the four regular markets held there until the late nineteenth century.[46] The bulk of the Cromartie estates' wealth came in the rents, which were paid, predominantly in kind, by the tenants. Amongst Lord Tarbat's first developments were modern water-mills for grinding the tenants' grain at Milton. He also built girnels [storehouses] there and at Portmahomack and

10. New Tarbat Castle (demolished).

Cromarty.[47] The latter survives only in small fragments but the girnel at Portmahomack remains intact.

The climax of Lord Tarbat's changes was his rebuilding of the old Munro castle at Milton that had caught Foulis' eye as a seat for his heir. His architect may have been James Smith (*c.* 1645–1731), who was responsible for New Hailes and Yester in the Lothians.[48] At New Tarbat (Fig. 10) Smith did his best to convert an existing fabric into a balanced palladian facade. The result, a three storied house with a central doorway and regular ranks of windows and matching towers at the corners, was perhaps not totally successful as an architectural composition, but it can claim to have been the first classical house in the Highlands. Inside the house, instead of bare stone walls covered with tapestries, this new sort of house was wood-panelled and contained the first sash windows ever seen in the Highlands. The gardens were equally remarkable, for Lord Tarbat was an enthusiastic gardener. The grounds were set out in the elaborate and symmetrical style of the period and contained such exotic plants as the first lime tree ever seen in the region.

Tarbat's improvements show him as a man both of his time, and ahead of it. The changes must have seemed strange, even bizarre, to his tenantry and neighbours, but they were the way of the future. Despite his astuteness, however, sometimes even Lord Tarbat's ideas outran reality. When in 1712 the Earl's Edinburgh coach was shipped by sea to Tarbat its wheels were taken off. And so it remained, because when it arrived it was found that there were no roads for it to run on.

NOTES

1. R. Franck, *Northern Memoirs Calculated for the meridian of Scotland to which is added the contemplative and practical angler, writ in the year 1658*, new edn. with an introduction by Walter Scott, Edinburgh, 1821. The passages relating to the Cromarty Firth occur on pages 207–215.

2. I. D. Whyte, *Agriculture and Society in Seventeenth Century Scotland*, Edinburgh, 1979, p. 9.

3. R. W. Munro, *Tain*, p. 72.

4. W. Macgill, *Old Ross-shire and Scotland as Seen in the Tain and Balnagown Documents*, Inverness, 1909, vol. I, no. 493.

5. Monica Clough has based these estimates for the population of Cromarty and the Black Isle on hearth tax figures; 'Cromarty and the Grain Trade' (typescript of a lecture delivered at Cromarty in 1980; generously lent by the author). In Cromarty there were 352 hearths and 247 males of military age; the total for the rest of the Black Isle was 818 hearths, with perhaps an average of four inhabitants for each dwelling.

6. It is possible to gain an idea of the relative importance of the Cromarty area burghs by the taxes they paid in 1697 compared with other Scottish towns: Edinburgh (the largest town in the country) paid £33, Glasgow £15, Aberdeen £6/10, Dundee £5/5/8, Perth £3/17, Inverness £1/16, Tain 7 shillings, Dingwall 2 shillings, Cromarty and Fortrose 5 shillings each.

7. J. R. Ross, *The Great Clan Ross*, 2nd edn., np, Canada, 1972, p. 85.

8. Macgill, *Ross-shire*, vol. 1, no. 902 (1572).

9. *Ibid.*, no. 677.

10. *RPC*, vol. 2 (1569–1578), pp. 409, 443, 594–5.

11. Macgill, *Ross-shire*, vol. 2, no. 1006.

12. *RPC*, vol. 3, pp. 361–2 (1581).

13. From evidence given to the Scottish Mussel and Bait Beds Committee by Alexander Mackenzie, Registrar at Cromarty, *Report*, (1889), p. 15, queries 470–1. I am indebted to R. W. Munro for pointing out this evidence. Hugh Miller also records a local tradition of southern plantation at Cromarty by James VI: see Miller, *Tales and Sketches* pp. 148–9.

14. Ross, *The Great Clan Ross*, p. 89.

15. The detailed charges of the case against Lady Foulis are given in the indictment of her trial in 1590 (based on depositions made by the condemned in 1577) and are printed in R. Pitcairn (ed.), *Ancient Criminal Trials in Scotland*, Edinburgh, 1833; vol. 1, pp. 185–91. The trial is also described in R. Chambers, *Domestic Annals of Scotland*, vol. 1, Edinburgh, 1859, pp. 202–9. The case has long attracted attention and has even been the subject of a novel: E. Sutherland, *The Eye of God*, London, 1977.

16. Pitcairn, op. cit., vol. 1, p. 197 article 21.

17. For a discussion of this case as it concerns Coinneach Odhar see E. Sutherland, *Ravens and Black Rain: The story of Highland second sight*, London, 1985. The name Brahan Seer was invented by Alexander Mackenzie, in his *Prophecies of the Brahan Seer*, Inverness, 1877.

18. Traditionally, it is claimed that Robert the younger outlived his father by eight months, but in fact the reverse is true, see R. W. Munro, *The Munro Tree (1738)*, p. 16, note R/1. Another confusion in the Foulis case is the venue for the trials, which is unspecified. Most authors have assumed that they took place in Edinburgh. It seems, however, from the composition of the juries, who were predominantly from Tain or nearby, that the trials took place in that town, thus making conviction even more unlikely.

19. *RPC*, vol. 4 (1585–1592), pp. xliii and 467 (note).

20. These figures are based on the list of cases and tables in C. Larner, C. H. Lee and H. McLachlan, *A Source book of Scottish Witchcraft*, Glasgow, 1977.

21. C. MacNaughton, *Church Life in Ross and Sutherland from the Revolution, 1688, to the Present Time*, Inverness, 1915, p. 15.

22. Larner, *et al.*, p. 276: from an unpublished manuscript of the Boyds of Tochrigg in Glasgow University Library.

23. MacNaughton, *Church Life*, pp. 145–6. As late as 1845 a case of 'cutting above the head' occurred at Portmahomack when a fisherman wounded an old woman he believed had bewitched his boats. Barron, J., *The Northern Highlands in the Nineteenth Century*, vol. 3, Inverness, 1903–13, p. 85.

24. MacNaughton, *Church Life*, pp. 199–206.

25. J. Munro, 'The clan period', *RC Book*, p. 138.

26. Colonel Robert Monro, *Monro his expedition with the worthy Scots regiment (Called Mac-Keyes Regiment) levied in August 1626 . . . collected and gathered together at spare houres,* London, 1637 (Another edition was published in 1644).

27. *Ibid.*, p. 6. The service of the Highland regiments under the King of Sweden had at least one long-term reciprocal consequence around the Cromarty Firth: the introduction of Gustavus as a common Christian name.

28. Macgill, *Ross-shire*, vol. 1, no. 6.

29. *Ibid.*, no. 8.

30. *Calendar of Munro of Foulis Writs, 1299–1823*, Scottish Record Society no. 71, Edinburgh, 1940, no. 77.

31. Munro, 'Clan period', *RC Book*, p. 135.

32. Macgill, *Ross-shire*, vol. 2, no. 1013.

33. *Monro's expedition*, p. 5.

34. C. I. Fraser, *The Clan Munro*, p. 26.

35. These details of the decline of the estate of Cromarty after 1650 are taken from W. Ferguson, 'The Urquharts of Cromarty' by 'J. McK' in *The Scottish Genealogist*, vol. 6, no.2 (1959), pp. 16–18; vol. 6, no. 3, pp. 1–14.

36. Sir William Fraser, *The Earls of Cromartie; their kindred, country and correspondence*, Edinburgh, 1876, vol. 2, p. 429. A merk was 2/3 of a pound (thirteen shillings and fourpence), hence the purchase price was in excess of £73,000 Scots. By the time of the Union of 1707 the Scots pound was probably equal to 1/12 of an English pound.

37. Macgill, *Ross-shire*, vol. 1, no. 540.

38. *Ibid.*, no. 628 (misprinted as 228).

39. *Ibid.*, no. 585.

40. For example *Ibid.*, nos. 565–7; SRO GD 305/1/160, no. 35.

41. *Dingwall Presbytery*, pp. 310, 314.

42. Macgill, *Ross-shire*, vol. 1, no. 224.

43. Much of the following discussion is based on the work of Monica Clough in the Cromartie papers. She has published some of her findings in 'Making the most of one's resources: Lord Tarbat's development of Cromarty Firth', *Country Life*, 29 September 1977, vol. 162, pp. 856–8 and in 'The Cromartie estate, 1660–1784: aspects of trade and organization', in *Firthlands*. I am also grateful to Mrs Clough for discussing her conclusions with me.

44. P. Hume Brown, *Early Travellers in Scotland*, Edinburgh, 1894, p. 175.

45. C. W. J. Withers, '"The shifting frontier": The Gaelic-English boundary in the Black Isle, 1698–1881', *Northern Studies*, vol. 6, no. 2, 1985, p. 135. Fortrose was also English-speaking by this time.

46. G. S. Pryde, *The Burghs of Scotland, a Critical List*, Glasgow, 1965, pp. 76–8. For Milton see H. M. Meldrum, *Kilmuir Easter, the history of a Highland parish*, Inverness, 1935, pp. 5–6. Other burghs of barony founded in the area during the seventeenth century were: Balblair [Kirkmichael] (1678: founded by Dallas of St Martins), Culbokie (1678: Mackenzie of Findon), Obsdale or Alness (1690: Macintosh of Torcastle) and Foulis (1699: Munro of Foulis).

47. For the Cromartie and other girnels see M. Clough in *Firthlands*, and E. Beaton, 'Late seventeenth and eighteenth century estate girnels in Easter Ross and South East Sutherland', in the same volume, especially pp. 92–3, 136–8.

48. Details of the rebuilt New Tarbat are based on an eighteenth century drawing of the elevations in SRO RHP 45193. The architect employed at Tarbat is a subject of debate, but recent opinion tends to credit the building to James Smith: see H. M. Colvin, 'A Scottish origin for English Palladianism?', *Architectural History*, vol. 17 (1974). I am grateful to Ian Mowat of the University of Hull and Dr James Macaulay, of the Mackintosh School of Architecture, Glasgow, for discussing this subject with me.

3

'Learned and full of Faith'

In St Duthus Memorial Church in Tain there is a Victorian stained glass window. It shows John Knox reading the Confession of Faith at the Reformation Parliament of 1560. Among the members of the assembly shown in the window are the two local lairds who attended this meeting and voted for the abolition of papal authority, Catholic baptism and the mass: Nicholas Ross, provost of Tain and abbot of Fearn, and Robert Munro of Foulis. The window was placed there when the church was restored in the 1880s. It is striking evidence of the conventional nineteenth century view of the Reformation as a complete and rapid abandonment of the old church under the influence of Knox's vehemence, a revolution that came swiftly and was immediately accepted by all the people of Scotland yearning for freedom after long centuries of spiritual oppression.

The Reformation did indeed come quickly in 1560, but its acceptance and implementation throughout Scotland was a much slower process. It would take nearly a century and a half before the presbyterian system of church government ordained by John Knox and his successor, Andrew Melville, was achieved. In that process the religious history of the Cromarty Firth is both a reflection and an exemplar.

Protestant influences had been present in Scotland for some time before 1560. One of the earliest Scottish Lutherans was Patrick Hamilton, Commendator of Fearn, who is also commemorated by a tablet in St Duthus Church:

> Learned and full of Faith,
> He was the first preacher of the Reformation in Scotland,
> And the first to seal its doctrine by a martyr's death,
> Being burnt at the stake in St Andrews, twenty eighth February 1528
> His principles quickly spread over Scotland
> Their influence was felt in the neighbourhood of his monastery
> And was early and decidedly manifested within these walls
> Where this tablet is erected in his memory.

Patrick Hamilton was indeed one of the early protestant martyrs, but he was not the first, and despite his position as Commendator of Fearn there is no evidence that he ever came to the area. Related to the king, Hamilton was a young aristocrat who was given his commendatorship in order to finance his studies at the University of Paris. There is some evidence that his reforming principles led him later to resign the commendatorship.[1] After taking his degree he returned to Scotland at about the time the Scottish crown began to be active against heretics. The importation of Lutheran books was banned by Parliament and, when Hamilton began to preach these proscribed ideas, he was forced to flee abroad. He went to Wittenburg, where he met Martin Luther himself, before again returning to Scotland to teach at the University of St Andrews. Soon his lectures began to attract the unfriendly attention of the church authorities and he was summoned to answer thirteen charges of heretical teaching, ranging from justification by faith to the claim that the Pope was anti-Christ. He was found guilty and condemned to be burnt at the stake. The sentence was carried out swiftly while Hamilton's kinsman, King James IV, was in the north on a pilgrimage to the shrine of his favourite saint, Duthac of Tain, and unable to intervene.

Men supported the Reformation of 1560 for a variety of reasons, some like Hamilton due to genuine spiritual promptings, others for much more materialistic considerations. For example, Hamilton's eventual successor as titular abbot of Fearn, Nicholas Ross, was an ambitious man who saw the decline of the old church as a means to advance his own family. The other local laird who voted for the Reformation, Robert Munro of Foulis, was somewhat more disinterested in his support, although he too benefitted materially from the change. It was in those parishes most directly under Foulis' control that the Reformation took earliest root around the Cromarty Firth and throughout the subsequent centuries they remained noted for their religious fervour and radicalism.

With some notable exceptions the new church was to prove itself no friend to the traditional culture of the Highlander, precisely because the Reformation was such a radical and complete break with the past. In some senses it was only after the Reformation that many parts of Scotland were converted to the fuller aspects of Christianity for the first time. Before then, 'Christianity' in many areas owed more to pagan survivals than anything else. As late as the mid-seventeenth century the Presbytery of Dingwall was still experiencing problems in eradicating pagan practices such as the sacrifice of animals to 'Mourie' (a vestigial survival of the Celtic saint, Maelrubha), the use of spells, belief in holy wells, the practice of lighting Beltane fires, and witchcraft (although the presbytery tended to deal leniently with witches).[2]

The Church in the Highlands was to be an important factor in the greatest cultural failure of all, the decline of the Gaelic language from its position as the sole language of the entire region in the sixteenth century to its virtual extinction around the Cromarty Firth within the last few decades of this century.[3] The essential activity of the new resident parish clergy was preaching the gospel to their people in the vernacular language. In the Highlands, however, that language was Gaelic and, despite the publication of John Carswell's Gaelic version of *The Book of Common Order* in 1567, the Bible was not available in Gaelic until a version in classical Irish style was adopted for Scottish use and published in the 1690s. A Scottish Gaelic Bible did not appear until two centuries after the Reformation (the *New Testament* in 1767 and the *Old Testament* in 1801). This meant that in the Highlands both the teaching of religious truths and the expression of religious faith remained an essentially oral, non-literate process; ministers had to cultivate the skill of making their own simultaneous translations from the English *Bible* into Gaelic. The situation was not helped by the common identification of Gaelic with lawlessness by the authorities in Edinburgh, a sentiment enshrined in the 1616 Education Act, framed for the advancement of 'the trew religioun' in order that:

> the vulgar Inglishe toung be universallie plantit and the Irishe [Gaelic] language, whilk is one of the cheif and principall causis of the continewance of barbarities and incivilities amongis the inhabitantis of the Ilis and Heylandis, may be abolisheit and removit.

Furthermore Scots, or 'Inglishe', was the language of administration in the higher courts of the church, such as presbyteries and synods. The earliest surviving presbytery minutes for the region, those for Dingwall, commence in 1649 and are written in Scots, although it is probable that the actual proceedings were in Gaelic.[4] English was an essential qualification for active involvement in the courts of the church, but as late as 1727 the Presbytery of Tain could still find it necessary to order that someone competent in the English language must be found in the parish of Tarbat to become a ruling elder and attend presbytery meetings; the existing elders only understood Gaelic.[5] In 1792 there were complaints about a case heard in English before the Kirk Session of Kilmuir Easter because only one of the ten members of the body understood the language.[6]

More immediately, the dominance of Gaelic exacerbated the difficulties of filling Highland parishes with suitable clergy in the years after 1560.[7] The 1562 General Assembly complained that 'the north countrie for the most part [is] destitute of ministers.' Some of the old clergy, such as George Duncan at Kilmuir Easter, conformed to the new church, as did the vicar of Dingwall, a cousin of Munro of Foulis. The archdeacon of the pre-Reformation Diocese of the Isles, Donald Monro the son of the laird of Kiltearn (and another cousin of Foulis), returned to his native parish as reformed minister. Monro had had a distinguished career in the old church. His account of his 1549 journey around the Hebrides is one of the earliest descriptions of this part of Scotland.[8] Monro's new home — for according to tradition he lived in the former seat of the Bishops of Ross at Castlecraig on the Black Isle — may have been more comfortable than the conditions he had been used to in the Isles, but for a man of about sixty years of age he still faced enormous challenges in his work. The reformers were so concerned that their new ministers should be the best men for the position that they were prepared to allow parishes to remain vacant rather than have them filled with inadequate clergy. This sparse complement of reformed ministers was assisted by temporary 'Readers' and 'Exhorters'. Thus, when the pre-Reformation vicar of Cromarty refused to conform, his curate, who had become protestant, was not apparently qualified to become minister; instead, he served as Reader and Schoolmaster of the burgh. Another way around the problem of lack of qualified clergy was to link parishes. Donald Monro's charge of Kiltearn was soon joined with Lemlair, and later with Alness, and he was assisted in covering this wide area by local Readers. By 1570 the thirty-five parishes of Ross had at least three ministers and nineteen Exhorters or Readers.

Another problem was finance. By the time of the Reformation all thirty-five churches in the diocese of Ross were appropriated with their revenues diverted away from the parish and the church served by a stipendiary priest. The non-resident vicar of Alness at the end of the fifteenth century was a grammarian at the new University of Aberdeen,[9] and his successor at Alness and Nigg at the time of the Reformation was John Davidson, Principal of Glasgow University, who after his conversion to Protestantism in 1559 became a leading reformer.

Finding the funds to pay ministers was a piecemeal process. Henry Sinclair, appointed bishop of Ross in 1558 but not consecrated until 1561, was largely an absentee but still diverted £50 from his own revenues to pay the 'prechar of the kirkis of Nyg and Terbat.'[10] In 1561 the Treasurer of the diocese of Ross provided one hundred merks from his own stipend to support the new reformed ministers of Urquhart and Logie Wester. Such piecemeal arrangements were not enough; a national system of finance had to be found.

Despite the radical nature of the Scottish Reformation and the violence of much of its rhetoric the end of the old church was a largely peaceful and, in some respects, a kindly one. Not only were monks allowed to live on in their crumbling monasteries until their death or to retire abroad, but existing benefice holders were also allowed to retain their revenues so that the pre-Reformation vicar of Lemlair was still collecting his in 1584. In 1562, however, it was agreed that these existing benefice holders should retain only two thirds of their revenues, with the remaining third going to support the clergy of the new church. At Alness, for example, the old rector, Thomas Ross the son of Abbot Nicholas, continued to draw his reduced funds while the church was served, from at least 1562, by an Exhorter apparently funded by some of the revenues the reformer John Davidson continued to draw from Alness and Nigg. The 'thirds of benefices' system never worked well, but it did help create a resident parish clergy in Ross. In 1561 only £379 was assigned from central funds for ministers' stipends; eight years later this amount had risen to £1,666, suggesting a complement of about fifty Ministers, Readers and Exhorters.

Another problem was how the church was to be organised on a regional basis. Bishops had not been abolished, but now were expected to act as 'Superintendents' of the areas of which they had once been diocesan. In Ross this system broke down when Henry Sinclair was succeeded in 1566 by a Catholic, the historian John Leslie. He was appointed by Mary Queen of Scots and, although forfeit when the Queen was deposed in 1567, continued to exercise his episcopal office intermittently in the 1570s and '80s.[11] In the immediate aftermath of the Reformation the lack of a resident Bishop or Superintendent led to the General Assembly appointing Donald Monro as Overseer of Ross in 1563, charged with the planting of kirks within the region and overseeing the life and work of the parish clergy. He held the position for twelve years, despite doubts about his lack of preaching ability and his command of spoken Scots.[12]

Within a decade of the Reformation the outlines of a reformed system of church government were in place. The parishes were slowly being filled by suitably qualified clergy and rudimentary Kirk Sessions, as ordained in John Knox's *First Book of Discipline* (1561), were perhaps already in being in some areas. The establishment of Presbyteries and Synods would come later. Yet for all this innovation it is impossible to know what the consequences of the Reformation were for ordinary people. In some respects little changed for them; they were still expected to pay their teinds [tithes] of food and animals to support the clergy, although it appears that some people attempted to use this obligation in order to get a better deal for themselves. The parishioners of Kiltearn, for example, apparently refused to pay the old vicar's stipend until 'ordour be put into the kirk.'[13] In other ways the changes brought by the Reformation to the lives of the people were profound. From now on the minister would be resident, living and working amongst the people of the parish. He, and the Kirk Session, would be responsible for the maintenance of Christian order and, in time, their oversight included nearly all aspects of life, from commerce to sexual morality.

The Kirk was a Godly Commonwealth made up of all the people of Scotland. Knox claimed that the Scottish Reformation was the purest reformation 'upon the face of the earth.' This idea of the special relationship of the people of Scotland with God was given more extreme expression by Andrew Melville's concept of the 'Two Kingdoms' — the claim not only that church and state were two separate entities, but that the church was superior to the state. It was Melville who called James VI 'God's sillie vassal' and was the first to demand explicitly the creation of Presbyteries (charged with overseeing the life of a group of parishes) and the abolition of Bishops. It was from Melville more than Knox that the idea came of a church of sanctified believers, set apart, and obliged by their state of grace to resist ungodly civil power. The existence of such religious fifth columns was something that no government could countenance, and was the reason such men as Mackenzie of Rosehaugh ('Bloody Mackenzie') acted as they did — because they believed that the power of the state was supreme over such sectarian enthusiasms: Mackenzie once even joked that whoever thought they had an independent church in their breast should conceive of their heads as steeples and hang bells therein. From such basic and irreconcilable differences came much of the intractable religious conflict and sectarian bitterness of the seventeenth century and after.

So long as the wily James VI remained king, however, there was little chance that the Melvillian system of church government could come into effect. The problems began with James's insensitive son, Charles I, who tried to impose a fully-blown episcopalian system in Scotland, modelled on that of England. When the Bishop of Ross attempted to use the so-called 'Laud's Liturgy' in his cathedral the schoolboys of Fortrose Grammar School burst into the church and attempted to burn the book on Chanonry Point. Resistance to Charles's policies resulted in the adoption, in 1638, of the National Covenant, a letter claiming that Charles's policies were an abrogation of the legally established and guaranteed status of the Scottish Church. After the initial signing of the Covenant in Edinburgh further copies of this letter were sent about the country for endorsement. Amongst the local notables promising 'to adhere to and defend the . . . true Religion' were Lord Lovat, Balnagown, Foulis and a number of Black Isle lairds. Later in the same year a General Assembly in Glasgow went further, deposing bishops and renouncing episcopal government. The stage was set for nearly half a century of intermittent and often bitter warfare, with changes in policy marked by changes in religion. Scotland was, by turns, episcopalian until 1638, then presbyterian until 1663, then episcopalian again until the Revolution of 1689 that brought the protestant William and Mary to the throne of Scotland.

It is possible to see something of the local consequences of these changes in the events that took place in the religiously sensitive parishes of Alness and Kiltearn in the second half of the seventeenth century. In 1652 the church of Kiltearn fell vacant. The Kirk Session called Andrew Munro but the appointment was opposed by Foulis and it failed to take effect. The church remained vacant for another year before Thomas Hog, chaplain to the covenanting Earl of Sutherland, was called to the charge. According to the Dingwall Presbytery Minutes Hog was 'acceptable to the godly of the west country' [i.e. the people of Kiltearn] and, what was even more important, to the laird. In October 1654 Thomas Hog preached in Gaelic and English before the Presbytery, was approved and admitted to the charge.[14] Backed by a sympathetic patron, Sir Robert Munro of Foulis, Hog set about the total spiritual reform of his parish. The laird had served in the protestant armies of Europe and this experience was perhaps reflected in the militant religious system introduced by his chosen minister of Kiltearn. The changes brought about by Thomas Hog at Kiltearn led ultimately to the area being nicknamed 'The Holy Land'.

Thomas Hog espoused a 'severe scholastic Calvinism' centred on the need for personal experience of conversion and continuous striving by the individual for assurance of salvation.[15] This perpetual self-examination was aided, under Hog, by the working out of a long series of questions he used to assess the spiritual state of his parishioners. The rigour of his system is indicated by the infrequency of communions held during his time at Kiltearn and the small number of people who actually felt themselves sufficiently in a state of grace to be able to receive the elements. During the later seventeenth century, under ministers such as Hog, the communion service began to assume the form it would have in the Highlands over the next two centuries, large but infrequent gatherings for sermons and exegesis, lasting several days and sometimes attracting people from long distances. Very few of those attending the communion season would actually take communion on the final day.

Much of Hog's teaching, and all of his preaching, would be extemporaneous not only because of the lack of published Gaelic devotional material but also the need to show forth the direct inspiration of God. Sanctity was often identified with prophetic gifts, a Christian borrowing of Highland second sight. Hog had this gift, as did the Kiltearn crofter, John Munro (Caird), the earliest of 'The Men' of Ross-shire, who came to prominence during Hog's incumbency.

By the eighteenth century 'The Men' had become virtually a lay confraternity, noted for their spiritual qualities and their ability to expound the truths of religion in simple terms that ordinary people could understand. In time, too, they came to have a distinctive appearance, long blue cloaks and handkerchiefs tied about their long hair. They played an especially important role during the regular fortnightly Fellowship Meetings that were also an innovation of Thomas Hog[16] and which became a major feature of church life in eighteenth century Easter Ross. Many of 'The Men' first came to the attention of the minister and his congregation as a result of their testimony during these Fellowship Meetings. Thereafter their gifts would be encouraged by the ministers, who not only saw the need to control this manifestation of popular religion within the church, but who could also see the value of 'The Men' as expositors of popular religion. The Fellowship Meetings were always presided over by the minister, but after opening with prayer and scripture readings a member of the meeting would propose 'The Question' that would then be replied to by one of 'The Men'. In time, too, they became favoured speakers at the Friday meetings preceding communions.[17]

Stories about the powers of John Munro and others of 'The Men' were manifold and became an important part of the region's folklore. After episcopacy was restored in 1663 and Thomas Hog deposed, John Munro became virtually the religious leader of the people of Kiltearn. A story from this period illustrates his prophetic gifts.

In 1679 the covenanter Walter Denoon, minister of Golspie, was captured and taken south. The distraught people of Kiltearn came to John Munro to ask what to do. He was silent for some time, before he said; 'Be quiet sirs, for I am persuaded, though Mr Walter be taken, he shall neither go to prison, nor die at this time . . . God would rescue him out of their hands.' And so it happened; Denoon was rescued by sympathetic Fife lairds and returned to Kiltearn.[18]

The restoration of episcopacy meant that a number of deprived ministers created what was virtually an unofficial, parallel church in some parishes around the Cromarty Firth. The wife of John McKillican, the minister of Fodderty, held land at Alness and he retired there, after being deprived of his charge, and continued to hold services. Thomas Hog, after his deprivation, spent some of his time at his family home in Moray, although he remained active in Kiltearn, supported by his patron, Munro of Foulis, who continued to pay his stipend until ordered to cease by the civil courts. Kiltearn's new episcopal minister, John Gordon, had a hard time of it. His stipend was not paid, and he met with resistance and antagonism from at least a hard-core minority of parishioners (it is impossible to know what proportion of the parishioners of Kiltearn supported Hog, although given the lead of Munro of Foulis it was probably considerable). Both Hog and McKillican continued to hold 'conventicles' (illegal religious services) within the parish and some families were prepared to allow their children to die unbaptised rather than bring them into the established church for the ceremony.[19]

It was a hard and uncompromising time, made worse by growing intransigence, bitterness and cruelty on both sides. Matters came to a head after the passage of an Act of Parliament forbidding conventicles. Thomas Hog, who ignored the Act, was captured in 1677 and imprisoned on the Bass Rock. At about the same time McKillican and the 'outed' covenanting minister of Cromarty, Hugh Anderson, performed communion in the house of the dowager Lady Foulis at Obsdale. The Bishop of Ross ordered out the soldiers but they arrived after the conventicle was over. According to tradition, McKillican was hidden from the soldiers under the voluminous cloak worn by the portly Sir John Munro of Foulis.[20] Eventually McKillican was captured in the house of Hugh Anderson at Cromarty and was also sent to the Bass Rock. After two periods of imprisonment McKillican was allowed to return to his wife's lands at Alness where he built a small chapel and continued to hold services until the restoration of presbyterianism. Thomas Hog, too, had been released, but was rearrested in 1684 following the swearing of a warrant against him by Sir George Mackenzie of Rosehaugh. He was summoned before the Privy Council in Edinburgh and sent into an exile that would take him eventually to Holland where he met, and impressed, William of Orange.[21]

It may have been in retaliation for the capture of Thomas Hog that in the same year a claim was raised before the Presbytery of Dingwall that Mr Gordon the minister of Kiltearn was the father of an illegitimate child; he in turn claimed that one of the witnesses against him had been offered a bribe by the laird of Foulis and the charge was dropped.[22]

McKillican died before he could be restored to Fodderty, but both Hugh Anderson of Cromarty and Thomas Hog of Kiltearn were returned to their churches after 1689. Anderson survived until 1707, Thomas Hog died in 1692. On his gravestone by the door of Kiltearn church is written the last of his prophecies: 'This stone shall bear witness against the parishioners of Kiltearn, if they bring ane ungodly minister in here.'[23]

In many respects this small group of Ross-shire covenanters were an unrepresentative group for their centres at Cromarty, Kiltearn and Alness were surrounded by more numerous episcopalian parishes. Nevertheless, the restoration of presbyterianism ensured the triumph of the religious system espoused by men such as McKillican and Hog. Their covenanting legacy was to shape the religious life of the Highlands until well into the present century, providing not only the theology and practice of the church but its mythology as well. Thomas Hog, too, has his nineteenth century memorial in St Duthus' church:

> That great and almost apostolical servant of Christ . . .
> Wandering, intercommuned, imprisoned, exiled,
> He ceased not to teach and preach Jesus Christ
> By his holy life and doctrine winning many souls for his Lord.
> In exile he won the friendship of King William III, then Prince of Orange
> Who consulted him on Scottish affairs
> Restored to his parish in 1690 he died there in 1692
> This tablet is erected to his memory
> Within the walls where in youth he worshipped.

The tablet is evidence of the power of the covenanting tradition two centuries after Hog's death; by the mid nineteenth century the tradition had taken on a new power during the 'Ten Years' Controversy' that led to the Disruption of 1843 and the establishment of the Free Church of Scotland. In the eighteenth century the tales told of Hog, McKillican, Anderson and others began to be supplemented by the writings of such church historians as Robert Wodrow. Hugh Miller, for example, grew up with such stories and used them with great effect in his own writings, while later in the nineteenth century *The Days of the Fathers in Ross-Shire* by the Rev. John Kennedy of Dingwall went through numerous editions and was required reading in any pious household in Ross and Cromarty until well into this century.[24]

Yet the triumph of this covenanting mythology can disguise the fact that the actual implementation of the Hog tradition was by no means swift and widespread. Hog and Anderson were unusual in that they survived episcopacy and were able to return to their original parishes. Elsewhere around the Cromarty Firth many episcopalian ministers remained in their charges, often without conforming and taking the necessary oath of allegiance to William and Mary, until well into the eighteenth century. Indeed, with the exception of Cromarty, most of the Black Isle and much of the central part of Easter Ross remained major centres of episcopacy until well into the nineteenth century.[25]

The fact was that, with exceptions such as Cromarty and Kiltearn, the triumph of presbyterianism in 1690 was not popular in the Highlands and in most areas 'the episcopalians had general support and were the Church of the people.'[26] Dingwall, for example, was noted for its episcopalian and Jacobite sympathies. In 1704 the town's long-serving and beloved episcopalian minister, John Macrae, died. Munro of Foulis had long had a strong influence on the town council of Dingwall, but not even he dared to move until Macrae was dead and the burgh magistrates were safely out of Dingwall. The Sunday following Macrae's death:

> Fowlis and his presbyterian minister with three or four score of men armed, came to the Town, brake open the Church doors and sett a guard thereupon. The magistrates of the village being near two miles out of the town in the next adjacent church [Fodderty], at Sermon, and that the whole people being of episcopal persuasion, the women and servants did raise a mobb, and chased the minister with Fowlis and his armed men out of the town, with little or no hurt: only two or three women of the town being wounded at the beginning which was what insensed the mobb.[27]

Four years later a second riot ensued when another attempt was made to present a presbyterian minister to the church at Dingwall. Presbyterian efforts were only crowned with success in 1716 but by then the general position of the episcopalians had changed drastically.

Until the death of Queen Anne the question of obtaining oaths of loyalty from episcopalian clergy had not been pursued with any diligence in the Highlands. In 1712, an Act of the new United Kingdom Parliament had granted toleration to Scottish episcopalians producing widespread anger amongst the presbyterians who saw this as an abrogation of their status as the national church guaranteed in the 1707 Act of Union. The succession of King George I in 1714 ended any chances of a peaceful restoration of the House of Stuart, and in 1715 came the first major attempt to restore the Stuarts by force. Many episcopalians were deeply involved in the rebellion and its failure brought a rapid deterioration in their position. In 1716 all meeting houses in Scotland where divine service was said without prayers for King George and his family were ordered to be closed. In 1719 episcopalian clergy who did not take the oath of loyalty to the House of Hanover were forbidden to officiate before a congregation of more than nine persons.

These penal laws, although they were not regularly enforced, eventually broke the power of the episcopalians. Nevertheless, there continued to be pockets of episcopalianism in the region throughout the eighteenth century. Robert Forbes, the episcopal Bishop of Ross, visited large congregations at Muir of Ord and confirmed believers amongst the followers of the laird of Cadboll during his visitations of his diocese in the later eighteenth century. Nevertheless, the decline of the episcopal church was inexorable: by the time of the compiling of the *Old Statistical Account* in the 1790s, for example, there were said to be only ten episcopalian families in Dingwall.

The growth in the presbyterian church in the Highlands was nurtured by this conflict with the episcopalians. The religious ideals represented by Thomas Hog and 'The Men' were of vital importance in this struggle, as was the influence of the 'Great Awakening' (or the 'Evangelical Revival'), a series of religious revivals that spread through Britain and the American colonies in the 1730s. The Cambuslang and Kilsyth Revivals of 1742 are usually seen as the beginning of this new, enthusiastic spirit in Scotland but three years earlier there had been a precursor in the remarkable religious revival at Nigg.

The origins of the Easter Ross revivals may lie in the prayer meetings ordered by the Presbytery of Tain to be held in the parishes of Edderton, Tarbat and Logie Easter in 1724; but the move towards spiritual renewal was given focus by the work of the Rev. John Balfour (*Maighstir Balfour Mór*), who was presented to the parish of Nigg four years later. The Nigg Revival of 1739 grew out of many of the elements introduced by Thomas Hog such as Fellowship Meetings, example and exposition by 'The Men', an active evangelising eldership, and the emotion and spiritual concentration of the communion meeting. The need for spiritual reassurance that lay at the root of such revivals may have been further encouraged by nature itself: 1739 was a year of bad harvests and widespread destitution, combined with a notable hurricane and an eclipse of the sun. Immediately the Nigg Revival spawned similar events throughout the region. There were revivals at Rosskeen in 1742 and Rosemarkie a few years later. These later Easter Ross revivals drew not only on the example of Nigg, but Cambuslang and Kilsyth as well. Indeed, the saintly John Porteous, minister of Kilmuir Easter, visited the 'work' at Kilsyth in 1742.[28] As has been said, 'It was the Evangelical piety of Easter Ross, fortified by the revivals of the third and fourth decades [of the eighteenth century] which eventually captured the whole of the Northern Highlands.'[29]

Another notable revival took place at Kiltearn in 1785, but by this time the strain of Highland piety associated with revivalism, weeping, shouting, crying, was diverging from the growing 'moderatism' in the rest of the Scottish Church. Such enthusiasm was seen by Moderates as dangerous and in bad taste. Nevertheless, the tradition of revivals continued to play a crucial role in local society. In the first half of the nineteenth century, for example, the Rev. John MacDonald of Ferintosh was famous for the power of his preaching. His communion services could be attended by as many as 10,000 people and were noted for their emotionalism. At one communion MacDonald reached the climax of his sermon urging the acceptance of Christ, and asked, 'Wilt thou go with this man?' A woman stood up and cried, *Théid, théid, O théid*, ('I will go, I will, Oh, I will') and MacDonald replied, 'God grant thee that grace and to all present here this day,' amidst weeping, crying and high emotion.

The fervour and emotion of Highland religion was, at least partially, a means of providing solace in the midst of social and cultural breakdown, the failure of the last Jacobite revolt in 1745–6, mass emigration, the introduction of sheep farming and the clearances. The Church began in this period to become a major critic of the social consequences of the new order in the Highlands.

It is possible to glimpse something of the reality of late eighteenth century church life in the pages of the diary of the Rev. John Calder, minister of Rosskeen between 1775–1783.[30] Calder was a son of the minister of Croy, in Nairnshire, and like his brother Charles (minister at Urquhart, 1774–1812), he was educated at Aberdeen University. He served first as minister of the Perthshire parish of Weem before being called north to succeed Hector MacPhail at Rosskeen (Fig. 11). MacPhail had been noted for his strong pastoral concerns; the minister on his small grey pony was a familiar sight in his far-flung parish.[31]

Calder, too, was deeply concerned to serve the people of Rosskeen to the fullest extent of his powers. His diary was written largely as a means of spiritual self-examination. He is preoccupied throughout with what he saw as not only his own lack of spiritual enthusiasm, but that of the church as a whole: 'The coldness and formality in religious matters that pervades in this corner of our degenerate church.' Yet, in the midst of these spiritual musings, there emerges a vivid picture of parish life in the Cromarty Firth area in the later eighteenth century: the minister on his rounds, visiting the sick, catechising, examining the local schools and concerned with the consequences of the War with America and the harvest failure of 1782. There are comments on the relative success of his English and Gaelic sermons, and when the members of the Presbytery of Tain come to Rosskeen to look into repairs to the manse, Calder is delighted to report that Sir John Gordon sent down a dozen bottles of claret for the brethren (temperance was a thing of the future). The laird also provided accommodation for visiting ministers at Invergordon Castle during a communion and (Calder proudly reports) Sir John assisted in the distribution of the elements. There are fortnightly Fellowship Meetings and individual spiritual conferences with parishioners: 'Conference in the forenoon with a woman under a serious concern about her eternal salvation.' And then there was the other side of the coin: 'Had some disagreeable session enquiries after the Catechising at Nonikil relating to a dumb woman with child and the young man pointed out by her denying any Connection with her.'

John Calder of Rosskeen may not have been one of the great ministers of Easter Ross, but he emerges from the pages of his diary as a sincere, conscientious and striving minister: 'Oh, for the Wisdom of the Serpent and the Innocence of the Dove in this and in several other Parochial Concerns coming now in my way or to come soon in my way if spared — Elders — Communicants — Charity — School — Catechists — a stated Visitation of Families — Irregularities . . .'

While attending a communion in his brother's parish he hears 'a most Masterly Testimony against Patronage assented to by the Elders etc and by

11. Rosskeen church (now disused).

the principal Heritor [landowner] residing in the Country.' When Calder repeated the gist of this testimony to his own principal heritor, Sir John Gordon, however, he was given short shrift. Patronage was a sensitive question, and one that was to be at the centre of the next period of the church's history in the Cromarty Firth. There was, in fact, opposition in the parish to the man Sir John Gordon named as Calder's successor.[32]

The right of the congregations as a whole to choose their ministers had been laid down in John Knox's *Book of Discipline:* 'It appertainest to the people, and to every several congregation, to elect their Minister . . . For altogether [it] is to be avoided that any man be violently intruded or thrust in upon any congregation.' Patronage had been abolished in 1690 and then, in 1712, reinstated by Act of Parliament. On the whole, patrons around the Cromarty Firth were careful to choose men acceptable to the congregation, but even this sensitivity could not obscure the fact that in the eyes of the Church a fundamental right had been abrogated.

There had been problems with patronage from the seventeenth century. Sir Thomas Urquhart was frequently in conflict with the minister of Cromarty, and worse was to come when the parish had a Catholic laird and patron in the mid eighteenth century. But the most notorious patronage case in the region occurred when the great Mr Balfour of Nigg died in 1752. The people and Kirk Session chose Mr John Bethune to succeed him. It was unusual for the patron to demur in such cases, but at Nigg the Crown, as patron of the living, insisted on presenting the Rev. Patrick Grant. The case was fought through the church and civil courts for three years before Grant was finally presented.[33] Virtually all of the congregation then left and formed a seceder church. It was said that Patrick Grant never preached to more than sixty of a congregation during his thirty-two years as minister. Even after the more acceptable Alexander MacAdam (who had been minister in the Gaelic chapel at Cromarty) was presented to Nigg in 1788 only about a third of the parishioners returned to the church. Nigg became, in fact, a rather contentious (not to say litigious) parish, and continued to be so until the present century.

The immediate result of the Nigg patronage case was, however, to harden local attitudes towards the practice. By the early decades of the nineteenth century the question of patronage (or 'non-intrusion') had become the focus for a wide range of discontents within the church. At stake was the still unresolved question of the relationship of church and state that stretched back to Andrew Melville's 'Two Kingdoms.'

By a strange turn of fate the Highland evangelical tradition, with its emphasis on a strong personal religion, found itself returning to a more central position within the Church of Scotland as a whole, with the rise of the evangelicals in the early nineteenth century.

The period of heightened religious feelings leading up to the Disruption of 1843 and the creation of the Free Church was marked by another series of revivals throughout Scotland, including a number in Easter Ross. At Rosskeen the Rev. David Carment reported in 1841: 'I have been enabled and preach frequently . . . to attentive, impressed and weeping congregations, who flock by night and day to hear the word.'[34] Evangelical leaders in the Lowland church, such as Thomas Chalmers, were equally concerned with the preaching of a living faith, expressed not only in individual testimony of salvation but in a strong social concern. In the case of the Lowlands this usually centred on the massive social problems created by the rise of industry and the explosive growth of cities such as Glasgow. In the Highlands the church's social concern was focussed on the rising tide of land clearance; David Carment ended his 1838 account of Rosskeen in the *New Statistical Account* with a critical note on the economic, social and moral consequences of the Clearances on both landlord and tenants. It is no concidence that he and other men destined to become luminaries of the Free Church of Scotland, such as the Rev. Donald Sage of Resolis and Hugh Miller, were amongst the most severe critics of the Clearances; the Free Church itself was a major force in bringing the whole problem before the wider audience of Scotland and Britain as a whole.

With the exception of Hector Bethune of Dingwall, all the ministers of the parishes ringing the Cromarty Firth joined the Free Church in 1843. At Cromarty there had been a meeting even before the final break was made to plan for the consequences of The Disruption; the town was divided into twelve districts and collectors appointed to raise funds for the new church building.[35] In the months after the first meeting of the new General Assembly of the Free Church of Scotland the ministers and their congregations left their old manses and churches, to find new meeting places as best they could. Hugh Miller recalled the scene at Cromarty on the day when seat rents in the old church were due. Instead of turning up to pay their rents, the congregation of the new Free Church instead took their seats away, although as yet they had no building in which to place them.[36] Within weeks of the split the Free Church congregation at Tain was worshipping in a temporary wooden structure.[37] Donald Sage and the congregation of Resolis met for worship in the disused girnel at Ferryton (Fig. 12), but the building was so dark and uncomfortable (and the congregation so large) that they only used it in inclement weather when it was impossible to worship in the open air.

With the exception of Munro of Teaninich no substantial laird joined the Free Church and there were equally few adherents amongst substantial farmers, except for the Middleton family in the Black Isle. Munro of Teaninich gave land and built a Free Church at Alness, and MacLeod of Cadboll swiftly gave a site for Rosskeen Free Church at Achnagarron which was opened in April 1845[38] and later gave the site for the Free Church hall in Invergordon itself in 1861. Moreover, he donated 60 guineas towards the building costs, but threatened to withhold 6 guineas if the spire was not built.[39]

Unlike some parts of the Highlands, no local laird refused to give land for new churches although some did create difficulties. The Cromarty Free Church Committee, for example, were refused permission to quarry stone for their new church on a local estate.

The year 1843 was a great dividing line in peoples' lives. It was said in the late nineteenth century that if you asked the age of an Easter Ross fisherman he would calculate it as 'so many years when the church came out.'[40] The Disruption divided families and communities and there was great bitterness often expressed in rather petty ways. Yet, at the same time, there was a strong sense that the new church was actuated by principles that stretched back to the earliest days of the reformed church. David Carment, a descendant of covenanters from the southwest of Scotland, gloried in the open air meetings of the early days of the Free Church, seeing them as being in the tradition of those seventeenth century defenders of the Church of Scotland's freedoms.

12. Ferryton girnel on the Black Isle.

The problems faced by the remnants of the Established church were equally acute. At Kiltearn, for example, only two or three people were left.[41] Only one member, the aged minister of Fearn, remained in the Presbytery of Tain. By joining together with the presbyteries of Dingwall and Chanonry, the Tain Presbytery of the Established Church was able to resume activities although sometimes these were risky. In September 1843 when representatives of the Presbytery went to induct the new minister at Rosskeen they were met at the door of the Established Church by a riotous mob of between two and three hundred people and threatened with violence. The mob occupied the church and spent the night ringing the church bell, while the Presbytery had to retire to a nearby farmhouse for the induction ceremony.[42] There were similar violent scenes elsewhere around the Firth which the civil magistrates seemed incapable of controlling. At Resolis a woman was arrested following disturbances during the induction of the new minister to the Established Church and taken to Cromarty Gaol. She was rescued by a mob, whose ringleaders were later arrested and tried before the High Court in Edinburgh.[43] In October 1843 HMS Greyhound and a detachment of two hundred men of the 87th Irish Fusiliers were sent to Invergordon to restore order.

Eventually, the excitement died down, and over the years the fervour and idealism of the Free Church underwent inevitable change towards being 'more ecclesiastical than religious.'[44] To some it seemed that success bred a certain rigidity: from being a radical force in the religious life of Scotland the Free Church became, almost imperceptibly, a conservative one. Perhaps this was inevitable, but some of the consequences of this change were unfortunate.

In 1874 patronage was abolished, but instead of bringing about reunion there began instead to be increasingly insistent demands for the disestablishment of the Church of Scotland as well. Large and heated disestablishment meetings are regularly reported in the *Ross-shire Journal* from the time the paper began publication in 1875.

At the same time, however, there also began to be a subtle shift in spiritual emphasis. The move was away from the God of Law, capable of sending, 'Ane to heaven and ten to hell, A' for thy glory!' towards a religion in which the emphasis was on a God of grace and love. A major influence in this change was the revivals held in Scotland by the American evangelists Moody and Sankey, beginning in 1873–4. They held a revival service in the Free Church in Tain in October 1874, and fifty-four conversions were recorded in the kirk session minutes in that same year. Their meetings in Inverness were widely attended, with specially-run trains coming from all over the Highlands, as another revival of religion swept the Highlands.[45] In 1891 Moody and Sankey returned and this time held a week's mission in Dingwall (which included a visit by Moody to Cromarty to hold services), assisted by ministers from both the Free and Established Churches.[46]

It was not just the spirit of the church that was changing, so too was its practice, symbolised by the introduction of organs in the Established Church for the first time since the Reformation. The innovation had begun in the Lowlands in the 1850s but took much longer to be accepted in the Highlands. Moody and Sankey were also a major influence in this change, for their meetings featured hymns composed by the two evangelists and sung by specially trained local choirs. In 1883 the Church of Scotland congregation of Tain began to sing hymns[47] and, despite protests by some, in 1890 an organ was introduced into the church.[48] In Invergordon the church authorities ordered anthem books shortly after the union with the United Presbyterians, but they were not used immediately. In 1906 twelve dozen church hymnaries were purchased, and by 1910 instrumental music (a harmonium) was being used, especially during the 'sailors services' which began to be held over the next few years. In 1914 the church's precentor retired and a 'choirmaster' was appointed.[49] Following Moody's 1891 service in Cromarty, when an organ was used in the Free Church, letters had been written to the local paper urging the permanent installation of an organ there.[50] Such innovations produced intense reactions. A 'Free Church Defence Association' had been formed in 1883, largely because of the introduction of music into church services despite a statement by the Free Church authorities in 1883 that 'there is nothing in the word of God or in the Constitution and laws of this church to preclude the use of instrumental music as an aid to vocal praise'. Certainly the proposals for an organ in Cromarty Free Church came to nothing.

And yet change was coming. At the end of the 1890s plans were brought forward for a union between the Free Church and the United Presbyterian Church (which stemmed from the union of the earlier Secession and Relief churches in 1847). The plan was the child of Principal Robert Rainy of the Free Church, and was supported by such notable local ministers as John Kennedy of Dingwall. The proposals, however, provoked violent reactions by other Free Church ministers who viewed them as a falling away from the ideals and principles of the Disruption. Presbytery of Dingwall meetings on the subject of church union became heated and, often, personally abusive.[51] At last, however, in 1900 the plan was carried through and a new United Free Church created. Nevertheless, a significant number of people remained out to form a continuing Free Church. In the Cromarty Firth parishes of Dingwall, Fearn, Alness, Rosskeen, Kilmuir Easter and Tarbat 2,867 joined the United Free Church while 2,191 remained with the Free Church.[52]

That was not the end of the story. As in 1843 feelings again ran high. When supporters of the new United Free Church church attempted to hold a meeting in the Jubilee Hall at Evanton in late November 1900 there was a serious riot and police had to be summoned by telegraph from Dingwall to deal with the disturbance.[53]

The bitterness engendered by the union of 1900 in the remnant Free Church remained for years. In *My Uncle George*, an affectionate memoir of life in the Free Church manse of Fearn in the 1920s and '30s, Alastair Phillips recalled:

> I was raised on the iniquity, the grasping worldliness and the vindictive chicanery of the Reverend Principal Robert Rainy of the Free Church College . . . I must plead guilty of a charge of partial counsel if I describe Principal Rainy as a trimmer, lax in discipline and principle, a subverter of constitutions, and an opportunist . . . for I picked up these epithets when I was at my most impressionable.[54]

This bitterness grew not only out of the circumstances of union, but out of the case brought by the post-1900 Free Church claiming title to the property and endowment of the former Free Church. After being rebuffed by the Scottish courts the Free Church took the case to the House of Lords and in 1904 their Lordships determined that the Free Church was 'a closed financial trust' and that by the creation of the United Free Church this trust had been broken.[55] The Free Church was declared possessor of all the endowments of the pre-1900 Free Church.

The decision was greeted with dismay in Scotland. Around the Cromarty Firth the Free Church moved quickly to recover the property of which they had been judged legal possessors. Interdicts were issued against United Free congregations and once again the area was witness to the scenes of congregations being forced from their churches. At Achnagarron there was a congregation of five hundred at the United Free Church on the last Sunday before the Free Church took possession of the church and manse. The minister in his sermon referred to the memorial slab by the door with the inscription, 'Blessed are the Peacemakers' and remarked that he did not know how the congregation that would worship here next week could look on it after what they had done.[56]

The extraordinary consequences of the Free Church case were eventually dealt with in the Churches (Scotland) Act of 1905 that arranged a more equitable distribution of the ten million pounds worth of buildings and endowments of the former Free Church. In the Highlands where the Free Church was such a major force this readjustment was not accepted easily. In Dingwall, the UF congregation, which had worshipped in the Masonic Hall since their interdict, had to break down the doors of their old church in order to return.[57]

Despite such denominational conflict, however, by the end of the nineteenth century there was a growing sense that, rather than concentrating on points of difference, there was in fact an underlying unity of doctrine and government amongst presbyterian churches that was much more important. In 1877 the first General Presbyterian Council was held in Edinburgh, bringing together churchmen from presbyterian churches throughout the world. If presbyterians from around the world could come together, why should there not be similar unity amongst the churches of the homeland? It was not until 1929, after long years of negotiation and voting by individual parishes, that the Established Church and the United Free Church at last joined together to form the Church of Scotland.

With one or two exceptions the union was accepted around the Cromarty Firth. A minority of the United Free Church declined to enter the union; one such was the church in the fishing villages of Shandwick and Balintore.[58] At Nigg, early in 1930 tension and bad feeling came to a head when both denominations claimed Chapelhill Church and announced services in the building for the same time.[59] Soon the quarrel widened to include accusations about the way the ballot for union had been conducted, charges that were found to be baseless.

Despite its strong Free Church tradition, the two congregations of Cromarty voted 75% for the union, but there was a reluctance to depart from the old Free Church that had meant so much to the people of the town. It was agreed that when the new united congregation came together in 1934 it should worship on alternate Sundays in the Old Church and the former Free Church.[60]

So much of the history of the church has been concerned with matters of doctrine and practice that it is easy to overlook the social role of the church, and yet it may be that in this sphere the church had its greatest influence. John Knox's *First Book of Discipline* ordained that the church should be responsible for the 'honest' poor and poor relief became the legal responsibility of the kirk session in 1597. Money was raised from regular collections, fees for the use of the mortcloth [funeral pall] and the occasional gift or legacy: in Kilmuir Easter, for example, the Earl of Cromartie had made an annual gift of five bolls of wheat to be distributed amongst the poor. This system was perhaps adequate in normal times, but when there was harvest failure and famine it broke down. Nevertheless, poor relief, administered by the minister and the kirk session, survived until the Disruption made the administration of a parish-based system unworkable. A Scottish Poor Law creating a national, secular system was passed in 1845.

Knox's *Book of Discipline* also ordained that every parish was to have a school, and the Church — and voluntary bodies — remained responsible for Scottish education until the establishment of a uniform state system by the Education Act of 1872. There was a pre-Reformation school in the monastery at Beauly and, probably, Fearn, as well as a grammar school in the cathedral town of Fortrose.[61] There may also have been burgh schools at Tain, Cromarty and Dingwall.

In the years after 1560, there is evidence that educational provision around the Cromarty Firth actually declined. Although the grammar school at Fortrose continued, the monastic schools ceased, as did Dingwall burgh school, and perhaps Cromarty and Tain as well. The beginnings of a school system around the Cromarty Firth only began with the 1649 law requiring heritors to pay for school buildings and the schoolmaster's salary. In that same year the presbytery of Dingwall appointed a committee of laymen to set up parish schools.[62] The heritors dragged their feet, but, nevertheless, the first parish schoolmaster was appointed in Urquhart in 1649, and a replacement schoolmaster appointed at Alness in 1650, suggesting that a school had been in existence there for some time.[63]

In the later seventeenth century some parish schools were founded and there were also 'Adventure Schools' run by free-lance teachers of variable and sometimes doubtful quality. One of the consequences of the religious revivals of the 1730s and '40s was that the people involved in them wished to learn to read and write; the heightened religious consciousness of the period demanded more educational provision. It has been estimated that by the mid-eighteenth century about half the population could write, although probably more could read; as late as 1770, for example, only one of the five elders at Alness could do both.[64]

In 1701 a committee of Edinburgh gentlemen was formed to help support schools in the Highlands, a body that eventually became the 'Scottish Society for the Propagation of Christian Knowledge in the Highlands and Islands of Scotland and Foreign Parts of the World' (SSPCK). Queen Anne headed the Society's subscription list when it was opened in 1707. The Society's schools grew from twelve in 1711 to three hundred and twenty-three in 1795, and their development was crucial in supplementing the work of the parish schools around the Cromarty Firth. At first instruction was entirely in English, geared towards the reading of the Scriptures and the eradication of 'barbarities and incivilities' amongst the Gaelic-speaking pupils. By the later eighteenth century there was recognition that this policy had failed; Gaelic-speaking children might read the English Bible but few of them understood it. The SSPCK then produced the Gaelic *New Testament*; in 1782 John Calder mentions receiving letters from the SSPCK asking him for a collection at Rosskeen towards the cost of this work.[65] On the whole, however, the SSPCK Schools still equated English with virtue, and the bulk of their teaching continued to be in that language. In 1811 the Gaelic Schools Society began founding schools where instruction was in that language, and there was also a certain amount of teaching in Gaelic in the Highland schools established by the Church of Scotland General Assembly beginning in the 1830s.

Despite this late change of direction, there can be little doubt that the spread of schools was perhaps the single most important cause of the decline of Gaelic. By the 1790s the majority of the children around the Cromarty Firth were receiving at least some education in parish, SSPCK or adventure schools, and the ministers' accounts in the *Old Statistical Account* make it clear that virtually all the young people understood English to some degree and that their knowledge came through schooling. By the time of the *New Statistical Account* in the early 1840s, the educational and linguistic situation had moved even further, although the first language of something like three quarters of the population was still Gaelic.[66]

In 1840 the minister of Urquhart felt that Gaelic had not lost ground because the scriptures were now taught in this language; and within those narrow parameters he may have been right. But it was the minister of Kiltearn who perhaps came closer to the truth. Writing in 1839, he suggested that the foundation of Gaelic schools, in fact, had hastened the decline of the language:

> This may appear paradoxical, but it is actually the case. Those children that had learned to read Gaelic found no difficulty in mastering the English: and they had a strong inducement to do so, because they found in that language more information suited to their capacity and taste than could be found in their own.[67]

Despite such problems, however, from the eighteenth century onwards Scottish literacy was, even in Highland areas, high by European standards. After the Disruption of 1843 Free Church schools were founded throughout the Highlands and the educational provision improved even further. The church's emphasis on reading the Bible produced a literate population at an early date.

This literacy was also encouraged by the foundation of local libraries. There had been a fine library at Beauly before the Reformation, and perhaps at other religious houses and centres, but all had been scattered and destroyed after 1560. Highland libraries were the brainchild of James Kirkwood, a Scottish episcopalian who was rector of a Bedfordshire parish in the late seventeenth century. He had spent time as a private chaplain in Breadalbane and his experience there had convinced him of the need for not only a Gaelic Bible but also for the creation of parish libraries.[68] The idea was taken up by the SSPCK and the General Assembly of the Church of Scotland. Initially, three libraries were set up in Ross. Essentially, these were ministers' libraries supplemented by other donations. The one at Alness was looted by the Jacobites in 1715 and 1716 and the legal proceedings that followed this event indicate that it contained works on theology, Latin authors such as Caesar, Cicero, Livy and Virgil, as well as a few medical books. The Jacobites were said to have sold the looted books to the local people; what they made of them is not recorded. In 1824 the Church of Scotland began to encourage the foundation of Sabbath schools with attached libraries. By 1833 a number of such local libraries provided the church authorities with borrowing details for the previous two and a half years. They included Scotsburn (53), Muirtown (136), Glenglass (14) and Clare (109).[69]

In the burgh of Cromarty there seem to have been fairly high literacy rates from an early period and a wide readership for books. This was, of course, because the parish was mainly English-speaking from at least the seventeenth century, and therefore had direct access to a huge range of English books (as late as 1850 there were only about 350 Gaelic titles in print).[70] By the early nineteenth century it was not unusual in Cromarty for quite ordinary people to possess substantial libraries; Hugh Miller's uncle had one hundred and fifty books and his father's smaller collection included religion, travel and fiction. In the educated laity of early nineteenth century of Cromarty it is possible to see the culmination of Knox's dream of a 'virtuous education' for the people of Scotland.

In 1872 the state took over responsibility for education, building on the basis of the parish and voluntary schools. Something of the nature of both the church's achievement and the state's new responsibility can be seen in the description of Cromarty's two successive schoolhouses. The burgh school that Hugh Miller attended in Cromarty was a long, thatched building, with a mud floor and an unlathed roof. Yet, from this unpromising source came not only Miller himself, but a stream of able men. Some left Cromarty and became doctors and educators; others remained at home. One such was the eighteenth century Cromarty fisherman who surprised the laird and two friends when they spoke to him in Latin, by replying in the same language.[71]

In 1873 the burgh of Cromarty elected its first school board. They found that the town had four hundred children aged between five and thirteen, and so they commissioned a new schoolhouse in the French Gothic style (Fig. 13) from the firm of A. Maitland and Sons of Tain. In 1876 the new 'bright' and 'cheerful' schoolhouse, with its 'chaste tower', was opened at Cromarty. A fisherwife was heard to say, 'The like o' the Cromarty school was never seen north o' Aberdeen afore.'[72]

Despite the church closures and unions of the past decades, the modern landscape of the Cromarty Firth is rich in church towers and buildings: the ruined medieval church of Kirkmichael, the early seventeenth-century churches at Nigg and Cromarty (Fig. 14), the classical town church of Dingwall (Fig. 15), the magnificent Gothic Free Church at Achnagarron, near Invergordon, built in 1900 (Figs. 16, 17) to replace the 1845 structure. From

13. Cromarty school.

the seventeenth century, at least, the church was perhaps the major influence on the lives of all the people of the region. If the church's direct influence is less today than it was, its legacy is of continuing importance.

14. Cromarty church.

15. Dingwall by J. Clarke.

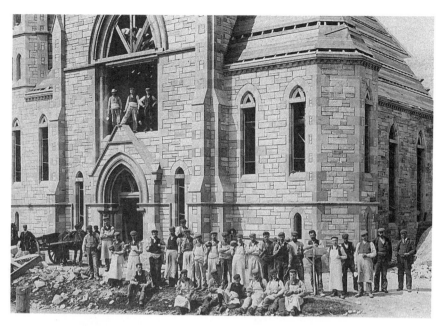

16. Achnagarron Free church under construction.

17. Achnagarron church.

66

NOTES

1. M. Dilworth, 'The commendator system in Scotland', *Innes Review*, vol. 37, no. 2 (1986), p. 64.

2. *Dingwall Presbytery*, for example pp. xl–xli, 154, 181.

3. As late as the 1960s eight copies of the Gaelic version of the Church of Scotland magazine, *Life and Work*, were still delivered to the villages of Balintore and Shandwick. SWRI Nigg, 'The Parish of Nigg', 1967, p. 17.

4. As late as 1877 a meeting of the Presbytery of Chanonry was conducted primarily in Gaelic. *RJ*, 27 April 1877, p. 3.

5. C. MacNaughton, *Church Life*, p. 144.

6. W. Macgill, *Ross-shire*, vol. 1, no. 108 (p. 72).

7. Much of the following discussion of the immediate consequences of the Reformation in the Cromarty Firth area is based on J. Kirk, 'The Kirk and the Highlands at the Reformation', *Northern Scotland*, vol. 7, no. 1 (1986), pp. 1–22.

8. This account has been printed a number of times, but the most recent and fullest version is *Monro's western isles of Scotland and genealogies of the clans, 1549*, edited by R. W. Munro, Edinburgh, 1961, from which I have taken most of the details discussion of Donald Monro's career.

9. L. Macfarlane, *Bishop Elphinstone and the Kingdom of Scotland, 1431–1514*, Aberdeen, 1985, pp. 365, 368.

10. *Monro's Western Isles*, pp. 10–11.

11. D. E. R. Watt, *Fasti Ecclesiae Scoticanae Medii Aevi*, 2nd edn, St Andrews, 1969, p. 270.

12. In 1570 the minister of Urquhart was assigned by the General Assembly to help Monro 'because the said Commissioner was not prompt in the Scottish tongue'. Some writers, have suggested that this means that Monro was deficient in Gaelic, despite the fact that the common word for Gaelic in the late sixteenth century was 'Irish'. It seems unlikely that Monro, a native of Gaelic-speaking Kiltearn who had spent his career as a church official in the Gaelic-speaking Hebrides, should not be able to speak the language. It is much more probable that, despite being able to read and write Scots (the *Description* is written in that language) he was not able to speak it with any fluency.

13. Kirk, 'Kirk in the Highlands', p. 11.

14. *Dingwall Presbytery*, pp. 244–5, 250, 258–9, 263–4.

15. Much of this discussion of Hog's influence is taken from J. MacInnes, *The Evangelical Movement in the Highlands of Scotland, 1688–1800*, Aberdeen, 1951, p. 176ff.

16. *Ibid.*, p. 212. Hog had attended similar meetings when he was a student at Aberdeen, and transferred the practice to Kiltearn.

17. Much of this discussion of 'The Men' is based on the account in J. Kennedy, *The Days of the Fathers in Ross-shire*, Inverness, 1897, p. 85ff.

18. D. MacLean, 'The presbytery of Ross and Sutherland, 1693–1700', *Records of the Scottish Church History Society*, vol. 5 (1953), p. 255.

19. *Dingwall Presbytery, int. al.,* pp. 305, 320, 322, 338–9, 344.

20. The conventicle at Obsdale is commemorated by a stone monument at the side of the B817 north of Dalmore Distillery.

21. M. Macdonald, *The Covenanters of Moray and Ross*, Inverness, 1892, p. 117ff.

22. *Ibid.*, p. 349, 351-2, 356-7, 360.

23. H. Miller, *My Schools and Schoolmasters*, p. 563.

24. See, for example, A. Phillips, *My Uncle George*, Glasgow, 1984, p. 23.

25. I. Mowat, *Easter Ross 1750-1950: The Double Frontier*, Edinburgh, 1981, p. 13.

26. A. L. Drummond and J. Bulloch, *The Scottish Church: 1688-1843*, Edinburgh, 1973, p. 15.

27. From an unpublished legal proceeding (1709) in the Cromartie papers (SRO GD 305/1/161 no. 85). I am grateful to Mrs Monica Clough for drawing my attention to this incident and making her transcript available to me.

28. *Ibid.*, p. 28.

29. MacInnes, *Evangelical Movement*, p. 156.

30. NLS, MS 14279.

31. Kennedy, *Days of the Fathers*, p. 53.

32. Mowat, *Easter Ross*, p. 120.

33. MacNaughton, *Church Life*, pp. 207-39.

34. T. Brown, *Annals of the Disruption*, new edn., Edinburgh, 1893, p. 11.

35. *RJ*, 21 July 1982, p. 7.

36. *Annals of the Disruption*, p. 227.

37. J. Barron, *Northern Highlands*, vol. 3, p. 27.

38. *Ibid.*, p. 75.

39. Fraser, *Invergordon*, p. 4.

40. A. Ross, 'Social Life among the Easter Ross fishermen', *The Highland Monthly*, 1889-90, p. 164.

41. Brown, op. cit., p. 650. The consequences of the Disruption can be seen thirty years after the event by the number of communicants in the established Church of Scotland out of the total population, published in the *Ross-shire Journal* on 39 May 1879:

Parish	Established Church	Total population
Alness	18	1,053
Dingwall	121	2,443
Kiltearn	55	2,720
Urquhart	28	2,803
Fearn	23	2,135
Kilmuir Easter	32	912
Nigg	10	1,201
Rosskeen	49	3,808
Tain	60	3,221
Tarbat	21	2,182
Cromarty:		
English	44	2,180
Gaelic	40	
Resolis	29	1,527

42. *RJ* 29 October 1943 (quoting *The Times* account of 1843).

43. Barron, *Northern Highlands*, vol. 3, pp. 34, 40.

44. Phillips, *My Uncle George*, p. 33.

45. *RJ*, 19 January 1877.

46. *Ibid.*, 11 December 1891; *CN* 10 December 1891, p. 2.

47. *RJ*, 17 August 1883, p. 5.

48. MacNaughton, *Church Life*, pp. 436–7.

49. C. I. Fraser, *Invergordon Church*, pp. 75–7.

50. *CN* 24 December 1891, p. 2; 31 December 1891, p. 3; 7 January 1892, p. 3; 21 January 1892, pp. 1, 3; 28 January 1892, p. 2; 11 February 1892, p. 2; 18 February 1892, p. 3.

51. See, for example, *Ibid.*, 28 October 1898, pp. 7–8; 7 September 1900, p. 7.

52. *Ibid.*, 30 June 1905. Resolis adhered to the Free Church in 1900.

53. *Ibid.*, 30 November 1900, p. 8. See also F. Maclennan, *Ferindonald Papers*, Evanton, n.d., pp. 36–7.

54. Phillips, op. cit., pp. 32–33.

55. J. R. Fleming, *A History of the Church in Scotland, 1875–1929*, Edinburgh, 1933, pp. 66–70.

56. *RJ*, 7 April 1905, p. 6.

57. *Ibid.*, 3 August 1945, p. 6.

58. *Ibid.*, 26 June 1931, p. 6. Balintore was part of Fearn parish.

59. *Ibid.*, 16 May 1930, p. 5.

60. *Ibid.*, 16 April 1943, p. 4.

61. Much of the following discussion on early schools is based on W. MacKay, 'Education in the Highlands in Olden Times', originally published in *CM*, vol. 14 (1905–6), pp. 109–37.

62. *Dingwall Presbytery*, pp. 156, 162–4.

63. *Ibid.*, p. 192.

64. Mowat, *Easter Ross*, p. 130 and the same author's 'Literacy, libraries and literature in eighteenth and nineteenth century Easter Ross', *Library History*, vol. 5 (1979), p. 2.

65. NLS manuscript 14279, f. 134.

66. Mowat, 'Literacy', p. 2.

67. *NSA*: Ross and Cromarty, Parish of Kiltearn, p. 323.

68. D. MacLean, 'Highland Libraries in the eighteenth century', *TGSI*, vol. 31 (1922–4), pp. 70–97.

69. Report of the Committee of the General Assembly for increasing the means of education and religious instruction in Scotland, 1833, p. 18.

70. Mowat, 'Literacy', p. 9. For a more detailed discussion of schools between 1750 and 1850, see Mowat, *Easter Ross*, pp. 122–36. There was also a library at Nigg in the 1840s supported by the Seceder congregation; Cameron, 'Sanitary Condition', pp. 10–11.

71. H. Miller, *Scenes and legends of the North of Scotland*, pp. 408–10.

72. *RJ*, 19 May 1876.

4

'Any man offering . . . to inclose . . . shall be preferred'

In 1790 Sir John Sinclair, the improving laird of Ulbster in Caithness, sent a printed letter to the nine hundred parish ministers of Scotland, asking their help to procure information on history and antiquities, language and culture, religion, natural phenomena and population as well as the agricultural and industrial development of their parishes. The result was the twenty volume *Statistical Account of Scotland* which appeared between 1791 and 1798 and which subsequently came to be known as the *Old Statistical Account*. The coverage and range of this parish-by-parish account of Scotland in the late eighteenth century has led to the *Old Statistical Account* being called the Scottish Domesday Book.[1] The ministers' accounts of the parishes around the Cromarty Firth capture the area at the 'hinge of great changes which transformed not only the agriculture but also the society of the northern and western Highlands.'[2] The *Old Statistical Account* provides the first detailed and comprehensive picture of life around the Cromarty Firth.

On the fertile plain of the parish of Fearn considerable agricultural improvement had taken place by the 1790s. Although there had been little actual enclosure, large farms were being created from smallholdings: land now managed by one farmer had previously been worked by between four and ten family units. The creation of large farms had led to a decrease of population, and many of those who remained in the parish worked on farms only as day labourers. Many others went south to work on farms during the summer, and a significant number of men enlisted in the army. The parish produced a surplus of food, which was exported and sold to neighbouring towns such as Tain, or sent to the military garrison at Fort George. Barley was distilled locally or sent to Ferintosh, and locally spun hemp was sent to the hemp factory in Cromarty. Otherwise the economic life of the parish was self-sufficient. The account lists sixteen weavers (with five apprentices), thirteen tailors (with four apprentices), five joiners or wrights (with three apprentices), two coopers, two masons, eight millers, one wheel wright and one merchant, within the parish. In the fishing villages of Hilton and Balintore, there were six deep-sea fishing boats and a deckless, flat-bottomed coble for inshore fishing. Over the past seven or eight years the price of fish had risen as the fishermen had had to go further afield to find their catches.[3]

In the neighbouring parish of Nigg, the minister painted a similar but bleaker picture. Here, too, farms were being thrown together and the population was declining. Most farmers did not hold their land by lease but at the will of the landlord (or, increasingly, his factor or farm manager) so there was no incentive to improve their holdings. For centuries the inhabitants had summered their cattle and horses in the Highland shielings, but this practice was dying out owing to the creation of sheep farms. The large number of sheep formerly kept in the parish was being reduced by enclosure and tree planting on the Hill of Nigg which had begun as early as the 1760s.[4]

The parish of Kilmuir Easter presented an altogether brighter picture. Over the previous forty years the population had grown from 1,055 to 1,975: the most spectacular increase in the region. There were a number of reasons for this. The parish had been the seat of one of the most active of the Easter Ross 'Improvers', Admiral Sir John Lockhart Ross of Balnagown. He financed the work of improvement at Balnagown from the taking of naval prizes while cruising off the coast of Portugal and Spain. In 1780 he wrote to his factor, 'I have taken six more ships . . . you should now repair the steading at Rhines, as also the work on the Castle as discussed . . .'. Work on transforming his farms and woods was said to have cost £10,000 and had provided employment for scores of workers, many of them incomers from the Highland areas.

These changes on the land produced new industries. The quarries at Balnagown and Scotsburn began to be exploited commercially during this period and twelve masons worked within the parish. In the summer twenty lime makers gathered loads of shells from the Firth at low tide which were burnt and ploughed into fields to increase fertility.[5]

By the time the *Old Statistical Account* for Kilmuir Easter was compiled, therefore, many of the improvements begun over the previous decades were beginning to bear fruit. The woods planted by Sir John and his predecessors were now mature. They provided materials not only for export but for local building work as well, as witnessed by the six house carpenters listed amongst the parish tradesmen who, the minister reported, had built fifty new houses in the past four years. At Milton a number of local entrepreneurs were involved in encouraging the development of manufactures, notably the merchant John Montgomery who had introduced flax-spinning to the area thirty years earlier. The venture had been a success.

Altogether, John Matheson, minister of Kilmuir Easter, could look with satisfaction upon his prosperous parish. He took great pride, for example, in the three hundred acres of the unimproved Muir of Delny that had been brought into cultivation by smallholders known as 'cottars' or 'mealers' (or 'mailers', from the Scots word 'mail' or rent). Cottars had long been familiar figures in the Scottish countryside, agricultural workers who were given a house and kailyard as part of their wages and who often pursued ancillary trades as tailors, weavers, shoemakers or wrights.[6] By the time the *Old Statistical Account* for the parishes around the Cromarty Firth was compiled, however, their status had changed. Now they were families dispossessed by the creation of large farms who were encouraged by their landlords to take up small patches of unimproved land. While working as agricultural day-labourers they could devote their spare time to bringing this new land into cultivation. The difference between the old and new-style mailers was not only the fact that they were deliberately being used to create arable land but also that they worked this land under quite specific conditions. On average mailers had seven years to bring about three acres into cultivation during which time they held the land rent free. Thereafter they rented the land at a value based on their improvements.

The ministers all speak favourably of the cottars and mailers as small, independent cultivators of the soil. The prevailing ethos of the late eighteenth century was to keep the rural population on the land. Emigration was discouraged, indeed regarded by most landlords as a sign of failure. The minister of Rosskeen claimed that:

> From their labour and their industry and their wives and children, they live more comfortably, than those in a supposed superior class, and they enjoy perfect independence.[7]

But, in fact, the creation of new holdings for mailers was only a short term solution to the falling demand for agricultural workers. Delny Muir was a convenient local overspill area, a limited asset that had largely disappeared by the 1840s. The fact that cottars usually improved common land, that is undivided land belonging to landlords, would lead to problems later on. Despite the encomiums of the ministers, the mailers and cottars of the 1790s slowly changed from the sturdy and independent smallholders of the ministers' and landlords' imaginings and became instead the poverty-stricken crofters of the nineteenth century.

Mr Urquhart's account of the cottars of Rosskeen is part of his disappointingly brief description of the parish. He does describe the plantations carried out by Sir William Gordon which had transformed the appearance of the land around Invergordon Castle, the seat of the family. His son, Sir John Gordon, had hopes that his new 'village of some extent at Ness of Invergordon' might become an industrial and trading centre but, although a certain amount of linen spinning was done, there were, as yet, no 'manufactories' in the parish, and the population had dropped from 1,950 to 1,700 over the previous forty years. By the time this account was written MacLeod of Cadboll was the laird of Invergordon. He was attempting to populate the village by encouraging settlers to undertake spinning and granting them perpetual feus for houses and gardens in the new town.[8] There was no harbour, but there was a 'dry, healthy beach where vessels of one hundred tons can lie in safety most seasons of the year.'

The account of Alness parish to the west was dominated by the extraordinary developments that had taken place on the estate of Novar under the nabob Sir Hector Munro.[9] From the time he obtained the estate of Novar in the mid 1760s Sir Hector was said to have spent over £100,000 on the improvement of the ancestral lands and the acquisition of adjoining estates, until by the mid 1780s he owned two thirds of the parish.[10] Over one hundred men were employed rebuilding the seventeenth century House of Novar and turning the land, 'of a poorer soil than almost any spot I am acquainted with . . . swamp and bog abounding' into rich farmland and policies.[11]

But such a transformation, although it produced much good, also brought social and economic dislocation in its wake. The Rev. Harry Robertson, minister of Kiltearn, was greatly concerned with the human consequences of improvement. His parish included the seat of Munro of Foulis, one of the earliest improvers. The minister's account is detailed, thoughtful and sympathetic, a reflection of the writer himself.[12] While he recognises the undoubted benefits brought by improvement, Mr Robertson also comments tartly on the growing disparity of wealth: 'In no country, perhaps, are the gentlemen better lodged, and the tenants worse accommodated, than in this parish.'[13] The houses of the common people were built of turf over a wooden cruck frame. After standing for five or seven years they would be razed and added to the contents of the dunghill. Robertson also foresaw that the salaries provided by lairds such as Foulis and Novar during the initial period of improvement would not last and suggested that manufactures would have to be established to provide paid employment, especially for females, after the work of improvement was completed. A small bleachfield had been established near the village of Drummond and in 1790 over 2,000 yards of linen were bleached.

The account of Dingwall differs from its neighbours because of the parish's predominantly urban status. Although not yet the officially recognised county town, Dingwall had enjoyed modest growth over the previous decades and its population (1,379, of whom seven hundred and forty-five lived in the burgh) contained a sprinkling of professionals, especially writers (lawyers), and the only physician mentioned in any of the accounts for the parishes ringing the Firth (although a doctor is known to have lived at Kilmuir Easter between 1755 and 1773). There were also large numbers of domestic servants and tradesmen.[14]

Across the Firth, the neighbouring parish of Urquhart, with nearly 3,000 people, was the most populous in the region, as a result of the 'Ferintosh privilege' which exempted locally produced whisky from excise duty.[15] The origins of the privilege went back to the Revolution of 1688, when the lands and distilleries of Ferintosh had been ravaged by the Jacobites (supporters of the soon-to-be-deposed King James VII). As compensation to the Whig proprietor, Forbes of Culloden, the government had exempted his distilleries from duty for payment of forty Scotch merks per annum. As a result Urquhart became the centre of large-scale whisky distilling. A warehouse for Ferintosh whisky was even built in London.[16]

In 1782 it was calculated that the 100,000 gallons produced at Ferintosh would have brought in £20,000 in duty and that was before construction began on a large new distillery in the parish. The 'Ferintosh privilege' continued for nearly a century and gave duty-free Ferintosh whisky an unfair market advantage that ended only in 1786 when the government redeemed the privilege for £20,000. The end of the Ferintosh privilege was lamented by Robert Burns (soon to be an excise officer himself) in 'Scotch Drink'.

Thee Ferintosh! O sadly lost!
Scotland lament frae coast to coast!
Now colic grips, an' barken *hoast*   [*cough*]
   May kill us a'
For loyal Forbes' chartered boast
   Is taen awa'.

In Ferintosh distilling had been organised on such a large scale that it provided full-time employment for about a thousand men. Although Forbes provided some help for these people, and about thirty licensed distilleries were set up after the ending of the privilege, the change was still a devastating one for the local population. Some men left to work in other distilleries, but those who remained suffered a severe fall in their standard of living. As in other parishes around the Firth the preferred solution was not emigration but instead settlement on unreclaimed land, in this case the western part of the seven thousand acre unenclosed common of the Mulbuie that stretched along the spine of the Black Isle.[17] From about 1789 the population of the parish began to increase again as people, with the encouragement of local landowners, began to settle on these marginal lands.

The Rev. Robert Arthur (1744–1821) of Kirkmichael and Cullicudden (Resolis), brother-in-law of the improving Munro laird of Poyntzfield, was a noted improver himself and in his *Old Statistical Account* entry mentions with some pride the ploughing experiments he had carried out on his own glebe. He, too, looked to the undivided common of the Mulbuie as the answer to many of the problems improvement brought to his parish. Mr Arthur claimed that the Mulbuie needed only ploughing to bring it into cultivation, and that it could be planted with fir, larch and oak. By the 1790s this process of resettlement was well underway for the inhabitants of the parish were divided between the families of seventy one farmers and one hundred and nineteen mailers and tradesmen.[18] Aside from the enclosed and improved mains around the houses of Newhall, Braelangwell and Poyntzfield, the remainder of the farms in Mr Arthur's parish were small, between ten and fifty acres. Until 1782 there had been no long leases, but now leases for between nineteen and twenty one years were being granted by the proprietors of Poyntzfield and Newhall, the latter's including provisions for enclosing and bringing the moorland into arable.

The Rev. Robert Smith's account of Cromarty catches the town at a turning point in its history, a history that differed considerably from the rest of the rural parishes around the Cromarty Firth, yet was inextricably linked to them due to the town's position as the main port for the region.[19]

In Cromarty, too, there had been rural depopulation owing to the consolidation of farms and many agricultural workers were driven south to find seasonal work. Others, however, migrated into the thriving little town, for in the later eighteenth century Cromarty was experiencing a marked revival of fortunes under the merchant William Forsyth. It was Forsyth who had first recognised the town's potential as an entrepôt, a place from which the old established export trade in agricultural produce, fish and timber, could be matched by an import trade in manufactured goods and luxuries for the population of the Cromarty Firth and beyond.[20] Like Kilmuir Easter, Cromarty was an economic growth point and attracted workers from outside the district; in 1783 George Ross, the laird of Cromarty, built a Gaelic chapel for the Highland workers who came to work in his various enterprises in the town. By the time of the *Old Statistical Account* the consequences of this import trade had descended the social scale to the ordinary people of Cromarty for the minister remarks that one of the greatest of recent changes had been the replacement of homespun clothing by printed cottons of English or Scottish manufacture.

Despite all this change the local population around the Cromarty Firth did not greatly increase. Between 1755 and the first official census of 1801 the population of Scotland grew by one quarter (and this leaves out the loss of population due to emigration).[21] Between 1755 and the early 1790s the population of the parishes around the Firth scarcely grew at all: the unofficial census carried out in 1755 by the Rev. Alexander Webster gives the total population for the parishes of Tain, Nigg, Kilmuir Easter, Rosskeen, Alness, Kiltearn, Dingwall, Urquhart, Kirkmichael and Cullicudden [Resolis] and Cromarty as 15,733; forty years later the population is given in the *Old Statistical Account* as 16,759.[22]

There were a number of reasons for this almost static population. One factor was disease, especially smallpox, which periodically visited the region with devastating results, although increasingly the people were coming to accept inoculation.[23] Harvest failure and starvation were still features of local life. There had been a devastating famine in 1740–1, when people were found dead by the roadsides and in the fields. In 1782–3 a less severe harvest failure brought hunger but little actual starvation because of prompt action by local proprietors and the government who brought in cargoes of meal and pease.[24] But disease and famine were minor factors in the demographic history of the Cromarty Firth region; of much more importance was widespread internal migration which benefited the 'urban parishes' of Dingwall and Cromarty as well as such 'industrial' parishes as Kilmuir Easter and Urquhart (Ferintosh). External emigration was also important. Many people from the Cromarty Firth region went to work on the farms and in the factories of the south of Scotland. Others, notably from Fearn and those parts of the region with a well-established military tradition, such as the Munro lands of Ferindonald, joined the army. Others emigrated to America, particularly during the 1760s and '70s. It was probably during this period that the position of Cromarty as a major port of departure for Highland emigrants was established. These eighteenth century emigrants were not usually poverty-stricken and dispossessed but were instead more often relatively well-off smallholders, tacksmen and tradesmen. One such was Gilbert Barkly, the son of a Cromarty tacksman, who emigrated to Philadelphia, probably in the 1750s, and became a successful merchant. His Loyalist sympathies, however, led him to act as a British spy during the revolution and he lost his fortune.[25]

America may have involved one Cromarty man in a revolution but for those who remained at home there had been a revolution as well. In little over a century the appearance and the social structure of the Cromarty Firth had been transformed beyond all recognition. It was the beginning of the end of a social and economic order that was hundreds, if not thousands, of years old. Two hundred years earlier the land had been bare, unenclosed; virtually the only human features were the lairds' houses, the small, scattered 'fermtouns' where the vast majority of the people lived, and 'roads' that were little more than meandering and muddy tracks. There were few field boundaries except, occasionally, a stone or turf dyke marking the division between lands or the extent of a park about a laird's house.

The earliest detailed map of the Cromarty Firth region was drawn by John Gordon of Straloch in the 1640s, a few years before Franck's visit. The map, now in the National Library of Scotland, shows no woods in the lowland areas around the Firth; only in the distant Highland glens did small stands of the ancient Caledonian forest survive. Small amounts of deal timber from these ancient stands of trees were being exported by this time.[26] One of the major changes in the seventeenth century was the beginning of the deliberate creation of wooded parks about the lairds' houses, and later, widespread afforestation. It was a centuries-long process which had begun in the late sixteenth century when James VI passed an act of parliament 'against the destroyers of planting hayning [enclosed planting] and policee' [stands of trees].[27] The scarcity of wood was so serious that even single trees were regarded as a valuable asset. In 1615, for example, John Finlayson in Alness was summoned under this act before the Sheriff at Dingwall to answer a charge that, having been given permission by a local landowner to cut down an alder tree, he had cut down two. For that he was fined £20 Scots.[28] The cutting of immature woods (often allied to poaching fish and deer) was a recurring problem throughout the seventeenth century. Thus in 1627 charges of poaching, including 'slachter of blackfish and cutting of grein wood' were brought by the procurator fiscal against fifty-nine men in the justiciary court in Tain.[29]

By the second half of the seventeenth century the emphasis had shifted to the planting of trees, a process begun in 1661 by the passage of what has been called 'the first improving act', requiring proprietors of land worth more than £1,000 Scots to enclose and plant at least four acres of land over the next ten years which would then be free of taxation for nineteen years.[30]

Despite its proximity to the Highlands, seventeenth century agricultural life around the Cromarty Firth was essentially Lowland in its age-old organisation and methods. Slowly, over the centuries, land had been cleared and taken into cultivation. In 1449, for example, a charter was issued allowing a group of tenants in Cromarty to bring burgh lands outside the town into cultivation; these new fields eventually became 'Newton' farm.[31]

The basic agricultural unit was the estate, but within that framework the yearly working of the land was based on arable farming and the grazing of beasts. Around the laird's house or the fermtoun was the 'infield', good, intensively cultivated land. Each year about one third of the infield would be manured, using dung, kelp, the remains of turf houses and (by the end of the seventeenth century) lime, and planted with bere, a quick-growing variety of barley suited to the short and uncertain growing season. During the following two years this third of the infield would be planted with oats, without being manured.

The 'outfield' was less fertile land but it, too, was used for crops, mostly grass, grown on areas that had been slightly manured by the pasturing of stock within temporary folds. The outfield also supplied the turf used for buildings and dykes as well as nearby grazing for the beasts. Around the Cromarty Firth there were, in addition, three major stretches of common land: the Hill of Nigg, Delny Muir or Moss and the Mulbuie. These commonties were used for grazing beasts, for cutting turf and (as local sources of peat became increasingly scarce) as a source of illicit wood for fuel. Hugh Miller described one such landscape, on the Black Isle farm of Meikle Farness (Fig. 18):

> Towards autumn, when the fields vary most in colour, it resembled a rudely executed chart of some large island, — so irregular were the patches which composed it, and so broken on every side by a surrounding sea of moor, that here and there went winding into the interior in long river-like strips, or expanded within into friths (*sic*) and lakes.[32]

The methods by which this seemingly chaotic and illogical landscape was farmed were in fact determined by a mixture of practical considerations and centuries of tradition. The yearly life of the fermtoun was 'organized with stricter regard to equality than efficiency.'[33] There was, for example, the annual allocation of rigs or strips of arable, based on their relative fertility, so that over the years each tenant would have equal shares of the good and bad land. This led to tenants being responsible for working small strips of land scattered over a wide area.

Once the spring plantings were over, it was common for the women and girls to take the stock to the summer shielings in the Highlands. Despite the encroachment of sheep runs, and later deer forests, the use of common grazing survived, in some areas, into the twentieth century.[34]

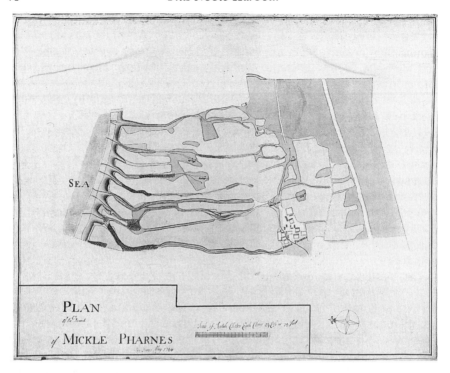

SEA

PLAN
of the Estate
of MICKLE PHARNES

18. Plan of Meikle Farness.

A good deal of the yearly round of work had to be communal. This was seen most clearly in the use of the large and ponderous old Scotch plough. The weight of the plough was necessary to cut through the heavy, undrained soil, but it also meant that the plough required several men to guide it and teams of up to eight or ten oxen to pull it. These teams were often composed of beasts belonging to several inhabitants of the fermtoun. Such ploughs were made mainly of wood, the only available material in a country where iron was a scarce and valuable commodity. Only such essential parts as the share or stock, the coulter and the chain for attaching the draught animals were made of precious iron. It is scarcely surprising that in some of the early farm inventories oxen and the metal parts of the plough are given pride of place. For example, in 1606 Alexander Ross Johnstone of Easter Rarichies had eight oxen and two ploughs 'with their irons.'[35]

If ploughing and the late spring planting of the low-yielding seed went well and the fields were not destroyed by bad weather during the short summer growing season, the crops could be harvested in the autumn. A good harvest meant survival for another year, food for man and beast to last the winter and to pay the rent.

Rents were paid in various ways: in money, kind, or labour. The age-old pattern of rent payment can be seen in the 1590 'Rental of the hail Fermes, Maills and Kanes, within the Earldom of Ross and Lordship of Armeanach', due to the Queen, Anne of Denmark, from a large number of farms along both shores of the Cromarty Firth. Swordale and Fyrish paid rents in kind, beer and meal, cattle, sheep and poultry. The Heights of Fodderty, however, paid both a money rent (twenty-three shillings) and two chickens. By and large, the money rents came from mills or brewlands (lands producing barley that could be sold to make ale) and the rents in kind accrued from purely agricultural lands.[36] Tenants were also responsible for certain services. These included harvest labour, cutting and leading of peats, road building and repair, and carriage services, such as transporting goods to and from local towns or their rents to the landlord's girnel. Wheeled transport was almost unknown, largely due to the lack of decent roads. Instead horses, carrying panniers or pulling wheel-less slypes, were used. By the 1780s crude carts were used to carry stones, manure and peat, but all corn was still carried on horseback; strings of horses tied nose to tail in a line would bring corn to the mill.[37]

Tenants' rents and obligations could be exploited by unscrupulous landlords. One such was the sixteenth century Andrew Munro of Milton, notorious as 'Black Andrew of the Seven Castles', whose violent temper, cruelties and oppressions have passed into local legend. Amongst other things he was said to have forced his female tenants to harvest his crops naked and to have executed tenants who crossed him. Centuries later, bones excavated from the base of the gallows hill and the site of his castle were claimed to have been those of his victims.[38] Whatever the truth of that story, there was certainly conflict between some local proprietors and their tenants. A well documented instance concerns Andrew's descendant, Andrew Munro of Newmore, who managed to obtain extensive lands from supporters of Mary, Queen of Scots after she fled to England.[39] In 1569 his new tenants at Meikle Suddy called him before a Justiciary Court, held by the Regent of Scotland, sitting at Inverness, 'for chargeing thame with extraorbitant cariage and for spoliation fra thame of ten oxen.' The Regent found the charges of forcing the tenants to perform excessive carriage service unproven and ordered the tenants to acknowledge Munro as their overlord; on the other hand, he ordered Munro to return the oxen to the tenants.[40]

There were other rights that pertained to the landlords. All tenants on the estate were 'thirled' to bring their meal to be ground at the landlord's mill, to pay the miller a 'multure', a fixed proportion of the grain, and to help with keeping the mill in repair. On some estates, too, tenants were required to use the landlord's blacksmith. Such tied services were unpopular and a rich source of conflict. Millers were particularly unpopular figures in rural Scotland. In 1660, for example, the baron court of the Balnagown estate at

Ardmore heard a case of reciprocal accusation between the tenants and Jean Stewart, miller of Westray, over 'ill service, extraordinar exactiones and measures of the said milne.'[41]

Despite such tensions, both landlord and tenants were locked into a common system and, on the whole, they had a mutual interest in making it work with the minimum of friction. Life was too precarious to permit the luxury of open or long-term conflict. Indeed, there was sometimes little to distinguish the laird from his tenant; often both worked together, or the laird (and his wife) personally supervised the work of the estate. In June 1686 the wife of Ross of Balnagown wrote to her husband, reporting that the weather had been so bad that no peats had been cut and she herself had had to go out to Edderton to oversee the clip of his wedders. No grass had been cut, so she was having 'to send all of your horses to the heilands for want of oats . . .'[42]

Balnagown was a huge estate, greatly exceeding Foulis and New Tarbat in size and wealth. Below this triumvirate were smaller estates held by related cadet branches of the local families, such as the Munros of Novar, Culcairn, Teaninich, and Newmore. The Reformation had led to an explosion in the number of secular landowners. In 1644 there were one hundred and sixty four proprietors in Easter Ross, many of them holding very small estates which would disappear as a result of estate consolidation during the early period of improvement.[43]

Within individual estates there could be a hierarchy of landholding. Below large proprietors were a class of men called tacksmen, often kinsmen of the landlord, who held their land in tack [lease] from the landlord. There were also a number of smallholders, some with lands of only a few acres, held on short term leases of usually between three or five years. The overwhelming majority of the rural population had no written lease or tack, at all. This lack of legal status was offset, in the Highlands at least, by the real or imagined bonds of kinship between the chief and his followers and the convention that a landlord's wealth and status was measured not only in the amount of land he possessed but also in the number of tenants and followers he could call upon. In fact, this usually meant that clansmen were required to follow their chiefs into battle. By the seventeenth century, clansmen might join the professional companies raised by their chiefs. This practice was particularly prevalent in Ferindonald, the land of the Munros. In return for such service the clan chief had an obligation to look after the welfare of his people.

These personal links were reinforced by the legal rights of landlords over their tenants. These rights could be 'regalian' in scope, allowing the landlord to hear all the pleas of the crown, murder, arson, rape, in his own court. Sometimes, legal rights were specifically delegated by the crown. A unique local example of the fusion of royal and local legal authority concerned the Mackenzies of Tarbat who, by their purchase of the Cromarty estates, became hereditary sheriffs of this small and ancient shire. In 1685 an Act of Parliament joined the family's scattered estates to Cromarty to form a single shire of scattered lands across Ross. In this new, enlarged shire of Cromarty, the Mackenzies had a dual legal status as royal sheriff and owner.[44]

Most of the great landowners, however, had more restricted jurisdictions, extending only over a single estate and commonly exercised through their baron court. These courts were mainly concerned with protecting the rights of the landlord and dealt with such matters as fixing and collecting arrears of rent, trespass, boundary disputes, dykebreaking and damage to property. Amongst the problems that local baron courts were most concerned with were poaching of game and the protection of young trees, especially following the passage of the 1661 Act. Small plantations of trees were beginning to make tentative appearances in the Scottish countryside, usually in enclosed parks about the laird's houses. In 1670 Thomas McIntyre of Little Farnes (Farness) appeared at Cromarty before the Sheriff-Substitute charged with destroying greenwood although he was able to prove that he was only clearing out undergrowth.[45]

This case is interesting, for it provides an early instance of what might be called modern farming methods at work. By the end of the seventeenth century there are, in fact, a few scattered evidences of the beginnings of changes that were to transform the region in the following century.

Perhaps the most important of these was the establishment of regular trading links with the outside world. Shipping points are found throughout the Firth in the seventeenth century. Some of the more important were at Nigg Sands, New Tarbat, Ness of Invergordon, Alness, Foulis Ferry, Ferryton and Balblair and, of course, Cromarty. It is clear that by this time, and probably even earlier, a number of local lairds had well-established trading links for local produce with distant markets. Salmon, for example, was being shipped to Edinburgh merchants by the middle of the sixteenth century[46] and there were regular trading links with other North Sea ports. In 1591 Andrew Munro of Newmore was once again engaged in litigation, this time over various legal fees due to him as 'mair' [*maor* or local judicial representative] of the earldom of Ross, fees that included payments to him for every sack of corn brought to the shore to be shipped.[47] One of the most important grain cash crops was bere. From at least the late seventeenth century lairds from about the Cromarty Firth were sending regular shipments of the grain to Edinburgh brewers and to England and the continent.[48]

The parliamentary union of 1707 allowed access to English markets and the north east ports enjoyed a small boom.[49] Evidence for this trade survives in the girnels that still fringe the Cromarty Firth. Lord Tarbat built the earliest of these, at Portmahomack and Cromarty and also used to store grain in the Baron Court House at New Tarbat.[50] In the eighteenth century other storehouses were built at Nigg, Ankerville, Balnagown, Portleich (Barbaraville) Invergordon, Alness Point, Foulis Ferry (Fig. 19), and Ferryton.[51]

Land transport, on the other hand, was still extremely primitive. Even in the eighteenth century many travellers claimed that there were no roads worthy

19. Girnel at Foulis Ferry.

of the name north of Inverness although this seems to be an exaggeration.[52] There were bridges over some major streams. The Water of Averon (Alness River) had been bridged from at least the mid fifteenth century, and the Peffery, by at least the mid seventeenth.[53] A bridge at Balnagown was probably built at about the same time.[54] These stone bridges indicate that there was a regular and well-used route along the north shore of the Cromarty Firth between Dingwall and Tain but until the parliamentary Act of 1669, creating the statute labour system, there was no method of maintaining such roads. This Act ordained that arable land adjacent to roads should be enclosed by a ditch, dyke or hedge, and that local heritors (landowners) should be assessed for road maintenance, the money being used to buy road-working tools with the actual work carried out by tenants.[55]

Thus the beginnings of a system of land transport were laid during the seventeenth century. General Roy's maps of *c.* 1750 show three main roads through the region; on the north shore of the Firth the route between Dingwall and Tain is well established, while on the Black Isle there is a road running between Fortrose and Cromarty, and another connecting the two ferry crossings at Kessock and Balblair. It seems likely that these routes were old ones and well maintained by the standards of the time.

Despite the importance of sea transport for the Cromarty Firth region in the seventeenth and eighteenth centuries, the development of roads was perhaps even more crucial in the long term. Not only did they allow easier access to shipping points, they also allowed access to local towns and markets and the beginnings of a more diversified and flexible local economy. Growing trade helped to pay for agricultural change.

Money was still in short supply. Despite some attempt at converting rents into money payments, development around the Cromarty Firth in the late seventeenth century was inhibited by the lack of specie. One of the great advantages of the series of 'improving' parliamentary Acts passed between 1661 and 1695 was that they allowed the lairds to develop their lands through statutory labour or remission of taxes, rather than large capital outlays. These Acts not only encouraged the planting of trees and the repair and maintenance of roads, but also the straightening of boundaries and marches prior to enclosure (1669), the consolidation of runrig holdings and the division of common lands (1695).

Tree planting and enclosure around the laird's house were the first steps in creating not only the landscaped gardens and lawns of the eighteenth century estate but also the improved mains (home) farm, which became the catalyst and exemplar for improvements on the rest of the estate. It is not clear when this process of change began around the Cromarty Firth, but Gordon of Straloch's sketch map of *c.* 1640 shows what may be planted enclosures around the castles at Milton (New Tarbat), Inverbreakie (Invergordon), Delny and Achnacloich. The map does not extend to Foulis, but it seems likely that plantation and the enclosure of a park around Foulis Castle also took place early, perhaps at about the same time that the newly-created Viscount Tarbat was laying out his gardens at New Tarbat. Lord Tarbat's innovations were certainly the main inspiration for early planting and improvement around the Firth. Indeed, the gardens at New Tarbat were the sole source for seeds and seedlings until the establishment of further nurseries at Allangrange, Novar, Cromarty and Balnagown in the eighteenth century.[56]

Besides the enclosing of parkland and the consolidation of the mains farm, tree planting on a large scale also began to take place on the open land and hillsides. By the early eighteenth century wood from Balnagown was regularly being shipped south to Edinburgh and agents from the south were coming into the region to look for trees to purchase.[57] Along with Ross of Balnagown and Lord Tarbat, Munro of Foulis was certainly one of the earliest of the local lairds to practice widescale afforestation; Sir Robert Munro (d. 1746) planted over five hundred acres of moorland and these are clearly shown on Roy's map of *c.* 1750, planted in a neat square with radiating avenues on the slopes of a hill to the north west of Foulis Castle.[58] The map also indicates that enclosure had taken place on a few farms and there are parks around such major seats as Findon, Ardoch (Poyntzfield), and Teaninich. Relatively few plantations are shown, however: only Invergordon, Balnagown, New Tarbat and Sheeppark, north of Newhall on the Black Isle.

Outside the major estates, the process of change was slow. Agricultural improvement was, in fact, a carrot and stick process. In 1735 the laird of

Balnagown found it necessary to take a strong line with his reluctant tenants in Balnagown, Rarichies and Westray. He ordered that their gardens were to be fenced and, moreover, that they were to get twenty trees from the nurseries at Balnagown and plant them five feet apart in their gardens or else there would be dire consequences:

> All good and sufficient tenants who shall enclose and endeavour to improve their possessions shall be continued in their tacks without removeall, but if they fail, any man offering . . . to inclose . . . shall be preferred.[59]

It is not clear if this promise of continuance worked. On the whole Balnagown, and other landlords, preferred to encourage improvement by the granting of longer leases (commonly of nineteen years) which contained clauses stipulating not only what improvements were to be carried out but land use as well. Such enforced improvement also drove people from the land. It was natural that they would react strongly against symbols of this feared and barely-understood change. In 1733, for example, five hundred people armed with dirks and cudgels pulled down newly-planted trees and a feal [turf] dyke built by Sir William Gordon's factor at Blackstand near Cromarty, and then 'beat and bruised' the workmen.[60]

This confrontation may have been exacerbated by the fact that the Gordons were relative newcomers to the district. Originally from Berwickshire, they had settled in Sutherland before arriving in the Cromarty Firth area in the seventeenth century. In 1634 Sir Adam Gordon of Kilcalmkill had served in Germany under Sir Hector Munro of Foulis.[61] It was his namesake and descendant, Adam Gordon of Dalpholly, and his wife Anne, the daughter of Alexander Urquhart of Newhall, who were the progenitors of the Invergordon family. Adam Gordon of Dalpholly made a fortune in trade and in 1695 was able to buy Ardoch (later Poyntzfield) in his wife's native Black Isle. The family fortunes were based on commerce and the acquisition of public office; for three generations the Gordons regularly held the influential local office of Inverness Collector of Customs, which covered the ports of the Cromarty Firth as well. It was Adam's sons, William, Alexander and another Adam, who laid the basis for the family's position in the Cromarty Firth. Alexander became laird of Ardoch and another, possibly Adam, became the Inverness Collector of Customs. Around 1700 William acquired the lands at Inverbreakie (Invergordon) from the MacLeods in lieu of a debt owed to his father.

William Gordon was a successful London banker and friend of the financier John Law of Lauriston, founder of the Bank of France and the West India Company, designed to exploit the riches of the Mississippi Valley. Law eventually went bankrupt but William Gordon realised a fortune from speculation in his friend's ventures as well as the South Sea Company. He also drew a regular salary of £500 from a government appointment. His income was perhaps supplemented by Adam's somewhat unorthodox activities as Collector of Customs. It was said, for example, that he had attempted to force a Fraserburgh ship from Danzig to unload directly at Invergordon without first going through customs and quarantine at Cromarty and in 1710 he was accused of being involved in the deliberate grounding of an Alloway ship loaded with wine and brandy near Invergordon as part of large-scale smuggling he carried on in his brother's name.[62]

Sir William Gordon used his wealth to transform his estate on the Cromarty Firth. In 1723 he was a founder member of the Honourable Society of Improvers in the Knowledge of Agriculture in Scotland, the first agricultural society in Europe, and the progenitor of such bodies as the Highland Society. These clubs were major forces in the spread of the techniques of the new farming. With Ross of Balnagown, William Gordon was one of the first lairds to introduce an active programme of field drainage and fallowing of land.[63]

The results of his work may be seen in an estate map of *c.* 1750[64] showing a neat grid of enclosed fields and intersecting avenues around Invergordon Castle, with a large plantation of trees on the later site of Saltburn (Fig. 20). Like many improving landlords, Sir William adopted the practice of naming his fields after family members, in this case, his children.

Indeed, not the least of Sir William's contributions to the family fortunes was his large family of eight children. One son, Charles, succeeded to the estate of Newhall. His daughter, Isabella ('Bonny Belle Gordon') made an advantageous marriage in 1724 to the future Earl of Cromartie, bringing with her a dowry of 20,000 merks. Another daughter, Anne, married Robert Dundas of Arniston; her son Henry Dundas, became Lord Melville, ('King Henry'), the political manager of Scotland at the end of the eighteenth century. This was a family alliance that was to prove of crucial importance.

Before the end of his life, however, there is evidence that Sir William Gordon was in financial difficulties and he died bankrupt in 1742. These financial problems were inherited along with the land and title by his son John.[65] By 1744 attempts were being made to sequester the Invergordon estate,[66] which was sold for debt in 1751 to Thomas Belsches, who conveyed back part of it to Sir John and part to his brother.[67] The rest of Sir John's life was to be a struggle against financial embarrassment. He was a peppery character, ambitious, often unscrupulous, yet loyal to his family, with a wide range of interests, including politics. He was Member of Parliament for Cromarty between 1742–7 and 1754–61 and had considerable political influence. He needed every bit of influence he possessed when, in 1745, the Jacobite revolt broke out.

The Gordons, Rosses and Munros were staunchly Hanoverian. Soon after Prince Charles Edward landed a company of Munros marched off to aid the government forces. Sir John's factor, John Gorry, however, refused to allow men to be recruited for this company from the Invergordon estates. It was a stand with which Sir John agreed: 'I did not see any room for ruining the tenants by carrying them off from their harvest . . .'[68] With his brother, Charles, Sir John organised local defence against the Jacobites, and he also

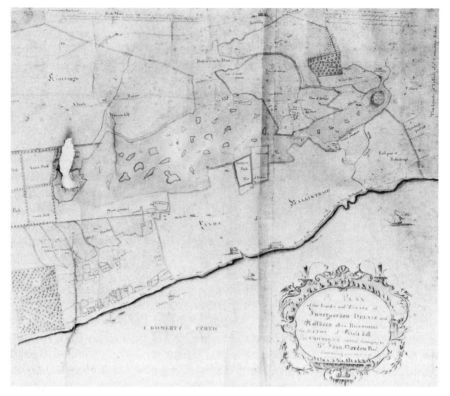

20. Invergordon estate map of *c*.1750.

attempted, unsuccessfully, to dissuade his brother-in-law, Lord Cromartie, from joining the rebels: on one occasion Cromartie took a diplomatic nap in order to avoid speaking with Sir John when he called at New Tarbat. In mid October 1745 the Earl and his eighteen year old son, Lord MacLeod, joined Prince Charles's army, along with two other local lairds, Alexander Ross of Pitcalnie and MacCulloch of Glastullich.[69] There was little local popular support for the Jacobites although Lord Cromartie managed to raise a few men for the Prince's army from his estates.

Although the Cromarty Firth was regularly visited by government and Jacobite ships during the Forty-Five the countryside escaped relatively lightly. Cromarty itself was briefly occupied and looted by a body of Highlanders who were then frightened off when a ship came into the bay. Indeed, the town suffered more when Lord Loudoun's government troops crossed Nigg ferry and took away all the local boats to prevent pursuit.[70]

Lord Cromartie was appointed chief Jacobite military commander north of Beauly early in 1746 and made his headquarters briefly at Dingwall before marching north into Sutherland.[71] He was captured at Dunrobin at just about the time the people of Cromarty were watching the progress of the Battle of Culloden from the hill above the town. Lord Cromartie was brought to Inverness two days after the battle and sent for trial in London. He was condemned to death, along with the Earl of Kilmarnock and Lord Balmerino, and his estates forfeited to the Crown.

Cromartie and his son were spared the fate of their fellow Jacobites largely by the long and tireless efforts of Sir John Gordon. His frequent letters to his sister, Anne Dundas, chronicle his campaign to save Cromartie and 'the boy' (Lord MacLeod): 'Everything is doing that can be thought off (*sic*) or attempted by Me and My Friends . . . but what will be the success God only knows . . .'[72] He used every trick he could think of to excite sympathy, including dragging his heavily pregnant sister, the Countess, to kneel before the King to beg mercy for her husband. Horace Walpole claimed that the Prince of Wales agreed to spare Cromartie in gratitude for Sir William's having come 'out of his death bed [in 1742] to vote for Sir Robert Walpole in the Chippenham parliamentary election' in which the Prince had spent £12,000.[73] Lord Cromartie was given a conditional pardon in 1753, but his estates remained in government hands and he spent the rest of his life living in genteel poverty in Devon.

Lord MacLeod had been given a free pardon late in 1746, on the condition that he resigned his claim to his father's estate. Sir John was both relieved and angered: 'This is an odd condition, but I did not then object to what I afterwards shall. I was willing to take what I could get . . .'[74] After a delay of some years Lord Macleod (Fig. 21) took the restoration of his fortunes into his own hands and, despite his uncle's disapproval, went abroad in 1749 and joined the Swedish army to begin a distinguished military career. He remained in close touch with Sir John and his aunt Dundas, who helped him over the years to redeem his position. In 1759 he returned briefly to Scotland and began to put his lands around the Cromarty Firth in order and in the following year he appointed Leonard Urquhart, Sir John's man of business and brother-in-law, as his factor. On the eve of his departure for India in 1778 he authorised Sir John to buy local estates on his behalf and began petitioning for restitution of the Cromartie estates.[75]

Sir John Gordon kept a 'pochetbook', a daily aide-memoire, which survives only for the period 1753–9, during part of his second spell as Member of Parliament for Cromarty.[76] Its entries provide a window on the mind of this extraordinary man. Sir John's interests moved from the fantastical ('A Table to find the Moon's age') to the practical; for example, recipes for medicines and cleaning white silk stockings, a list of the contents of his cellar, his brother's debts and the cost of a trip from Edinburgh to London in 1755. The bulk of the entries, however, are concerned with matters of estate management. He was keen to have the estate surveyed, so that he could plan further changes, such as the enclosure of larger farms and the '. . . removal of the Mealers — one tenant in their Room.'[77]

His plans for his castle and new town occupy a good deal of space in his notebook. Invergordon Castle was being rebuilt in classical style by 'Adams the architect' (almost certainly John Adam) and a concomitant of that change was the creation of the first planned village in Easter Ross, Invergordon. In 1753 he reminds himself 'To Consider the Biggins at the Ness and at Balblair', presumably buildings connected with the Ferry.[78] Two years later a book of plans of his estate is said to include one showing 'Invergordon Shoars with draught for Piers, Ferries and Fisher Houses and for a shell fishing.' Although a pier at Invergordon would not be built for another sixty years Sir John was the first to understand that regular sea access to distant markets was crucial in the development of local agriculture and commerce. He must also take the credit for first seeing the tourist potential of Invergordon as a centre of 'sea bathing', then just coming into fashion.[79]

Sir John's notebook is full of jottings relating to road building and repair, including the list of heritors bound to pay for road maintenance. Ultimately, he felt that the public should pay the cost of building and repair, and he hoped the government might take over the ferry at Invergordon, which was a regular drain on his finances.[80] In this he was unsuccessful and the running of Invergordon ferry continued to be a costly problem for successive lairds of Invergordon for over a hundred and fifty years.

The consequences of the Cromartie forfeiture still concerned him. In 1751, at the instance of Sir John, the Countess of Cromartie had been awarded a pension of £200 by the Barons of Exchequer in Scotland,[81] and his notebook has several entries relating the payment of the Countess's jointure. A more immediate problem, however, was his relationship with the government administrators appointed by the Commissioners for the Forfeited Estates to administer Cromartie's lands at New Tarbat since the forfeiture of Cromartie had left the respective rights of local landowners ill-defined in such places as the commonty of Delny. In 1757 Sir John wrote a note to himself to find out 'To whome since Cromartie's forfeiture must the vassals of the barony of Delny pay their feu duties.'[82] As Delny Muir had been divided in 1739, Sir John was constantly attempting to assert his rights, usually in the face of the Commissioners' local agent, Captain John Forbes of Newe, who also wished to bring it into cultivation. To Sir John, Delny represented an opportunity not only to house his dispossessed mealers, but also a welcome means of increasing his rent rolls.

The notebook is also full of financial calculations on how to cut down his living expenses and regular promises to himself 'to clear all my debt.'[83] But the truth was that, in addition to inheriting his father's debts, Sir John added many of his own. As well as Invergordon Castle Sir John had two houses in London, and unlike his father he apparently had no interests beyond politics to fund his activities. Moreover, he was said not to have increased rents on his estate for forty years. His financial position had always been perilous but it became

21. John, Lord Macleod.

irretrievably disastrous after the long legal case in which he became involved with the new owners of the Cromarty estate in 1763.

Sir John was caught in a financial trap that was all too common amongst eighteenth century improvers. Such radical changes required massive injections of cash over a long period of time before any real return could be expected. Sir John did not have the necessary capital.

In the end the economic regeneration of the Cromarty Firth would depend on massive amounts of money from outside sources, often from natives of the area who had made their fortunes abroad and then returned home. One of the earliest was the Baltic merchant 'Polander' Ross who bought the estate of Ankerville in the early eighteenth century;[84] but the most remarkable and successful of these returning native sons was George Ross, who had made his fortune as an army agent before purchasing the Cromarty estate. Success as an improver not only required money, time and ability, but also a large amount of luck. Not even government-sponsored attempts at improvement, such as those carried out by the Crown Commissioners of the Forfeited Estates, established in 1752, could guarantee success.

The Commissioners planned that the rents and profits of the annexed estates were to be ploughed back into their development and the creation of a prosperous and loyal population. After initial surveys were carried out to assess the potential of the fourteen estates under their control, the Commissioners had appointed local agents. Thus, in 1755 Captain Forbes of Newe presented the findings of an initial survey of the Cromartie lands to his masters. New Tarbat, he said, was not a typical Highland estate. Already there was some industry connected with Milton and some improvement, although this was mostly connected with the Mains Farm. He found 'the people . . . more industrious than in any other part of the [Cromartie] estate . . . sober, honest.'[85] Forbes recommended the granting of long leases with improving conditions, as well as the establishment of an English school and a spinning school at New Tarbat. As part of his programme he composed a letter to the tenants of the Cromartie estates and ordered local ministers to read it in church in both English and Gaelic. In it, he urged the people to 'obey the laws, apply themselves to agriculture, manufactures, the education of their children in the Protestant religion and to speak and read English, knitting stockings etc.'[86]

The work of the Commissioners for the Forfeited Estates was the first major government-sponsored attempt to deal with some of the intractable problems of the Highlands. In many ways it anticipates the Highlands and Islands Development Board set up two centuries later. New Tarbat was, in fact, an early form of enterprise zone.

Some of the Commissioners' plans, such as the establishment of a fishing station near the Cromarty Firth, came to nothing, as did an elaborate scheme to establish a 'manufacturing station at the house of New Tarbat,' covering all stages of linen-making from raising the flax to the final bleaching. As a result the house of New Tarbat was left to decay during the years that the estate was controlled by the Commissioners.[87] It had been planned to spend more than £4,000 over nine years to train nine hundred girls to spin and one hundred and ninety-two apprentices who would learn the trades of heckling, scutching, bleaching and weaving. Nevertheless, a spinning school was established and trade with the outside world was encouraged by the building of a girnel at

Portleich (Barbaraville). There were plans, too, for a pier but these were abandoned due to cost.[88]

The Commissioners, like private landowners, were also interested in creating new towns and settlements. In 1757 a report suggested New Tarbat as a likely place for the introduction of English-speaking outsiders and an ambitious programme of building and enclosure was started for the 'industrious manufacturers' who would settle there. Instead, forty-one retired soldiers and a number of ex-sailors and their families arrived.[89] William Forsyth, as the local agent of the British Linen Company, was responsible for supplying the new-fangled spinning wheels, which were rapidly replacing the distaff, to the soldiers' wives. It was hoped that the sailors would form the nucleus of a fishing community. Six sailors did accept a boat and nets for herring fishing at a cost of £6. The boats, however, were too small and the fishermen (and most of the other incomers) soon left New Tarbat.[90]

By the time of the compilation of the *Old Statistical Account*, all but two of the soldier families had gone and their lots were 'now occupied by a more industrious set of people.'[91] Despite these attempts at improvement, the Commissioners ultimately brought little change or benefit to the estate of New Tarbat. The development of the parish outlined in the *Old Statistical Account* came largely from private landlords and from manufactories already in existence, such as linen spinning and lime burning.

Nevertheless, the Commissioners for the Forfeited Estates did play a small part in the transformation of the Cromarty Firth. For example, they helped George Ross with the cost of building the pier at Cromarty and also built the gaol and courthouse there (Fig. 22), at a cost of £350.[92] After the affairs of the Commissioners were wound up early in the nineteenth century, the remaining funds were transferred to the Commissioners for Highland Roads and Bridges and were used on such local projects as the Dingwall Canal, ferry piers at Invergordon and Balblair, and the long-planned fishery pier at Balintraid.

With the exception of the period when New Tarbat was managed by the Commissioners for the Forfeited Estates, virtually all the development of the Cromarty Firth region in the eighteenth century was the work of individuals. At least one improver was a woman, Henrietta Gordon, the heiress of Newhall who, with her second husband, David Urquhart of Braelangwell, transformed her Black Isle estates. She was an especially enthusiastic planter. The farm of Henrietta Park began as a plantation named for her and both Henrietta and her husband attempted to encourage local industry. Gordon's Mill (*c.* 1790) was built by them as a snuff manufactory, and later was used as a water-powered wool carding mill.[93]

But of all improvers, none was more remarkable than Sir Hector Munro of Novar (Fig. 23). He had had a military career, beginning with service in a Company commanded by his kinsman, Sir Harry Munro of Foulis, in 1747. In 1760 he went with his regiment to India and made his fortune during the conquest of Bengal for the East India Company. Four years later he commanded

22. Court house at Cromarty.

an army that defeated a confederation of Indian princes at Buxar. His prize money was the enormous sum of twelve lakhs, which was 120,000 rupees.

When he returned to Scotland, Sir Hector took over the Novar estate,

23. Sir Hector Munro of Novar.

although not the heir, and set about its transformation. Novar was known for the poverty of its soil and was utterly barren of trees. Over the next decade Sir Hector set about the creation of the enclosed and wooded landscape that survives to this day, while his neighbours watched in astonishment. The

24. Novar.

seventeenth century house was rebuilt as a classical square, painted yellow
and topped off with white chimneys.[94] The axis of the new house (Fig. 24) was
turned ninety degrees, so that its public rooms faced out over the Firth and, in
order to improve the view from his windows, Sir Hector had several small hills
levelled.[95]

   This remaking of the landscape to suit the taste of man is the key to Sir
Hector's improvements at Novar. An estate map of 1777 (Fig. 25) shows that
field boundaries had been laid out, although the curved rigs of the old fields
still show in some of the enclosures, along with the names of their soon-to-be-
improved tenants. The mansion and Novar Inn were complete, along with a
scattering of 'Oblisks thro' the Policy' which included a statue of Mercury and
the Eagle (the Munro crest) as well as several Indian-style temples. The
walled garden north of the house had the factor's house attached to the north

25. Novar estate map of 1777.

west corner; beyond it were the Nursery Gardens and the Kennels. To the northeast of the House was the Home Farm, built round a square with a bell-tower over the entrance. On the hill slope to the north, roads led to the moss and the quarry through 'The Large Firr Plantation of Fyrish' and a sheep park.

It was said that Sir Hector Munro spent £120,000 on the transformation of Novar. He was obliged to return to India to earn another fortune in order to run the estate.[96] This time his military career was less fortunate for there were serious disagreements with Sir Eyre Coote, the commander-in-chief. Nevertheless, he did return with a second, smaller fortune from his battles, which had included the defeat of Hyder Ali and the capture of Negapatam. While Sir Hector was away, the estate was in the hands of one of the many Lowland factors who were coming into the Cromarty Firth area in the later eighteenth century, Thomas Baird from Dalkeith.

In the years after his second return from India, Sir Hector Munro brought his plans for Novar to completion. An estate map of 1788 (Fig. 26) shows the fields and buildings as they are to this day. A small cartouche in the top right hand corner is surrounded by drawings of captured guns and pennons; one cannon (facing towards the fields of Novar) is firing. Some improvers literally shot out tree seedlings from guns. There is no evidence that Sir Hector ever did this; nevertheless, the landscape of Novar was most certainly brought forth from the mouth of a gun.

Unlike his neighbours Sir Hector did not name his fields after his children, but instead after battles and places in India: Bombay, Madras, Negapatnam (*sic*), Calcutta, Buxar. In some ways this shows his egotism and also his honesty about what had made the transformation possible; in a real sense, the fields of Novar *were* his children.

The transformation was crowned, in all senses of the word, by the millions of trees Sir Hector planted on Fyrish Hill, including the first larch trees ever seen in the district.[97] The hill was surmounted by a white-painted copy of an Indian city gate.[98] According to tradition the local people were suffering want, either from famine or from the ending of work on the estate, and Sir Hector built the folly to provide work for them. This would accord well with the mixture of paternalism coupled with family and military pride that was so much a part of Sir Hector's character. But there is more to it than that. The folly is an aesthetic statement, literally a centrepiece in a series of improvements that transformed this part of the Cromarty Firth. Although no longer painted white to contrast with the green trees surrounding it, the Fyrish Monument (Figs. 27, 28) still performs its original function of drawing the eye up through the woods of Fyrish to the hilltop and the sky beyond.

Fyrish is also a monument to a conception of land ownership that still owed something to the old clan feelings of responsibility for the kindred; Sir Hector was a Highlander through and through (it was said that in India he sent especially important communiques in Gaelic).[99] Elsewhere around the Cromarty Firth, however, the old bonds of Highland society were dying, and with them went an entire way of life. A major blow to the clan system had been the abolition of the chief's legal powers ('heritable jurisdictions') after the Forty-Five. The pacification and occupation of the Highlands also made the old military function of the clans obsolete although some clan leaders managed to convert this service into new forms. Ironically, the most successful example of this change concerned the umquhile Jacobite, Lord MacLeod who, after rising to become a Marshall of Sweden, returned to his native country and in 1778 sailed to India ('the land of Rupees') with a regiment of clansmen. His service there completed his rehabilitation as a loyal servant of the Hanoverians and made him a modest fortune.[100]

In other respects, however, the changes that occurred after 1750 could not be bonded onto the old ways, or seen as anything except a complete break with what had gone before. Sheep farming, for example, began to be

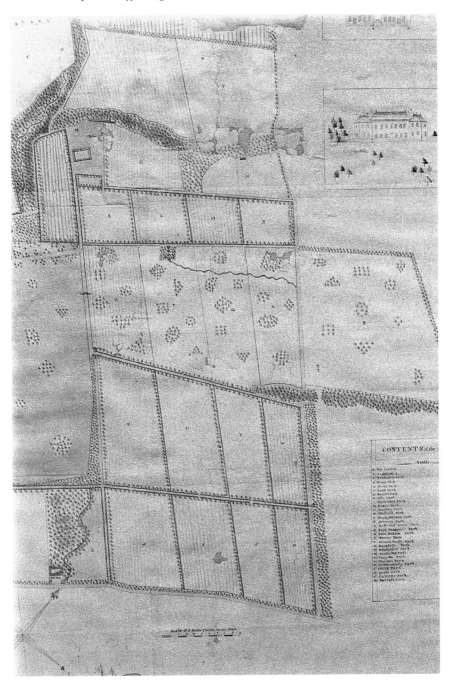

26. Novar estate map of 1788.

27. Fyrish monument.

introduced into Easter Ross in the 1760s. The ever-optimistic Sir John Sinclair claimed that the introduction of sheep in Highland pastures would force the low-country tenant 'to a better system, rotation of crops, sown grass etc.'[101] But this was too facile. At issue was not just whether cattle of sheep should be the foundation of the Highland economy but also whether a communal peasant society would survive or be swept away by the forces of entrepreneurial capitalism.

The man responsible for initiating this change around the Cromarty Firth was Sir John Lockhart Ross of Balnagown, a man who, despite his surname, had little family connection with the area. The estate had come to the family by an extremely dubious purchase following the death of the last of the Rosses of Balnagown in 1711. The Lockhart Rosses had extensive estates elsewhere, notably in the Borders where sheep-farming was well-established by the mid-eighteenth century. Lockhart Ross had already been sheep-farming in the area for some years before he brought in Mr Geddes, a southern sheep farmer, to his lands at Strathoykel in 1781–2. After a number of tenants were displaced, Mr Geddes and his sheep were subjected to harrassment and open violence from the local people.[102]

The resistance at Strathoykel was part of a pattern of local rural protest that went back at least to the overthrowing of the dykes at Blackstand in 1733; it was to reach a climax in 1792, 'The Year of the Sheep'. Why Easter Ross should be the breeding ground for such a tradition of protest is difficult to explain. Perhaps because contact with the outside world was frequent, radical ideas were in circulation. Hugh Miller recalled how the French Revolution of 1789 brought a questioning of the accepted order to Cromarty. A group of

28. Fyrish monument.

young hotheads even formed a Jacobin Club and paraded the Tree of Liberty through the streets of the town[103] and in 1792 a French consul was established in the town. The lairds who suppressed the rising believed that the men responsible for the sheep drove were directly influenced by the ideas of the French Revolution, perhaps with some justification. A more important element, however, may have been religion. Stories of the stands taken for righteousness by such men as Thomas Hog were part of local folklore. Certainly the protest, posted on church doors throughout the region, was couched in Old Testament terms:

> That the Curse of the Children not yet born, and their generations, would follow such as would not cheerfully go and banish the Sheep out of the Country.[104]

The flashpoint for 'The Year of the Sheep' was the settling in 1791 by the laird of Culcairn of two brothers named Cameron on a sheep farm at the head of Loch Morie, a move which necessitated the removal of a number of sitting tenants.[105] Immediately, there was conflict between the new farmers and the men of Strathrusdale over the curtailment of their traditional grazing rights at Kildermorie. The Camerons regularly captured cattle straying onto their land and fines had to be paid before they would be released. Events reached their first crisis when, in June 1792, Strathrusdale cattle that had strayed into Kildermorie lands were impounded. A group of men from Strathrusdale and Ardross, led by a local leader named Alexander 'Big Wallace,' marched to the pound at the end of Loch Morie where the cattle were held. Captain Cameron had armed himself and threatened the mob with shooting and transportation to Botany Bay. Instead, he was disarmed, severely beaten and the freed cattle returned to Strathrusdale.

Cameron tried to bring his assailants to court but a group of witnesses travelling to Alness (or, in some accounts, to Tain) were forcibly prevented from appearing.[106] A few days later there was a wedding in Strathrusdale in the course of which plans to drive the sheep out of the Highlands were laid.

In response to the call posted on church doors, about two hundred people gathered at Brea in Strathoykel four days later. From there men set out to drive the sheep into a central gathering spot. Eventually, as many as 10,000 sheep were brought together and set on a drove south. On Saturday 4 August they were at Boath, at the bottom end of Loch Morie; it was planned that the flock would stay here until other sheep still being collected could be added to it. Instead, three companies of the Black Watch, dispatched from Fort George at the urgent request of the Sheriff of Ross, MacLeod of Geanies, and led by Sir Hector Munro of Novar, arrived at Boath on the morning of 5 August. Eleven men were captured and 'The Year of the Sheep' ended as suddenly as it began.

A number of trials followed at Inverness. Eight men, charged with riot and assault on the Camerons at Kildermorie, were found not guilty. Charges against three men of attempting to prevent the appearance of witnesses were only slightly more successful. Of the men charged with capturing and driving sheep, one had the charge dismissed, one was fined £50 and imprisoned for a month, two were banished from Scotland for life, and one imprisoned for three months. These sentences were, by the standards of the time, extremely light, suggesting that there was a good deal of sympathy for the men. The two ringleaders were sentenced to seven years transportation, but were allowed to escape from gaol and, after a brief period in hiding, spent the rest of their lives in Moray.

Everyone seems to have recognised that 'The Year of the Sheep' was some kind of watershed. Both sides in the conflict were concerned about the consequences of widescale sheep farming. Ross of Balnagown, like many improvers, was convinced that it was possible to introduce sheep and still maintain the population; he founded the village of Edderton to serve as a woollen mnufacturing centre that would receive its raw materials from the surrounding sheep farms. Sheriff MacLeod of Geanies, too, was concerned about the consequences of the introduction of sheep; he had settled some of the dispossessed on his own lands, and it may have been because of this (or fear of his authority) that his flocks remained untouched in 1792.

With hindsight it is possible to know that, as the men of Strathrusdale feared, sheep farming could not be accommodated to the traditional way of life. It may have seemed to the lairds that their actions had restored the status quo, yet things were changing so rapidly that within a few years even the certainties by which they lived their lives would be swept away, as surely as the people of Strathrusdale were also doomed to disappear.

NOTES

1. For Sir John Sinclair and the background to the *Statistical Account* see R. Mitchison, *Agricultural Sir John*, London, 1962, especially Chapter 10.

2. E. Richards, 'Agrarian Change, Modernisation and the Clearances', in *RC Book*, p. 160.

3. *OSA*, vol. 4, pp. 288–301.

4. *Ibid.*, vol. 13, pp. 13–22. Summons for division were issued in 1763; See 'Plan of hill of Nigg, as divided', [dated 1763] SRO RHP 680; Division took place in 1770. See SRO 'Directory of Commonties', vol. 2, p. 208.

5. *Ibid.*, vol. 4, pp. 183–96. Lime-making apparently went back at least to the early eighteenth century. In 1707 William Ross, merchant in Milton claimed eight bolls of lime, or the equivalent price, from Agnes Lindsay the widow of James Allan of Balintraid. Cromartie MSS, SRO GD 305/1/154 no. 14.

6. I. Whyte, *Agriculture*, p. 38.

7. *OSA*, vol. 2, pp. 558–64. An earlier, more detailed, view of these same mealers on the Gordon of Invergordon estates is found in A. Wight, *Present State of Husbandry in Scotland*, Edinburgh, 1778–84, vol. 3, p. 250. They are said to have three acres for every man and have seven years rent free, and the landlord supplies each of them with

twelve shillings for furnishings, plus two spades and mattocks and enough oats to sow half an acre. The mealers are to bring into cultivation half an acre each year and enclose the whole with stones from the fields.

8. The Invergordon Chartulary, 1918 (an estate record book kept by the MacLeods of Cadboll) contains a copy of one feu charter in Invergordon dating from the late 1780s, p. 13.

9. *OSA*, vol. 19, pp. 234–40.

10. W. L. Brown, 'Alness in the eighteenth century', *TISSFC*, vol. 6, 1900–6, p. 20.

11. Wight, op. cit., p. 243ff.

12. *OSA*, vol. 1, pp. 261–298.

13. *Ibid*., pp. 288–9.

14. *Ibid*., vol. 3, pp. 1–20.

15. *Ibid*., vol. 5, pp. 203–17.

16. Much of this discussion of the Ferintosh privilege is based on I. Mowat, *Easter Ross*, pp. 58–60.

17. Lord Elibank, Laird of Cromarty, attempted to divide the Mulbuie in 1764, but the process was not complete until 1814–1828. SRO 'Directory of Commonties', vol. 2, pp. 205–6.

18. *OSA*, vol. 14, pp. 88–106.

19. *Ibid*., vol. 12, pp. 245–61.

20. 'A true story of the life of a Scotch merchant', in H. Miller, *Tales and sketches*, pp. 295–389.

21. T. C. Smout, *History of the Scottish People*, London, 1969, p. 159ff.

22. Both sets of statistics are given in *OSA*, vol. 20, p. 616.

23. *Ibid*., vol. 1, p. 265 (Kiltearn); vol. 3, p. 1 (Dingwall).

24. See Richards, 'Agrarian change', pp. 159–60.

25. For Barkly, see G. Seed, 'A British Spy in Philadelphia: 1775-77', *The Pennsylvania Magazine of History and Biography*, vol. 85, no. 1 (January 1961).

26. Thomas Tucker (1655) quoted in P. Hume Brown, *Early Travellers in Scotland*, Edinburgh, 1891, p. 175.

27. Macgill, *Ross-shire*, vol. 1, no. 211.

28. *Ibid*.

29. *Ibid*., vol. 2, no. 1070.

30. Whyte, *Agriculture*, p. 101. Much of the following discussion of seventeenth century agricultural practices and conditions is based on this work and A. Fenton, *Scottish Country Life*, Edinburgh, 1976.

31. W. M. Mackenzie, 'The royal burgh of Cromarty and the breaking of the burgh', *Cromarty Literary Society*, 1924, pp. 12–13.

32. 'The salmon fisher of Udoll', Miller, *Tales and Sketches*, p. 137.

33. Whyte, op. cit., p. 138.

34. See for example, Balnagown MSS, SRO GD 129/2/24, 129/2/30.

35. Macgill, *Ross-shire*, vol. 1, no. 425.

36. The rental is printed in Cromartie, *A Highland History*, Berkhampstead, 1979, pp. 153–6; 'Fermes, Maills' are farm rents. 'Kanes' (sometimes spelt 'Cain') are rent paid in kind. Ardmeanach is the old name for the Black Isle, but the lands were much more extensive, including Meikle Allan, Calrossie, Glastullich, Drumgillie, Meikil Meddat, Wester Pollo, Balintraid, Delny, Kincraig, Culkenny (Rosebank), Milcraig,

Novar, Balcony, Culcairn, Katewell, Scatwell, Culbokie, Balblair, Kessock, Suddy, Rosehaugh and Redcastle.

37. J. MacDonald, 'On the agriculture of the counties of Ross and Cromarty', *THASS*, 4th series, vol. 9 (1877), pp. 67–209.

38. For 'Black Andrew' see A. Ross, 'Munros of Milntoun, *CM*, vol. 10 (1885), nos. 110–13, also H. M. Meldrum, *Kilmuir Easter, the history of a Highland parish*, Inverness, 1935, pp. 102-2 and A. G. R Robertson, *The Lowland Highlanders*, Tain, 1981, pp. 45–8.

39. The lands had belonged to David Chalmers who was forfeit after the Battle of Langside, and included the toun and lands of Suddy, with the brewhouse, croft and mill, the toun and lands of Auchterflow and Meikle Tarrel. Munro also obtained the lands of Meikle Allan after Bishop Leslie was forfeit; Ross, 'Munros of Milntoun', *CM*, vol. 10, no. 112 (1885), pp. 156–7.

40. *RPC*, vol. 1, p. 672.

41. Macgill, *Ross-shire*, vol. 2, no. 1099.

42. *Ibid.*, vol. 2, no. 1039.

43. Mowat, *Easter Ross*, p. 7. By 1756 there were only 94 landowners in Easter Ross.

44. *Ibid.*, p. 4ff. Following the Cromartie forfeiture and the abolition of heritable jurisdictions the county of Cromarty was linked with Ross under the Sheriff of Ross: Mackenzie, *A General View of the Agriculture of the Counties of Ross and Cromarty*, London, 1810, p. 13.

45. Macgill, op. cit., vol. 1, no. 213.

46. *Ibid.*, vol. 1, no. 453.

47. Meldrum, op. cit., p. 105.

48. See for example, Cromartie MSS, SRO GD 305/1/96, 305/14/15.

49. T. C. Smout, *Scottish Trade on the Eve of Union*, Edinburgh, 1963, pp. 142ff.

50. M. Clough, 'The Cromartie Estate', in *Firthlands*, p. 92. At Strathpeffer the ground floor of Castle Leod was used as a storehouse.

51. E. Beaton, 'Late seventeenth and eighteenth century estate girnels', *Firthlands*, pp. 133–151. Mrs Beaton does not, however, mention the surviving girnels at Balnagown or Ferryton. Both must be assigned to the eighteenth century on architectural grounds.

52. Mowat, *Easter Ross*, pp. 74–5. Captain Forbes, the Factor for the Commissioners of the Forfeited Estates at New Tarbat reported in 1755 that the roads there were very good. V. Wills, *Reports on the Annexed Estates*, Edinburgh, 1973, p. 38.

53. The bridge over the Averon at Alness is mentioned in a charter of 1439: Acts of the Lords of the Isles, Scottish History Society, Edinburgh, 1987, no. 29 and p. 85; Dingwall Presbytery, pp. ix, 161.

54. Macgill, *Ross-shire*, vol. 1, no. 490; contract for the repair of the stone bridge at Balnagown, dated 1699.

55. Whyte, *Agriculture*, pp. 103, 177.

56. For eighteenth century nurseries see Mackenzie, *Agriculture*, p. 107; *The Fowlis Case*, Section V, p. 44; Macgill, *Ross-shire*, vol. 2, no. 1116.

57. Balnagown MSS, SRO GD 199, numbers 199, 208, 209, 238, 241, 248.

58. Wight, *Husbandry*, p. 239.

59. Macgill, *Ross-shire*, vol. 2, p. 1116.

60. *Ibid.*, vol. 1, no. 786.

61. Much of the following discussion of the Gordon family is based on notes compiled by the Manpower Services Commission Scheme in Invergordon, 1986-7.

62. J. M. Bulloch, *The family of Gordon of Invergordon, Newhall, also Ardoch, Ross-shire, and Carroll, Sutherland*, Dingwall, 1906, p. 14.

63. Mowat, *Easter Ross*, p. 9.

64. SRO RHP 37985.

65. See Dundas MSS, SRO GD 238/8/1 no. 25; a letter from Anne Gordon Dundas to her brother: '. . . for God sake let not that infatuation so fatal to your father Prevail with you. Let no Chimeral Schemes nor hopes divert you from settling your private affairs'. (1743).

66. Dundas MSS, SRO GD 235/8/2, no. 2.

67. Session Papers, vol. 148, no. 14.

68. Sir John Gordon of Invergordon, *Correspondence on the occasion of the rebellion, Autumn, 1745, containing some particulars of those times*, Edinburgh, 1835, p. 8.

69. F. Maclennan, *Ferindonald Papers*, p. 52.

70. Miller, *Scenes and Legends*, p. 320 claims the ships were burnt; the log of the 'Shark' says the boats were seized or made unseaworthy (see Chapter Seven).

71. Cromartie, *History*, pp. 224-5.

72. Dundas MSS, SRO GD 235/9/4 no. 13.

73. Bulloch, *The Gordons*, pp. 23-4.

74. Dundas MSS, SRO GD 235/9/4 no. 27.

75. Dundas MSS, SRO GD 235/8/13 nos. 21, 11.

76. NLS, MS 106. 'Pocket Book of Sir John Gordon of Invergordon, begun 1753'.

77. *Ibid.*, p. 42. A letter from Henry Dundas to Sir John in 1773 shows that he was still hoping to build a pier: SRO GD 235/8/6 p. 37.

78. NLS, MS 106 p. 39.

79. Mowat, *Easter Ross*, p. 68.

80. NLS, MS 106, pp. 90, 345.

81. Cromartie MSS, SRO GD 305/1/154 no. 140, 305/1/159 nos. 33-4, 37-8, 40, 75; Dundas MSS, SRO GD 235/8/2 nos. 19, 20.

82. NLS, MS 106, p. 310. The Commissioners for the Annexed Estates also took over Cromartie's lands at Strathpeffer.

83. For example, *Ibid.*, p. 479.

84. Meldrum, *Logie Easter*, p. 95.

85. Wills, *Annexed Estates*, p. 38.

86. *A Selection of Scottish Forfeited Estates Papers*, ed. A. H. Millar, Edinburgh, 1909, p. 78.

87. A. Smith, *Jacobite Estates of the '45*, Edinburgh, 1982, pp. 113-14. The abandonment of Tarbat House was seen locally as the fulfilment of a prophecy made by the Rev John Porteous of Kilmuir Easter that if Cromartie joined the rebellion the house would become roofless and abandoned to the nettles.

88. *Ibid.*, p. 209.

89. Mowat, 'Moray Firth Province', *Firthlands*, p. 73.

90. Mowat, *Easter Ross*, p. 50.

91. *OSA*, vol. 6, p. 189.

92. Wills, *Annexed Estates*, SRO, E 721/18.

93. The planting of Henrietta Wood and the subsequent building of the farm square and Gordon's Mills are documented in a series of estate plans at Newhall House: 'Plan of the Mains of Newhall' (1788 and 1799). I am grateful to Mr John Shaw of Tordarroch for allowing me to see these plans.

94. The west facing wall of Novar House still bears a date stone of 1634. I am grateful to Mr and Mrs Arthur Munro Ferguson for showing me Novar House and especially the two estate maps of 1777 and 1788 at Novar House upon which much of the following discussion is based. (Copies of the plans are deposited in Register House, Edinburgh: RHP 10671, 42696.) Mackenzie, *Agriculture*, p. 69.

95. *Ibid.*, p. 109.

96. R. Southey, *Journal of a Tour in Scotland in 1819*, London, 1929, p. 120.

97. Wallace Brown, 'Alness', *TISSFC*, pp. 24–5.

98. Mackenzie, *Agriculture*, p. 109.

99. A. M. Cain, *The Corn Chest of Scotland: Scots in India*, Edinburgh, 1986, p. 19.

100. SRO GD 235/8/11 no. 10; See Cromartie, *History*, pp. 255–6 and MacLennan, *Ferindonald*. Lord MacLeod in fact served (unhappily) under Munro of Novar in India. His estates were restored in 1784, by which time they also included Invergordon. His uncle, Sir John Gordon, had died childless in 1783 and had made MacLeod his heir. He did not hold the Invergordon estate long, however, before he sold it to the Macleods of Cadboll, who had owned it in the seventeenth century and who remained Lairds of Invergordon until after the first world war. Lord MacLeod removed the ruins of New Tarbat and began the construction of New Tarbat House, but died in 1789 before it was completed.

101. J. Sinclair, *General View of the Agriculture of the Northern Counties and Islands of Scotland*, London, 1795, p. 72.

102. E. Richards, *A History of the Highland Clearances*, London, 1982 and 1985, Vol. 1, p. 186.

103. Miller, op. cit., pp. 477–9.

104. K. Logue, *Popular Disturbances in Scotland*, Edinburgh, 1979, p. 61 (quoting from a Justice Court indictment against one of the rioters).

105. *OSA*, vol. XIX, p. 236. Amongst the obscurities about 'The Year of the Sheep' perhaps the most fundamental is exactly which laird was responsible for the introduction of the Camerons. Part of the problem lies in the fact that there are two Culcairns — one in the parish of Kiltearn, the other in Rosskeen. These places are often also confused with Culrain (since the estates were at various points held by the same family of Munros). Eric Richards assigns the estate of Culcairn to Munro of Novar (*Clearances*, Vol. 1, p. 255), Kenneth Logue to Munro of Culcairn (*Disturbances*, pp. 58–9). Although Munro of Novar later owned Culcairn, he was not the possessor at the time of the Year of the Sheep. I am grateful to R. W. Munro for helping to trace the ownership of Culcairn during this period.

106. Richards, *Clearances*, Vol. 1, p. 256; Logue, *Disturbances*, p. 60.

5

'No longer an independent peasantry'

In the immediate aftermath of 'The Year of the Sheep' it seemed as if everyone held his breath as both sides tried to assimilate what had happened and to wonder what kind of future would result from the events in Strathrusdale.[1] This short hiatus was an understandable human reaction but it solved nothing. The Cromarty Firth region was locked onto a course that, over the next century or so, would see the creation of the essentials of modern life in the area. Gaelic was replaced by English as the dominant language of the region. A modern communications network was established, centred on road and, later, rail so that the total dominance of sea transport ended, although there was a kind of compensation in the increased use of the Firth by the Royal Navy, culminating in the establishment of a dockyard port in the Cromarty Firth in 1913. Internal and external migration continued, rising to periodic peaks in times of extreme social and economic dislocation, such as the 1840s, after which decade the population of the region began to fail.

The visible signs of this century of change are the towns and roads, fields, farms and harbours of the present day. Although set against a background of Highland hills and the sea, the Cromarty Firth region presents essentially a Lowland landscape for it was during the nineteenth century that the position of this most favoured portion of Easter Ross as the northernmost outlier of Lowland 'high farming' was established.

If 'The Year of the Sheep' was a practical failure, it nevertheless had important consequences. For half a century memories of this conflict informed the regular outbursts of social protest and violence that marked the modern transformation of the region:

> The Highland fringe of Easter Ross was the scene of more popular disorder — riots against clearances, against the induction of unacceptable ministers, and against food exports — than any other part of the north in the following half century.[2]

In 1792, however, this could not have been foreseen. Instead, the protesters regarded the future with a kind of vague dread while the landlords saw the revolt as a negation of their belief in progress and change as the keys to human improvement and happiness.

Some landlords did try to strike a human balance; certainly all the tenants involved in the creation of the Campbell brothers' sheep farm were resettled 'on other farms.'[3] But such landlord benevolence towards their dependents had nothing to do with 'the rights of the people' then being trumpeted in the streets of Paris — and Cromarty. The great advocate of improvement, Sir John Sinclair, never questioned the idea that the people should remain on the land — but on his terms, not theirs. Thus, he could describe the mealers who undertook the slow and painstaking work of bringing their marginal lands into cultivation as the 'great enemies of enclosure' and 'the *aborigines* of improvement in this country' but with no suggestion that they should be dispossessed because of what he saw as their backwardness.[4]

There were still local landowners who believed it was possible to reconcile improvement with an active concern for their tenants. One such was Captain Hugh Munro of Teaninich, who, after being blinded at the siege of Njemingen in 1794, returned to transform his estate (Fig. 29), a process that included the consolidation of farms and their letting on long leases, as well as the founding of Alness and the building of Teaninich Distillery in 1817. Much of the Captain's life (and that of his heirs) was spent in the straightening of the course of the River Alness to prevent its frequent and devastating flooding. The identification of the Munros of Teaninich with the community was reinforced when they became virtually the only influential local family to join the Free Church in 1843. In 1845, too, they gave room to victims of the Glencalvie clearances. There is also a tradition that Sir Alexander Munro of Novar, who succeeded his brother Sir Hector in 1805, warned his tenants to take out double leases (i.e. for thirty eight years) as a protection against his dilettante son and heir.[5] Sir Alexander was an old man who had returned to his Highland homeland late in life after a long career as Consul-General in Madrid, and it seems that he recognised that his feelings towards his tenants belonged to a different century and a different society than the one in which his son lived.

Already by the middle of the eighteenth century there had been other, harsher, voices speaking out against this conservative view of society. One such was the improver Sir George Steuart Mackenzie of Coul (1780–1848), whose *General View of the Agriculture of the Counties of Ross and Cromarty*, published in 1810, breathes a new spirit of ruthless determinism into the question of agricultural change.

> The humane feelings which were excited by the prospect of distressing an indolent and almost useless population, cannot be blamed [i.e. faulted] . . . [but] the true value of land is to be found, not in the number of ignorant and idle people who can continue to live upon it, but in the number of cattle and sheep and in the quantity of corn it can produce . . .[6]

According to Mackenzie, the Highlander had not the intelligence or (more crucially) the capital to improve the land and Gaelic was an enemy to improvement. The mealers on Sir George's estate had, he claimed, been more concerned with smuggling and poaching than with improving their holdings.

29. Teaninich House.

In the end he had evicted them. The Highlander was expendable. Cockburn Ross, the improving laird of Shandwick, agreed. According to him the future lay with 'south country tenants of skill and real capital . . .'[7]

This is exactly what happened around the Cromarty Firth in the late eighteenth and early nineteenth centuries. Some of these new 'south country tenants' came from Moray, but more were from the Lothians and England. Like the ambitious feudal settlers of the middle ages these new farmers were attracted by the unexploited potential of the region, the relatively cheap farming tenancies and the chance to make their fortune during the buoyant economic conditions produced by the war with France. The value of arable land rose by thirty per cent in the few years before 1809, mostly due to the arrival of new farmers from the 'opulent south.'[8]

Perhaps the best known of these southern farmers was George Middleton, from Tynedale in the north of England, who was invited by the laird of Cromarty to settle in the parish in the 1790s.[9] There was no wheat grown in the parish until Middleton began to grow it and he was the first to export it in commercial quantities. Forty years later it had become the staple product. He built the first threshing mill seen in the parish and also established a slaughter house in the burgh to revive the flagging export trade in pork. Middleton was the progenitor of an influential dynasty who set the pace of farming in nineteenth century Easter Ross. In 1844 George Middleton of Fearn was amongst the first to import guano as a fertiliser although he and his partner kept quiet about it until success was assured because they feared ridicule. Another descendant, Jonathan Middleton of Clay of Allan, pioneered steam cultivation in the late 1860s.

Such south country farmers were major agents for the introduction of new ideas and techniques. They were also a highly visible, and unpopular, symbol of the changes feared by the great mass of the local population. Sir George Mackenzie, however, was prey to no such doubts; the manifest changes around the Cromarty Firth were all the justification that was needed for his beliefs. Yet it is doubtful if the agricultural 'take-off' of the region would have been quite so spectacular and successful if it had not been for one major, yet unforeseen, event. In 1793 France declared war on Britain and, with the exception of the year's peace following the Treaty of Amiens in 1802, there would be war with France until 1815. The changes which took place around the Cromarty Firth during the first quarter of the nineteenth century were both accelerated and distorted by the demands and stresses of a war economy. By the time peace returned in 1815 the pattern of the future was set.

War meant that foreign imports were drastically cut, leading to an increased demand for domestically produced food and raw materials and a dramatic rise in prices for both.[10] This in turn forced up land prices and rents, which provided the bulk of the money to pay for the capital investment required for the new farms. Agricultural labourers, dependent on a daily or weekly wage, were even more at the mercy of the fluctuation of the market and the growing season. During the bad year of 1802 many were forced to eat seed potatoes and emigration fever reached new heights. During the buoyant year of 1812, on the other hand, when more land was being taken in to provide for the growing demand for wheat and with extensive drainage works being undertaken in Strathpeffer, farm workers could demand and get high wages. Nevertheless, the final result of the war period and its immediate aftermath around the Cromarty Firth was to make the lot of the bulk of the population even more precarious.

For the lairds and substantial farmers, however, the period was one of rapid and sustained expansion, despite disastrous growing seasons in 1802 and 1806-7. Vast amounts of new and, in many cases, marginal land were brought into cultivation. New techniques and tools were introduced, such as the lightweight iron swing ploughs which could be operated by only one man and a team of horses. These tools were now mass produced in southern factories, such as the Carron Iron Works, or copied by local blacksmiths and agricultural manufacturers. New crops were grown, particularly wheat for export and turnips for wintering stock, and experiments were carried out with selective breeding and new methods of stock rearing. Soon local beasts were not only finding their way south to London and Edinburgh but further afield; in 1813 Balnagown cattle were sold to Hudson's Bay.[11]

Such developments were encouraged by such bodies as the Highland and

Agricultural Society of Scotland, which offered prizes and premiums for essays on agricultural improvements and new techniques, to be published in the Society's *Transactions*. The work of this national body was supplemented on a local level by the foundation of the Ross-shire Farmers' Society in 1794, with committees in Tain, Dingwall and Fortrose. It was superseded in 1811 by the Easter Ross Farmers' Club, mainly composed of substantial tenant farmers, with a sprinkling of landlords.[12] In 1812 the Easter and Wester Ross Farmers' Clubs held their first ploughing match followed in the next year by their first agricultural show at Alness.[13] In 1835 the Black Isle Farmers' Club was founded.[14] Through their meetings and shows these clubs encouraged the exchange of ideas and experiments with new agricultural techniques, and were especially important in encouraging the breeding of new, improved stock. By 1813, for example, the Easter Ross Farmers' Club was offering prizes for stallions.

In the early 1800s the rate of agricultural development begun by the eighteenth century improvers began to accelerate. By the end of the nineteenth century the last vestiges of run-rig would have disappeared and been replaced by the regular and enclosed agricultural landscape of much of the present day Cromarty Firth region. The key to this change was land drainage and field consolidation. It was an undertaking on a truly heroic scale. Besides drainage, in some cases new land was literally created. For example, some of the lands of Pitglassie were claimed from the tidal reaches of the upper Cromarty Firth in the 1770s. Here Davidson of Tulloch created fields first by surrounding the land with a turf dyke, then draining and enriching the soil using shell marl brought as ballast from the west coast on a returning meal ship.[15]

But the part of the country most affected by drainage and reclamation was the huge, prairie-like expanse of land north of the Bay of Nigg. In the summer of 1760 Bishop Richard Pococke of Ossory in Ireland, an inveterate traveller, crossed the plain in the course of his journey from Tain to Cromarty. He dismissed the future 'Garden of Ross' as a 'vale which is a Morass, and high spring tydes do sometimes come into it.' Nevertheless, he could see some potential for development for he thought that the local shale beds would provide a 'most admirable Manure for Corn.'[16] Another visitor, Andrew Wight, sent north in the early 1780s by the Commissioners of the Forfeited Estates to report on agriculture, suggested that the plain should be traversed by a transport canal, with lateral cuts for drainage, five hundred years after the first drainage channel had been dug by the canons of Fearn Abbey.[17]

Cargo-carrying ships never appeared on the plain of Nigg, but drainage work on a massive scale was begun by the Lanarkshire landowner, John Cockburn Ross, who succeeded to the estate of Shandwick in 1790.[18] He found the land unenclosed and badly farmed by tenants who were mostly in arrears of rent. In 1792 he sent north three Lowland farmers with horses and equipment to begin work but eventually realised that he would have to supervise personally his intended improvements. Soon after his arrival in 1799 Cockburn Ross began building the castellated dwelling house of Shandwick (succeeded in the present century by Shandwick House) which became the centre for the improvements he effected on his farms at Cullisse, Rarichie, Balaphueil, Old Shandwick and Ankerville.

Ankerville had been bought in 1721 by 'Polander' Ross, the former soldier of the King of Poland, who had risen in the royal service more by his capacity for drink (which exceeded his Majesty's) than for his military abilities. He returned to Scotland and bought the estate, 'built and lived too greatly for it . . . and died much reduced in his finances' in the mid eighteenth century.[19] 'Polander' Ross must have had a damp retirement, and even the drainage works of his improving successor, David Ross, Lord Ankerville, were not completely effective. Cockburn Ross found that Ankerville was still subject to sea flooding during spring tides. He built an embankment with internal ditches to drain the land and two sluice gates. The farms of Cullisse and Rarichie were also subject to flooding by runoff from higher ground. He drained these lands by making a canal seven feet deep and three miles long to Nigg Sands.

The improvements by Cockburn Ross did not stop there for new farm offices were built and plantations were undertaken at Shandwick and on the Hill of Nigg. These new farms were then let on nineteen year leases for three times their previous rents to south country farmers. By the 1840s the farms of Wester Rarichie and Cullisse were farmed by one man where once there had been seventeen farmers.[20]

At the same time, immediately to the north of Shandwick, Hugh Rose was busy on the land he had bought out of the profits made supplying the British fleet in the West Indies.[21] His new estate was extensive, including Calrossie, Bayfield and Tarlogie, north west of Tain. Rose, too, was an active improver, draining the land, enclosing fields, as well as planting over forty miles of thorn hedges and several elegant avenues of beech trees. Soon after his marriage to the beautiful Miss Phipps in 1799 he began to build a house on a farm appropriately called 'The Bog' which Rose renamed 'Arabella' after his bride.[22]

Indeed, the period of agricultural improvement, and especially the three decades after 1792, saw the largest creation of new place names in the region since, perhaps, the arrival of the Vikings a thousand years before. Some new names clearly reflect the times, such as the farms of 'Waterloo' near Dingwall and 'St Vincent' near Tain, for example. Other new names, like their Viking, Gaelic and Pictish precursors, described physical appearance or agricultural use: Crosshills, Broomhill (Kilmuir Easter), and Bayfield (Nigg). Some new names, such as Poyntzfield, were self-conscious statements of a new order replacing the old. Ardoch was renamed Poyntzfield by George Gun Munro (d. 1785) in honour of his wife Charlotte (or Mary) Poyntz, the daughter of the Rt. Hon. Stephen Poyntz. Although there seems to be some vagueness about

30. New Tarbat House.

the lady's name, there does not seem to be much doubt that she brought the money to the marriage that allowed the process of improvement on this Black Isle estate to begin.[23]

In addition to new and improved farms, names had sometimes to be invented for the new towns and planned villages that were springing up around the shores on the Firth in the early decades of the nineteenth century. These settlements were built by local proprietors as homes not only for people displaced from the land but as centres for business and communications. Several of the seventeenth century burghs of barony were reorganised during this period. Milton had been replanned in 1786 by James MacLaren in connection with the building programme of New Tarbat House (Fig. 30) by Lord MacLeod and Culbokie was reorganised and expanded before 1833.[24] But the real prototypes for these new nineteenth century towns were Cromarty and Invergordon.

Cromarty, although an ancient town with an ancient plan, had what was, in effect, a new town grafted on to it by George Ross. The harbour, brewery (Fig. 31) and ropeworks buildings survive to the present day as symbols of this new kind of urban environment: an ordered landscape for life and work.

Invergordon's development was a good deal less ordered although Sir John Gordon had commissioned plans from one of the Adam brothers for buildings in his new village. In fact, little appears to have been done in a systematic way until the MacLeods of Cadboll took over the estate in the late 1780s. Invergordon enjoyed a small boom during the Napoleonic period; a hemp factory was established there and a number of shopkeepers and tradesmen set up businesses. Despite the lack of a pier, the town became an important shipping centre for local produce.

31. The brewery at Cromarty.

In 1813 the MacLeods of Cadboll hired a local land surveyor to survey their estates. His work included surveying and planning every new farm, as well as laying out the town of 'Ness of Invergordon' and Saltburn.[25] Ninety-eight feus were laid out at Invergordon, probably all lining 'The Street', which became the modern High Street.[26] The modern pattern of cross streets intersecting 'The Street' probably followed a few years later as part of the arrangements necessary for the building of Thomas Telford's new ferry pier in 1818 and MacLeod of Cadboll's construction of the first harbour pier in 1828.[27]

The consolidation of Cadboll's farms inevitably meant that people had to be removed and resettled. At 'Ault-na-Tallen' a new town was created. Thirty feus along the shore were created, with room for further expansion, possibly for people displaced from the newly laid out farm of Ord or from other new farms in mid-Ross.[28] The community's new status is reflected in the abandonment of its Gaelic name for its English equivalent — Saltburn.[29]

Despite the growth of Invergordon, however, Cromarty still dominated the commercial and social life of the region in the 1820s (Fig. 32). It had long been the customs port for the Firth and was the centre for seaborne communications. Ships of between 400 and 500 tons could lie safely in the harbour, and the town boasted two shipowners and a shipbuilder.[30] By the 1820s the herring fishing was enjoying a boom; amongst the occupations listed in *Pigot's*

32. Cromarty by William Daniell, 1821.

Directory (1825–6) for the town were eighteen fishcurers. Other businesses catered to the general needs of Cromarty's population, including bakers, shoemakers, grocers, tailors, drapers, a hardware dealer and even a watch repairer. In addition the town had a surgeon, a druggist, a housepainter, a cabinet maker and eight haberdashers. Cromarty also served as a commercial centre for its Black Isle hinterland, and boasted a small genteel society, predominantly made up of dowagers and maiden ladies from important local families and retired army and navy officers.

Invergordon during the same period was a more workaday place, just beginning to grow 'from a few scattered houses to a respectable village.'[31] By 1825–6 the town boasted two hemp manufactories, eight grocers, a linen draper, baker, flesher, two blacksmiths, two house carpenters and a nail maker. There were regular coach services to Inverness and Wick and boats to Cromarty 'occasionally'.

West of Invergordon two other planned villages had been founded shortly after 1800. Evanton was laid out to supersede the ancient fermtoun of Drummond by Alexander Fraser of Balcony who, like other new lairds in the region, had made his fortune through government supply contracts in the West Indies.[32] There had been a small settlement to the west of the bridge over the Averon from at least the 1770s[33] but it was Captain Munro of Teaninich who was responsible for the feuing of Alness, a burgh of barony since 1690, on ninety nine year leases in the early 1800s. By the 1830s Alness was sufficiently big to warrant the appointment of a village constable. There were three annual fairs and a monthly cattle market between April and November to supply the Falkirk Tryst. There were also a number of thriving local businesses including bakers, a blacksmith, a tea dealer, a timber merchant, a nail maker, a tin-plate worker, and a customs officer for the distillery.[34]

These planned settlements were commercial centres, linked to their hinterland by sea and, increasingly, by roads. In the last three decades of the eighteenth century hundreds of miles of roads were built in Easter Ross by the Commissioners of Supply for the county, although there were no metalled roads before 1807.[35] Such expansion, however, placed increasing strains on the statute labour system so that by 1794 Sheriff Depute MacLeod of Geanies suggested its abolition and replacement by a money assessment on landowners and major tenants. Although there was general acceptance of the idea, little was done until adequate financial arrangements were made in the first decade of the nineteenth century.[36]

Compared with other parts of the Highlands, the Cromarty Firth region benefitted only slightly by the passage of the Act for Highland Roads and Bridges (1803), although Thomas Telford was later to build the piers at Invergordon Ferry and Balintraid. Instead, in 1805 a separate Parliamentary Act was passed allowing for a new system of assessment for roadbuilding in the county. This Act, however, was ineffective and was superseded two years later by a further Act that, at last, ended the statute labour system. Soon work began on a turnpike road between Beauly and Dornoch, with toll gates every six miles. This was an ambitious and expensive undertaking since a large number of bridges had to be built, including the stone bridge across the Conon near Dingwall begun in 1807.[37]

There was a similar development in the Black Isle too. From at least the 1760s there had been plans for a statute labour road along the north shore, but it was only in the early nineteenth century that the new 'County Road' was laid out between Dingwall and Cromarty. The line of this road survives virtually intact as the modern B9163, just as until recently the route of the early nineteenth-century 'Parliamentary Road' between Dingwall and Tain formed part of the A9 until the construction of bypasses around Evanton and Alness. Between Dingwall and Evanton the mid-eighteenth-century road followed the course of the modern secondary road between Tulloch, Foulis and Drummond. Originally this road passed uncomfortably close to the northern main entrance of Foulis Castle. In 1790–1 the route was moved to its modern alignment, following a wide loop south of the castle, so that 'travellers will not only pass through the middle of rich fields, and fine plantations of trees, but will also have a fine view of that ancient and elegant mansion'.[38] Further to the east the 'Scotsburn Road' follows the line of the earlier turnpike road.

Roads were vital in the economic and social transformation of the region.

Not only did they allow the movement of crops to shipping points, they also facilitated the growth of local markets. In 1806, for example, a monthly corn market was established in Dingwall; before this time corn agents had had to travel about local farms to buy crops.[39] By the first decade of the nineteenth century, too, regular sheep and cattle markets were being held at Beauly and Fort William[40] and in 1820 the first cattle market was held at Bridgend of Alness. With the older established market at Kildary it was to become an important and regular feature of the local cattle trade in the nineteenth century.[41]

Roads also helped to link the region with the outside world. In 1808 the first carrier between Dingwall and Tain began to operate and in June the following year the first public stagecoach, a four in hand, began to run between Inverness, Beauly, Dingwall and Tain.[42] Soon a regular mail service was established and the price of postage plummeted. Within a decade a coach service was running from Inverness to Wick and Thurso.[43] For the first time Britain was linked by public transport from one end to the other.[44]

The development of roads and coach travel was, of course, paralleled by the development of sea transport. By 1804 there were regular sailings every three weeks by smack between Inverness, Cromarty and London.[45] After 1811 ships sailed every ten days although the voyage could vary in length from between three and fourteen days depending on winds.

There is no doubt that the Cromarty Firth boomed during the Napoleonic Wars. The need to provide military uniforms led to a dramatic rise in wool prices although a number of local sheepfarmers were ruined by the hard winter of 1807–8; it was from this time that the trend began towards the wintering of sheep in lower pastures.

With the defeat of Napoleon in 1814 the Ross-shire reporter to the *Farmers' Magazine* wrote, 'We must no longer look for war prices' and by the end of the year he reported that, although there had been a good season, cattle prices had fallen sharply and this had led to a number of farming failures.[46] For over a generation agriculture had been fuelled by war; now it would be starved by peace. Britain was reopened to cheap foreign imports and overextended local agriculture could not compete. Around the Cromarty Firth all work of draining, liming and reclamation came to an end. Land reverted to disuse. Prices plummeted. Rents on grass pastures fell between twenty and thirty per cent in a single year. Many tenants faced disaster. Some landlords chartered ships to bring in food for their tenants and reduced rents. MacLeod of Cadboll, for example, reduced his tenants' rents by up to thirty per cent. Nevertheless, the farming failures continued. The corn agents who had swarmed over the region during the war stayed away and local farmers had difficulty in finding markets for their grain. Local distilleries, and some in Ireland, took up the slack trade in barley and some farmers began to make their own arrangements with factors in Leith and elsewhere in the south to ship their grain and livestock, creating a trade pattern that would remain throughout the century and be a major factor in the growth of Invergordon harbour.

Roads and harbours may have been the symbols of the region's newly found war prosperity; now they became avenues of escape for the people. Cromarty was one of the main ports of embarkation, not only for local migrants, but for the growing flood of dispossessed from throughout the Highlands. Many of these people were victims of evictions in Sutherland but by 1820 clearances were taking place much closer to home. In that year on the Novar estate of Culrain (in Kincardine parish) six hundred people were served with writs of eviction.[47] Unlike the contemporary Sutherland Clearances, no provision was made for giving them new homes or employment. *The Scotsman* reported the people's reactions in some detail:

> On notice being given to these poor creatures to remove, they remonstrated, and stated unequivocally, that as they neither had money to transport them to America, nor the prospect of another situation to retire to, they neither could nor would remove, and that if force was to be used, *they would rather die on the spot that gave them birth than elsewhere.*[48]

In the first week of March 1820 twenty-five members of the Ross-shire Militia and forty constables marched to Culrain to enforce the evictions. Instead, they were attacked by a mob of between three and four hundred, led (as so often in these cases) by women. Shots were fired and some of the women were injured, as was the Sheriff. The Culrain riots helped to bring the problems of the Highland evictions to a wider public but solved little for the people involved. The land continued to be cleared and the people dispersed. Some were given refuge by local landowners, others found work on local farms, but many were forced to emigrate, either to the growing industrial cities of the south or abroad.

By the time of the Culrain evictions the brief boom of 1819 was over. It had been fuelled by a good growing season and the revival of the herring fishing, which had made it difficult for farmers in seaboard parishes to get enough labourers to bring in their abundant harvest. This brief revival, however, did nothing to solve the underlying problems of post-war agriculture. Perhaps the major distortion of the war had been the spectacular and overwhelming rise in the amount of wheat grown. By 1821 it was clear that overproduction was forcing wheat prices down. The following year the *Farmers' Magazine* reported that the 'state of the Tenantry in this quarter [is] worse and worse' and claimed that the only solution was a reduction of rent.[49]

The reporter also commented darkly on the growing tendency of landlords to be absentee, seeing this as a contributory factor in local distress. Perhaps he was thinking of Novar and, certainly, this trend was to become more and more marked throughout the century. There were, however, some exceptions. One such was Sir George Gun Munro the laird of Poyntzfield. As the depression headed towards its nadir in 1825–6, he set about building a new estate village, Jemimaville, named in honour of his new wife, Jemima Graham of the family of Graham of Drynie.[50] Munro may have been inspired by the changes that were taking place in Invergordon at about this time and hoped that Jemimaville could become the commercial and social centre of his estate. A regular market was established there and continued into the early years of the twentieth century. In 1841, for example, a ship of 80 tons was launched from a shipyard in the village, built from wood grown on the Poyntzfield estate.[51]

Despite such optimistic developments as Jemimaville, however, the 1820s remained a time of uncertainty and discontent. One way in which this new mood was expressed was in the growing tide of agitation for political reform, especially of the electoral system.

The vote was confined to those who held land directly of the crown to the value of £400 Scots (£33 sterling).[52] Throughout the eighteenth century, as estates were consolidated, the number of voters decreased so that on the eve of the Reform Bill in 1832 the total electorate around the Cromarty Firth could be counted in scores. Votes were controlled by local magnates, such as the earls of Cromartie or Munro of Foulis. In 1710, for example, Robert Munro younger of Foulis was elected Member of Parliament for the Northern Burghs, and he set about building up a power base at the expense of Cromartie. Control of burgh council membership ensured control in parliamentary elections, so this particular political struggle centred on Dingwall, a small and impoverished burgh, where the patronage and bribery connected with local and parliamentary elections provided a badly needed supplement to town finances.[53] Thus, from 1710 onwards Munro and his brother, Munro of Culcairn, alternated as provosts of the burgh. When, in the burgh election of 1721, a precursor to the parliamentary election of 1722, the Mackenzies attempted to regain their lost power the brothers mounted a military expedition to the town, arrested three councillors, and ensured that Munro of Culcairn was again elected provost. This raid led to Foulis being tried and fined but he was not disbarred from being Member of Parliament for the Northern Burghs. In the parliamentary election of 1740, the Munros again marched in force to the town, arrested ten members of the town council and carried them off to Tain. After riots in which the wife of one of the arrested men was killed and several women and children were injured, the Munros succeeded in gaining the election.

The forfeiture of Cromartie and the death of Munro at the Battle of Falkirk in 1746 ended this particular rivalry. Votes were gained, lost, and controlled by the exercise and practise of 'interest.' Sir John Gordon's notebooks are full of notes of the favours he owed to various local families in return for support in parliamentary elections.

Causes célèbres such as the Cromarty case led to demands to reform the system but change was postponed by the war with France. As Hugh Miller recalled, the Jacobin spirit of Cromarty died with the coming of war: 'Whigs forgot everything but that they were Britons . . . till at length the Battle of Waterloo, by terminating the war, reduced them to the necessity of seeking, as before, their enemies at home.'[54]

Nevertheless, reform of the electoral system did not come quickly or easily.[55] As late as 1826 the Edinburgh writer and publisher Robert Chambers reported that the houses of Cromarty had recently been whitewashed by one of the candidates in the parliamentary election and remarked ironically: 'Cromarty came cleaner out of the election business . . . than perhaps any other town in his Majesty's dominions.'

In the 1831 election there was a three-cornered fight in the county of Ross between candidates all in favour of reform, although Cromarty itself was won by the anti-Reform candidate, Davidson of Tulloch, who defeated MacLeod of Cadboll by eight votes to seven. After the votes were counted the pro-reform *Inverness Courier* commented: 'But for the unlucky absence of one of Mr MacLeod of Cadboll's voters, which threw the county of Cromarty into the hands of an anti-Reformer, we should have been able to boast that every county north of the Highland Border was consecrated to Reform.'[56]

The 1832 Reform Act gave the vote to owners of property valued at £10 or more, as well as to tenants of £10 properties holding leases for life (or at least fifty-seven years), or £50 properties on leases of at least nineteen years. The Scottish electorate was increased from just over 7,000 to 65,000. New constituencies were created including a new combined single constituency of Ross and Cromarty. Around the Cromarty Firth the bulk of the new electors were landowners, substantial tenant farmers and members of the professions, such as ministers and lawyers, although the new voters' roll also contained merchants, grocers, bankers, schoolmasters, gardeners, blacksmiths, house carpenters, carriers, shoemakers, as well as the shoremaster at Invergordon and a salmon fisher from Alness.[57]

Many Scots saw the widening of the franchise as a kind of political millennium, and there was the inevitable sense of anticlimax when it was found that the Act fell far short of expectation. Because the ballot was still not secret, tenants remained subject to the political control of their landlords. As Hugh Miller remarked; 'The Reform Bill . . . had the effect of considerably modifying the tone of their politics. They began to discover — will it be believed? — that all men are not born equal, and that there exists an aristocracy in the very economy of nature.'[58]

Even as the Reform Act was passing through Parliament, the people of the Cromarty Firth had a much more immediate problem to cope with: in the summer of 1832 the Firth was made an official cholera quarantine station.[59]

The disease had spread through Russia from India, and arrived in the north east of Scotland on ships arriving from the Baltic ports, as Hugh Miller recalled:

> Day after day vessels from the Baltic came sailing up the bay, and the fears of the
> people . . . began to wear out. The first terror, however, had been communicated
> to the nearer parishes, and from them to the more remote . . . The whole country
> talked of nothing but Cholera and the Quarantine port.

It was not the first time that the Firth had been used for quarantine and, as
before, fear bred rumour and rumour bred fear. Cromarty fishermen were
unable to sell their catches because, it was said, the bodies of cholera victims
from the quarantine ships were thrown overboard and poisoned the fish, and
in Nigg the tale is still told of Thomas Vass who saw the disease floating in a
yellow cloud above the ground and was able to capture it in a sack and bury it
under the 'cholera stone' in the churchyard.[60]

In fact, the disease arrived on the mainland around the Firth not as a yellow
cloud or from the quarantine ships but from the crews of a government
revenue cutter and fishing ships from the south.[61] Hugh Miller, an eye-witness
to the epidemic, reported on the consequences of the disease in the seaboard
villages of Easter Ross in August 1832. In Portmahomack one fifth of the
population died; in Inver there were fifty-three deaths in a population of
about one hundred. Cromarty cut itself off from the outside world; in late
September a group of Inverness gentlemen were 'seized and smoked
[fumigated]' before they were allowed to enter the town.[62] In Nigg a Board of
Health had been set up six months before the disease arrived.[63] Inspectors
were sent round to report on the cleanliness of the parish; the inhabitants
were encouraged to remove their dunghills from near their homes and the
heritors were solicited for funds to buy blankets, medicines and lime to
whitewash houses. In March the Health Board decided that the storehouse by
the ferry would act as the hospital, since it was convenient for visits by the
doctor from Cromarty. A quarantine station for people coming into the parish
without clean bills of health was also set up and provision made for the burial
of victims of the disease.

Because of its early and well-planned response to the cholera epidemic,
Nigg escaped lightly compared with its neighbours. By September the worst
was over and the last victim was recovering. Watchmen were appointed early
in October to prevent people from coming over from Cromarty where the
disease did not disappear until early November.

By the end of the year life returned to normal; but, in fact, the 1830s and
40s were to turn out to be anything but normal. Many of the ministers of
parishes around the Firth who contributed articles to the *New Statistical
Account* in the late 1830s were openly critical of the social changes they saw
going on about them. The minister of Nigg, for example, remarked on the
consequences of the large farm system that had been introduced about forty
years previously:

> Many families were driven from their homes, a few strangers were introduced in
> their room, and poverty succeeded in the train of almost all the actors and

sufferers on the scene. The writer [believes] that those proprietors who expel the inhabitants from their properties are depriving themselves of some of the highest enjoyments in life — the luxury of doing good . . .[64]

In Rosskeen, the Rev. David Carment also commented on these changes in characteristically prophetic vein:

> In many respects, this parish had been improved within the last forty years, but the population of the country by large farms is a serious evil, and is likely to bring along with it consequences which the landed interest seem not to have contemplated. There is no longer an independent peasantry. The morals of the people are deteriorated by the loss of independence, and their spirits embittered by what they deem oppression. The ties which united master and servant are severed; and when the time comes, to which we look forward with fearful anticipation, it will, we fear, be found, that an error has been committed, by grasping too much, at the risk of sooner or later, losing all.[65]

The 1830s were a period of continued economic slump and there was serious crop failure in 1836–7, only mitigated by the swift and efficient relief organised mainly by local landlords. The rural population began to fall. Many landlords were now absentees and as early as the 1820s local estates began to be bought by southern speculators,[66] interested more in sport than in agriculture. Deer forests began to be created in the 1820s[67] and by midcentury there were extensive deer forests at Balnagown, Ben Wyvis, Kildermorie and Ardross.[68] The creation of regular land and sea communication during the early nineteenth century laid the basis of the Highland tourist industry. Invergordon enjoyed a small boom, with visitors arriving there by sea en route to sporting estates or the new spa at Strathpeffer. Was Sir John Gordon's dream of the town as a centre for sea bathing to become a reality?[69]

Some local people found work in the growing towns but most employment continued to be on farms. In 1831, for example, the farm of Arabella, already one of the largest and most advanced in the region, employed on a regular basis ten ploughmen, two cattlemen and a boy (who looked after both cattle and the young farm horses), two carpenters, four male and ten female labourers.[70] By the early 1840s the average number of servants per farm on Easter Ross was four or five, with occasional seasonal labourers brought in for particular jobs. Women would be hired for hoeing and reaping, men for trenching, draining and fence building.[71] The trend was towards greater production done by fewer people preforming more specialised jobs.

In common with the rest of rural Scotland, Easter Ross witnessed during this period the emergence of a new rural sub-class, landless workers, dependent on wages for seasonal or daily work in the land (or piece work in such industries as the hemp manufactory in Cromarty) to eke out their lives. Illness, injury, old age or death in the family could lead to total destitution, although sometimes this was alleviated by poor relief administered by the established church in each parish. After the Disruption of 1843, however, this rather inadequate poor relief system broke down. A Parliamentary enquiry into the Scottish Poor Law was set up in the summer of 1843 and the answers they obtained from Easter Ross ministers and lairds, factors and schoolmasters paint a dispiriting picture.[72]

The Commissioners found that the bulk of the rural population was without even the minimal security enjoyed by crofters, who at least possessed land even if they often paid disproportionate rents for it. Although some had houses, many of which were not weather-tight, few possessed land on which to raise the potatoes which were the staple of their diet. They supplemented their scanty income derived from seasonal work by collecting dung (road-scrapings and kelp) and selling it to local farmers and by regulated begging; for example, Saturday was set aside as begging day in Dingwall.[73]

In some parishes benevolent landowners, such as Munro of Teaninich, Davidson of Tulloch and Hay-Mackenzie (Cromartie), supplemented the Poor Law funds with extensive private charity, providing medical help, fuel and clothing to the needy as well as regular pensions to former servants. Elsewhere it was a different story. Many heritors were non-resident and unhelpful. As David Carment of Rosskeen said: 'I know of a proprietor in the parish who draws £2,000 or £3,000 a year and contributes only £3 to the poor's fund.'[74]

Without exception the ministers who gave evidence to the Commissioners blamed the rise of this new, insecure and poverty-stricken proletariat on the new farms; as the minister of Kiltearn said: 'I believe that the principal cause of the poverty of the people is the enlargement of the farms.'[75]

The enquiry led to the creation of a new national system of poor relief but did little to solve the problems of the poor of Easter Ross. Farm consolidation continued and soon, too, there would be the unforeseen disaster of the potato blight. Emigration was the answer for many, although as David Carment had said in his evidence, this was always a final desperate expedient for Highlanders attached to their native soil. There was much seasonal migration, when workers went south to work on farms at seed and harvest time. This practice was especially popular with people from Sutherland and the Black Isle but many recognised this practice as a sad stopgap. In 1828 the *Inverness Courier* reported seeing one such group walking south behind a piper: 'The sound of the bagpipes seemed to give a tone of gaiety to the scene, but there was often more of sorrow than of merriment in the strain.'[76] By the 1820s, however, these Lowland agricultural jobs were increasingly filled by Irish labourers, a human tide that became an overwhelming flood after the Irish potato famine of the mid 1840s. For others, the move south was permanent as they sought work in the growing industrial centres of Scotland and England.

Throughout the 1830s and '40s a growing number of emigrant ships sailed each summer from Cromarty bound for Canada (Fig. 33), Australia, New Zealand and even South America. In 1831, for example, seven vessels carrying over 1,500 people left Cromarty for Canada, and the number would have

NOTICE TO PASSENGERS FOR QUEBEC.

THE FINE A. I. SHIP SALAMIS, Capt. Royal, is now at CROMARTY, and will po-it vely Sail on the 25th inst., direct or QUEBEC. Passengers must therefore be on board a few days previous.

The CLEOPATRA, Capt. Morris, may be expected at Cromarty about 25 h, and will Sail on the 1st June.

These Vessels are in place of the CORSAIR and CLIO, formerly adver:ised. but could not be got ready in sufficient time. Exper.enced Surgeons are engaged for both.

Agents, John Mowat, Jun., Cromarty; John Fraser, Dornoch; and William Gordon, Pittentrail, Rogart.

Leith, 13:h May, 1831.

The Brig ZEALOUS, Capt. Bell, is also fitting out, and will call at Cromarty if required.

33. Notice of passage for intending emigrants, 1831.

been even greater but that some held back because of rumours that the government was planning to introduce assisted emigration.[77] By the end of the decade emigration was a highly organised business, much of it in the hands of local agents such as Duncan MacLennan of Inverness. In 1840, for example, he sent a 'Notice to intending emigrants to the British settlements of North America' announcing the sailing on 20 April of the 'Osprey' from Cromarty by way of Scrabster Roads to Pictou and Quebec. The ship was 381 tons, copper bottomed and carried a surgeon.[78]

Emigration was spurred on after 1846 by the potato famine and the growing number of clearances. There had been trouble again at Culrain in 1840–1 when the local tacksman attempted to evict his tenants. Instead the law officers were deforced and the writs and tacksman's home burnt.[79] Throughout the 1830s and '40s there were continuous evictions from the Balfour estate of Strathconon to make way for sheep farms.[80] Many victims of these removals settled on the Mulbuie common where they took over small crofts, cleared them, and nursed their grievances. By the 1880s perhaps as many as three quarters of the crofters at the western end of the Mulbuie were Strathconon people. Mackenzie of Gairloch also took in people removed from Strathconon as did, apparently, Shaw-Mackenzie of Newhall. An estate map of 1849 at Newhall shows clusters of small crofts of between three and eleven acres lining the county road between the Bog of Cullicudden and Resolis, thus creating the settlement pattern of small croft houses that survives to this day along the county road between Cullicudden and Balblair. These Newhall crofts were rent-free for twenty-five years and 2/6 an acre thereafter, an arrangement followed with resettled tenants elsewhere as, for example, on the Cromartie estate.[81]

Some of the clearances around the Cromarty Firth, such as the removal of twelve families from the Hill of Nigg in 1841 to make room for trees, attracted little interest and have left scarcely any record or memory.[82] Other evictions further afield, however, attracted great publicity. One such was the clearance at Glencalvie, an estate belonging to the absentee Robertson of Kindeace. His factor, James Falconer Gillanders, who also acted for other local lairds, had been attempting to clear these lands for a sheep farm since 1842. Gillanders specialised in evictions.

The Glencalvie case began to attract attention in 1843 when Gustavus Aird, the new Free Church minister of Creich, took up the people's cause and reporters from *The Times* and *Scotsman* arrived on the scene.[83]

In the spring of 1845, Gillanders removed sixteen families from Newmore, shortly before the Glencalvie people were finally evicted. A few found refuge on the lands of Munro of Teaninich and others were said to have been settled at Shandwick, while a long-standing oral tradition in the parish of Nigg records a smack landing people evicted from Bonar Bridge and Ardgay on the sands at Nigg, who then sailed from Cromarty in a schooner bound for America.[84]

The Cromarty Firth region did not suffer as severely from clearances and the potato famine as other parts of the Highlands, yet it was here that the first and most violent reactions to sheep farms and clearance occurred. Culrain was a prototype for the Battle of the Braes and other incidents during the so-called 'Crofters' War' of 1882. All these conflicts began with immediate, and ill-organised, reaction to threats of eviction. Often officers of the law would be attacked and the writs of eviction destroyed. In the actual battle women and boys commonly played a leading part. Justification for resistance was usually expressed in biblical terms.

The final manifestation of this tradition of social protest around the Cromarty Firth itself was the series of meal riots that erupted along the north eastern Scottish coast between Aberdeen and the Pentland Firth in the first months of 1847. The Cromarty Firth was no stranger to meal riots. As early as 1740–1, during a time of famine, a local mob from Cromarty had raided a Greenock ship beached on Nigg sands which was being loaded with local grain.[85] Later, in 1796, a mob of about one hundred marched behind a piper and members of the local volunteer militia from Dingwall to Foulis Ferry to prevent shipment of meal at a time of food scarcity and rising grain prices.[86] The leaders of the mob had taken the precaution of getting the key to the

Foulis storehouse before they set off. When they found little grain in the girnel they returned peaceably to Dingwall and that was the end of the affair, except that memories of these protests were, doubtless, added to those of 'The Year of the Sheep' in the popular consciousness of the people. They would surface again half a century later when in August 1846 it became clear that, in common with the rest of the Highlands, the Easter Ross potato crop had failed. Despite the fact that local agriculture was a good deal more diversified than elsewhere in the Highlands and the rest of the harvest was good, many people were dependent on the potato. By early winter some sections of the population were destitute and facing starvation.[87] Some landowners began to buy in grain to sell at cost to their tenants, while others, such as Davidson of Tulloch, bought bread for immediate distribution. Early in January there were meetings in Inverness and Dingwall to make plans to deal with the emergency but by then trouble had already begun.[88]

What seems to have precipitated the riots were reports of actual starvation on the west coast, coupled with the beginning of a steep rise in local food prices early in 1847, partially due to some local farmers holding crops back in hopes of getting high famine prices later. Exceptionally severe weather in February exacerbated the problem since work on local farms, which would have provided wages to buy grain, could not begin.

The riots began in Banffshire in mid-January and the first outbreak in the Cromarty Firth occurred on the nineteenth and twentieth of that month when a mob at Evanton (where there is some evidence of price speculation by local growers and agents) warned a local farmer that they would prevent his grain wagons getting to Invergordon for shipment.[89] A week later there was a riot in Cromarty, when the Provost, Dr MacDonald (who was also a local farmer), purchased twenty bolls of oatmeal from a retailer in the town. It was believed that the Provost was hoarding the meal in the hopes of fetching famine prices later. A mob, led by women and young boys, marched out to MacDonald's farmhouse and broke several windows before capturing a dog cart and returning to town where the cart was flung off the quay into the sea. Then the mob broke a few windows in the retailer's house before being dispersed by promises that the meal would be returned to town and sold to the people. The following day a group of farmers met at the Court House and agreed to provide a sufficiency of meal for local needs.[90]

This meeting seems to have defused the situation in Cromarty for the moment, but over the next few days shipments were prevented at Foulis Point and Balintraid and anonymous notices were sent through Rosskeen urging 'All lovers of their country to stop shipments of corn, potatoes, fish and eggs.' In February a mob of about one hundred people prevented the loading of one hundred and thirty-nine barrels of cured haddock on a London-bound steamer at Invergordon.[91]

By now large crowds were roaming about the countryside, turning back wagons, and patrolling the various ports along the Firth to prevent shipments.

There were threats to open potato pits to help themselves. Ross-shire had no police force to deal with the mobs and the special constables, claimed to 'consist principally of old pensioners',[92] were reluctant to act against friends and neighbours. The garrison at Fort George was too small to cover all the affected ports, although troops were called out to Avoch and other harbours on the south shore of the Black Isle in February. In any case, the local authorities were both powerless and reluctant to act since there was a good deal of sympathy with the people's fears. As Sheriff Jardine wrote to the Lord Advocate on 5 February, the situation arose 'from no lawless or mischievous disposition of the people but from a *serious apprehension* of there not being sufficient food reserved for the maintenance of the people.'[93]

A county meeting was called for 11 February, to arrange for a sufficient quantity of corn to be retained in the county for local needs. In the event, however, the meeting only agreed to keep back a quantity of grain and put aside £600 to buy grain to be sold at 'prime cost' [i.e. at cost]. The Procurator Fiscal in Dingwall feared that this was insufficient to cure the fears of the mob[94] and he was right. Neither side expected relief supplies of grain to be free but there was a growing feeling by the people that there was a 'morally tolerable price for food' and that this had been exceeded by the rapid rise in grain prices.[95]

By the beginning of March trade around the Cromarty Firth had been at a standstill for over a month but soldiers from Edinburgh Castle had, at last, arrived in the north to protect shipments. The mob knew that they could not win any direct confrontation with the military so they changed their tactics and began mixing the grains to render them unfit for export (although still edible).

Around the Cromarty Firth the climax came at Invergordon on Tuesday 2 March when the long-promised soldiers, numbering just over one hundred, finally arrived by sea in the town at three o'clock in the afternoon.[96] Andrew Baxter, farmer at Rosskeen, had been trying for some time to ship grain. That day he had sent six carts into Invergordon. These were met by a mob on the west side of town, turned back to Rosskeen, and forcibly unloaded. The newly disembarked troops were rushed to the farm, along with the Sheriff, where the Riot Act was read and the soldiers succeeded in arresting two men and two women. The carts were loaded again and brought back into Invergordon under military escort and the grain loaded on the ship at about eight o'clock at night. The mob, now numbering between four and five hundred, followed, led by a 'party of pressing women', who failed to be deterred by a further reading of the Riot Act, a charge by the soldiers at the quayside and the taking of over a dozen prisoners.[97] The empty carts were set upon outside town on their way back to Rosskeen, broken up and dumped into the sea. Only two carts arrived back at Andrew Baxter's farm intact.

After the ship was loaded the magistrates and officers brought their prisoners to their lodgings at the Commercial Inn and the mob followed. By now it was led by John Munro, a twenty-three year old carter from Newmore, who had come to Invergordon that day on business. He had met the mob at the Bridge of Rosskeen when it had first turned back the carts, but had refused to join it despite being taunted as a coward. This obviously rankled for, when he had finished his business, John Munro became drunk and joined the crowd at the quayside where his may have been the voice, heard in the winter darkness, denouncing the Sheriff, Mr Jardine, and others 'as the enemies of the people for bringing the soldiers.'[98] After the carts were destroyed at the Bridge of Rosskeen, Munro harangued the crowd, urging them to march back into the town 'like soldiers' and rescue the prisoners. He led the mob to the Inn where, with the women to the fore, the door was broken in with a carriage pole taken from Sir James Mackenzie's phaeton. In the confusion two prisoners succeeded in escaping but John Munro was captured. A military guard was put on the Inn and there was no further trouble that night.[99]

The following day, however, there was a final explosion of violence. When a local farmer attempted to bring grain into the town the carts were met at the Bridge of Rosskeen, the sacks cut open and the grain emptied on the road before the carts were broken up and thrown into the sea. The Sheriff and troops arrived to a scene of devastation and high excitement. When the Sheriff attempted to read the Riot Act to the mob, the paper was snatched from his hand, and he was told, 'It would suit you better, Sheriff, to read the 65th Psalm, where corn is promised in abundance by a Higher Authority than even you . . .'[100] The Biblical tone, and the outright destruction of the grain, are both signs of a new spirit, a strange and heady mixture of euphoria and desperation.

By now the crowd was augmented by 'an army of eight hundred navvies, headed by a piper' and far outnumbered the Sheriff and his forces.[101] Military reinforcements were sent for but in the meantime the mob dashed through Invergordon towards Saltburn and the road to Balintraid pier where it fell upon a large convoy of carts. When the soldiers arrived to escort the carts into Invergordon, they were only able to stop the mob after a bayonet charge in which at least one man and one woman were wounded.[102]

The bayonet charge may have stopped the mob at Balintraid but small groups continued to roam about the countryside that day breaking into granaries and destroying their contents.[103] That night at Foulis Point grain was destroyed by being mixed with coal and lime and in Invergordon an angry mob once again besieged the officers at the Commercial Inn. A distraught magistrate wrote from there: 'A mob collected in front of the Inn this evening and the worst possible Disposition is shown by the people — while I write riotous parties are assembled before the Inn.'[104]

Two days later a mob attacked a boat unloading stones on the beach near Cromarty and tore away its ropes, sails, blocks and rudder. Then they seized another small boat and dragged it 'furiously' through the streets of the town. The vessels belonged to Donald Urquhart, a quarrier from Cullicudden, who had helped to load a meal ship in Cromarty Roads with grain from Findon. The motive for these attacks was, quite simply, revenge.[105] Ironically, on at least one occasion the mob prevented the sailing of ships bearing relief supplies for the western Highlands where starvation was real and not just anticipated.[106]

And then, quite suddenly, the riots ended. Within a few days of the Invergordon disturbances shipments of grain began again throughout the Cromarty Firth despite fears that this was but a temporary calm.[107] John Munro came to trial in June and pleaded guilty to being in the mob that attacked the officers of the law and helped the prisoners to escape from the Commercial Inn.[108] He claimed in mitigation that he was sincerely contrite for what he had done when drunk and produced a certificate from the minister of Rosskeen and another signed by eighty-five inhabitants of Invergordon testifying to his favourable reputation although 'he was easily imposed upon and misled.'[109] He was sentenced to nine months imprisonment.

The reasons for the abrupt end to the meal riots are unclear. In part, perhaps, it was simple exhaustion on the part of the mob unable to sustain the high excitement and purpose of early March. The actions of those last few days in destroying grain and carrying out revenge attacks certainly suggest a kind of hysteria stemming from a realisation that shipments could no longer be prevented. During February, Davidson of Tulloch had promoted a well-circulated pledge amongst local landowners in which they promised to set aside a certain proportion of their crop, and seed, until the next harvest. Another reason may have been, quite simply, an improvement in the weather which allowed farm work to begin and wages to be paid. A great deal of local labour was also absorbed by the large-scale improvement then just beginning at Ardross under its new laird, Alexander Matheson.

Two decades earlier Ardross had been sold by the last Gaelic-speaking *Fear Ard-rois*, Murdo Mackenzie, to the Marquess of Stafford (soon to become the Duke of Sutherland). Little evidence remains of the Sutherland period of tenure beyond the placename, Stittenham, which derived from the family's English lands. The Sutherlands seem to have used the estate primarily for shooting and some tenants were evicted when the Duke built a sporting lodge at Tollie. Then, in 1846, the estate was sold to Matheson for £90,000.

The new laird of Ardross had been born in 1805 into the family of an impoverished tacksman in Wester Ross who, by the time Alexander became a young man, had been forced to sell Attadale, the last of the family lands. Alexander's uncle, Sir James Matheson of the Lews, was a partner in the firm of Jardine Matheson and Company, and it was he who found a place for his nephew in his far eastern business. Much of the company's profits came from the opium trade. When Alexander Matheson retired at the age of forty with a huge fortune he returned to Scotland and began buying property in the Highlands.[110]

Ardross became the centre for what can only be described as a huge piece

of social engineering; an attempt by a single landowner to reverse the decline
of the Highlands by the use of massive amounts of private capital. Perhaps
because of his own family's history Sir Alexander Matheson (he was knighted
in 1882) seems to have had two main aims in his programme at Ardross: to
improve the land and the life of the existing tenants and to use the
transformation of the estate as the means of bringing more people back to the
land. When he became laird there were nineteen tenants at Ardross (a total of
one hundred and nine people) with farms of between six and twenty acres
held at the will of the landlord without written leases. Their homes were the
traditional blackhouses and 'the cattle sheds stood as if they had dropped
from the heavens.'[111] No tenants were evicted as a result of improvement since
the new landlord needed all the workers he could find. Between March 1847
and January 1848 Matheson was said to have spent over £30,000 mostly on
wages and to have employed about two hundred and seventy men.[112]
Eventually, the local labour pool was so depleted that labourers had to be
brought in from further afield and a special barracks accommodating two
hundred men was built. Many of these labourers were Irish refugees from the
potato famine, and it was they who named the estate village 'Dublin'.

Even the way work was organised at Ardross was experimental. The jobs
were arranged on small contracts, not only because this was cheaper than
letting to a single large contractor, but because the competition it engendered
amongst the various squads of workmen led to speed and increased efficiency.
In all of this there was a strong thread of paternalism, and it is possible that
some of the estate agents used the situation to their own advantage. There is a
tradition that the factor, for example, ran a truck shop at which all estate
workers were obliged to trade.[113] Nevertheless, the changes at Ardross were
remarkable. Over the next nine years 2,600 acres of arable land were improved
by trenching, draining, and liming. Sixty seven miles of dyke, eleven miles of
barbed wire fence and twenty eight miles of roads were built. Over three
thousand acres of land were enclosed and planted. The shooting lodge at
Tollie was replaced by the baronial pile of Ardross Castle and its gardens
were reclaimed from bog (Fig. 34). By the end of nine years twenty-four new
and compact farms had been created, ranging in size from thirty to three
hundred acres, as well as fourteen crofts of up to twenty acres. All were held on
nineteen year leases. This mixture of large and small holdings was a deliberate
policy because it was believed that there was 'a great mutual advantage in
having a due proportion of large and small farms in a country.'[114]

By 1856 the large sheepruns in Strathrusdale and Dibidale were being
broken up to create eight further farms, which would be linked to the main
estate by a twelve mile road, and the permanent population of the estate had
increased threefold to 429.[115] The total cost of the Ardross improvements was
estimated to be £230,000.

Ardross was a remarkable exception. Other local estates were smaller and
operated on a much more restricted scale. By the late 1840s Teaninich, for

34. Ardross Castle.

example, had fifteen regular servants, including a grieve, cattleman, shepherd, miller and ten labourers.[116] The farm was a mixed one, with the added elements of a commercially organised salmon fishery and the distillery, which used local peats and grain, and in turn provided chaff and dregs for use as manure on the farm. Cinders from the distillery were used to line the cattle yards and pig sties. With the exception of the export of livestock, salmon, wheat and whisky, the purchase of seeds from a merchant in Invergordon and the import of coals, bricks and tiles (for a hot house at Coul), malt and a certain amount of artificial fertilisers, Teaninich was largely self-sufficient. The imported coal was supplemented by local peats; the guano and artificial fertilisers from the factory in Invergordon were used with sea clay gathered at low tide, and horse and cow dung scraped from the road.

Despite the fact that by the end of the 1840s agriculture was at last pulling out of its slump, the laird of Teaninich was apparently in some financial difficulties; the daily farm diary he kept mentions having to sell crops for ready money.[117] The impression gained from the Teaninich diary is of a closely integrated system of farming with little room for mistakes or failure, such as the mysterious disease (perhaps tuberculosis) which struck some of the cattle and the continued failures of the potato crop from 1846 to 1849.[118]

On the other hand the diary also shows a yearly round of farming life that was shared by everybody, the work, the highdays and holidays such as Old New Year (12 January), communions and harvest home.[119] The laird was responsible for the well-being of the people on the estate; he notes, for example, the regular deliveries of coal and potatoes made to the poor in the village of Alness.[120] This social cohesion was reinforced by a common church affiliation; in 1848 Munro of Teaninich was a commissioner to the General Assembly of the Free Church.[121]

Despite local fears amongst landlords and farmers about the consequences of the abolition of the Corn Laws and the growth of free trade, agriculture grew to new prosperity in the 1850s and remained in a thriving state for over two decades. For the Cromarty Firth region an important element in this new buoyancy was the arrival of the railway.

From at least 1848 there had been plans for an extension of the line from Inverness to Wick.[122] In the event it was the advocacy of Alexander Matheson of Ardross that brought the railroad to Invergordon in 1863, seven years after it arrived in Inverness.[123] Originally it was not thought practicable to build a line from Inverness to Dingwall because of the expense of bridging the Ness. It was proposed instead to run a connecting steamer from a railhead at Nairn to Invergordon and build the line north from there. In 1860, however, Matheson secured the passage of the Inverness and Ross-shire Railway Act and the first sod for the new line was cut at Inverness by his wife. In March 1861 the contract was signed for the thirteen miles between Dingwall and Invergordon.

The *Invergordon Times and General Advertiser* reported the slow progress of the railroad in great and expectant detail. When the line to Invergordon was opened on 25 March 1863 the paper proudly reported that the town now marked 'the northern extremity of the line on Bradshaw's map.'[124] Yet already there were plans to extend the line beyond Invergordon to Tain, and thence to Bonar Bridge,[125] and within a few months navvies had arrived at Invergordon to begin work on this extension, which was completed in October 1865.[126] (In 1878 a small spur line was built from Alness to Dalmore distillery).

The effect of the arrival of the railway in Easter Ross was immediate and touched all sections of the local population. For example, Cromarty fishermen no longer had to walk or sail to Dingwall to sell their wares; instead they came to Invergordon and completed the journey by rail.[127] Within a few months the horse-drawn mail coaches between Dingwall, Invergordon and Tain disappeared.[128] The relationship between the Cromarty Firth and the world beyond changed completely. As one citizen of Evanton succinctly put it: 'Ferindonald was thus but a day's journey from London.'[129] And now, too, the world could come to Easter Ross. When the Channel Fleet paid a visit to the Firth in August, 1863, the railroad company ran many special excursion trains to Invergordon.

Easter Ross became infected with 'railway mania.' A line from Dingwall to the west was begun in 1868 and, as early as 1865, there had been talk of a branch line in the Black Isle[130] although nothing was done until the late 1880s. In 1890 a line from Muir of Ord was begun and by 1894 it reached Fortrose and there it stopped.[131] By 1887 another line along the north shore of the Black Isle to Cromarty was proposed, primarily to ship local fish to southern markets.[132] Plans had been drawn up in 1896 as a result of the passage of the Light Railway Act[133] but the railroad company was not floated for another sixteen years. The scheme was popular and £96,000 was subscribed by local authorities and local people. Construction began in the late spring of 1913. The line was laid as far as Jemimaville and at Townlands Park in Cromarty a huge hole was dug for the station and turntable.[134] Some rolling stock ran on the line although the Cromarty Railway never carried passengers. During the war the rails were requisitioned and taken to the Western front[135] and the line was never completed. In 1926 the Cromarty and Dingwall Light Railway went into voluntary liquidation.[136]

The 'railway mania' that struck Easter Ross in the 1860s was but one symptom of a buoyant economy. From this time Easter Ross became a prime area for fattening cattle and growing seed potatoes for the southern markets opened up by the railway. These changes in agricultural practice were to lessen the local consequences of the national slump in grain prices of the 1870s and 80s. About 1866 prices for sheep and mutton began to drop.[137] By the late 1870s agriculture was in a state of severe depression due to bad harvests and cheap imports of American grain so that soup kitchens were established in a number of towns in and around the Cromarty Firth while the landlords compensated for the loss of income by the further creation of deer forests and grouse moors and the sale of land. British agriculture did not really recover until the outbreak of the Great War in 1914.

During the difficult times of the 1880s emigration rose again. The railroad allowed local emigrants to travel south to Liverpool and other ports instead of leaving from Cromarty. Regular advertisements for sailings to America and the empire appeared in the *Invergordon Times* and the *Ross-shire Journal*, but not all emigrants went out of desperation. Perhaps the most extraordinary migrant from the Cromarty Firth in the 1880s was Murdo Mackenzie. He was the clever son of a tenant farmer of Balnagown, who returned from a period working in a bank in Tain to become assistant factor on the estate. In 1885 a visitor to Balnagown asked Mackenzie if he might be interested in the job of assistant manager in a newly formed Dundee-based company investing in the cattle ranches of the American West. Mackenzie eventually became manager of the three-quarter million acre Matador Ranch in west Texas. The lessons he had learned about careful estate management at Balnagown stood him in good stead.[138] It was said that you could not buy a hobble rope on the Matador but in Dundee they wanted to know if the expense was justified.

Mackenzie, however, was an exception to the general social and economic gloom of the 1880s; the crofters and cottars of Clare and elsewhere were much more typical. Crofters' holdings of between one and five acres were usually on the moor or a remote corner of a large farm or estate and in order to survive

> they generally have recourse to some trade, or labour occasionally with neighbouring farms. Their lot is precarious, for their 'wee bit' may, they know not how soon, be incorporated with the 'big farm' and little or no encouragement is given them toward building or improvement.[139]

For these small tenancies crofters often paid rents that were comparable to those of their larger and more prosperous neighbours; and these rents continued to rise over the decades. In the 1880s one Mulbuie crofter wryly remarked '. . . they [the crofters] began by paying a hen, and now they had to pay a shilling for every feather in the hen.'[140] At the same time the crofters' tenure became even more precarious. As late as 1875 — at the same time as Matheson was returning the common grazings at Dornie to his tenants — cottars were being evicted from a newly-enclosed common in Logie Easter by Sir Charles Ross of Balnagown and other local proprietors.[141] An article from the *People's Journal* (reprinted in the *Ross-shire Journal*) warned against the bad policy of such actions even though the people might have no rights at law.[142]

In the 1880s, however, the cottars and crofters found a new voice and what they had to say would change the shape of Highland history forever. In part they were galvanised by events in Ireland, where violent protest had led to a measure of land reform, but more immediately they were aided by the passage of the Third Reform Bill of 1885 which gave the vote to smallholders like themselves and increased the Scottish electorate to half a million. Led by such men as John Murdoch, the editor of *The Highlander* and a frequent speaker to crofters' groups around the Cromarty Firth,[143] as well as such local organisers as Bailie Thomas Nichol and John Macrae of Dingwall, local crofters and smallholders began to demand reforms, including security of tenure and compensation for improvements.

In fact the crofters' demands found much sympathy amongst some local landlords and many large tenant farmers; a meeting of the Easter Ross Farmers' Club in October 1881 voted in favour of just such reforms, although there was disagreement whether they should be enforced by Parliamentary legislation or not.[144] But the situation David Carment had prophesied half a century before had now come to pass; the people's 'spirits embittered by what they deem oppression' had totally broken 'the ties which united master and servant.' The day had come when 'by grasping too much' all was indeed lost. The crofters not only had genuine grievances, they also had a sustaining mythology that emphasised their oppressions and rights, as well as the lack of identity between crofters and farmers and landlords. There was a time, so the myth ran, when all the land had belonged to the people in common but these rights had been usurped by landlords. Around the Cromarty Firth the most fervent maintainers of this myth were the crofters of the Mulbuie, yet they themselves were relatively recent incomers, striking evidence that historical change often depends on what is believed to be true rather than what is the truth.

By the early 1880s there were a number of active branches of the Highland Land League around the Cromarty Firth, in places such as Alness, Culbokie and the western end of the Mulbuie. Most of these groups came into being as a response to the appointment of the Napier Commission in 1883. In mid September 1883 local crofters held meetings to delegate men to give evidence to the Commissioners when they came to Dingwall on 10 October.[145] The Napier Commission raised high expectations and in the wake of its local sittings a number of formally constituted branches of the Highland Land League were set up. At the Mulbuie, although the majority of the League's members were Gaelic speakers and the club had a Gaelic bard, most of the business was conducted in English and the minutes were kept in that language. Evidence, perhaps, of the crofters' sense that they were part of a movement that had ramifications well beyond the Gaelic-speaking Highlands? The branch enrolled both men and women and its meetings regularly attracted enthusiastic audiences of between one and two hundred. By 1884 it was busy gathering local land-holding statistics, agitating for the extension of the franchise and urging that no landlord should be elected as Member of Parliament in the forthcoming general election. By now it was clear that the findings of the Napier Commission fell short of expectation and that in any case the government was unlikely to act upon its recommendations. The activities of the branch became more political. In the autumn of 1884 the Mulbuie crofters were making plans to attend the first Highland Land League convention in Dingwall. The members marched behind a piper carrying banners urging 'Remember who stole the Mulbuie Common' and 'Success to Reform.'[146]

Despite the election in other Highland constituencies of five Crofters' MPs, the General Election of 1884 in Easter Ross went to a Liberal laird, Munro Ferguson of Novar, who although committed to land reform, was anathema to such groups as the Mulbuie Crofters. The General Election of 1885 brought a revolution to Highland politics. With the exception of Sutherland, every one of the Highland constituencies returned a Crofters' Party Member to Parliament. In Ross and Cromarty Dr Roderick MacDonald was elected. John MacLean, the Mulbuie bard, sang in praise of him:

> However I would sing the hero's praise
> Wherever I would drink a dram;
> However, I would sing the hero's praises.
>
> This Dr MacDonald of whom I speak
> Is undoubtedly a crofter's son;
> He defeated the laird of Novar,
> He kept him out of Parliament . . .

> Truly, I love that hero
> Who won the great esteem of the Gaels;
> He defeated his enemy
> And he will reduce the land-rent for us . . .[147]

Gladstone's majority in the new parliament was so narrow that the Liberals were forced to meet the demands of the Crofting Members of Parliament. In 1886 the Crofters Act was passed, granting security of tenure, the right to pass land on to the family, and compensation for improvements. The Act also set up a Crofters Commission, a regulatory body with the power to fix fair rents.

The Crofters Act was both revolutionary and reactionary; it transformed the nature of land holding, and to a large extent agricultural practices, throughout much of the Highlands but at the same time it 'froze' the agricultural landscape in a way that was to have both good and bad consequences. Around the Cromarty Firth the Act did not have quite the decisive effect it had elsewhere. The provisions of the Act were not extended to the seaward parishes of Fearn and Cromarty; it was claimed that this omission had a bad effect on local fishing and agriculture.[148] At Ardross Sir Alexander Matheson's small tenants had already gained these rights and therefore refused to come under the provisions of the Act; elsewhere there were no crofters left. All around the Firth an agricultural landscape something like that already in existence at Ardross came into existence; a mixture of large farms and small crofts.[149]

Despite the failure of the 1886 Act to change radically local farming or to meet all the demands of the crofters, it remains a landmark in the history of the Cromarty Firth. In 1792 the people of Strathrusdale had been defeated in their attempt to turn back the sheep and maintain their traditional ways. Nearly a century later, the Mulbuie crofters echoed these feelings when they vowed to work 'until all rights have been restored to the people.'[150] In reality, there could be no return to a golden age, not least because the golden age had never existed. Nevertheless, the Crofters Act was an act of tardy justice which brought the process that had begun in Strathrusdale to some kind of end; it was a victory, of sorts. As in 1792, it was equally clear in 1886 that things would never be quite the same again.

NOTES

1. G. Mackenzie, *Agriculture*, p. 294.
2. E. Richards, *Clearances*, vol. 1, p. 281.
3. *OSA*, vol. 19, p. 236.
4. J. Sinclair, *General View*, pp. 58–9.
5. From information provided in an interview with W. W. Munro, Clashnabuaic, 9 November 1986. Sir Alexander only held Novar for a few years, dying in 1809 at

Ramsgate, aged 83. His son, H. A. J. Munro was a noted art collector, a patron and friend of the reclusive artist J. M. W. Turner. Turner visited Novar in 1831 and it is said that one of his Carthaginian paintings, 'Mercury and Argus' (now in the National Gallery of Canada) was inspired by the visit. See *Turner and Scotland*, Aberdeen Art Gallery, 1982, pp. 61–2. Novar wrote: 'Cromarty, I believe, is only famed as a good harbour. Turner thought by enlarging something might be made of it . . .' From notes on H. A. J. Munro supplied by R. W. Munro.

6. Mackenzie, *Agriculture*, p. 295.

7. Quoted in *Ibid.*, p. 107.

8. *The Farmers' Magazine*, vol. 10 (1809), p. 562.

9. This account of the Middletons is based on material from Sinclair, *General View*, p. 63; *NSA* Cromarty, p. 13; I. Mowat, *Easter Ross*, p. 39; J. MacDonald, 'Agriculture', pp. 92, 95, 150; J. A. Symon, *Scottish farming past and present*, Edinburgh, 1959, p. 146 (quoting the Aberdeen *Press and Journal*, 24 January 1939).

10. Most of the following discussion of changes around the Cromarty Firth is based on the quarterly accounts for the region published in *The Farmers' Magazine* between 1800 and 1825.

11. J. Barron, *Northern Highlands*, vol. 1, pp. 63–4.

12. Mowat, *Easter Ross*, pp. 39–40.

13. Barron, *Northern Highlands*, vol. 1, pp. 50, 68.

14. D. P. Willis, 'A century and a half of Black Isle Farmers', 1986.

15. A. Wight, *Husbandry*, vol. 4, pp. 236–7. The scarcity of manure at this period is indicated by the fact that the lands were also spread with powdered lime from old houses. See also, MacDonald, 'Agriculture', p. 124.

16. R. Pococke, *Tours in Scotland, 1747, 1750, 1760*, ed. D. W. Kemp, Scottish History Society, 1887, p. 174.

17. Wight, *Husbandry*, p. 267; Gordon, 'Nigg', Farming II, p. 7.

18. Mackenzie, *Agriculture*, pp. 97ff. Cockburn, the son of an Edinburgh lawyer and laird of Rowchester, near Greenlaw in Berwickshire, married Jane (or Joan) Ross, niece of Hugh Ross ('The Entailer') last laird of Shandwick. He was killed in a duel in London in 1790. Cockburn took his wife's name on succeeding to the estate. He died in 1827 and is buried in Fearn Abbey. I am grateful to Mr Nevile Reid of Shandwick for showing me Old Shandwick and explaining the family's genealogy to me.

19. Pococke, p. 174.

20. Cameron, 'Sanitary Condition', pp. 12ff.

21. Hugh Rose was born in Creich, Sutherland, in 1767, the fifth son of the Rev. Hugh Rose and his wife, Mary MacCulloch of the Easter Ross family of Glastullich. Subsequently his father was transferred to Tain. I am most grateful to Sir John and Lady Hayes for making available to me their notes about the history of Arabella House.

22. The house was built around an earlier dwelling named 'Drummeddat' — the element 'drum' strongly suggesting that it was one of the few high (and dry) spots in the Nigg plain. Rose also named a newly created (but now disappeared) farm Phippsfield. I. Fraser, 'Place names', *RC Book*, p. 228. By 1839 Phippsfield had a brick and tile works, supplying amongst other things the tile drains needed for further drainage work throughout this part of the Cromarty Firth region. Barron, *Highlands*, vol. 2, p. 278. There are a number of local traditions connected with Arabella Phipps Rose. One is that she was murdered by her husband's discarded West Indian quadroon

mistress who came to Easter Ross, concealed herself in the attic of the mansion, and eventually succeeded in pushing Arabella downstairs. Arabella's tombstone, however, states that '. . . in the act of preparing medicine for the relief of a sick and indigent family [she] suddenly expired on the ninth of November 1806 aged 27.' See Gordon, 'Nigg', Law and Order III, Civil Matters, p. 4. There is another local tradition that Barbaraville was named for one of Arabella's sisters. In fact, the name predates 'Arabella.' Barbaraville was named for Barbara Munro of Culrain who was betrothed in the mid-eighteenth century to William MacLeay of Pollo and Portleich. When she died a few days before the wedding her brokenhearted bridegroom decided to commemorate her by renaming Portleich 'Barbaraville.' See A. Mackenzie, *History of the Munros of Foulis*, Inverness, 1898, pp. 203–4.

23. From genealogical notes provided by R. W. Munro. The house of Poyntzfield dates from 1757, with additions of 1775 and 1790. See E. Meldrum, *The Black Isle* (Local History and Archaeology Guidebook, no. 3), Inverness, 1984, p. 27.

24. Mowat, *Easter Ross*, p. 69.

25. 'Contents and estimate of the estate of Cadboll,' vol. 2 (Rosskeen, Kilmuir and Tarbat), copy in possession of Miss J. Gill, Brucefield.

26. *Ibid.*, pp. 14–17.

27. *The Inverness Courier* reported on 8 January 1818 that the piers were to be built that season at a cost of £1,000; see Barron, *Northern Highlands*, vol. 1, p. 135.

28. 'Contents and estimates of the estate of Cadboll', pp. 22, 19–20. Mrs Jane Durham, Scotsburn, has suggested that the first inhabitants of Saltburn came from Ord, while I. R. M. Mowat believes that they were resettled from mid-Ross.

29. *Ibid.*, p. 19.

30. The following account of Cromarty and Invergordon is based on *Pigot's New Commercial Directory of Scotland for 1825-6*, London, 1826.

31. *Ibid.*, p. 638.

32. Mowat, *Easter Ross*, p. 69 (where, as R. W. Munro has pointed out, Alexander is misnamed Simon); and information supplied by Duncan Murray, Evanton.

33. It is clearly shown on Taylor and Skinner's *Maps of the roads of North Britain or Scotland*, 1776, Plate 23.

34. *Pigot and Company's National Commercial Directory of the whole of Scotland*, London, 1837, p. 740.

35. Mowat, *Easter Ross*, pp. 75ff.

36. Sinclair, *General View*, pp. 44–5; Mowat, *Easter Ross*, p. 80.

37. Mackenzie, *Agriculture*, p. 270; Barron, *Northern Highlands*, vol. 1, p. 6.

38. *Fowlis Case*, Section V, p. 4 (Court of Session Business Proof 8 February 1834, pp. 9–10). A surviving bridge from this realignment bears the date 1791 and the names of Sir Hugh Munro and Forsyth the builder; see *Clan Munro Magazine*, vol. 15 (1979), p. 22.

39. *Farmers' Magazine*, vol. 7 (1806), p. 118; the prime mover behind the Dingwall mart was Sir George Mackenzie of Coul.

40. Barron, *Northern Highlands*, vol. 1, p. 15.

41. *Ibid.*, p. 185.

42. *Ibid.*, pp. xxi–ii.

43. The first stage coach left Inverness at 6 am on Monday and arrived (with luck) by noon on Thursday; the coach was a four in hand to Tain and thereafter a fly. See L. Gardiner, *Stage Coach to John O'Groats*, London, 1961, p. 95. By the early 1820s

three coaches left Inverness daily for the Cromarty Firth region: two coaches for Dingwall, travelling via Beauly and Kessock, with connections for Cromarty and Tain and a third coach for the Spa Hotel at Strathpeffer.

44. Barron, *Northern Highlands*, vol. 2, p. xxii.

45. *Ibid.*, p. xxv.

46. *Farmers' Magazine*, vol. 15 (1814), p. 393.

47. Once again the confusion between Culrain and the two Culcairns has caused this episode to be misplaced. It is clear, however, that the evictions were on the lands of Culrain in Kincardine parish, since after the initial report of the conflict appeared in the *Inverness Courier* it was the minister of Kincardine who wrote to the paper about the events. See Barron, *Northern Highlands*, vol. 1, pp. 179, 181.

48. Quoted in Richards, *Clearances*, vol. 1, p. 220.

49. *Farmers' Magazine*, vol. 23, 1822, p. 119.

50. From genealogical notes supplied by R. W. Munro. The marriage took place in 1822 and one of the houses in the village bears the date 1825. There is an octagonal lookout tower at Poyntzfield House named 'Jemima's Tower'. E. Meldrum, *The Black Isle*, pp. 26–7.

51. Barron, *Northern Highlands*, vol. 2, p. 298.

52. J. Fergusson, '"Making interest" in Scottish County Elections', *SHR*, vol. 26, 1947, pp. 119–20.

53. W. Ferguson, 'Dingwall burgh politics and the Parliamentary franchise in the eighteenth century', *SHR*, vol. 38, no. 126, October 1959, pp. 89–108.

54. H. Miller, *Scenes and Legends*, p. 486.

55. Quoted in Barron, *Northern Highlands*, vol. 2, p. 45.

56. *Ibid.*, vol. 2, pp. 97–8.

57. Details from 'Book for the combined counties of Ross and Cromarty, Polling place, Tain, 27 December 1832', from a copy in the possession of Mrs Rosemary Mackenzie, Tain.

58. Miller, *Scenes and Legends*, pp. 486–7.

59. The most complete account of the cholera epidemic in the Cromarty Firth Region is found in Miller's *Scenes and Legends*, Chapter 16, but the following account has been supplemented from Barron's *Northern Highlands*, vol. 2, pp. 98ff.

60. S.W.R.I. Nigg, p. 15 (an account largely drawn from Hugh Miller).

61. Barron, *Northern Highlands*, vol. 2, p. 116.

62. *Ibid.*, pp. 118–19.

63. For the cholera epidemic at Nigg, see J. R. Martin, 'Church Chronicles of Nigg', n.p., 1967, pp. 41–3 as well as S.W.R.I., 'Nigg', and Gordon, 'Nigg'.

64. *NSA*, Ross and Cromarty, pp. 27–8.

65. *Ibid.*, p. 279.

66. Barron, *Northern Highlands*, vol. 2, p. 3.

67. *Ibid.*, p. xxxvi; J. Mitchell, *Reminiscences of my Life in the Highlands*, Newton Abbot, 1971, vol. 1, p. 72.

68. A. Grimble, *The Deer Forests of Scotland*, London, 1896, pp. 239, 286; G. K. Whitehead, *The Deer Stalking Grounds of Great Britain and Ireland*, London, 1960, pp. 302, 374; W. Orr, *Deer Forests, Landlords and Crofters*, Edinburgh, 1982, pp. 168–9, 172. Ben Wyvis and possibly Balnagown were old hunting grounds; other local deer forests, such as Kildermorie and Ardross, were created in the 1830s, '40s and '50s.

69. The pump room in Strathpeffer was opened in 1819. Barron, *Northern Highlands*,

vol. 1, p. 165.

70. 'Weekly state of labour on the farm of Arabella from Monday 28 November 1831', MS in the possession of Mrs Gill, Rosskeen Farm.

71. Cameron, 'Sanitary Condition', pp. 13–14.

72. The evidence is printed in *PP* 1844, vol. 21, pp. 1–64.

73. *Ibid.*, p. 22.

74. *Ibid.*, p. 45.

75. *Ibid.*, p. 23.

76. Barron, *Northern Highlands*, vol. 2, pp. 53–4.

77. *RJ*, 21 July, 1931, p. 4.

78. *Ibid.*, 5 April 1940, p. 4.

79. Richards, *Clearances*, vol. 2, p. 321.

80. *Ibid.*, vol. 1, pp. 394ff. Clearances began at Strathconan from the early years of the nineteenth century but the pace accelerated after the Balfour family acquired the estate in 1839. The grandson of the purchaser, Arthur Balfour, was Secretary of State for Scotland at the time of the 'Crofters' War' in the 1880s and, later, British Prime Minister.

81. C. J. Shaw of Tordarroch, *A History of Clan Shaw*, Chichester, 1983, pp. 274–5; *PP* 1844, vol. 21, p. 56. An estate map at Newhall, dated 1813, shows the beginning of enclosure and improvement on the estate, but there is no indication that it was planned to create smallholdings, rather the reverse, since large fields have been laid down over rigs in such places as Castlecraig and Cullicudden. This change in estate planning between 1813 and 1849 appears to have been a direct response to clearance elsewhere in the region.

82. S.W.R.I., 'Nigg', p. 16.

83. For details of this clearance, see Richards, *Clearances*, Vol. 1, pp. 370ff.

84. Gordon, 'Nigg', The population, p. 1; Sea Transport, p. 3. The incident is dated here to 1819 but there were no contemporary clearances involving Ardgay in that year and it seems possible that the tradition is a conflation dealing with the fate of the Culrain and Ardgay people.

85. *Ibid.*, War and Strife, p. 2.

86. K. Logue, *Popular Disturbances in Scotland, 1780–1815*, Edinburgh, 1979, pp. 43–6.

87. Barron, *Northern Highlands*, vol. 3, p. 115.

88. The following discussion is based on E. Richards, 'Riots', and the reports sent to the Lord Advocate in Edinburgh from local legal agents throughout the spring of 1847 (SRO AD 56/308/1–6) and the precognitions taken before the trial of the Invergordon rioters (SRO AD 14/47/136).

89. SRO AD 56/308/5 no. 2; a memorial drawn up in February 1847 by 69 inhabitants of Evanton claimed that they were living entirely on turnips; Barron, *Northern Highlands*, vol. 3, p. 124.

90. SRO AD 56/308/1 no. 1 Letter from Procurator Fiscal in Cromarty dated 4 February 1847, and SRO AD 56/308/5 no. 1 letters from Sheriff Substitute at Tain dated 30 January 1847.

91. SRO AD 56/308/1 no. 2 Letter from the Procurator Fiscal, Tain, dated 4 February 1847.

92. SRO AD 56/305/6 no. 48.

93. SRO AD 56/308/5 no. 4.

94. SRO AD 56/308/4 no. 60.

95. Richards, 'Riots', p. 47.

96. Soldiers had been expected at Invergordon since the middle of February, SRO AD 56/308/2 nos. 31, 32, 67. Part of the reason for the delay was lack of suitable accommodation. The 'old manufactory' which had been used for the soldiers who came after the Disruption riots in 1843 was no longer wind and weather tight. SRO AD 56/308/5 no. 4; AD 56/308/2 no. 85.

97. SRO AD 56/308/6 no. 48 report of Lt. Col. Goodman commanding the 27th Regiment at Invergordon to the Assistant Adjutant General.

98. SRO AD 14/47/136 p. 57.

99. SRO AD 56/308/2 no. 68 (Letter written from the Commercial Inn, 3 March 1847), and SRO AD 14/47/136.

100. From an article in the *RJ*, 28 January 1922, quoted in Richards, 'Riots', pp. 24–5.

101. It seems likely that these hundreds of navvies were, in fact, men working on the improvements at Ardross.

102. The *RJ* informant claims that the woman later died, but her recovery is reported in contemporary newspaper accounts. SRO AD 56/308/6 no. 41. The Procurator Fiscal reported to the Crown agents that the man and woman's wounds were not serious, 5 March 1847: Richards, 'Riots', p. 25 and note 73. The newspaper account also claims that there were fifty carts in the convoy, of which only six arrived safely in Invergordon; the officer commanding the troops wrote on the day of the affair that thirty carts were escorted into Invergordon. SRO AD 56/308/6 no. 48.

103. Procurator Fiscal (in Invergordon) to Crown agent, 4 March 1847: SRO AD 56/308/6 no. 103.

104. SRO AD 56/308/3 no. 68.

105. SRO AD 56/308/6 nos. 13, 39.

106. SRO AD 56/308/6 no. 60. Letter dated 27 February reporting that carts bound for Foulis Point and a ship for Loch Broom were turned back.

107. SRO AD 56/308/6 no. 35; Letter from the Procurator Fiscal, Tain, to the Crown Agent, 9 March 1847.

108. *The Scotsman* 30 June 1847. Donald Holme, Bridgend of Alness (who had escaped from the Commercial Inn) was tried in his absence and outlawed.

109. *Ibid.*, 30 June 1847.

110. Matheson's other properties around the Cromarty Firth included Dalmore, Culcairn, Delny and Balintraid. A. Mackenzie and A. Macbain, *History of the Mathesons*, Stirling and London, 1900, pp. 72ff. By 1882 his possessions in the county of Ross extended to 220,000 acres, worth £773,020.

111. W. Mackenzie, 'Report of improvements at Ardross', *THASS*, new series, 1857–9, p. 133; much of the following discussion of the Ardross improvements is taken from this source.

112. Barron, *Northern Highlands*, vol. 3, pp. 148–9.

113. Mackenzie, 'Improvements', pp. 138–9; Interview with W. W. Munro, Clashnabuaic, 9 November 1986.

114. Mackenzie, 'Improvements', p. 136.

115. *Ibid.*, p. 148.

116. Much of the following discussion is based on the manuscript copy of the Teaninich farm diary, 1 January 1848–12 March 1850, in the possession of W. W.

Munro, Clashnabuaic. (Copy also available in Scottish Working Life Archive, Royal Museum of Scotland, Edinburgh).

117. *Ibid.*, p. 135.

118. *Ibid.*, pp. 6, 73, 152–7; for example, p. 163; '. . . the potatoes in the potato cellar below the straw barn found to be almost altogether rotted, emitting a strong and most offensive stench. I had them taken out and carted to the midden on the river field — they are quite black and so entirely rotted that the pigs would not touch them'.

119. *Ibid.*, pp. 9, 56, 70. In 1855, at the height of the Crimean War, there were strenuous attempts to abolish local celebrations of the Old New Year. At a meeting in Tain in December 1855 it was claimed that Russia was the only other great power to keep the old style and 'we ought to show that we were opposed to them on this as well as on other occasions', Barron, *Northern Highlands*, vol. 3, p. 342. In fact, the Old Style New Year was still being celebrated around the Cromarty Firth until well into the present century.

120. *Ibid.*, pp. 12, 160.

121. *Ibid.*, p. 35.

122. *Ibid.*, vol. 3, p. 68.

123. H. A. Vallance, *The Highland Railway*, Newton Abbot, 1963, p. 6.

124. *Ibid.*, 25 March 1863, p. 2. It seems likely that the new line did not carry passenger traffic for a few months. It was only in July 1863 that the *IT* reported that the line was open and timetables had been published. *Ibid.*, 8 July 1863, p. 2.

125. *IT*, 12 February 1862, p. 4; 12 March 1862, p. 4; 19 March 1862, pp. 4ff.

126. Vallance, *Highland Railway*, p. 27.

127. *IT*, 13 May 1863, p. 3.

128. *Ibid.*, 17 June 1863, p. 2.

129. F. Maclennan, *Ferindonald Papers*, p. 29.

130. *IT*, 23 August 1865, p. 3.

131. A. J. Beaton, *Illustrated Guide to the Black Isle Railway*, Dingwall, 1894; Vallance, *Highland Railway*, pp. 41–2. In 1951 the line was closed to passenger traffic. Goods traffic ceased in 1960 and the track was lifted by January 1963. *Ibid.*, p. 181.

132. See *RJ*, 26 April 1889, p. 2, 17 May 1889, p. 3.

133. RHP 17882 ('Bound plans and sections of the Cromarty and Dingwall Light Railway, 1896').

134. This account of the Cromarty railway is based on Jessie Munro, *Recollections of a Bygone Age*, Thurso, 1974, p. 17, as well as articles appearing in the *RJ*, plus Register House Plans 18087–8, 11750, 44269–73, 3094/1, and an interview with Donald Ross in Cromarty 10 December 1986. For the subscription of shares and the date construction began, *IC* 25 March 1913, p. 4.

135. W. M. Mackenzie, the Cromarty native and historian, claimed that the rails ended up in Thessalonia in northern Greece. Information supplied by R. G. Cant.

136. *RJ*, 12 February 1926, p. 4.

137. D. Turnock, *Patterns of Highland Development*, London, 1970, p. 57.

138. C. L. Douglas, 'Cattle King of Texas; Mackenzie of the Matador', *The Cattleman*, vol. 23, no. 8, January 1937, pp. 13–17. Mackenzie eventually became a cattle baron in his own right, running ranches in South America. For the Matador, see W. M. Pearce, *The Matador Land and Cattle Company*, University of Oklahoma Press, Norman, Oklahoma, 1964.

There seems to have been a strong connection between Ross-shire and the American West. There were regular advertisements for ranch and farm workers in Texas and other Western states in local papers during the 1870s and '80s. Some went permanently, others spent a season or several years working on Western ranches before returning to Ross-shire. Interview with W. W. Munro of Clashnabuaic, 9 November 1986.

139. Cameron, 'Sanitary Condition', p. 13.

140. Mulbuie Highland Land League Minute Book (1884–99), p. 20, MS in the possession of Mr A. Cameron, Wellhouse, Muir of Ord. I am most grateful to Mr Cameron for allowing me to see this minute book on which much of the following discussion of crofting in the 1880s is based.

141. SRO Directory of Commonties, vol. 2, p. 208; summonses were first served in 1843, but division was not carried out until 1867.

142. *RJ*, 18 June 1875, p. 3; 30 April 1875, p. 2.

143. See *Ibid.*, p. 2 and 25 June 1875, p. 2 for Murdoch speaking at the Sabbath School at Alness on 'Highland Education'. For the general background see R. Gibson, 'Crofter power in Easter Ross; the Land League at work, 1884–8', Highland Heritage Educational Trust, Dingwall, 1986.

144. *RJ*, 28 October 1881, p. 3.

145. *RJ*, 28 September 1883; for the background to the Napier Commission see A. D. Cameron, *Go Listen to the Crofters*, Stornoway, 1886. The evidence given by local witnesses at Dingwall is printed in *PP* (1884) vol. 20, nos: 40231–40924.

146. Mulbuie Minute Book, pp. 6–11.

147. Translation by Dr Donald Meek, Department of Celtic, Edinburgh University.

148. *RJ*, 17 May 1889, p. 2.

149. J. Tivy, 'Easter Ross, a residual crofting area', *Scottish Studies*, vol. 9, 1965, p. 64.

150. Mulbuie Minute Book, p. 25.

6

'Cromarty a sort of depôt for the whole'

For the earliest peoples of the Cromarty Firth the sea was a highway and a provider. It had been the avenue by which the earliest inhabitants of the region had arrived, and until the coming of all-weather roads and the railway in the nineteenth century it was virtually the only means of transport. The core of this early system of sea transport was the ferries that criss-crossed the Firth and also provided access to the outside world.

The earliest documented Cromarty Firth ferry was the Nigg-Cromarty crossing, but Inverbreakie (Invergordon), Alness and Foulis were probably all ancient crossing places.[1] Following the building of Dunskeath Castle in 1179 the ferry revenues were assigned to the upkeep of the castle; hence the name 'King's Ferry' that came to be applied to the crossing.[2] Nigg remained perhaps the most heavily used of the Cromarty Firth ferries until modern times, only yielding pride of place to Inverbreakie with the rise of Invergordon and the construction there of Thomas Telford's ferry slipways in 1817. Used in conjunction with the Kessock or Ardersier ferries Invergordon ferry cut a full day from the journey between Invergordon and Nairn or Inverness.

The Telford piers at Invergordon and Balblair were an improvement, although at certain states of the tide passengers still often had to disembark well out into the Firth and either wade or ride horses ashore (Fig. 35). As late as 1825 passengers on the Nigg-Cromarty ferry had to be brought ashore in the traditional Highland manner, on the backs of women who waded out to meet the boat.[3]

Beyond the confines of the Firth there were, certainly by the middle ages, growing links with other Scottish ports. Indeed, in some senses the sixteenth and seventeenth century Cromarty Firth was the northernmost outlier of the east coast 'Golden Fringe' of trading burghs and harbours that extended from the Firth of Forth to Aberdeen and beyond.

In 1524 a merchant named 'Oliver' and the master of a ship 'from Flanders or Celand' [Zeeland] were arrested and clapped in Cromarty Castle by a group of 'friends and servants' of the laird, Thomas Urquhart, because the unfortunate Flemings did not have a safe-conduct from the boy-king, James V.[4] The Regent Albany had recently concluded an alliance with France which cut Scotland off from her major trading partners in the Low Countries. The fate of the Flemish mariners, their ship and cargo, is unknown. In fact the arrest looks suspiciously like a 'put up job' with the laird of Cromarty using his office as hereditary Sheriff and his admiralty rights, and the excuse provided by Albany's policies, as a pretext to seize the ship's cargo. Whatever the truth behind the story of the Zeeland ship, however, the incident provides a striking

143

35. Tidewaiters at Invergordon.

illustration of the kind of trading links there were between the Cromarty Firth and North Sea ports from a very early period.

It may be, too, that such Low Country ships first brought Protestant ideas into the Cromarty Firth. Protestant books had certainly appeared in East Coast ports further south in the early 1520s. In the year following Urquhart's seizure of the Zeeland ship the Scottish Parliament passed its first act against Lutheran heresies.

The evidence for foreign trade around the Cromarty Firth in the sixteenth and seventeenth centuries is sparse but there is no doubt of its regularity and importance. In 1624 two new church bells for Tain and Nigg were ordered from Middleburg in Holland. The bells arrived safely in Cromarty but in the course of a drunken fight on Nigg ferry the bell destined for Tain fell overboard and was never recovered.[5] The ancient Scandinavian trade, too, continued to be important throughout the seventeenth century. For example, in 1621 the bailies of Tain entered into an agreement with an agent in Bergen for a shipment of bere[6] and in 1685 an Edinburgh merchant chartered a ship to Lord Tarbat to sail from Edinburgh to Tarbatness and thence to Bergen.[7]

There was, of course, the other side of the trading equation: local merchants who went abroad. The most famous was 'Polander' Ross, but there were others. James Mowat, merchant in Paris, who acted as foreign banker (in the days before banks) for Sir George Mackenzie in the 1660s and '70s, may well have been a local man.[8] In the following century there was James Baylie of Migdie, who became a merchant in Rotterdam but returned home before his death in 1747 and lies buried under an elegant headstone in Kilmuir Easter church. He was but one member of a diaspora of local merchants, managers and brokers that began in the seventeenth century and exploded after 1707. By the 1780s, for example, Robertson of Kindeace had a son in London, another in India, while a third was managing an estate in the West Indies and a fourth was in business in New York.[9]

By the seventeenth century much of the trade around the Firth was being organised by local lairds bent on exploiting the resources of their estates to support increasingly ambitious and elaborate life-styles. The leader in these developments was Lord Tarbat, who set the pace for his fellow Easter Ross lairds. In the last decades of the seventeenth century, for example, he was exploiting his woods to the full[10] and his neighbours at Balnagown and Pitcalnie followed suit. By the early eighteenth century there were a number of local timber mills[11] where wood shipped from the surviving stands of native forest, such as Strathoykel, was cut up and planed. Some of this timber was used locally, but by this time wood was also regularly being shipped to Edinburgh and London, and southern agents were coming into the region to negotiate contracts for timber shipments.[12] Shortly after the Union of 1707 the Laird of Pitcalnie wrote from London to ask the Laird of Culrain if he would sell his oak woods cheaply, since he was 'thinking of trying an iron mill' and needed a cheap local source of charcoal.[13] Nothing came of the idea.

Nevertheless, Pitcalnie's plans are indicative of a growing desire on the part of local lairds and a growing body of professional entrepreneurs such as William Forsyth, the Cromarty merchant, to create local industries. There was already the distillery at Ferintosh and later in the eighteenth century Forsyth's initiative, and his position as local agent for the British Linen Company, would lead to the establishment of linen spinning and bleaching at a number of places around the Firth. But perhaps the earliest example of industrial processes concerned the salting and export of fish.

Salted fish, mostly salmon, was being shipped out of the Cromarty Firth regularly from at least the sixteenth century, but since the whitefish and salmon trade was a monopoly of royal burghs and salting required some expertise, the trade was usually farmed out by local lairds. The common practice was for merchants to pay in advance for the catch, or to take a tack [lease] of the laird's boats or yairs for a specific period. In 1679, for example, Sir George Mackenzie granted a tack of 'my fishe boat of Castlehaven alias Portmahomack as my brother Keneth had . . .' to a local laird.[14]

This tack was a simple agreement but increasingly the granting of fishing rights, especially the highly desirable Conon salmon fisheries, became a complex and lucrative business. In 1700, for example, Lord Tarbat farmed out his salmon boats on the Conon to the son of the provost of Inverness, for £172/2/6 Scots.[15]

However, the staple in local trade was bere and oats. Doubtless there had always been local coastal shipping of grain around the Cromarty and Moray Firths. It seems likely that in the seventeenth century the bulk of the Cromarty Firth's grain exports went to European North Sea and Baltic ports rather than elsewhere in Scotland.[16] From the middle of the seventeenth century, however, Tarbat and other lairds were making regular arrangements for the shipping south of local produce, much of it bought up by brewers and maltsters in and around Edinburgh.[17]

The trade followed a seasonal pattern. Rents were paid at Candlemas (2 February) and the grain was gathered into the girnels. The local chamberlains in Easter Ross would then report on the size and quality of the year's crops. By March Lord Tarbat and the others would be negotiating with local and southern merchants and brewers for the sale of their crop. Usually the laird was responsible for chartering the ships to carry his grain south. The normal agreement stipulated that the skipper would bring his ship to port, usually Dingwall, Nigg Bay, Cromarty or Portmahomack, and take on board a specified amount of grain during ten weather-work days.[18] In the meantime the estate chamberlains would have had the crop bagged and engaged local shore workers to transport the cargo out to the ships. After the construction of Lord Tarbat's harbour at Portmahomack in the early 1690s ships could be berthed there but the practice elsewhere was for ships to be beached and loaded at low tide. Sometimes things did not go according to plan; for example, there was the unfortunate *Rose of Aberdour* which beached on Nigg Sands in 1690. Her master, Robert Bell, later claimed that Tarbat's chamberlain had 'put him off from time to time without ane reason . . . so that he could not get any cargo.'[19] Elsewhere ships might be loaded in deep water anchorages such as Cromarty Roads. In 1636, for example, John Johnstone, ferryman at Cromarty, was paid for transporting crops to a ship anchored off shore.[20] Once loaded the ships set off south.

In return, luxuries, manufactured goods and such necessities as salt, lime and coal were shipped north.[21] The building of New Tarbat also acted as a stimulus for trade, for not only did southern ships arrive with fixtures and furniture for the new house, they also brought north men with new skills such as painters, glaziers, gardeners and nurserymen.[22] Lord Tarbat's many enterprises also stimulated local enterprise. Alexander Urquhart, master of *The Blessing* of Cromarty, became a prominent local skipper in part through a profitable charter business he ran for Tarbat. Urquhart first appears in 1675 engaged in a coastal trade bringing Caithness and Dunrobin slates to the Cromarty Firth for use at New Tarbat.[23] By 1685 he had the contract to transport south Tarbat's entire 1684 grain crop, which included 400 bolls of bere and 72 bolls of meal. Urquhart was careful to reserve his perquisites as Captain of one boll of meal and eight gallons of ale.[24]

There is some evidence that by the early eighteenth century this southern grain trade was falling off and would not revive until mid century when Britain would change from being a surplus to a deficit grain producer.[25] On the other hand, there was growing local trade. From the late seventeenth century the distillery at Ferintosh provided a local market for grain as did, after 1748, the building and garrisoning of Fort George.

Indeed, by the early eighteenth century not only is there evidence of extensive local trade but it is also possible to see in some detail how it worked. Local landlords still chartered ships or maintained small coasters of their own.

One such was the new boat bought by Pitcalnie's factor in 1752, after the wreck at Cadboll of the laird's previous boat, while carrying bere from Portmahomack to Beauly:

> [The] Crew and their ffamelys were starveing and declared they'd be forced to goe elsewhere to find a way to Labour for their Bread . . . I went to Cromarty and Bought a handsome new Boat. It was made in August last by Williamson in Chanorie [sic]. All her keels and intimber are Oak and very strong and well built. She carries 20 bolls and six men can draw her anywhere . . .[26]

In the seventeenth and early eighteenth centuries the bulk of external trade was in the hands of Inverness and Elgin merchants. Tain and Dingwall were small, local centres with little commerce beyond their immediate hinterlands.

Another aspect of local trade was the control of the customs service by local lairds. The tenure of the office of Inverness Collector of Customs by successive members of the Gordon family of Invergordon was most lucrative. There were regular claims by other lairds that the family deliberately lured ships onto the rocks in order to be able to claim their cargoes as wrecks.

Following the Union of Parliament in 1707 the Scottish Customs were reorganised on a more professional basis. The records of the Inverness area show Cromarty's exciseable exports and imports to be flour and salt, much of it from Spain and Portugal. The arrival of a trading ship was the signal for local agents to ride posthaste to Inverness. Thus, early in July 1716 the Inverness salaries incidents' book reports a payment of eighteen pence to 'David Simson for coming express 12 miles and ferrys from Cromarty advising of a Danish ship being on ye coast with wine brandy and salt'. An official would then be sent out to deal with the cargo. The regular arrival of the 'East Country Fleet' (the Dutch fishing busses) meant that an official from Inverness and several boatmen would travel to the burgh for the duration of the stay. Other 'tydesmen' were sent out to patrol the coasts of the Moray Firth against smugglers.[27]

Cromarty grew in importance in the first half of the eighteenth century to become 'the most active centre of population in the whole area' acting as 'the entrepôt port for much of the north of Scotland . . .'[28] and there is evidence of a full-time customs officer in the town by the early 1740s.

The man who, more than any other, was responsible for beginning this great change was the merchant William Forsyth. He represents a new, professional and entrepreneurial spirit but his father was the real pioneer. James Forsyth had come from Moray to work as a mason in Cromarty during its first great herring boom in the reign of Queen Anne. He opened a shop in the town and his son William took over the business following his death in 1739. By this time the herring had disappeared and Cromarty was in decline as a fishing port. William Forsyth, however, realised that:

Cromarty, although a bad field for the retail trade, might prove an excellent one for the merchant. Its valuable though at this time neglected harbour seemed suited to render it, what it afterwards became, the key of the adjacent country . . . The bold and original plan of the young trader, therefore, was to render Cromarty a sort of depôt for the whole, to furnish the shopkeepers of the several towns with the commodities in which they dealt, and to bring to the very doors of the proprietors the various foreign articles of comfort and luxury with which commerce alone could supply them. And launching boldly into the speculation at a time when the whole country seemed asleep around him, he purchased a freighting boat for the navigation of the three friths (*sic*), and hired a large sloop for trading with Holland and the commercial towns in the south.[29]

Unlike the Cromarty skipper Alexander Urquhart, however, Forsyth was not just content to carry cargoes; he set about generating business by the creation of local industry. He attempted to revive the herring industry by gathering together a group of local gentlemen and merchants who, amongst other things, offered a bounty on the first barrel of herring caught each year in the Moray Firth. The scheme failed when the herring once more deserted the local seas. Forsyth was more successful in his encouragement of local kelp gatherings but the real basis of Cromarty's economic take-off under his direction was the flax spinning. Flax was imported, probably from the Baltic,[30] and then distributed in Forsyth's boats to local spinners and weavers. From at least the 1750s flax spun in Cromarty and around the rest of the Firth was being shipped out in Forsyth's boats.

Forsyth's enterprise laid the basis, after 1772, for the developments of George Ross the new laird of Cromarty, 'probably the most far-sighted and unselfish landlord to hold property in the area . . .'[31] Ross's new pier built in 1785, his ropeworks, brewery, nail and spade factory and the export trade in pork which he encouraged added to Cromarty's growing importance as an industrial entrepôt, a position reinforced by the reappearance in the 1790s of 'those Heaven directed strangers, the Herrings.'[32] At the end of the eighteenth century Cromarty reached the apogee of its prosperity and it took on something of the appearance it has retained to the present day (Fig. 36): a grid of streets with the fishertown and small houses for the workers and artisans punctuated by larger classical houses lived in by men such as Forsyth.

This revival did not last. Across the Cromarty Firth the town of Invergordon was, by the early nineteenth century, growing in importance. Robert Southey, who stopped there for breakfast in 1817, called it 'an ugly village in an important situation' and he was absolutely right. Despite its lack of a proper harbour, Invergordon's more sheltered position within the Firth and its location at the centre of the complex of the richest and largest of the new farms were important elements in its growing commercial predominance. Invergordon's rise as a port (Fig. 37) was also partially due to the improvement in land communications. The town was on the main route between Dingwall and Tain. An indication of the change in the relative positions and prosperity

36. Church Street in Cromarty with Hugh Miller's house in the centre.

of Cromarty and Invergordon may be seen in the comparative rentals for the two parishes as revealed in the *Old* and *New Statistical Accounts*. Cromarty's rose from £2,500 in the 1790s to £3,300 in the 1830s; the valuation of Rosskeen rose 350% to £7,000 over the same period.

Not even the slump in agricultural prices after the end of the Napoleonic Wars could halt this progress, which was enthusiastically encouraged by the laird, MacLeod of Cadboll, who owned the harbour. Two stone piers (one straight, the other L-shaped) were completed in 1828 just in time for the beginnings of steam navigation.[33] By the mid 1830s there were regular steamship links between Invergordon, Inverness, Aberdeen, Leith and London as well as the west coast of Scotland. The *Duchess of Sutherland* sailed once a fortnight to London, and there were plans for a second ship for the route. The *Brilliant* sailed once a week between Invergordon, Cromarty, Inverness, Aberdeen and Leith, while the rather inaptly named *Velocity* plied the same route once a fortnight.[34] In addition, at least one of the thrice-weekly steamers through the Caledonian Canal (which had opened in 1822) to Inverness, continued on to Cromarty and Invergordon.[35] Local farmers began to use steamships, or specially chartered sailing ships, to transport grain, potatoes and livestock south to Edinburgh and London markets.

The stone piers of Invergordon were found to be inadequate virtually as soon as they were completed and a wooden extension added in the mid-1830s to allow a draught of ten feet at ebb tide was so badly engineered that it was useless. In 1857–8 two large wooden piers were added at a cost of £5,000.[36] Even these piers were found to be inadequate for some steamers and within a few months of completion there had been several groundings, and steamships often still preferred to offload goods and passengers standing off from the pier.[37]

On 28 June 1858 an indignant letter appeared in the *Invergordon Times*:

> Sir,
> This fine steamer landed a considerable number of passengers at this port on Saturday last. It is a subject of comment and remark that she has not as yet availed herself of the facility offered by the new jetty. Among the passengers were several children and delicate ladies, to whom the passage from the South was nothing to the annoyance and anxiety of descending the side of the vessel, and being landed in an open boat during the rough weather of Saturday . . . There is something wrong here which demands explanation from the Company.
> Your obedient Servant,
> A Party Interested

It was the coming of the railway in 1863 that supplied the final element in Invergordon's takeover from Cromarty as the premier port not only within the Firth but for the whole of Easter Ross as well. Within days of the line opening to Invergordon a regular coach link began to run between Cromarty and Balblair to connect with the Invergordon Ferry crossing; Cromarty had become a 'feeder' into the main port for the region.[38] Later, this link would be superseded by a direct ferry between Cromarty and Invergordon, which was running by at least 1872.[39]

Despite the revival of fishing at Cromarty and the building in 1880 of a new pier that extended twenty feet out from the breakwater to allow loading in

37. Invergordon from the harbour.

most states of the tide, Cromarty was no longer the main port for the Firth. Even the timbers used in the construction of the new pier had to be floated down from Invergordon.[40]

Aside from Invergordon and Cromarty a number of other harbour works were completed within the Firth during the nineteenth century. As early as 1724 the Dingwall town authorities had petitioned the Convention of Royal Burghs for help in building a harbour. A small one was built at the mouth of the Peffery, but this 'harbour of sorts' was hampered by the mud-flats of the upper Cromarty Firth.[41] In the early nineteenth century, therefore, an Act of Parliament for the construction of a canal was passed and work began in 1815. By the time it was completed two years later over £4,000 had been spent on diverting part of the River Peffery to allow access by small craft to Peter's Bridge, close to the centre of the town.[42] The canal was opened amidst scenes of great excitement, with bands, speeches and a banquet. Ships carrying timber and grain, coal and lime did use the canal and its small piers, but within a few years the channel was beginning to silt up and the sea wall was being worn away by the action of the tides. In 1824 a further Act of Parliament vested control of the canal and harbour of Dingwall in a Board of Commissioners but by the mid-1830s the harbour was generating only £130 a year, which was insufficient to keep the canal in repair. In 1856, when bids were taken at Dingwall for the normally lucrative office of Collector of Shore Dues, there were no takers.[43] In 1868 work began on deepening the canal and building a 151 foot extension of the existing piers in Danzig timber[44] but these improvements were subverted by the coming of the railway. Not only did it take away traffic, but the construction of a railway bridge across the Peffery rendered the upper part of the Dingwall Canal useless.[45] The Harbour Commissioners found costs outrunning their resources. The contractor for the work was still trying to recoup his money fourteen years later.[46]

Aside from these major works, a number of other, smaller, piers were constructed around the Firth in the first half of the century. Balintraid, with its associated workers' cottages, was built by Thomas Telford in 1817 primarily as a fishing port, although a small amount of import and export trade was also carried on there.[47] Further up the Firth a pier was built at Belleport, for the export of wood from Ardross, after its purchase by Alexander Matheson in 1845.[48]

These piers and harbours were an integral part of the economic life of the region. Not only did they allow quicker communications and access for local products to external markets, they also opened up Easter Ross to outside manufactures. Thus, for example, when the new extensions to Invergordon harbour were opened in 1858 the occasion was marked by the arrival of a new steamship, *The Dundalk*, carrying the first Hormby portable threshing machine to be seen in the region. This 'threefold novelty' attracted a large crowd to see the boat arrive in harbour.[49]

Some idea of the impact of the increasing diversity and sophistication of Cromarty Firth trade and transportation can be glimpsed in the pages of a farm diary kept by Munro of Teaninich. Like many other local farmers Munro of Teaninich shipped wheat, oats, wool, sheep, cattle and salmon. He also regularly shipped whisky from his distillery to the south. In March 1848, for example, he noted: 'sent 60 hogs to London for sale by the steamer . . .'[50] and a year later he wrote sadly that an accident on a ship taking his beasts south meant that they were injured and did not sell well.[51]

The growth in trade meant that 'southern manufacturers, for the first time, [were able] to make a major penetration of the Easter Ross market, all but destroying the locally based rural industries and greatly increasing the area's dependence on the outside world.'[52] One such local industry to disappear was agricultural tile-making, so that in 1849 Teaninich had to import bricks and tiles from Aberdeen for his new hot house at Coul.

Virtually the only local industry to survive, and benefit by easier access to markets, was distilling. In 1839 another distillery was built, at Dalmore. Distilleries depended on outside sources of coal and, occasionally, barley and malt. The Teaninich diary is full of references to coal shipments both for the distillery and domestic use. Sometimes the coal boats dumped their cargoes on the sands below the farm; often they would come into the pier at Dalmore (Belleport) and a small procession of farm carts would be sent out to collect the coal. In August 1848 Teaninich wrote: 'coal from Captain Hall at Dalmore to farm servants to the house . . .'[53]

James Hall of Belleport (Dalmore) was born about 1795 at Limekilns, Fife, and had first visited the Cromarty Firth on an apprentice voyage.[54] He must have been attracted by the growing prosperity of the Firth and after he gained his first command he began to establish trading links with the region before coming to live there in the mid 1830s. Based at Belleport, Captain Hall, 'Coal and Wood Merchant', built up a thriving business as a shipowner, merchant and local agent. He exported grain, livestock and timber and imported coal, lime, guano and other fertilisers as well as manufactured goods. Hall regularly carried cargoes for farmers such as Teaninich and Andrew Baxter at Rosskeen Farm, and also exported wood from the Ardross, Balnagown and Novar estates. One of the mainstays of Hall's business was the export of locally cut pitprops to the mines of County Durham in return for coal and lime.

Like the agricultural improvers before him Captain Hall named his fleet of ships after his family; *William, Jane, The Sisters* and the *Hall*. The last named was built at Sunderland[55] but some of the smaller sailing ships in Hall's fleet were built locally. In 1841, for example, the *Anne* of 120 tons and built of Novar timber was launched at Belleport.[56]

James Hall died in 1864, a year after the railroad arrived at Invergordon. In a way his death was symbolic of a changing order. Captain Hall was the last in a line of the old merchant captains of the Cromarty Firth that stretched back to Alexander Urquhart. Hall's house, with its large glass windows looking out to Belleport Pier and the Firth beyond, survives today as a witness to a vanished way of life.

It may not have been clear to all just what kinds of changes the railway was to bring. During its construction materials were supplied by sea: there are accounts of railway sleepers, wagons, coal, lime, slates and timber regularly being offloaded at beaches and piers around the Firth. For a time local shipping boomed. Then there was a period of sharp decline as the novelty of the railway consumed everyone's attention. By midsummer 1863 the shipowners began to fight back by drastically lowering their freight charges and, later, their passenger rates, as well. Shipping slowly revived as it was realised that it still remained a cheaper, if not a quicker, method of transport; the rail fare to Edinburgh was 10/— while the same trip by steamer could cost as little as 5/—.[57]

Within a few years some of the railroad euphoria had worn off; the practices and prices of the local railway company aroused some hostility. When in 1876, for example, there were yet further plans to revive Dingwall Harbour the *Invergordon Times* remarked that such developments were to be encouraged since sea transport cost so much 'less than . . . the all-engrossing railway.'[58]

In fact, the later decades of the nineteenth century were the great days of Cromarty Firth shipping. In addition to the regular steamboats there were hundreds of other sailing ships calling in and out of the Firth at all times of the year. In the depths of the winter of 1856 the *Invergordon Times* reported that:

No fewer than sixteen vessels ten of which are now in harbour, have called at the port within the last week. Some are loading with wood, corn and potatoes, while others are engaged in discharging coals, meal, etc. The harbour has an unusually busy appearance.[59]

Local exports also included grain and whisky. Imports commonly included fertilisers (much of it imported South American guano for the fertiliser mill in Invergordon), Baltic timber, tiles, coal, salt and luxuries such as books, drapery, clothes and musical instruments. By the 1860s, for example, shops in Invergordon were selling ladies' hats from London and Paris.[60] In addition to regular steam and sailing vessels, there were also increasing numbers of excursion steamers and pleasure boats, bringing groups of tourists and day visitors. One such was the steamer *Queen* from Findhorn which brought a pleasure party of tourists to Invergordon in July 1856.[61] Later, excursions would run on local holidays or to take spectators to such local events as the Black Isle Show.[62] The growth of steam navigation and easier access to the south created a small land boom in Easter Ross.[63] and many wealthy new landowners and visitors came into the Firth on their private yachts. One such was Prince Napoleon who, in July 1856, arrived to meet his yacht anchored in the Firth. The visit caused some excitement — and some chagrin — as the *Invergordon Times* reported:

> He came from Inverness in a close carriage, drove straight down to the quay and immediately embarked for his yacht, not even inspecting the town, which some of the inhabitants think so much of.[64]

Not even the agricultural slump of the 1870s and '80s seems to have had a negative effect on local shipping except that now agricultural produce was often being imported rather than exported. American grain was delivered at Dalmore distillery and Teaninich imported Baltic grain in 1881.[65] In 1882 local farmers made at least one attempt to reverse this trend when they chartered a vessel to carry local potatoes to New York because the British potato market had collapsed.[66]

But the prosperity of Cromarty Firth shipping was gained at a price. There were frequent accidents and sinkings; for example, the sloop *Friendship*, that sailed from Invergordon loaded with guano and bound for Fraserburgh, early in February 1858, disappeared without trace.[67]

Without a doubt the most famous shipwreck victim in the Cromarty Firth was Prince Henry of Prussia who was cast ashore at Nigg in May 1891. He and his bedraggled companions were turned away from Dunskeath House before being given refuge by Mrs Christina Ross at the Ferry Inn. She was later presented with a scroll and photograph of the young prince, recording the event.

Shipping on the east coast of Scotland had to contend with one of the most dangerous and inhospitable coasts in Europe, despite attempts to make local navigation safer.

The first lighthouse in the region was built at Tarbatness in 1830 by Robert Stevenson and was the highest lighthouse then built in Scotland. It was said that in a gale the tower swayed enough to stop a pendulum clock. Stevenson's son, Alan, designed the two other local lights, both opened in 1846, at Cromarty and Chanonry Point.

It was probably during these middle decades of the nineteenth century that the local Customs and the Coast Guard were put on their modern footing. There had been customs officers, of a sort, in the region since the late seventeenth century. By the mid eighteenth century officers were active in Cromarty and the seaward villages, attempting to control smuggling and illicit whisky distilling.[68] By the 1820s there was a customs office in Cromarty, and an officer at Alness to oversee bonding and excise at Teaninich distillery.

The Cromarty Customs Office may have been established after the old system of riding or preventive officers had been changed into the Coastguard in 1822. The new organisation was, initially, under the control of the Customs Service (a few years later it would be transferred to the Admiralty) and had two branches, cruisers and riding officers, both charged with stamping out smuggling and dealing with wrecks.[69] By 1844 Cromarty was one of ten Coastguard districts in Scotland and had a complement of eight officers and men.[70] By the middle decades of the century the Coastguard was also becoming involved with setting up lifeboat stations. Although the first Royal National Life Boat stations in Scotland were set up at Fraserburgh (1858) and Lossiemouth (1859) and by the early 1860s there were further north-eastern lifeboats at Thurso, Banff, and Buckie,[71] the first station at Cromarty was run by the Coastguard. In 1867 a 'new lifeboat' was delivered there by the Coast Guard cutter *Eagle*. The *Invergordon Times* described the Cromarty boat as being twenty-four feet long and four feet wide, with an air-tight inside cylinder fore and aft, and fitted with two masts and pulling four oars.[72]

In addition to lifeboat stations, the government was actively interested in creating 'harbours of refuge' along the dangerous east coast of Scotland. A Parliamentary Select Committee was set up to look into the question in 1857. Although some of the witnesses claimed that the Cromarty Firth already served in this capacity, there were problems. For instance, its 'inland' position took longer to reach and the general direction of autumn winds made it difficult for sailing ships in certain parts of the Moray Firth and beyond to run through the Sutors into the safe waters beyond.[73] In 1859, therefore, the Committee recommended the creation of a harbour of refuge at Wick and another at Peterhead.[74] This decision may, in fact, have helped to ensure that the nineteenth century fisheries in and around the Cromarty Firth never achieved their full potential. The failure to be designated an official harbour of refuge was only one part of the long and chequered history of Cromarty Firth fishing.

From earliest times the sea was a source of food for the people of the Firth. The shell-middens found around Nigg Bay are evidence of prehistoric exploitation of the mussel scalps and oyster beds that remained an important source of food and bait until well into the nineteenth century. There was also some kind of deep sea line and net fishing, both within the Firth itself and around the Sutors, from a very early period.

Fishing and fishing rights formed an important part of the feudal rights of local landlords. In 1698 the charter granting Sir George Mackenzie the barony of New Tarbat included:

> fishings . . . together with the salmon-fishing, and power of killing and catching other fishes, as well small as great . . . as well upon the sands of Nigg as upon and near the said lands of Milnton, with power . . . to have and build yairs and stells [stake nets] in any part of the said lands and of having and keeping boats, nets and other materials for that effect . . . and all and whole the full power warrant, right, and title of planting and preserving oyster scalps, one or more, within the Bay of Cromarty, from the two Sutors thereof as far as Cullicudden, on both sides of the said bay of Cromarty, and particularly within the barony of Tarbat, with the sole privilege of fishing and taking oysters within the said bounds . . .[75]

This unusually comprehensive grant was to be exploited fully by Mackenzie and was to influence the fishing history of the Cromarty Firth for several centuries.

In the seventeenth century, however, fishing around the Firth was an ill-organised and *ad hoc* affair. Herring, unless it was salted, spoiled quickly. Both it and whitefish had to be sold locally. Nevertheless, it was clear that fishing was potentially very lucrative. The Dutch had had a large, and profitable, fishing fleet in Scottish waters from at least the fifteenth century. By the seventeenth century they were sending out large, covered boats, an early form of factory ship called 'busses', that were capable of staying at sea for up to two months and had facilities for salting down the fish on board.[76]

By the seventeenth century (and probably much earlier) there were a number of fishing settlements within the Cromarty Firth at such places as Balnapaling, Balnabruaich (at Nigg), Portleich (Barbaraville), Balintraid and, most important of all, in Cromarty itself. Nothing is known of their origins, whereas the fishing communities at Inver, Portmahomack, Rockfield, Balintore, Hilton of Cadboll and Shandwick, seem to have been deliberately created. Certainly Hilton was originally the home of the fishers who supplied the Abbey of Fearn (and lived rent free) before the Reformation.[77] An earlier name for Balintore, *Port an Ab* (Abbot's haven) suggests that Fearn Abbey may have also been the original founder of this seaboard community. The settlement of Inver may date from the late seventeenth century; in 1678 Sir George Mackenzie complained that Robert Gray of Arboll and others were building small 'fisher houses and bothies' on the lands of Lochsline and Inver.[78]

From the first these seaboard fishing villages were distinctive communities, set apart from their countryside neighbours not just because of the peculiar demands of fishing, but also possibly because the lairds introduced their populations from outside the Cromarty Firth region. The strong local tradition that common fisher names such as Patience, Fidler, and Hossack were introduced in the seventeenth century may have a basis in fact, although whether they were originally Cromwellian soldiers is another matter. Certainly such settlement by outsiders took place later; a number of Mackays, displaced by the Sutherland Clearances of the early nineteenth century, settled in the fishing villages.

Fishing was a livelihood that consumed all the energies of the community. The men crewed the boats and their sons would join them from about the age of fourteen. The women were responsible for collecting bait and attaching it to the lines; the fishwives of the seaboard villages regularly walked the six miles to Nigg Sands and back to collect mussels in their creels (Fig. 38). They also helped to launch and beach the boats, as well as carrying the men out to the vessels. Once the catch came in they gutted and dried or smoked the fish and, in many cases, sold the catch to local merchants or from door to door. Even until the late 1930s fishwives from Cromarty and the seaboard villages tramped the country selling their menfolk's catch. Because fishing involved the whole family as an economic unit, marriages tended to take place early and within the community. Families were large.

James Cameron, the Tain surgeon who reported on local conditions for Edwin Chadwick's *Report on the sanitary condition of the labouring population of Scotland* (1842), said of the fishers of Shandwick and Balintore:

> They have the reputation of being a very prolific race; intermarriages with the rural populations are very uncommon; and it is seldom that the children deviate from the perilous craft of their fathers. They are characterised by peculiar notions and practices; and they have a certain feudal spirit, or *pride of order* which tends to preserve them as a *separate* community, and to promote concord among themselves.[79]

Part of this 'pride of order' was a deep religious faith. The fisherfolk were conscientious and enthusiastic church goers and although illiterate in English, they regularly read their Gaelic *New Testament*. The various schisms in the nineteenth century Church of Scotland left their mark on the villages so that by the 1890s all the inhabitants of Hilton and most of Balintore belonged to the Free Church, while the people of Shandwick were United Presbyterians and dates were often reckoned by such events as The Disruption of 1843.[80]

The fisherfolk's religious practices were but one expression of an almost ritualistic view of life: the daily and yearly round of life and work was strictly organised along traditional lines. If certain practices were not followed, bad luck would ensue. At weddings, for example, the actual ceremony had to be preceded by a *reiteach* or covenant and the ceremonial washing of feet on the night before the service. On the day of the marriage the bride's party led the procession since it was believed 'he follows her to-day but she is to follow him afterwards.' The Sunday after the ceremony the couple were 'kirked' and as

38. Fishwife Williamina Vass of Shandwick.

soon as the lengthy sermons were over the couple and their friends quickly marched the long road back to the village; whoever arrived first would 'get the blessing.'[81]

Such superstitious practices grew out of the precarious life of the fisherfolk; everything must be done in proper order so that catastrophe might be prevented. Thus, pointing the index finger at a sailing vessel was considered unlucky, as was the mention of the word 'salmon' while on the way to catch any other kind of fish.

The fishermen's year was highly structured as well. There were, first of all, the various fishing seasons for the herring and the whitefish. These seasons were punctuated by such events as 'ware day', at the beginning of April, when the whole community turned out to gather seaware or kelp to manure their small potato and kail yards. For days before the men would have their usual daily gathering to discuss village affairs, the weather and fishing; everything would be discussed except the coming kelp gathering. Then:

> One of the older men who is recognised as a leader, shouts at the pitch of his voice, in Gaelic, 'To the ware,' and in a moment every capable man and woman are seen rushing, hook in hand and creel on back, in the direction of the rocks. As a rule every householder confines himself to the rocks opposite his own house and any violation of this unwritten law is regarded with the greatest disfavour.[82]

Ware gathering was but part of the seasonal round. As late as 1891 the fisherfolk of Cromarty burned an old boat on Hogmanay, to ensure the return of the sun and the turn of the year[83] and New Year (Old Style) continued to be an important holiday until well into the present century.

It is scarcely surprising that the fisherfolk seemed almost a race apart. The novelist Jane Duncan wrote of the Cromarty fishers:

> I have never later in life, been so aware of the gulf fixed between two races of people as I was of the gulf between the land and sea peoples of Achcraggan [Cromarty]. The land people tended to be tall and fair of skin, the sea people short and sallow, the land people were soft and slow of speech, the sea people shrill-voiced and rapid; to the land people fish were repellently dirty and stinking, to the sea people dirt and stink were the main characteristics of farm animals.[84]

Cromarty was in some respects unusual because its fisherfolk lived within (although sharply separate from) a wider community. The seaboard fishing villages, by contrast, were physically separate from the agricultural areas of their parishes; even the houses faced away from the land and looked out to sea. A common saying went: 'Cod and corn dinna mix.'[85] Moreover, there was little landward contact amongst the three fishing villages themselves: until the present century no road connected Shandwick, Balintore and Hilton.[86]

This physical separation of the fishing villages from the rest of the population may also have been the result of deliberate landlord policy. Certainly in the seventeenth and eighteenth centuries the lairds in the seaboard parishes maintained a close and careful interest over their fisher villages. For example, at the small settlement of *Port an righ*, tucked into the cliffs of the North Sutor, the eighteenth century lairds of Kilravock and Balnagown kept close control of their exclusive rights to kelp and fishing there.[87]

In the late seventeenth century a number of northeastern lairds had even attempted to use the law to tie their fishermen to their jobs:

> Albeit the seamen of fish boats in the North Countrey are by the constant custom of the place tyed and obleidged to the same servitud and service that coall hewars and salters are here in the South, and it is not lawfull to any man whatsomever to resett [to receive stolen goods], harbour or intertain the fishers and boatmen which belong to another . . .[88]

Unlike the parliamentary acts that enslaved the colliers and salters in the course of the seventeenth century, however, the legal position of the fishermen was not reinforced by statute. It was merely customary but no less lacking in force for that.

Elements of the system lingered around the Cromarty Firth into the eighteenth century. In 1713 a group of lairds from the seaward parishes of Tarbat and Tain banded together to enforce an agreement which prevented 'our fishers' from leaving one master's boat for another:

> Therefor to prevent any such trouble or abuses wee severally do agree and condescend that none of any undersubscribing shall allow any of our men now in our possession to work or enter in another boat and if the same shall be done by [without] our knowledge that fisher aggressor shall be punished not only by the master he's bound to serve but also by the heritors or Tacksmen in whose boat he fishes . . .[89]

Throughout most of the eighteenth century fishermen were bound to serve fixed terms on boats provided by the lairds. These boats were locally made and seldom had a keel length of more than fifteen feet. The lack of harbours meant that ships had to be small in order to be beached easily and this in turn limited the range they could fish. Early fishing boats were open decked and although they could have a sail they were usually rowed. One such was the 'Great new boat with hir oars' that Sir John Urquhart of Cromarty ordered (but failed to get delivery of) from a builder in Strathoykell in 1670.[90] As late as the 1790s in the fishertowns of the parish of Tarbat the proprietor still furnished a new fishing boat every seven years although individual fishermen might own smaller inshore yawls. The crews were required to maintain the laird's boat during this term and, in return, they were allowed to keep one fifth of the fish they caught.[91]

Throughout the seventeenth century there had been various attempts to create joint stock companies to capitalise the Scottish fisheries. All these had foundered due to lack of money and endemic political instability. Nothing on this scale would be achieved until the creation of the British Fisheries Society in 1786 although its activities would have little effect around the Cromarty Firth. Some time before this, however, a number of local lairds were attempting to put their fisheries on a more regular and profitable footing. In 1721 the Earl of Cromartie came to an agreement with Thomas Robertson, merchant in Inverness, in which he 'sett [leased] to the said Thomas Robertson . . . his haill fishing boats for fishing of Cod, herring, and other white fishes . . .'[92] The fisheries included those on the earl's lands in Wester Ross where it was said he had between thirty and forty boats; no figures are given for the boats from Milntoun, Tarbatness and Wilkhaven, which were included in the agreement, so the fleets in Easter Ross were presumably smaller and less important.

As the Earl of Cromartie's tack suggests, there were two sorts of fishing in the eighteenth century. The autumn and winter line fishing for haddock, whiting and small fish was carried on close into shore with daily trips to the grounds. During the summer there was drift net fishing for herring somewhat further offshore. Fifteen miles was the outer limit. Because the herring spoiled easily they, too, had to be landed quickly, thus limiting the range of the fishing boats.

Herring fishing was a risky business, for the shoals appeared and disappeared without any apparent reason. In fact, their movements depended on a conjunction of factors including the presence of the plankton on which they fed, as well as currents and water temperature. They wintered in grounds on the edge of the Norwegian deep and came in July to their spawning grounds off the east coast of Scotland. Sometimes the shoals came right into the Cromarty Firth:

> In the autumn of 1780, a body of herrings was seen betwixt the Sutors, swimming up the frith (*sic*) with all the accompaniements of a large shoal, whales, porpoises, and flocks of seagulls. They passed through the roadstead of the port and the strait opposite Invergordon, beating the water for several miles into a foam and giving to it appearance it presents when ruffled by those sudden land squalls which blacken the surface, but die away before they furrow into waves. The shoal took up its spawning ground opposite Ardilly . . . within three miles of Dingwall and was fished in immense quantities within four hundred yards of the shore.[93]

At the very time the Earl of Cromartie was letting his fishings, the fishing fleet of Cromarty was enjoying its first boom: the great period of the 'herring drove.' The focus for the fishery was the Guilliam Bank halfway between Cromarty and Burghead, which attracted herring boats from all parts of Scotland.[94] Then, without warning, the herring left the Bank.

> After a busy and successful fishing, the shoal, as usual left the frith (*sic*) in a single night. Preparations were made for the ensuing season; the season came, but not the herrings; and for more than half a century from this time Cromarty derived scarcely any benefit from its herring fishing.[95]

Despite William Forsyth's attempts to encourage the herring fishing the shoals stayed away from the Cromarty Firth for nearly sixty years. By the mid-eighteenth century some local fishermen were going north to the Caithness fishing grounds, and the booming port of Wick, in pursuit of the elusive fish. In 1780 the herrings returned and then eight years later left the Firth again.[96] The fisherfolk endured a period of real hardship. By the early 1790s there were only three fishing boats (worked by six men) at Hilton, and three boats and a coble at Balintore and these fishermen were being forced to seek their catches further and further offshore.[97]

The herring returned later on in the 1790s and from that time onwards until the late 1820s the herring fishing of the Cromarty Firth was in a fairly prosperous (though fluctuating) condition. The end of the wars with France opened up new markets, especially with Germany, the Baltic and Russia, that were to be the basis for the growth in the Scottish fishing industry. With the development of fishing harbours along the Aberdeenshire coast, the main herring fishing grounds moved south again from Caithness to the Moray Firth.[98]

The Government, anxious to exploit and develop the fisheries, had set up a Scottish Herring Board. Its reports, beginning in 1809, were published in the *Parliamentary Papers* throughout the nineteenth century and provide a vivid and detailed picture of the somewhat chequered history of the fisheries of the Cromarty Firth. Indeed, one of the puzzles of the nineteenth century fisheries of the Cromarty Firth was why, relatively speaking, they were so unimportant. There were a number of developments that passed the Firth by, the creation of harbours of refuge for example, which may help to explain this failure. In the end, however, it may simply be that the region lacked another entrepreneur of the vision of William Forsyth or affluence of George Ross to capitalise the industry adequately. Thus, much of the history of fishing during this period is conditioned by inadequate resources and, it must be said, missed or delayed opportunities.

This failure, however, cannot be laid at the door of Government. By the 1820s a Fisheries Officer was based in Cromarty, with overall responsibility for the dozen or so fishertowns of his district that ringed the coast from Kessock Ferry to Inver. In addition to overseeing the landing, curing and packing of catches, the Fisheries Officer also helped with the administration of the system of branding the fish barrels (to ensure uniformity and quality for the new overseas markets) and administered the bounty paid on each barrel of herring as well as government grants paid to poor fishermen to improve their boats and gear. He also made regular statistical returns and reports. In 1826, the first year for which there are detailed reports for the Cromarty district, there were 284 boats of all sizes manned by nearly 1,300 fishermen and boys. Onshore there were 114 coopers, 22 fishcurers and over 1,000 people worked at gutting and packing in addition to 1,600 other labourers connected with the fishing. Although the figures fluctuate somewhat over the following quarter of a century, the only substantial difference in the figures for 1841 are that over 1,800 people were now employed in the gutting and there were nearly twice the number of labourers as before.

By the early nineteenth century the fishermen of Easter Ross had become owners of their own boats although the lairds continued to be the feudal superiors of the villages in which they lived. The boats themselves were usually owned by four partners. The common practice was for fishcurers to engage boats and their crews before the start of the fishing season, promising to buy the entire catch up to an agreed limit.[99]

Packing and curing were widely dispersed since the fishing boats still had to bring the catch to shore as quickly as possible. There was a fishcuring yard at Portmahomack, with a substation at Balintore, although this had closed down by the early 1840s.[100] With the development of larger and more sophisticated boats that could range over longer distances there was a growing trend towards fewer fish curing yards concentrated in fewer ports. Many local fishermen were cut off from this development by lack of harbours which meant their boats remained uneconomically small. On the other hand, many fishermen from around the Cromarty Firth went to work in other east coast ports or, beginning in the 1840s, journeyed to the growing west coast fisheries in the Minch.

By the early 1840s the average takings for the herring season were £70 per boat, which added to takings at the white fishing could reach £160 for the year's work. This was divided amongst the four owners. From this they commonly had to spend £20 on repairs and equipment for the boats, leaving very little for the support of the large fisher families.[101]

By the end of the 1840s, however, fishing was growing again in prosperity. Not only had the herring reappeared, so unfortunately had foreign fishermen from France, Germany and Scandinavia. It was from this time that Fishery Protection vessels begin to make their appearance in the area. Amongst the first was HMSV *Trident* under the command of Lieutenant Risk, who subsequently commanded other ships. His duties were various, ranging from recovering nets and fishing gear to sorting out problems with the foreign vessels.[102] The paddle steamer fishery protection vessel *Lizard* used the Cromarty Firth as its main coaling station in the early 1860s.

In 1863 herring shoals entered the Cromarty Firth itself once again[103] and there was general prosperity until the end of the decade when the herring again failed and Baltic markets were cut off by the French blockade during the Franco-Prussian War of 1870. But it seems that not even the relatively well-placed fishermen of Cromarty were able to benefit totally from the prosperous fishing of the 1860s.

In 1864 a parliamentary commission was set up to investigate the state of the sea fisheries. The two commissioners who visited Cromarty in late July were James Caird, MP, and the famous scientist, T. H. Huxley. They questioned three fishermen, Donald Manson, Alexander Finlayson, and George

Skinner, and the Fishery officer about their life and work.[104] Haddock was fished during the winter and herring from late July through August. After that the men would go away to the white fishing. A small amount of cod was caught in the autumn using small lines; once they had been plentiful but 'since the Buckie men have fished them in such great quantities they have diminished here.' Another witness blamed the men of Nairn 'who fish now upon our ground [off Tarbat Ness] who were not in the habit of doing so formerly.'

There were, in fact, only three boats engaged by curers for herring from Cromarty; the rest of the local fishing fleet (19 or 20 boats) worked 'upon their own account.' Manson felt that the rates of payment made by the curers were good but, nevertheless, was of the opinion that the fishing was not as good as it had been twenty years ago when 'we got twenty hundredweight of fish in a boat, and in almost a month's work you will hardly find that.'

The evidence given by the Cromarty fishermen catches local fishing at an interesting juncture. Clearly part of the problem was that stocks were being overfished not just by local fleets but by the larger and more sophisticated boats coming out of the east coast English ports and Aberdeenshire. It was about this time, too, that hemp nets began to be replaced by light-weight cotton, thus allowing a longer net train and the potential of a larger catch even for the small and relatively unsophisticated boats of the Cromarty and seaboard fleet. Between 1855 and 1880 the capacity of nets was doubled for the same weight.[105] Nevertheless, the relative smallness and simplicity of the Cromarty boats lay at the root of the problem as one witness made clear when he described an occasion when they had struck a shoal of herring so huge that they were unable to haul it in:

> I suppose we lost about £1,000 in one week what with material and fish . . . the fish struck so heavily that the boats were not able to make anything of them; the fish struck in a body and the nets got filled up with the fish. The consequence was that, as the boats were drifting, the nets became entangled with each other and became immoveable. If the gunboat had been here at that time it would have been of great use.

Another problem was bait. One witness said, 'Bait has got very scarce now . . .' And then, shifting the blame, he continued, 'The Buckie men have made a clean sweep of it . . . with a sort of dredge by means of which they dredge them up.'

For millennia the sands of the Firth, especially at Nigg and New Tarbat, had been the source of fishing bait. But the steady rise of the fishing industry put increasing pressure on this resource. The Earl of Cromartie, acting under the barony charter granted to his ancestor in 1698, effectively farmed the mussel scalps on Nigg Sands throughout the first half of the nineteenth century.[106] The accounts for this period are full not only of references to the prices obtained for mussels, and the cost of restocking the beds, but also the cost of employing men and boats to protect the scalps from poachers. Thus, in 1837 his Lordship's factor made payments to:

> Joseph Hossack, Expenses in ascertaining the bynames of the Cromarty fishers taken on the Scalps. Factor's Expenses with Forester going to Cromarty and capturing six boats with mussells, including spreading the mussells taken back to the Scalps.

Cromartie's desire to exploit a valuable resource collided with the fishermen's increasingly desperate search for bait and their strong belief that they had traditional rights to take mussels from Nigg sands. It was a situation that led to constant skirmishing between Lord Cromartie's agents and fishermen from Cromarty and other ports of the region.

Matters came to a head less than two years after the Parliamentary Commissioners had visited Cromarty, when the Duchess of Sutherland, as heir to the Cromartie estates, took a group of Cromarty fishermen to court. The case hinged on the fact that, although oysters were mentioned in the 1698 charter, mussels were not, and therefore rights to the mussels were still to be determined.[107] Despite the best efforts of the Duchess's lawyers the case was eventually decided in the fishermen's favour by the Court of Session.

The case excited interest in all the fishing communities around Cromarty and there is a local tradition that the fishermen of Avoch even contributed to the defence fund. It was a famous victory but a hollow one, since it solved nothing. The fishermen used the beds but made no attempt to restock. By the time of the Scottish Mussel and Bait Beds Committee report in 1889 the Nigg beds had been almost totally depleted and provided scarcely enough to furnish the thirty Cromarty boats engaged in the inshore line fishing.[108]

Nevertheless, the 1870s were a period of optimism in the local fishing. As a result of the inquiry of 1864 a Fisheries Act had been passed in 1868 that required, amongst other things, the registration of fishing boats as well as certain safety measures of which the most important was the carrying of lights at night. In 1870 the provision of the Factories and Workshop Act was extended to the fishing and helped to regulate conditions.

There was a brief boom in the garvie (sprat) fishing within the Cromarty Firth itself in the early 1870s.[109] In addition to selling them locally, large numbers of barrels were sent off by rail to the London markets; 300 barrels went from Dingwall in mid-February 1872.[110]

At about the same time an attempt was made to exploit the oyster beds of the Cromarty Firth. In the winter of 1871–2 a number of trawlers from Colchester entered the Firth and began to dredge for oysters.[111] The Duchess of Sutherland, whose title to her oyster beds at least was unambiguous, stopped them and then had a number of surveys carried out by English mussel cultivators. Their reports were cautious and not very encouraging;[112] nevertheless, an attempt was made to cultivate oyster beds in the Firth. As late as November 1873 the *Invergordon Times* was claiming that 'there is every hope that the oyster beds will turn out productive and make the enterprise in every way a success.' Nothing seems to have come from the scheme.

By contrast, the deep sea fishing was in a thriving condition in the 1870s. Boats were becoming larger and were now fully decked. Often, too, they were equipped with winches to haul the nets. In 1877 a boat of this type was ordered by a Cromarty fisherman from a Fraserburgh builder at a cost of £250. The *Ross-shire Journal* commented on the event as a 'sign of prosperity'.[113] But on the whole the boats remained small and the town of Cromarty was losing its position as the head port of the region to Avoch. In 1881 a special survey of boats in the fishing ports of the Cromarty area was carried out and printed in the annual report in the *Parliamentary Papers*. Avoch had 31 first class boats and 36 second class boats, compared to Cromarty's 18 and 25. For whatever reason the fishermen of Avoch were investing in larger boats that gave them access to the more distant fisheries and markets and it is from about this time that Avoch's position as the main fishing port for the region was established.[114]

By the early 1880s the market was over-supplied with herring. Between 1884 and 1886, as a result of record catches and the imposition of higher import duties in the main European markets, herring prices fell catastrophically. Because of the slump the herring curers ended the usual practice of buying catches at prices agreed and fixed before the season opened and began, instead, daily pierhead auctions of catches. In turn, the boatowners ended the old system of fixed wages and payment became a small proportion of the sale.

Yet as early as 1878 the *Ross-shire Journal* reported that no curing or engaging was taking place around the Firth because of the failure of the fishing.[115] There was also growing competition from Scandinavian fisheries so the high stocks meant that prices dropped further until the herring market failed completely.

Long before that time, however, the fishermen of the coastal villages had been in growing difficulties which by the early 1880s were combined with a rising militancy that owed a good deal to the crofters' example. In fact in 1883 a group of four hundred fishermen from Hilton, Balintore and Park, and Shandwick had presented a petition to the Napier Commission.[116] They claimed that they had very little land for growing crops and had to depend on the fishing but they were hampered by the lack of a suitable harbour or piers. This meant they could not use sea-going boats except at the time of the herring or when stationed in other harbours. The rest of the year they used small boats which had to be hauled beyond the water line at the end of fishing. The Commission's report included the recommendation that a harbour be built on this coast.[117]

In December 1884 a meeting was held in the Temperance Hall, Dingwall, attended by fishermen and their representatives from all around the Cromarty

Firth. The focus for discontent was the introduction of steam trawling, which local fishermen claimed was threatening the white fishing by destroying spawn and over-fishing.[118] Early in the new year further meetings were held in the villages of Portmahomack and Hilton. William Grant of Portmahomack claimed to have lost twenty-five shillings worth of lines to the trawlers: 'I have brought up fourteen of a family on one hook, and now I cannot keep myself and the cat.' Hugh Skinner of Inver claimed that he now had to go halfway to Buckie to find fish whereas 'my father never went three miles off Tarbatness.' He claimed that the fish had only moved away about four years ago when the steam trawlers came.

A few days later a more 'enthusiastic' meeting of between 200 and 300 fishermen was held at Hilton; the message was the same. Before 1878 whitefish had been caught in great quantities and since then catches had fallen so badly that the practice of engaging had been discontinued.[119]

Feelings against trawlers ran so high that late in January that year the master of an Aberdeen trawler was assaulted in the streets of Invergordon.[120] But steam trawlers were merely a focus for other grievances and problems, including what was probably the real problem — overfishing. By February a realisation was dawning that the problem was a good deal more complex than simply that created by the trawlers, although that was serious enough. The scale of the new fishing meant that the seaboard fishers were less and less able to compete. Boats and equipment had deteriorated and the fishermen could not afford to replace them on a scale sufficient to compete with the increasingly large and sophisticated trawlers that came north from Yarmouth and Aberdeen each season. At the end of the Hilton meeting Mr Wallace of Tulloch had proposed a subscription to buy a large boat for local use. Within a few weeks there were plans afoot to buy two large boats for £500, but eventually this idea was abandoned due to the lack of harbour accommodation.[121]

The condition of the Cromarty Firth fisherfolk became increasingly desperate. In 1885 Monro of Allan and the Inspector of the Poor had gone to the seaboard villages and found that the people had 'nothing to live upon.' In April of the same year the United Presbyterian minister the Reverend Mr Robson of Inverness urged his Presbytery to take a collection to relieve the destitution of the fishers of Nigg: 'had these people been crofters money would have been poured in upon them, but as they were quiet, uncomplaining fishermen, they were left to suffer extreme poverty and distress.'[122] The fisherfolk of Cromarty, which had a good harbour, were equally destitute.

At last, from this nadir in their fortunes came the will to build harbours in the seaboard villages. The fishermen of Hilton, acting perhaps out of desperation, began to build their own breakwater but the project ceased when the authorities refused to give help, perhaps because they were involved in building the long-promised harbour at Balintore.[123]

Construction of the road into Balintore in 1819 had first prompted moves to build a proper harbour there: an L-shaped stone pier to the north and a straight wall to the south. But despite further plans being drawn up over the next twenty years, nothing was done.[124] In 1845 a harbour was again proposed by Joseph Mitchell of Inverness, engineer to the Commissioners for Highland Roads and Bridges, to cost £8,000 of which two-thirds was to be paid by the Fisheries Board and one third by the landlord, Mr Rose of Tarlogie. But Tarlogie died and nothing further was heard of the scheme.[125] Finally, in 1888 a petition was sent to the Board of Trade, under the General Pier and Harbour Act of 1861, asking for authority to incorporate a body of Harbour Trustees who would be responsible for building a breakwater and quay and deepening the harbour. Plans were drawn up by the firm of David and Alan Stevenson and work began in 1890.[126]

The harbour took nearly six years to complete; there were problems with construction and with the tides.[127] At neighbouring Hilton a stone jetty was built about 1898–9.[128] These harbour works brought a modest revival in the fortunes of the seaboard villages but in some ways these improvements came too late; the fishing was changing. Despite the dislike by Scottish fishermen of steam trawlers, by the 1890s they were taking over from sail-powered 'Fifies' and 'Scaffies'. By the end of the 1890s steam drifters were a common sight in Cromarty harbour.[129] They came to dominate Scottish fishing in the years leading up to the First World War.

These steam drifters were large ships, over eighty feet long, and could carry up to 100 nets that could extend over two miles. The longer range of these boats (up to 100 miles) meant that fish curing could be concentrated at fewer centres. It was not long after the harbour opened that the fishcuring yard that had been opened at Balintore about 1880 closed down.

The introduction of long-range steam-powered trawling was the final blow to the engagement system. Increasingly, the fishermen of the Cromarty Firth had to take their catches to Wick, Fraserburgh, Peterhead and Aberdeen to sell. By the end of the nineteenth century all fish curers brought their fish by auction at the quayside. A new occupation, fish salesman, appeared on the scene with stations in all the major ports for buying fish and selling supplies. Steam trawlers were expensive. Fish salesmen began to buy shares in the boats, thus beginning another change in the pattern of boat ownership. By the end of the nineteenth century it was much more common for local fishermen to sign on as crews rather than to own the boat from which they fished.

The new patterns of fishing changed the lives of the women of the fishing communities as well. They began to travel to the new fishing ports to work at gutting and salting the fish. By the early twentieth century the pattern of this seasonal migration by the fisher lassies from Cromarty and the seaboard villages was well established. They would go first to Shetland usually between June and late September and then return home briefly before setting out by train for the English ports of Lowestoft and Yarmouth.[130]

The First World War was the great turning point in fishing as in so many other things. Many of the local fishermen were in the Naval Reserve and were called up. In any case, the use of the Cromarty Firth as a major naval base created insuperable problems to local fishing during the war, not the least of which was the boom set up between the Sutors in 1914, and the mining of the outer waters of the Moray Firth. After the War portions of the minefield were blown up and one eye-witness recalled that afterwards the surface of the sea was covered with stunned and dead fish. But it was the 1917 Russian Revolution that was the blow that finally destroyed the east coast herring fishery by closing off the major east European market for the fish; in 1913 eighty per cent of the east coast herring catch had gone to Europe, mainly to Germany and Russia.[131]

Those fishermen of the Cromarty Firth region who returned from the Great War found their world utterly changed. Between 1921 and 1931 the population of Cromarty itself fell by over thirty per cent (from 1,126 to 837) due almost entirely to the decline in fishing.[132] By the 1930s herring exports were being further affected by the financial crisis in Germany. There was scarcely any inshore line fishing carried out. Only a few crews still fished and only to supply the local market.

In the seaboard villages the position was a bit more hopeful but not much. Trade had been greatly reduced during the war and afterwards the financial position of Balintore harbour was so precarious that the Trustees resigned *en masse* in 1922.[133] Three years later the Board of Agriculture offered financial help in repairing the harbour and there was a modest revival. Herring fishing was not carried on but white-fishing enjoyed a small boom. Fish merchants set up in the villages, so that the fishermen were not totally dependent on what the fishwives could sell in the surrounding towns and countryside. Some merchants became part owners in new boats. Then, in the 1930s the seine-netters destroyed the spawn and the white-fishing died.[134] Many local men sought work on the land or joined the merchant Navy.

Today all that remains of the fishing industry in the seaboard villages is salmon fishing and small-scale shell-fishing, the final relic of a long fishing tradition that goes back at least to the late eighteenth century. Fifty thousand lobsters were caught in one year in the early 1790s around Tarbat Ness and sent south[135] and Nigg also exported lobsters to the London market until stocks became scarce.[136] After this period, however, there was little attempt to exploit this resource until the present century. In 1910 however a Hilton fisherman began lobster fishing and sent his catch to Billingsgate. The trade died with the First World War and was not seriously revived until the 1970s, when it was said 'there were lobster pots every twenty yards from North Sutor to Tarbat Ness.'[137]

Perhaps ironically, the fishery that has survived the longest is salmon fishing. When the large estates were sold after the First World War many of their salmon fishing rights were dispersed. The Crown Fishings, however, off the seaboard villages have survived intact and they are operated in much the same way as they were from at least the seventeenth century with the nets being leased out to the fishermen. One of the few visual survivals of the centuries of fishing around the Cromarty Firth are the salmon nets poking up out of the sea off the villages of Hilton, Shandwick and Balintore during the summer months. The nets may be nylon instead of hemp or cotton, but the basic technique does not change; the salmon yairs remain a small link with a maritime past that stretches back thousands of years.

NOTES

1. For further details see *RJ*, 10 March 1972, R. W. Munro, 'Black Isle Ferries'.
2. *Ibid*.
3. I. Mowat, 'The Moray Firth Province', *Firthlands*, p. 81.
4. Cromartie MSS SRO GD 305/1/127 no. 3.
5. Gordon, 'Nigg', *Chapels Churches and Graveyards*, p. 6.
6. M. Clough, 'The Cromartie Estate, 1660–1784', *Firthlands*, p. 90.
7. Cromartie MSS SRO GD 305/1/147 no. 32.
8. Cromartie MSS SRO GD 305/1/150 nos. 69, 82.
9. Mowat, 'Moray Firth Province', p. 84.
10. Cromartie MSS SRO GD 305/1/148 no. 195; 305/1/149 no. 34.
11. For example, Ross of Pitcalnie MSS SRO GD 199 no. 12 (mills at Ardmore and Kincardine).
12. See for example Ross of Pitcalnie MSS SRO GD 199, nos. 177, 199, 248, 210, 238.
13. Ross of Pitcalnie MSS SRO GD 199, no. 210.
14. Cromartie MSS SRO GD 305/1/162 no. 291: Kenneth Mackenzie was apprenticed to an Edinburgh merchant in 1658 (SRO GD 305/1/147 no. 2) and was active in arranging his brother's commercial affairs in Edinburgh in the 1670s (SRO GD 305/1/147 no. 20).
15. Cromartie MSS SRO GD 305/1/149 no. 150.
16. Mowat, 'Moray Firth Province', p. 82.
17. See for example Cromartie MSS SRO GD 305/1/147 nos. 28 and 38 (contracts with brewers dated 1684 and 1696) and the authorisation by a Leith maltman to his local agent to receive oats and bere from the laird of Cromarty, SRO GD 305/1/161 no. 4 (1661).
18. Much of this discussion is based on M. Clough, 'The Cromartie Estate', pp. 90–1.
19. Cromartie MSS SRO GD 305/1/158 no. 121.
20. Cromartie MSS SRO GD 305/1/160 no. 29.
21. Cromartie MSS SRO GD 199 no. 208 (salt); SRO GD 305/1/147 no. 43 (lime from Limekilns in Fife to Dingwall); *Ibid.*, no. 37 (coals from Wemyss to Cromarty).
22. For example, a painter appears in 1674 and a glazier two years later; William Frogg, gardener, appears at New Tarbat in 1691; Cromartie MSS SRO GD 305/1/147 nos. 16, 18 and SRO GD 305/1/149 no. 75.

23. Cromartie MSS SRO GD 305/2/147 nos. 6, 7, 11. For other contracts let to Urquhart by Cromartie see Cromartie MSS SRO GD 305/1/152 no. 45 (1675).

24. Cromartie MSS SRO GD 305/1/152 no. 173. Although there had been agreement in 1655 to standardise weights and measures in Nigg and surrounding parishes (SRO GD 305/1/147 no. 67) it is impossible now to know what was the local weight for a boll: the 'great Boll of Tarbat' which was used for local grain measurement was kept in the kirk of Tarbat until the early eighteenth century but its capacity is uncertain; a recent historian has suggested that it could have been anything between 308 and 672 pounds! Whatever its capacity Alexander Urquhart was responsible for shipping a considerable cargo.
For a discussion of the question of the Tarbat boll, see Clough, 'The Cromartie Estate', p. 91.

25. Mowat, 'Moray Firth Province', p. 82. Much of the following discussion of eighteenth century trade is based on this article.

26. Ross of Pitcalnie MSS SRO GD 199/75 no. 2.

27. SRO, CE 62/4/1.

28. Mowat, 'Moray Firth Province', pp. 75, 83.

29. H. Miller, 'A Scotch merchant', *Tales and Sketches*, pp. 303–4.

30. Hugh Miller claimed Forsyth obtained his flax from the Low Countries but this is denied in Mowat, 'Moray Firth Province', p. 77.

31. *Ibid.*

32. L. McCulloch, *Observations on the Herring Fisheries upon the North and East Coasts of Scotland*, London, 1788, p. 13.

33. R. and F. Morris, *Scottish Harbours*, Everton, 1983, p. 198.

34. *NSA* 'Rosskeen', p. 275.

35. I. Mowat, *Easter Ross*, p. 85.

36. Morris, *Scottish Harbours*, p. 199; *IT* 19 May 1858.

37. *IT*, 1 September 1858.

38. *IT*, 22 April 1863.

39. *RJ*, 10 March 1972 (ferry piers shown on 6" Ordnance Survey map 1872).

40. *IT* 11, 18 August 1880.

41. Morris, *Scottish Harbours*, p. 96.

42. This account of the Dingwall Canal is based on the *OSA, NSA*, Mowat, *Easter Ross*, pp. 83–4 and an article in the *RJ* 31 March 1950.

43. *IT*, 13 February 1856.

44. *IT*, 17 June 1868.

45. J. Lindsay, *The Canals of Scotland*, Newton Abbot, 1968, pp. 184–5.

46. *IT*, p. 5 July 1882.

47. Morris, *Scottish Harbours*, p. 192.

48. From information supplied by Duncan Murray, Evanton. Belleport is from Gaelic Baile puirt (Port town).

49. *IT*, 5 May 1856.

50. Teaninich Diary, p. 20.

51. Teaninich Diary, p. 113.

52. Mowat, *Easter Ross*, p. 85.

53. Teaninich Diary, p. 27.

54. The following discussion of James Hall is based on a collection of letters

possessed by James Hoseason, Belleport, that were brought to my attention by members of the 1986–7 MSC scheme in Invergordon, and Hall's obituary which was printed in *IT* 23 November 1864.

55. *IT*, 17 October 1860; 26 September 1860.

56. J. Barron, *Northern Highlands*, Inverness, vol. 2, p. 306.

57. *IT*, 11 November 1863.

58. *IT*, 31 May 1876.

59. *IT*, 24 December 1856.

60. *IT*, 4 November 1863.

61. *IT*, 30 July 1856.

62. See for example *IT*, 1 May 1878 (Tain Summer holiday) and 14 August 1878 (Black Isle show).

63. *IT*, 20 April 1859.

64. *IT*, 2 July 1856, p. 1.

65. *IT*, 9 January 1878; July 1880; 25 May 1884.

66. *IT*, 15 February and March 1882.

67. *IT*, 10 February 1858.

68. J. MacDonald and A. Gordon, *Down to the Sea*, np, reprint, 1978, p. 9.

69. W. Webb, *Coastguard! An Official History of H.M. Coastguard*, London, 1976, p. 23.

70. PP, 1844, xii.

71. *The Life Boat*, vol. 4, 1858–9, pp. 117, 148.

72. *IT*, 16 October 1867. The R.N.L.I. station at Cromarty was set up in 1911 when the Nairn station was closed (*The Life Boat* vol. 21, 1910–12, p. 309) and the original rowing boat was replaced by a motorboat in 1932; by that time there had been eight launches and two lives saved. *Ibid.*, vol. 28, 1930–2, p. 341.

73. The evidence is printed in *PP* 1857 vols. 14; 1857–8, vol. 17, 'Select Committee on harbours of refuge'; see also *The Life Boat*, vol. 4, 1858, p. 16.

74. *IT*, 16 March 1859.

75. *Cases decided in the Court of Session*, Third Series, vol. 6 (The Duchess of Sutherland vs James Watson and others, 1868) p. 199. I am most grateful to Jane Ryder, WS, for locating the records of this case for me.

76. J. R. Coull, 'The Herring Fishing, 1800–1914; development and interpretation of a pattern of Resource Use', MacDonald and Gordon, vol. 102, no. 1 (April, 1986), p. 5.

77. *Down to the Sea*, p. 6.

78. Cromartie MSS SRO GD 305/1/158 no. 165.

79. Cameron, 'Sanitary condition', p. 15.

80. A. Ross, 'Easter Ross fishermen', pp. 160–1.

81. *Ibid.*, pp. 163–4.

82. *Ibid.*, p. 162.

83. *CN*, 31 December 1891, p. 2.

84. J. Duncan, *My Friends the Miss Boyds*, London, 1959, p. 34.

85. J. R. Coull, 'Fisheries in the North-east of Scotland before 1800', *Scottish Studies*, vol. 13, 1969, p. 23.

86. MacDonald and Gordon, op. cit., p. 38.

87. Gordon, 'Nigg', Fishing and the sea, p. 2.

88. *A Source Book of Scottish History*, ed. W. Croft Dickinson, Gordon Donaldson,

2nd revised edition, London, 1961, vol. 3, pp. 388-9; T. C. Smout, *A History of the Scottish people, 1560-1830*, p. 182.

89. Ross of Pitcalnie MSS SRO GD 199 no. 6; the signatories include McCulloch of Glastullich, Ross of Little Tarrel and MacLeod of Cadboll.

90. Cromartie MSS SRO GD 305/1/155 no. 25.

91. *OSA*, Tarbat, vol. 6, p. 424.

92. Cromartie MSS SRO GD 305/1/139 no. 13.

93. Miller, 'Letters on the Herring Fishery', *Tales and Sketches*, pp. 159-60.

94. *Ibid.*, pp. 149-51; P. F. Anson, *Fishing Boats and Fisher Folk on the East Coast of Scotland*, London (reprint), 1971, p. 235.

95. Miller, 'Herring Fishery', *Tales and Sketches*, p. 150.

96. *OSA*, Nigg, vol. 13, p. 17.

97. *Ibid.*, vol. 4, pp. 292, 289-90.

98. D. Turnock, *Patterns of Highland Development*, op. cit., pp. 41-5.

99. Coull, 'The Herring Fishing, 1800-1914', p. 5; MacDonald and Gordon, op. cit., p. 23.

100. Cameron, op. cit., p. 9.

101. *Ibid.*, pp. 8-9.

102. *PP* Herring Board Reports for 1851, 1852.

103. *RJ*, 20 February 1885, p. 4.

104. The evidence is printed in *PP* 1866 vol. 18, 'Sea fisheries. Report of the commissioners. Minutes of evidence'.

105. M. Gray, 'The organisation and growth of the East Coast Herring Fishing, 1800-1885', *Studies in Scottish Business History*, ed. P. L. Payne, London, 1967, p. 208.

106. Cromartie MSS, SRO, GD 305/1/925 no. 1.

107. *IT*, 28/2/1866; for details of the Case see *Cases decided in the Court of Session*, Third Series, vol. 6, no. 51, pp. 199-217.

108. *RJ*, 12 April 1889, p. 3.

109. *IT*, 3 January 1872, p. 2.

110. *IT*, 21 February 1872, p. 2.

111. *IT*, 31 January 1872.

112. Cromartie MSS SRO GD 305/2/295 nos. 2-4.

113. *RJ*, 19 July 1877, p. 3; the Cromarty fishing fleet at this time consisted of 16 boats.

114. J. Hunter, *The Making of the Crofting Community*, Edinburgh, 1976, pp. 170-1.

115. *RJ*, 23 January 1885.

116. *PP*, 1883, vol. 16, Appendix A, LXXIV.

117. *RJ*, 23 January 1885, p. 3.

118. *RJ*, 26 December 1884, p. 3.

119. *RJ*, 23 January 1885, p. 3.

120. *RJ*, 30 January 1885, p. 3.

121. *RJ*, 6 March 1885, p. 4.

122. *RJ*, 17 April 1885, p. 3.

123. There had, in fact, been a landing place at Hilton, built between 1828 and 1851, with a bulwark added in 1855 by the landlord, MacLeod of Cadboll, and the Herring Fishery Board. (*PP* 1856, vol. 54, p. 397) but — it was later claimed — 'a harbour of a very unsubstantial character had been built at Hilton about sixty years ago, but it was

in such a position that it succumbed to the first great storm'. Ross, *Easter Ross Fishermen*, p. 158.

124. 'Plan of the proposed harbour at Balintore' (RHP 4280) is undated (but dated 1818 in the SRO list); it seems much more likely that the plan is contemporaneous with the road. Subsequent plans (all more or less showing the same proposed layout) include RHP 4281 (1828) and 4282 (1829). In 1829 a modified plan for a breakwater wall to the north (and no southern wall) was proposed (RHP 4283) and a similar plan was proposed ten years later (RHP 4282).

125. *RJ*, 23 January 1885.

126. SRO RHP 14954, David and Alan Stevenson.

127. MacDonald and Gordon, *Down to the Sea*, pp. 26, 32.

128. *Ibid.*, pp. 32–3.

129. *RJ*, 3 May 1935, p. 4.

130. *RJ*, 13 October 1903, p. 4.

131. M. Gray, *The Fishing Industries of Scotland 1790–1914*, Oxford, 1978, p. 212.

132. *RJ*, 21 August 1931, p. 4.

133. MacDonald and Gordon, *Down to the Sea*, p. 33.

134. *Ibid.*, pp. 3, 22.

135. *OSA* Tarbat, vol. 6, p. 424.

136. MacDonald and Gordon, *Down to the Sea*, p. 31.

137. *Ibid.*, p. 31.

7

'This noble harbour'

In 1706 the journalist and English agent Daniel Defoe was sent to Scotland on behalf of the prime minister of England to spy out the land while the negotiations for the parliamentary union between England and Scotland were in progress. His journeys took him as far as Caithness and on the way he was deeply impressed by the Cromarty Firth:

> North of the mouth of this River [the Ness] is the famous Cromarty Bay, or Cromarty Firth, noted for being the finest harbour, with the least business of, perhaps, any in Britain: 'tis, doubtless, a harbour or port, able to receive the Royal Navy of Great Britain, and, like Milford-Haven in Wales, both the going in and out safe and secure. But as there is very little shipping employed in these parts, and little or no trade, except for corn, and in the season of it some fishing, so this noble harbour is left entirely useless in the world.[1]

Defoe was almost certainly not the first person to see the naval potential of the Cromarty Firth, but he was among the first to advocate it in print: it was this sort of information that would be of interest to his English masters.

It would be well over a century before the Firth was visited by a full Royal Navy fleet, but there is evidence throughout the eighteenth century that small squadrons of naval ships did call into the Firth, to shelter or to take on water and supplies, and — sometimes — to press local men into the Navy.

Early in 1709, for example, a French privateer seized an Orkney sloop in Cromarty Roads and threatened the neighbouring coast. From the early eighteenth century there may have been small and primitive batteries on the Sutors. Their use and local defence was organised by Sir Kenneth Mackenzie of Cromarty and Colonel Charles Ross of Balnagown who, with the help of a brass gun belonging to the latter, were able to force the French privateer to surrender its prize.[2]

The fact that the enemy was France determined the siting of the string of naval ports around the southeastern coast of England. It was only during the Jacobite revolts that some Royal Navy attention was focussed on the north. Warships are known to have called in and out of the Firth during The Fifteen. The Hanoverian Sir Robert Munro of Foulis fortified his home and, with the Earl of Sutherland, established a camp at Alness which was strengthened by artillery borrowed from a warship then anchored in Cromarty Roads.[3]

It was a similar story during the last Jacobite revolt in 1745–6. In 1745, for example, HMS *Glasgow* entered the Firth in support of the government troops in the north under Lord Loudoun. Her log records the visit which began on Wednesday 9 October: 'Att Anchor att Cromiti . . . att 7 came to anchor in

21 fathoms water . . . att 11 . . . Lord Louden's going ashore saluted him with
11 guns.'[4] The *Glasgow* stayed in port for several days, and on 12 October: '. . .
att 2 pm prest two seamen from West Shore with yaull (yawl) Employed
Ditto.'[5]

The Firth was especially busy early in 1746 as the Jacobite Army marched
north following its victory at Falkirk on 17 January. Loudoun's Hanoverian
garrison left Inverness, retreating towards the friendly country of Sutherland,
pursued by Jacobite troops under the command of Lord Kilmarnock. In the
weeks leading up to the Battle of Culloden in mid-April the navy was busy
supplying and transporting Loudoun's men as well as taking off local
Hanoverian families threatened by the approaching Jacobites.

Amongst the naval ships to be active in the Cromarty Firth during this
period was HMS *Shark*, a sloop of ten guns.[6] *Shark*, part of Admiral Byng's
fleet of eleven ships, sailed north late in 1745 to join the general naval
blockade to stop French naval ships and privateers from supplying the
rebels. She arrived in the Cromarty Firth on 19 December and returned again
in February 1746 along with the *Vulture* and *Speedwell*. The *Shark*'s log
which records the crowded events of Lord Loudoun's retreat began on 20
February:

> This day Lord Loudon crost over the Ferry from Cromerty [*sic*] to the North side,
> with part of a Regiment being pursued by the Rebel Army.
> [21 February] At 8 AM His Majestys sloop Vulture weighed and sailed for
> Inverness by my order to assist the Speedwell convoying down a vessel with arms
> for Lord Loudons Army and two others with Plate jewells Furniture (etc) belonging
> to the inhabitants of Inverness and Cromerty; put on board for their Security,
> being in danger of being Surprized by the Rebells . . .
> [22 February] Arrived here the Vulture and Speedwell . . . with their convoy from
> Inverness.
> [23 February] Lord Loudon being informed that the Rebells were advancing
> towards him, with a large body at 3 AM he thought proper to retrite (*sic*) further
> to the Northward.
> At 5 . . . sent our boat with 15 men with the Speedwells and Vultures boat man'd
> to Bring off all the Fishing Boats from the Northside, by 10 they sent all the Boats
> on board to the number of 19, one being leaky so that she cou'd not swim, stove
> her and left her on shore.[7]

Three days later *Shark*, *Speedwell* and *Vulture*, along with three merchant
ships, weighed anchor and sailed from the Firth, perhaps with the Nigg fishing
boats in tow, although these may have been amongst the local vessels
commandeered by Loudoun's troops to help in their retreat.[8]

A few days after leaving the Cromarty Firth *Shark* encountered two
suspicious ships:

> Saw two boats coming from the shore [and] stood in toward them, the first that
> came on board asked if we belonged to France or England. I answered to the

French King, he said then he was right; told us that their prince, meaning the Pretender Charles had got a greater army than ever and seemed over joyhed (*sic*) at it; the second boat, when she came near the ship found her mistake, would have been glad to have got away ... but found twas but in vain, came alongside ...[9]

The capture of the two French ships yielded guns, prisoners, money and valuable information. Other French ships, however, managed to run the blockade and come into the Cromarty Firth. One such was *Le Hardi Mendiant* of Dunkirk (a captured English ship originally named *The Sturdy Beggar*) which sailed into the Firth on 16 April, the day of the Battle of Culloden.[10] Once the battle was over, the French ships began trying to find the Prince and take him back to France. *Le Hardi Mendiant* remained in local waters, returning to the Firth on the last day of the month, but the man of war *Bridgewater* came in and anchored between her and the Sutors. The French ship, however, was able to raise sail and slip safely out of the Firth.

By the late spring and early summer of 1746 local waters were again being patrolled by the *Glasgow*, which frequently came into the Firth to take on water and supplies and to carry out exercises. She ranged as far as the Hebrides, where she took on board a group of French prisoners from the Summer Isles. In late August on her way south with these prisoners, she came into the Firth one last time. The ship's log records that the captain 'exercised great guns and small arms' and 'read articles of war to ye ships company' before leaving for Sheerness on 3 September.[11]

The ending of the Jacobite threat also ended the first phase of the Cromarty Firth's connection with the Royal Navy. Up to now it was an *ad hoc* one, but the idea of using the Firth as an official base for the entire British fleet remained alive. In the early 1790s, just as the wars with France were beginning, Robert Smith, the minister of Cromarty, echoed Daniel Defoe when he wrote:

> Such is the vast extent of sea-room in this bay, and such the capacious description of its length, depth and breadth, that almost the whole British Navy might, with the greatest safety, ride within the view of this place [the town of Cromarty].[12]

As French conquests spread over the continent, so did a concern to establish coastal and naval defences further and further up the eastern coast of Britain. By 1803 it was said:

> The maritime frontier of the enemy, by commanding the United Provinces [Low Countries], and the whole of the coast from thence, it may be said almost to Constantinople, most impressively demands that exertions of the greatest magnitude should be directed to the improvement of the whole of the maritime frontiers of the British Islands.[13]

The war spread to the Baltic when Napoleon persuaded Russia, Sweden, Denmark and Prussia to form a League of Armed Neutrality. Denmark was the nearest to Britain of any League member, and early in April 1801 a British fleet defeated the Danish Navy in Copenhagen Roads. Although the Royal

Navy fleet which went to Copenhagen sailed directly there from Yarmouth, the Cromarty Firth was regularly being used by Royal Navy ships during this period. A number of naval officers who gave evidence as part of the survey and report compiled by Thomas Telford in 1802 for the Treasury, on the problems and potentials of the Highlands of Scotland, indicate that they had extensive personal knowledge of the Firth.

Telford proposed the creation of a system of Highland roads, bridges and piers, with the linchpin of this communications system being a canal through the Great Glen. Telford's report also gave serious consideration to the potential of the Cromarty Firth as a naval base. The first report, submitted in June 1803, derived most of its evidence on the subject from a Captain Duff of the Royal Navy, who went directly to the nub of the matter:

> Persons conversant in naval Affairs will be able to judge how far this Bay would be suitable for a Squadron destined to watch the mouth of the Baltic and to protect the coast. It would be singularly well situated for convoys of vessels coming from the westwards through the Caledonian Canal.[14]

Duff himself had been in and out of the Firth in all weathers; he estimated, for example, that even in contrary winds a ship of war could clear the headlands in forty-eight hours from leaving the Bay. The water in Invergordon was 'brakish' but there was a good well nearby that could be dammed and piped to the shore. He also felt that a small pier should be built at Invergordon to enable boats to take on the water barrels. The only other buildings needed were 'storehouses and some other conveniences which may be on a small scale, until the merits of the place have been fully proved: allow an Expense here of £5,000.'[15]

Captain Duff saw Cromarty as a base for large warships, the head port in a string of north-eastern naval stations. He suggested that Aberdeen harbour might be rebuilt to take frigates. The intervening small fishing stations of Peterhead and Fraserburgh could be developed as communication centres using light signals or a land express communications system could be set up via Nairn and the Black Isle ferries. Alternatively, 'a fast sailing Vessel would soon run with an Easterly wind from Frazerburgh (*sic*) to Cromarty.'[16]

The Treasury was interested and a further, more detailed, report was submitted a few months later. In this report Cromarty's claims were, for the first time, balanced against those of Leith and the Firth of Forth. James Dunbar, a post captain in the Royal Navy said:

> Ships of war at present frequent Leith Road as a Roadstead and Cromarty as a safe harbour . . . I have been six or seven times in the Bay of Cromarty in a ship of war and am of the opinion it is the best and safest Harbour I have ever frequented . . .[17]

And there were further advantages as well:

If ships of war were stationed at Cromarty, there would be from that part of the island a great supply to His Majesty's Navy of hardy men, accustomed to the sea [and the ships] would, in great measure, be the means of preventing Depredations upon the Revenues (i.e. smuggling).[18]

Captain Murdo Downie, a retired naval officer living in Aberdeen, concurred that the Firth was superior to Leith:

Cromarty is already so perfect a harbour in all natural respects, that it needs nothing to make it a most commodious resort for ships of every description, great and small, unless it be conveniences for holding stores and for ship's watering; the last of which is to be had upon the South shore of the harbour, about two miles west from the town [Cromarty], nearly opposite the Anchorage . . . [probably the stream at Shore Mill] It was there where ships usually watered when I visited the Place and the water was laid in by rolling casks to the stream . . .[19]

Nevertheless, there were critics of the plan to create a base in the Cromarty Firth. One of them, Robert Fraser, claimed that a naval base needed not only safe anchorage but also adequate local supplies and easy access to the sea. As for the Cromarty Firth:

Its situation is not near the open sea, its entrance narrow, vessels cannot get out of it in contrary winds, the country around it does by no means afford a natural source of provisions fit for the abundant supply of a fleet; to convert, therefore, such a situation into a principal naval station, appears to be absurd . . .[20]

Some of these criticisms were justified. The agricultural development of the region was just beginning and it would indeed have been difficult to supply a large fleet using local resources. On the other hand, the naval captains who gave evidence to the committee did not regard the narrow entrance and the difficulty of getting out of the Firth in contrary winds as insurmountable problems. Nevertheless, this remained a constant argument against using the Firth as a naval base and making it a harbour of refuge so long as the navy was powered by sail and the conservative Royal Navy long resisted the introduction of steam.

The Cromarty Firth continued to be used by the Royal Navy over the next few years, especially in 1807 when Canning, the Minister of War, sent a second British naval expedition to Copenhagen, but nothing was done to create a proper naval base.

Naval attention was directed northwards again with the outbreak of the Crimean War in 1854. Britain and France declared war on Russia in March and a naval blockade of the enemy's Baltic ports was mounted by a flotilla under the command of Admiral Sir Charles Napier, who became something of a popular hero. A music hall song of the period ran:

> France and England — one in counsel —
> Are impatient for the day,
> And off steaming to the Baltic,

Ripe and ready for the fray.
We have hearts that never fail us,
So look out for wounds and scars,
For there's Charlie Napier coming,
With his gallant Jack-Tars.[21]

When the Baltic was closed by ice in the winter of 1854–5 four steam frigates of the Baltic Fleet (with their gallant Jack-Tars but without Charlie Napier) wintered in the Cromarty Firth.[22] The *Inverness Courier*'s correspondent reported early in the New Year that the town's lack of a good eating house and a temperance hotel was causing problems. Sailors were allowed ashore in groups of fifty and could find nowhere to eat and could 'get little to drink except whisky.'[23] By mid-January the sailors were using the regular omnibus which ran between Cromarty and Kessock Ferry to make good-humoured if slightly tipsy visits to Inverness:

> It [the omnibus] is usually decked out with flags and ribbons and the whisky bottle is a conspicuous feature in the outside arrangements . . . The stock of ribbons in Inverness had been greatly diminished by the sailors, everyone of whom had some yards of brilliant streamers flying from his cap and button holes.[24]

And then, in mid February, the Fleet was withdrawn to south coast ports.[25] The Cromarty Firth's first brief experience of a visit by a Royal Navy fleet was over. This short episode left behind one memento: the inn at Cromarty was renamed 'The Admiral Napier Hotel.'

The Crimean War had revealed serious inadequacies in the Royal Navy as well as in harbour accommodation and coastal defences. In 1856 a report on the Scottish harbours was prepared by a Captain Westmacott, RN, which included the recommendation that a six gun battery should be mounted at the entrance to the Cromarty Firth.[26] Nothing was done.

By now, however, the age of steam could no longer be denied by the Royal Navy. A few years later the Parliamentary Select Committee on Harbours of Refuge (1857–8) considered the possible use of the Cromarty Firth as a permanent naval coaling station. Once again the Firth itself was claimed to be an excellent anchorage but its position within the Moray Firth meant that it would take time for the ships to steam out to meet the enemy.[27] However, by the early 1860s the government fishery protection vessels regularly came into the Firth to take on coal and water and were often stationed there for long periods.[28]

In the autumn of 1858 the Cromarty Firth was visited by a committee of army and navy officers, part of a Royal Commission delegated to report on naval ports. They could see the potential of the Firth, especially if used in conjunction with the Caledonian Canal, and recommended:

> Measures for the security of these waters, and to prevent access to them by an enemy, would be very desirable. Immediately after passing within the bold headlands, the land almost suddenly falls, forming a low, sandy beach backed by

banks about 10 to 30 feet high. On the South shore immediately fronting the town, a small heavily armed battery has been proposed with another of a similar nature on the opposite side. Both would directly command the entrance and should be supported by a small barrack-keep against surprize.[29]

When nothing resulted from this visit, the Town Council of Cromarty wrote to the War Office complaining of the unprotected state of the Firth.[30] Lord Ripon replied that 'measures have been under consideration for establishing defensive works . . .' but again nothing was done.

Nevertheless, from this time onward there was a marked increase in the use of the Cromarty Firth by individual naval ships and, eventually, whole fleets. In the summer of 1860 rumours swept the Firth that the Channel Fleet would visit Cromarty. The *Invergordon Times* commented hopefully that the visit would be good for local trade, shopkeepers and the steamer traffic.[31] This optimism was short-lived; the Fleet went to Yarmouth instead.

Over the next few years there were regular visits by Royal Navy ships into the Firth including, in May 1862, the frigate *St George*, with the Queen's son, Prince Alfred Duke of Edinburgh, aboard as one of the midshipmen.[32] There was great excitement ashore. The Cromarty Artillery Volunteers saluted the ship, which was opened up for visits by local people, and a party of officers came ashore for a cricket match in the grounds of Cromarty House.

And then, in 1863, the Channel Fleet, under the command of Admiral Dacres, paid the first official visit by a Royal Navy fleet to the Cromarty Firth. Nine ships with nearly 5,000 men arrived at the end of the second week in August as part of the Fleet's annual circumnavigation of the coast of Britain.[33] People came on special excursion trains to Invergordon. Many of the ships were open to visitors daily, including Sunday, which aroused the ire of the Free Church. The visit brought a small boom to the merchants and innkeepers of Invergordon and Cromarty. It was claimed that the Temperance Hotel in Invergordon served between two and three hundred meals daily while the Fleet was in.[34] On the whole the visit passed pleasantly and when the flotilla sailed the laird of Invergordon, MacLeod of Cadboll, travelled as far as Kirkwall as a guest on the flagship *Black Prince*.

This first Fleet visit seems to have had a galvanising effect upon the locals. Clearly, the better the local facilities, the more likely it was that the Channel Fleet would return in the future. For some time there had been complaints about the lack of proper lighting on the pier. Within a few weeks of the visit a meeting was held to discuss the matter. In return for a partial remission of rates MacLeod of Cadboll, as the owner of the harbour, agreed to see to the lighting and cleaning of the harbour area.[35]

At the time of the Fleet's first visit work was already under way to reclaim land at Chapel Bay on the harbour at Invergordon. About 40,000 cubic yards of clay from the railway cutting at the back of Invergordon were transported to the shore by means of a specially constructed tramway. A stone breastwork about two hundred and fifty yards long was built to protect the infill. After construction was finished the tramway was realigned to the edge of the new embankment and the existing road extended to run parallel with it, thus providing access from the railway line to the harbour for the first time.[36]

All these improvements may have been to no purpose since the Fleet did not return for eleven years. Nevertheless, there were regular visits by individual ships of the Royal Navy and occasionally foreign naval ships as well. In mid-September 1864, for example, a Danish warship called into the Firth to refuel before sailing to the west of Scotland.[37] There were regular visits, too, by fishery protection vessels, and coastguard and naval reserve ships.

When in 1874 the news came at last that the Channel Squadron was to visit the Cromarty Firth again, there was huge excitement. Elaborate plans were made for the Fleet's entertainment. Officers were invited to a garden party at Ardross Castle, a Navy cricket match against the local club was arranged at Invergordon Castle and a public ball was held in Inverness.[38]

The Channel Squadron returned the next year and this time rumours swept the area that Invergordon was to be made a naval station.[39] This did not materialise, but from this time onwards large-scale naval visits were frequent. The Channel Fleet returned in 1877, 1883, 1885, 1887, and 1888 (Figs. 39, 40).

The 1883 visit created wide interest. Before the Fleet arrived from Orkney two large coaling steamers entered the Firth. The Fleet's progress down the coast from Orkney was monitored by telegraph and large crowds gathered along the shore and jetties to see the eight ships enter in single file between the Sutors and then line up in pairs before sailing up the Firth to drop anchor. Invergordon's population trebled as over 2,000 visitors crowded the town. Special trains were run from Inverness and the steamer between Burghead, Cromarty and Inverness was packed with sightseers. The Black Isle steamer *Rosehaugh* ran special trips around the anchored Fleet.[40]

Two years later the Fleet returned in mid-October and although the *Ross-shire Journal* remarked 'such visits are not the novelty they once were' there still was considerable excitement. Local pleasure boats thronged the Firth, sailing amongst the huge ironclad vessels. There were the usual parties for officers at the local big houses, while the ratings held sports events and a sham fight at Balblair Park in Invergordon. One night the Fleet held a demonstration of electric search lights which were played about the buildings of the town and were reported to be 'especially effective on the Free Church steeple.'[41]

By 1888 Fleet visits had been relegated to the 'Local News' column of the *Ross-shire Journal* but, in fact, this visit was to be the last until the beginning of the twentieth century. When regular visits were resumed they would be markedly different, a reflection of a new spirit in the Royal Navy itself.

Beginning in the 1880s the attention of British naval strategists was increasingly focussed on the growing power and pretensions of Germany. Consequently, the creation of a naval base at Cromarty again began to be seriously considered to meet the German threat and to strengthen the navy in

39. The fleet at Invergordon harbour, 1887.

home waters. Naval surveyors were busy in the Firth in the summer of 1902,[42] and following the visit of the fifteen ships of the Reserve Fleet under the command of Sir Gerard Noel to Cromarty in that year the *Ross-shire Journal* reported:

> This is his fourth visit to Cromarty and he holds very strong ideas for the making of Cromarty a naval station. It may be remembered that he had reported very favourably to the Admiralty on the capabilities of the firth.[43]

An improved coaling facility was set up early in 1903 and there was talk again of fortifying the Sutors. There was also strong local feeling that the Cromarty Firth's chances of serious consideration as a naval station would be enhanced if the harbour accommodation, especially at Invergordon, could be improved.[44]

There were rumours that a new 'North Sea Squadron' was going to be created. In mid-February 1903 a Naval Conference was held at Westminster attended by naval personnel, Members of Parliament and other interested parties, including the Provost of Invergordon. He returned to report that there was little urgency in the matter: 'The creation of a new squadron is not the affair of a year.'[45] Within a fortnight, however, the decision had been made to create a first class naval base at Rosyth, including an anchorage and dockyard,[46] with Cromarty as a subsidiary 'shelter anchorage.' Once again local hopes had been raised only to be dashed.[47]

Nevertheless, Admiral Sir John Fisher, who had become First Sea Lord in October 1902, was a warm supporter of the Cromarty Firth over Rosyth throughout his career:

40. Sailors at Invergordon harbour, *c*.1880.

> As you know, I've always been 'dead on' for Cromarty and hated Rosyth, which is
> an unsafe anchorage — the whole Fleet in jeopardy . . . and there's that beastly
> bridge which, if blown up makes egress very risky . . . Also Cromarty is strategically
> better than Rosyth.[48]

The rapid development of the Firth in the first decade of the twentieth
century was a direct consequence of Fisher's appointment and his ideals.

It was 'Jacky' Fisher who, more than any other, was responsible for moving
the Royal Navy out of its century of stagnation and preparing it for the war
with Germany which he believed to be inevitable. Fisher initiated an urgent
programme of shipbuilding. The key to the new navy was the Dreadnought
class battleship, which was to be the largest, fastest and most powerful
warship afloat. The first Dreadnought was launched in February 1906 and
made its appearance in the Cromarty Firth in July of the following year.[49]
Fisher was also an enthusiastic proponent of submarines, as agents of coastal
and harbour defences, despite the conventional naval view that they were
'underhand, unfair, and damned un-English.' In 1908 the first submarine ever
seen in the area visited the Cromarty Firth.[50]

These new ships forced a reconsideration of how they were to be powered.
There had been Admiralty onshore coaling sheds at Invergordon for decades;
now they were supplemented by coaling hulks moored in the Firth.[51] Under
Fisher oil slowly began to supplant coal, although the latter remained
predominant until the Great War. Oil began to be shipped north by rail in
small quantities in anticipation of Fleet visits and as early as 1907 an oil barge
capable of holding 500 tons was stationed at Invergordon to supply the Fleet.[52]

Fisher's programme of reform for the Fleet included constant training
exercises and from the time he became First Sea Lord there were several
Fleet visits a year to the Cromarty Firth. In September 1904, for example, the
Channel Fleet under Admiral Lord Charles Beresford, soon to become Fisher's
arch-enemy and severest critic, was in the Firth. In the following month a

flotilla of six torpedo boats was to call, followed by the twenty-one ships of the Home Fleet.[53] In between times there were constant comings and going by small groups of ships or single vessels such as gunboats and coalers.

The Moray Firth, beyond the Sutors, was a favourite site for gunnery practice and manoeuvres, which caused increasing problems for local fishermen. Sometimes, too, there were onshore accidents. In November 1905, for example, the gunboat *Harrier*, then stationed in the Cromarty Firth, accidentally shelled Dunskeath and the Ferry Inn at Nigg.[54]

By 1906 the increased navy presence, and the gradual decline of small sailing schooners, led MacLeod of Cadboll to undertake a number of necessary changes at his harbour at Invergordon to improve berthing and discharging facilities (Fig. 41). The east jetty was extended to three hundred and fifty feet to create a berthing depth of between sixteen and eighteen feet, depending on the state of the tide, and tramway lines for the steam traction engine were extended along the whole of its length.[55]

Fleet visits were now well organised events, and they needed to be, for otherwise Invergordon and Cromarty would have been swamped by thousands of sailors who came ashore. During the visit of the Home Fleet in July 1907, 4,000 men and five bands took part in a naval review at Balblair Park under Lord Charles Beresford.[56] Three months later the Firth was even fuller, with twelve battleships, four armoured cruisers, two unarmed cruisers, two scout ships and twenty torpedo boats, a total complement of 14,500 men.[57]

In addition to naval personnel the area would also be full of sightseers, as well as officers' families who came north by train and took rooms in Invergordon and Cromarty. While the Fleet was in all sorts of temporary businesses set up shop. Naval outfitters opened their shops for the duration of the Fleet's stay; postcard companies, such as Valentines of Dundee, came north to take local views to sell to the sailors.

There were parades, games and reviews (Fig. 42). Groups of sailors came ashore to shop and sightsee or to use the sports facilities. For the officers there were parties at the local big houses, smoking concerts in town and meetings with the local Masonic Lodge. There were problems, certainly, with such things as gambling, drunkenness and inadequate public facilities, but on the whole visits by the Fleet were popular with the local community.

Relations between crews and the local population were cordial. Some ships that were regularly in the Firth came to be regarded as 'our ships.' One such was the repair ship *Cyclops*, whose return in the summer of 1911 was recorded by the *Invergordon Times*:

> Many poor in the town live to bless them. In their works of charity the last word has not been heard, and if the announcement of a concert for local charities does not take place shortly, it will be surmised that something needs 'repairing.'[58]

For some sailors the Cromarty Firth proved to be their last port of call. In 1901, for example, nineteen ships of the Reserve Squadron called into the

41. Invergordon harbour.

Firth. In the midst of shore leave and parties for the officers, a small funeral procession walked through the streets of Cromarty (Fig. 43). A stoker on the *Sanspareil* had died and was taken to be buried in the naval section of the cemetery on the hill overlooking the town.[59]

Fleet visits also became big business although even as late as 1902 when the Reserve Fleet visited the Cromarty Firth, there was little or no pre-planning. On arrival the caterers came ashore and bought out the Cromarty shops.[60] By 1906 regular contracts with local merchants were negotiated before the Fleet came in (Fig. 44). When eleven ships of the Channel Fleet visited in that year local contracts included 7,050 tons of beef, 10,600 pounds of vegetables and 7,660 pounds of bread.[61] Eventually contracts were negotiated from year to year with arrangements being made during one visit for the next one. In 1912, for example, William Gill at Tomich in Rosskeen gained the 1913 contract for vegetables not only for the Fleet at Cromarty and Invergordon but for the ships stationed at Fortrose and Scapa Flow as well.[62]

In July 1908 the German High Seas Fleet left its home ports in the Baltic and cruised in the Atlantic for the first time. In the spring of the following year the Germans moved half of their fleet from Kiel to Wilhelmshaven. The press began to demand the development of a northern naval base to counter this German threat, which was real enough, although the German menace also produced some early scare stories.[63] It was from this time that the 'German gypsies' began to be perceived as a threat and their bands were diverted from the Firth and escorted out of the area by the local constabulary.

Fisher resigned as First Sea Lord in January 1910 but one of his last acts in office was of great significance for the naval future of the Cromarty Firth. In

42. The proclamation of King George V at Invergordon, 1910.

1910 he managed to get the development of Rosyth delayed for four years and it is from this time that the build-up of facilities in the Cromarty Firth began to accelerate (Fig. 45). Fisher put his position clearly in a letter written in the summer of 1912:

> I still hate Rosyth and fortifications and East Coast Docks and said so the other day! But what we desire for Cromarty is for another purpose — to fend off German cruisers, possibly by an accident of fog or stupidity, getting loose in our small craft taking their ease or refuelling in Cromarty (oil will change this in time, but as yet we have for years coal-fed vessels to deal with) . . .[64]

Fisher's policies were enthusiastically continued by Winston Churchill, who became First Lord of the Admiralty in October 1911. Both men were proponents of the use of oil. In the summer of 1911 the Admiralty applied for permission from Invergordon Town Council to lay underground pipes from five oil tanks they wished to construct to the north of the town.[65] In May 1912 MacLeod of Cadboll feued five acres of land to the Admiralty for the tanks, now increased to ten, which were completed by the following summer, receiving their first oil shipment in May 1913.[66] Invergordon experienced its first invasion by a large, transient workforce as two hundred men arrived to build the tanks (Fig. 46). More workers were added when the Admiralty asked for a further twenty-five acres to build forty more underground tanks.[67] In

43. A sailor's funeral at Cromarty.

September 1913 the new, green-painted tanks were inspected by members of the Admiralty Oil Fuel Committee who arrived in the Firth on the steam yacht *Valiant* and immediately announced plans for even more.[68]

In retirement Lord Fisher chaired a Royal Commission on the use of fuel oil which in 1913 recommended the total replacement of coal by oil as naval fuel, providing regular sources and safe storage could be assured. Invergordon was already well on its way to being developed as a safe storage area and this, plus Commander Donald Munro's advocacy of floating repair facilities in the Firth, led to the 1912 decision by the Committee of Imperial Defence to recommend the creation of the Cromarty Firth as a 'floating second-class naval base and war anchorage . . . fortified on a scale sufficient to deter armoured attack.'[69] Winston Churchill announced these plans to the House of Commons on Monday 18 March 1912.

From now on there would be a permanent on-shore naval presence, so land was bought at Invergordon for a naval recreation ground and the site was chosen for an officers' club.[70] The most obvious result of the naval build-up in the town of Invergordon was a housing crisis, which was only slightly mitigated by the construction of the town's first council housing. In November 1912 the *Invergordon Times* reported that a house selling for £235 a few months before was now worth £1,000. The Admiralty attempted to alleviate the situation by buying land within the town on which to build its own houses.[71]

44. Victuallers to the navy, pre-First World War.

The growing naval presence led to a number of improvements and changes in the town. The Admiralty helped to put in a new water supply and sewage system at the same time as the first oil tank pipeline was laid. The town's roads began to be surfaced and by 1914 concrete pavements were being built and the town's first speed limit for motor cars was passed in 1912. New businesses sprang up: provision merchants, garages, machine shops. The Victoria Hotel was rebuilt and renamed 'The Royal.'

There were worries, too, about the harbour. Early in 1913 Invergordon Town Council passed a resolution about its unsatisfactory working and asking for a Board of Trade Inquiry.[72] The fact was that the harbour had outgrown the capacity of one man, or as the case now was, the Cadboll Trustees, to manage it, since it was subject now to the twin demands of commerce and defence. It was necessary, at the very least, to define respective interests and obligations concerning the harbour. Little was done, however, aside from some rebuilding and paving of the East Dock before war broke out and the matter was taken out of the hands of the Cadboll Trustees and the Town Council by the Admiralty.

If there were accommodation problems on land, there were similar problems in the Firth itself. The build-up begun by Churchill's House of Commons statement soon led to a realisation that even 'this noble harbour' was too small to hold all the ships needed in the North Sea. It was from this time that Scapa Flow began to be considered as an additional northern base.[73]

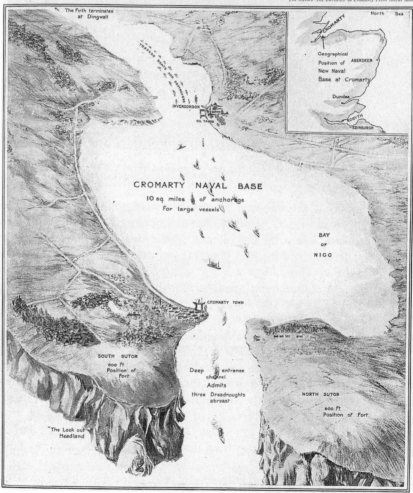

45. Bird's-eye view of the new naval base at Cromarty, 1913.

46. Invergordon from a crow's nest, *c.*1914.

For much of his information and advice about Scottish defences Churchill depended on Commander Munro (Fig. 47), who since 1911 had been Senior Naval Officer and King's Harbourmaster at Rosyth.[74] Churchill had already accepted Munro's recommendations for the fortification of the Sutors.[75] However, this plan fell foul of the endemic rivalry between the Army and Navy, who were jointly responsible for the defence of naval ports. Friction led to delay. When the War Office refused to pay for the proposed defences at Cromarty, Munro suggested to Churchill that the Navy should erect its own port defences to be manned by Royal Marines and thus be independent of the Army. Churchill agreed to come north with some members of the Cabinet to look into the matter. On Sunday 1 September 1912 the Admiralty yacht *Enchantress* appeared off Cromarty early in the morning and dropped anchor alongside the cruiser squadron that was in the Firth. At three in the afternoon Churchill, his wife and Commander Munro came ashore and spent three hours inspecting the site of the proposed defences on the South Sutor. The *Enchantress* remained in the Firth until Wednesday to watch manoeuvres.[76]

As a result of this visit Churchill asked Munro to draw up a detailed memorandum on his plans for the Sutors and the proposed floating dock.[77] Munro's ideas were revolutionary. Not only was the dock to be capable of being moved about according to requirements, it was also to include workers' accommodation in addition to workshops. Munro's proposed dock was never built, but in many ways its design and function anticipated the kind of technology that was later to be used in the building of North Sea oil platforms.

And this was not the only parallel with the later oil boom. There was also a sudden influx of large numbers of workers from outside the region. Many of the men who came to work on the fortifications on the Sutors were accommodated in specially built barracks at Nigg while in Cromarty they were housed in the old hemp factory. The Royal Marines who manned the fortifications on the Sutors were initially housed in an obsolete battleship, *Renown*, until permanent housing was built on land.[78] This sudden population explosion led to social problems as well. There were few amenities in Cromarty and when it was proposed to build a naval canteen there were objections that the town already had too many pubs and the canteen would increase drunkenness.

Surveying work began on the South Sutor defences by the end of 1912[79] and, despite poor weather and labour problems, construction was complete by early 1914. There were repeated attacks on the plans to man the fortifications with Royal Marines including claims that the guns to be used were antiquated and that the batteries themselves were indefensible against bombardment by sea or attack from the landward side.[80] Nevertheless, early in 1914 Munro was busy placing the guns and searchlights in position. The guns for the North Sutor were landed on the shore and those for the South Sutor landed at Cromarty harbour. Then, using specially built traction engines, they were taken up steep roads to the emplacements.[81] The two forts were equipped with electricity and telegraph cables. Power houses were built underground, along with smaller batteries, magazines and barracks. Churchill came north for the testing of the guns in mid-July 1914, just a few weeks before the outbreak of war.[82]

Amongst the other results of Churchill's first visit to Cromarty had been the decision to station a torpedo boat flotilla in the Firth. Moorings for it were laid down between Alness and Invergordon by the late spring of 1913.[83] Churchill was a great enthusiast for aviation and even took flying lessons. Early in 1913, therefore, a temporary hydroplane station was established on Cromarty Links for the summer naval manoeuvres, which would include aeroplanes from the world's first aircraft carrier, *Hermes*, commissioned earlier that year. These planes could take off from on board but had to have a proper landing place.

Two planes were offloaded at Invergordon for Nigg in late June[84] and in early July thirty men and officers arrived and erected canvas hangars on Cromarty Links for three hydroplanes. The first flight in the Firth took place at Cromarty on 14 July, watched by crowds of spectators. The aeroplanes flew as far as Lossiemouth and Dingwall, achieving altitudes of up to 3,000 feet and speeds of between 50 and 60 miles per hour. The town was besieged by

47. Commander Munro.

tourists, one of whom was arrested by Coast Guard officers for taking photographs.[85]

Both air fields proved to be short-lived. In October the hangars at Nigg were demolished and the aeroplanes from both stations were removed to a flying field near Fort George.[86] A few weeks before, however, Churchill sailed north again in *Enchantress* and was escorted into the Firth by hydroplanes from the Cromarty base. He inspected the work on the South Sutor and indulged his taste for excitement by making flights in biplanes and monoplanes over the Firth. The Farnam biplane in which he flew crashed the following day.[87]

The main purpose of Churchill's visit, however, was not to fly but to hold a naval conference. He had come north with Asquith, the Prime Minister, and while in the Firth met a number of naval leaders including the First Sea Lord, Prince Louis of Battenberg (Fig. 48) and two soon-to-be famous admirals, Sir John Jellicoe and David Beatty. Their discussions included plans to upgrade the Cromarty Firth base and led directly to an Admiralty Order in Council passed in December 1913 declaring the Cromarty Firth to be a 'Dockyard Port'.[88] In effect, this Order merely regularised much of what had already happened. Under its provisions the Admiralty took control of 'all the waters of the Cromarty Firth including all the bays, creeks, lakes, pools and rivers so far as the tide flows . . .' The powers of the Harbour Commissioners at Cromarty and the Cadboll estate at Invergordon were not affected. Following the outbreak of War in August 1914, however, the Admiralty took over the harbours of Invergordon and Cromarty and quickly built a jetty at Nigg.

Another consequence of the Order was that Donald John Munro was appointed Cromarty's first King's Harbourmaster.

Munro was responsible for the fact that the Cromarty Firth was the best defended of the East Coast ports upon the outbreak of war even if that was not saying a great deal. Despite all his best efforts to encourage the placement of the long-planned boom across the entrance to the Firth there was opposition. A few weeks before war broke out he received word from the Navy's Boom Defence Committee that their Lordships had decided that the project was unnecessary.[89]

Munro ignored the message and went on with his plans for the boom. On the night war was declared he marched to the Post Office in Cromarty to telegraph messages to the wood merchants and to the wire rope and winch makers whom he needed to make the boom.[90] When the Postmaster refused to keep his Post Office open after business hours Munro placed the coastguard in charge of the telegraph machine, sent his messages, and the next day removed the telegraph office to another building. At the same time Munro sent an officer to Buckie to hire twelve drifters to patrol the Moray Firth Coast and to report to the coastguard if they noticed anything unusual. In addition, a flotilla of eight minesweepers patrolled the navigation channels into the Cromarty Firth.

The great fear was submarines. Both Germans and British had under-estimated their potential range and destructiveness but within days of the beginning of hostilities a rash of periscope sightings, mostly imaginary, had occurred along the East Coast. A new disease called 'periscopeitis' was

48. Winston Churchill, First Sea Lord, with Prince Louis of Battenberg and
Admiral Beresford.

diagnosed. On 1 September in Scapa Flow, where the Grand Fleet now lay at
anchor, an unfortunate seal precipitated a full-scale naval bombardment. Five
days after 'The First Battle of Scapa Flow', however, comedy turned to
tragedy with the sinking of *Pathfinder* by a German U-boat off St Abb's Head.
Worse was to follow on the twenty second when three cruisers, the *Aboukir,*

Hogue, and *Cressy*, were sunk off the Dutch coast with appalling loss of life by a single, obsolescent U-boat.

It was against this background that Munro laboured, and the Cromarty Firth's very own submarine scare took place, the famous 'Battle of Jemimaville.' In late October the Battle Cruiser Squadron commanded by David Beatty, later to be Commander-in-Chief, was moved to Cromarty. As it steamed slowly into anchor a 'periscope' was sighted in the waters of the Firth. Accounts vary as to what it was; some claim it was simply the wake of a ship, others that it was a ten foot long fishing buoy that had broken loose in the Moray Firth and drifted into the Cromarty Firth.[91] Firing commenced, and shells landed on a number of houses in Jemimaville, injuring a baby. The afflicted family was visited by a naval doctor and officer who assured it that *three* submarines had been hit. Years later one of the naval officers present at the time recalled: '. . . no Bar [has] yet been issued for the Battle of Jemimaville, but for those who were present it remains a treasured memory of the lighter side of the war.'[92]

Spy scares were another tragicomic aspect of those early weeks of the war. The Cromarty Firth was no stranger to these, and there is no doubt that German agents were in the area, but Beatty's letters while his squadron was stationed in the Cromarty Firth verged on the hysterical: 'It is a fact that all over Scotland, anywhere there is a possibility of there being a naval base, the postmistress (not master) is a German.'[93] King's Harbourmaster Munro claimed that the local Cromarty spy who travelled the country as a Polish packman was well-known; whenever he came into the town they were careful to prime him with false information.[94] The German governess of the children of a naval officer was also suspected.[95] Whatever the truth of these assertions, these feelings fed a small spy hysteria in the opening days of the war: a German schooner in harbour was impounded and the crew of a German fishing boat (found to have radio equipment on board) were arrested and sent to Perth.[96]

But even as the search for spies and the Battle of Jemimaville took place, the war was assuming a much more serious face. The lack of defences at Scapa Flow had forced the Grand Fleet to leave this anchorage and sail to the west coast of Scotland (and later Ireland). Beatty's Battle Cruiser Squadron abandoned the Cromarty Firth, leaving the North Sea in effect unpatrolled.

The first boom was assembled at the Caledonian Canal Basin in Inverness and was in place between the Sutors by 15 October. The whole structure was completed eleven days later, held in place by trawlers moored across the entrance to the Firth. The day after the boom was completed Admiral Pears, Senior Naval Officer in the Cromarty Firth, sent for Munro to pass on a message from the Admiralty:

> It is understood Commander Munro, King's Harbourmaster, has constructed and placed in position an anti submarine defence in the entrance of the Cromarty

Firth. This officer is to immediately forward through you his reasons and by whose authority this work has been carried out.[97]

Munro failed to comply with this request owing to pressure of work; at the same time he was also involved in setting up a naval hospital in Cromarty. Eventually, he was summoned to London to explain himself.

But Munro had powerful friends. On 17 October 1914 David Beatty wrote to Churchill from his flagship *Lion* which was then skulking in a sea inlet on the Isle of Mull:

We have no base where we can with *any* degree of safety lie for coaling, replenishing and refitting and repairing after two and a half months of war . . . The one place that has put up any kind of defence against the submarine is Cromarty, and that is because at Cromarty there happens to be a *man* who grapples with things as they are, i.e., Commander Munro . . . If the Fleet cannot spare the time and labour, turn it over to Commander Munro and give him a free hand and he will do it in a fortnight.[98]

Munro was given to understand that his career stood in the balance for he had upset some in the Admiralty. Yet, after explaining his work at Cromarty, he was put in charge of all northeastern harbour defences and given an office in the Admiralty, although he knew that the bulk of his work would be at Scapa Flow. He surrendered his charge at Cromarty 'with deep regret' but returned one last time to arrange his affairs. After leaving the town he drove along the spine of the Black Isle and looking north he saw:

This noble port bathed in moonlight, with a mighty fleet lying peacefully at anchor and more dimly the floating dock where a glare told of the docking work in progress. On the twin headlands behind me the flashing of numerous searchlights proclaimed the ceaseless vigil over the open sea . . . Guns, large and small, searchlights, booms, floating docks, oil fuel tanks etc. — all the various paraphernalia of a great war harbour had sprung up; thus changing the Port Salutis (*sic*) of the Romans into a safe haven for the mightiest armada that had ever entered its waters.[100]

But what sort of war was this mighty armada expected to fight? The British public expected another Trafalgar, a speedy and spectacular defeat of the Germans. The Germans expected a strict blockade of their ports which would allow them to mount harassing attacks upon close range enemy ships. Instead, the British chose a distant blockade, shutting off the English Channel and the two hundred-mile channel between Orkney, Shetland and Norway, thus denying the Germans access and trade with the outside world.

The Germans had, therefore, to come to grips with a long-range enemy. U-boats were but a partial answer; soon the Germans were using a new weapon, mines. Worse was to come for at Coronel in the South Pacific a German fleet under Admiral von Spee destroyed a British fleet under Cradock. Jellicoe ordered *Invincible* and *Inflexible* to leave Cromarty and, after

49. The floating dock submerged.

refitting at Devonport, to join a fleet in the South Atlantic under Admiral Sturdee. The resulting British victory over the Graf von Spee in the Falklands early in December was, however, diminished by the German raid on Scarborough on 11 December in which eighty-six civilians died and four hundred and twenty-four were wounded. Naval intelligence had predicted the raid and detachments were ordered south, including four ships of Beatty's Second Battle Cruiser Squadron, now returned to the Cromarty Firth. Unfortunately, because of bad signalling and deteriorating weather they failed to engage the enemy; the best opportunity so far for a decisive battle in home waters was lost.

The press reaction was furious and to placate public opinion Beatty's Cruiser Squadron was moved from Cromarty to Rosyth on 21 December to be closer to the German naval ports. It was proposed to bring the Grand Fleet from Scapa to Rosyth as well but Jellicoe feared the Firth of Forth because of its frequent fogs and the danger of being trapped should the rail bridge be destroyed. The Grand Fleet remained at Scapa and the Cruiser Squadron at Rosyth while the Cromarty Firth became the main base for armoured cruisers, supplemented by occasional visits by ships from Scapa and Rosyth.

As it turned out, the shape of naval warfare in 1915 was not to be based on these large ships of the Grand Fleet but instead on submarine and anti-

50. The floating dock with *HMS Akbar*.

submarine warfare, and mine laying and minesweeping in off-shore waters. In this sort of war Cromarty's position as a safe anchorage midway between Scapa and Rosyth and its facilities as a repair base was crucial.

At the outbreak of war the Cromarty Firth's population rocketed. Hundreds of dockyard workers followed the floating dock (Figs. 49, 50) north from Portsmouth and were housed initially in a merchant ship captured from the Germans.[101] 'The village of Invergordon (population 1,100) was speedily transformed into an industrial town, and also became a playground for Jack ashore. Cromarty (population 1,200), less affected industrially, was crowded with sailors and soldiers.' There were probably 20,000 people living in and around Invergordon.[102] In addition, military camps soon ringed the Firth. Housing and recreation facilities for this new, overwhelming population quickly sprang up. Early in 1915 a YMCA canteen and hall (Fig. 51) accommodating 2,500 was opened in Invergordon and by this time, too, the town had three cinemas. All of normal life was subsumed by the demands of the war. When blackout was proclaimed early in January 1915 a Balblair crofter was fined for failing to observe it.[103]

It was during 1915 that the Cromarty Firth had its only real submarine scare. The cruiser *Caernarvon* was fired on by a submarine while in the Moray Firth. As she entered the Firth through the gate in the boom at nine in the evening in bright moonlight, two of the floats holding the boom were seen to sink and the gate was closed only with difficulty. When repairs were made to the boom it was found that over two hundred feet of net weighing over two tons had vanished, probably caught by the pursuing submarine which must in turn have sunk under the weight of the net outside the entrance to the Firth.[104]

And then, early in August 1915, the German armed auxiliary ship *Meteor*, disguised as a merchant ship, sank a British Navy armed boarding steamer and, under cover of fog, laid a large minefield outside the entrance to the Cromarty Firth. The intention appears to have been not only to bottle up the Firth but also to immobilise Jellicoe's flagship *Iron Duke*, which was in port at the time. Instead, Jellicoe used the minefield to add to the Firth's defences by ordering that only side channels should be cleared through the field; the Moray Firth thus became too risky for U-boats to move freely about in, and Jellicoe and his ship were able to slip quietly away to Scapa through one of the newly cleared channels.[105]

By 1915 the naval life of the Cromarty Firth had settled into a kind of routine. Patrols came and went, the repair docks worked day and night, until suddenly on the last day of the year, this routine was horribly broken when HMS *Natal*, a 13,000 ton armoured cruiser (Fig. 52), blew up at her moorings in the Firth, turned over and sank within five minutes.[106] A Hogmanay party for local guests had been arranged on board the ship although bad weather kept many away. A band played, and in the wardroom a cinematograph show was in progress. Amongst the guests were the factor of Novar, Mr Harry Dods, his wife and three children, along with three nurses from the naval hospital at Cromarty. The explosion was seen, and felt, throughout the Firth. Nearly four hundred people, more than half the ship's complement, plus the day's guests, died.

Immediately rumours began: it was a torpedo; it was sabotage by a German spy disguised as a dockyard worker; a whole party of school children had been killed (in fact only the factor's three children were on board). Rumour grew in part because wartime security required that details of the explosion could not be reported. Even the Procurator Fiscal in Dingwall was denied details of the civilian deaths and the *Ross-shire Journal* was only able to report that Dods and his family had been wiped out 'as a result of a painful and distressing accident.' More white crosses appeared in the growing naval sections of the cemeteries at Cromarty and Rosskeen. An equally poignant reminder of the tragedy and the scores of bodies that were never found was the overturned hull of the *Natal* which over the years slowly settled into the mud of the Firth bottom. Naval ships entering the Firth continued to salute it for decades. Even after decades of salvage work and attempts to reduce its

51. The opening of the first naval canteen at Invergordon.

bulk as a navigational hazard, the wreck of the *Natal* is still marked by an isolated danger buoy.

A memorial service was held over the site of the wreck on New Year's Day 1916, and two days later the survivors and wounded were taken south to the *Natal*'s home port of Chatham where, on 17 January, a court martial was convened.[107] Its conclusions were straightforward; the explosion was internal and most likely caused by faulty cordite. No blame could be attached to the officers and men of the *Natal*.

On 25 April 1916 another German raiding force bombarded Yarmouth and Lowestoft. Although the fleets at Rosyth and Scapa had again been tipped off in advance their progress south to intercept the enemy was hampered by bad weather and they arrived too late. Once again the public, and the Royal Navy, had been denied a decisive battle. It appeared to many that it was only the Germans who were prepared to wage offensive war: in fact both sides were effectively stalemated.

By the late spring of 1916, however, both the British and German commanders had developed plans designed to lure out the enemy into strategic submarine traps. British naval intelligence was able to inform Jellicoe of Admiral Hipper's plans to send one fleet to the south coast of Norway to draw the British out while another German fleet doubled back on the west side of the Grand Fleet to trap it. At last the German fleet was venturing into the open sea. The combined British fleet set sail even before the Germans left port, Jellicoe from Scapa Flow and Beatty from Rosyth.[108] The eight ships of

H.M.S. NATAL.
Armoured Cruiser, 13,550 tons.

Cost £1,200,000; Length, 480 feet; Beam, 73¼ feet; Draught, 27½ feet; Speed, 22½ knots. Armed with Six 9.2 in.; Four 7.5 in.; Twenty-nine Small Quick Firing Guns, and Three Torpedo Tubes.

52. HMS *Natal*.

the Second Battle Squadron led by Vice-Admiral Sir Martyn Jerram, in his flagship *King George V*, sailed from the Cromarty Firth at midnight on 30 May to join them. With Jerram were the four obsolete ships of the First Cruiser Squadron led by Sir Robert Keith Arbuthnott. They were part of the greatest armada the world would ever see, one hundred and fifty ships and 70,000 men engaged in a 'titanic, half-blind race in the darkness of the ocean trailing unseen clouds of black smoke' to find their long-elusive enemy.[109] The British and German fleets met west of Jutland Bank at six in the evening of 31 May.

The sailing of such a fleet from the Cromarty Firth was, of course, a secret that could not be kept. More than two dozen ships had vanished from the Firth and it did not take much imagination to conclude that the long-promised naval battle was at last to take place. Soon rumours of a great naval battle began to sweep the countryside and when the ships returned on 2 June word had spread in advance of their coming. Crowds of local people and naval personnel lined the cliffs of the Sutors and the shore of the Firth to watch their return. Some did not come back. Three of Arbuthnott's four ships were hit and sunk including his own flagship *Defence*, which went down with all 850 men on board. Years later local people recalled standing on the Sutors, waiting for the return of the ships that had survived and seeing the '. . . holes in their sides [that] appeared to be circled with paint . . .'[110] Once again, too, the small funeral processions formed up to go to local graveyards, this time with the bodies of sailors who had survived the battle only to die ashore from the effects of their wounds.

The two floating docks now moored in the Cromarty Firth were busy in the days after the Battle of Jutland[111] despite the fact that in May 1916 the decision had been taken at last to make Rosyth the primary base on the Scottish east coast. Until defences could be completed there in the spring of 1918 the Cromarty Firth remained of vital strategic importance and a reflection of this importance was the introduction of the system of state liquor control in the Spring of 1916. The origins of the system went back to the summer of 1915. The Minister of Munitions, Lloyd George, was deeply concerned about the consequences of drink on war production: 'Drink is doing more damage than all the German submarines put together.' A Central Control Board was set up in 1915 to supervise all aspects of the drinks trade and its provisions covered almost all of Scotland. In April 1916 a scheme of direct control was introduced to more sensitive areas such as Carlisle, Gretna (where there were munitions plants) and the Cromarty Firth. 'On' and 'off' sales were separated and 'off' sales permitted only to genuine residents of the area. The government acquired a number of hotels to control the bar trade, opening hours were reduced to four and a half a day, and to provide accommodation for naval officers and their families.[112] The system of state liquor control was to prove one of the most lasting legacies of the Great War, being abolished only in 1972.

By 1917 there were 3,000 dockyard workers in Invergordon (Fig. 53) including by this time a number of women, many of them former fisherlassies. After Jutland it was realised there would be no more great set-piece battles. The war would return to what it had been before, a struggle against the submarine menace and mines. Much of the work of the Invergordon dockyard after Jutland was refitting ships with anti-mine devices called paravanes and 'blisters' which rendered ship's sides immune from torpedo attacks.[113]

In the autumn of 1917 it was decided to lay barrages of mines across the English Channel and a 'Northern Barrage', two hundred and forty miles long, between the Northern Isles and Norway. The Americans, who had entered the war in April 1917, had developed a particularly powerful mine, and it was agreed that they should be primarily responsible for laying the Northern Barrage. Grangemouth became the British base for this operation and the Cromarty Firth was set aside for the Americans. Equipment was shipped from the United States to Kyle of Lochalsh and then taken by rail across Scotland to the Cromarty Firth. Dalmore Distillery, with its convenient rail spur, was taken over by the Admiralty in November 1917 and rebuilt to accommodate about 1,250 men.[114] A rail link was constructed between Dalmore (Fig. 54) and Invergordon harbour and an additional arm was added to the timber east pier in Invergordon for loading the mines on board ship. Construction began on an embankment and pier, still called 'The Yankee Pier', to the south of the distillery but these were not completed by November 1918.

53. Dockyard mateys leaving Invergordon, *c*.1916.

Before the Americans arrived, however, a British naval detail was sent to move some three hundred thousand gallons of whisky to other distilleries. Some of the barrels were transported on the newly laid railway line to Invergordon harbour while other consignments went by lorry. All were accompanied by an excise officer, but even so some ratings found that by

54. Mine assembly base at Dalmore Distillery.

pressing the barrels the staves would open and whisky could be leaked from the casks into buckets.

The American officers and ratings arrived in the Cromarty Firth early in 1918 and in May mines began to be delivered to the Northern Barrage when ten American minelaying ships arrived.[115] The American sailors were a novelty around the Firth. Their pay was high and this made them popular with local girls and unpopular with British sailors. There was a near disaster at Dalmore itself when a fire started during a party for local girls held in one of the former bonded warehouses. There were some marriages but there were also some fights and eventually the American sailors were confined to quarters. By the time of the Armistice thirty eight and a half thousand mines had been shipped from Dalmore and the Northern Barrage was nearly complete.

And then, quite suddenly, it was all over. The official announcement of peace came through the Post Office telegraph and, as the word spread on 11 November, bunting began to appear on houses and people met in the street and shook hands. In Invergordon the American sailors ignored their orders and poured into the town. Soon they were joined by men of the Scottish Rifles with pipe and brass bands. A wagon was drawn up near the fountain and from it Provost Macdonald addressed the crowd to great cheers.

The official celebrations would come later, in July 1919, and by then it was easier to see just what the consequences of the war had been for the Cromarty Firth. It was time to count the cost, and look to the future.

NOTES

1. D. Defoe, *A Tour through the Whole Island of Great Britain*, London, 1971, pp. 662–3.

2. Gordon, 'Nigg', War and Strife, pp. 1–2.

3. Cromartie, *A Highland History*, p. 223.

4. PRO ADM 57/4198.

5. *Ibid*.

6. PRO ADM/L/S 225, Log of the *Shark*. For the background to the *Shark*'s activities see W. E. May, 'The *Shark* and the '45', *Mariner's Mirror*, vol. 53, Cambridge, August, 1967. I am most grateful to Flt. Lt. P. D. R. Moriarty of Culcairn House, for drawing this article to my attention.

7. PRO ADM/L/S 255.

8. Cromartie, *History*, p. 244.

9. *Ibid*.

10. J. Gibson, *Ships of the '45*, London, 1967, p. 41.

11. PRO, ADM 51/4198.

12. *OSA*, Cromarty, vol. 12, p. 250.

13. R. Fraser, 'A Letter to the Rt. Hon. Charles Abbot, Speaker of the House of Commons, containing an inquiry into the most effectual means of improvement of the Coasts and Western Isles of Scotland and the Extension of the Fisheries', London, 1803, p. 41.

14. T. Telford, A Survey and report of the Coasts and Central Highlands of Scotland Made by the Command of the Rt. Hon. the Lords Commissioners of HM Treasury in the Autumn of 1802, PP 1802–3, vol. iii, pp. 10–11.

15. *Ibid*.

16. *Ibid*.

17. Fourth report from the committee on the survey of the coasts etc of Scotland: Naval Stations and Fisheries, June 1803, p. 86.

18. *Ibid*.

19. *Ibid*., Appendix no. 3.

20. R. Fraser, 'A letter to the Rt. Hon. Charles Abbot . . .' pp. 41–2.

21. 'Charlie Napier and the Baltic Fleet', broadside, published in Glasgow, 12 January 1855. I am indebted to Adam McNaughtan for drawing my attention to this song.

22. The ships included H.M.S. *Rosamund, Dragon, Basilisk* (six guns) *Vulture* and *Cossack* (twenty guns). See *IC*, 21 December 1854; 1 February 1855 and correspondence with the Admiralty and Vice Admiral Sir C. Napier respecting naval operations in the Baltic (1854). Navy Records Society, no. 88.

23. *IC*, 4 January 1855.

24. *IC*, 18 January 1855.

25. *IC*, 15 February 1855.

26. PRO, WO 33 (5): 'General Report of the Defence of Commercial Harbours in the United Kingdom'.

27. *PP*, 1857–8, vol. 14, Select Committee on harbours of refuge, Questions 2216–2220.

28. For the *Lizard*'s visits, see *int. al. IT*, 16 July, 3 September 1862; 22 July 1863.

29. PRO WO 33 (10), p. 39.

30. *IT*, 6 July 1859, p. 1.

31. *IT*, 20 June 1860.

32. *IT*, 21 May 1862.

33. *IT*, 5 August 1863. The ships were: *Black Prince* (iron), 41 guns, 6,109 tons, 1,259 horsepower, 650 men; *Emerald* (wood), 35 guns, 2,913 tons, 600 horsepower, 570 men; *Warrior* (wood), 40 guns, 6,109 tons, 1,250 horsepower, 650 men; *Royal Oak* (iron), 35 guns, 4,056 tons, 800 horsepower, 600 men; *Edgar* (wood), 71 guns, 3,091 tons, 600 horsepower, 750 men; *Liverpool* (wood), 39 guns, 2,656 tons, 600 horsepower, 600 men; *Defence* (iron), 16 guns, 3,720 tons, 600 horsepower, 600 men; *Resistance* (iron), 16 guns, 3,712 tons, 400 horsepower, 600 men, and the wooden gunboat, *Trinculo*, of 60 horsepower.

34. *IT*, 16 September 1863.

35. *IT*, 26 August 1863.

36. *IT*, 24 June 1863, p. 2.

37. *IT*, 14 September 1864.

38. *IT*, 19 August 1874.

39. *RJ*, 25 June 1875.

40. This account is based on *RJ*, 7, 13, 16 July 1883.

41. *IT*, 16 October 1885, p. 3.

42. *RJ*, 5 September 1902, p. 5.

43. *RJ*, 24 October 1902, p. 7.

44. *RJ*, 13 February 1903, p. 7; 20 February 1903, p. 7.

45. *RJ*, 20 February 1903.

46. B. B. Schofield, *British Sea Power: Naval Policy in the Twentieth Century*, London, 1967, p. 34; Inverkeithing High School, *The story of Rosyth*, rev. ed., 1982, pp. 85–8.

47. *RJ*, 6 March 1903, p. 6.

48. Letter dated 2 August 1912; *Fear God and Dread Nought; the Correspondence of Admiral of the Fleet, Lord Fisher of Kilverstone, 1904–14*, vol. 2, ed. A. J. Marder, London, 1956, no. 384.

49. *RJ*, 5 July 1907, p. 5.

50. R. Hough, *The Great War at Sea 1914–18*, Oxford, 1983, p. 29; *RJ*, 17 July 1908, p. 7.

51. See for example, *RJ*, 1 December 1911, p. 5.

52. *RJ*, 6 December 1907, p. 5.

53. *RJ*, 23, 30 September, 7 October 1904. In fact the Home Fleet's visit was curtailed. There were two main Fleets in home waters that regularly called into the Cromarty Firth during Fisher's period as First Sea Lord: the Reserve Fleet, based at Devonport, Sheerness and Portsmouth and the Home Fleet (renamed the Channel Fleet). In March 1909 all naval forces in home waters, except the Atlantic Fleet, based at Gibraltar, were combined into the Home Fleet, which was subsequently renamed the Grand Fleet at the outbreak of war in 1914.

54. *RJ*, 10 November 1905, p. 7.

55. *RJ*, 9 March 1906, p. 6.

56. *RJ*, 26 July 1907, p. 7.

57. *RJ*, 25 October 1907, p. 5.

58. *IT*, 23 August 1911.

59. *RJ*, 18 October 1901, p. 5.

60. *RJ*, 31 October 1902.

61. *RJ*, 3 August 1906, p. 4.

62. *IT*, 30 October 1912.

63. A. J. Marder, *From Dreadnought to Scapa Flow: The road to war, 1904–14*, vol. 1, Oxford, 1961, pp. 144, 216.

64. A. J. Marder, *Fear God and Dread Nought*, vol. 2, no. 385.

65. *RJ*, 21 July 1911, p. 5.

66. Invergordon Cartulary, no. 2, pp. 271–4; *RJ*, 13 September 1912; 5 August, 1913; *IC*, 20 May 1913.

67. *IT*, 28 May 1913.

68. *IC*, 9 September 1913, p. 7.

69. Marder, *Fear God and Dread Nought*, vol. 2, p. 415.

70. *IT*, 4 June 1913.

71. *IT*, 20 November 1912.

72. *IC*, 22 July 1913; 12 August 1913.

73. Schofield, *British Sea Power*, p. 37.

74. His account is to be found in D. J. Munro, *Scapa Flow; a naval retrospect*, London, 1932.

75. *Ibid.*, pp. 141ff.

76. *RJ*, 6 September 1912, p. 5.

77. Munro, *Scapa Flow*, pp. 153–6.

78. *Army and Navy Gazette*, March 28 1914, p. 278.

79. *RJ*, 17 January 1913, p. 7.

80. *IT*, 10 April 1913; see especially Major General Sir William Knox, 'The latest comedy in home defence', *The Nineteenth Century*, vol. 19, 1914, pp. 939–44.

81. Munro, *Scapa Flow*, p. 167.

82. *IC*, 21 July 1914; *IT*, 24 July 1914.

83. *RJ*, 16 May 1913, p. 7.

84. *RJ*, 27 June 1913, p. 5.

85. *IT*, 30 July 1913.

86. *RJ*, 2 January 1913, p. 7; 24 October 1913, p. 5.

87. *RJ*, 10 October 1913, p. 8.

88. Admiralty Orders in Council, 1913, no. 55.

89. Munro, *Scapa Flow*, p. 171.

90. The following account of the placing of the boom across the entrance to the Cromarty Firth and its consequences is based on *Ibid.*, pp. 180ff.

91. See Hough, *Great War at Sea*, pp. 171–2; 'Griff' (A.S.G.) *Surrendered: Some Naval War Secrets*, Twickenham, nd. pp. 183–4 (for the buoy story).

92. Admiral Sir Reginald Plunkett-Ernle-Erle-Drax, quoted in Marder, *From Dreadnought to Scapa Flow*, vol. 2, Oxford, 1965, p. 67.

93. S. Roskill, *Admiral of the Fleet: Earl Beatty, the last Naval Hero*, London, 1980, p. 88.

94. Munro, *Scapa Flow*, p. 174.

95. 'Griff', *Surrendered*, p. 17.

96. *RJ*, 14 August 1914, p. 8.

97. Munro, *Scapa Flow*, p. 187.

98. W. S. Chalmers, *Life and letters of Earl Beatty*, London, 1951, pp. 158–9.

99. Munro, *Scapa Flow*, pp. 187–8.

100. *Ibid.*, p. 190; The boom pioneered at Cromarty became the standard pattern for all ports in Britain, including Scapa Flow. *Ibid.*, p. 218.

101. J. Jellicoe, *The Grand Fleet, 1914–16*, London, 1919, p. 79.

102. H. Carter, *The Control of the Drink Trade*, London, 1919, p. 175.

103. *RJ*, 15 January 1915, p. 3.

104. Munro, *Scapa Flow*, p. 220.

105. Marder, *Dreadnought to Scapa Flow*, vol. 2, p. 368; *RJ*, 31 January 1919, p. 3.

106. The best account of the 'Natal' explosion is A. C. Hampshire, *They Called it Accident*, London, 1961, although the author's suggestion of long-range sabotage does not seem entirely credible.

107. The court martial records are in PRO ADM 1/8445/9.

108. There is no truth to the story that Jellicoe himself sailed from the Cromarty Firth to Jutland, although he rented New Tarbat House during the war, and was often in the Firth.

109. Hough, *Great War at Sea*, pp. 205, 214ff; the figures for the ships are based on Marder, *From Dreadnought to Scapa Flow*, vol. 2, p. 457. The Second Battle Squadron consisted of *King George V, Ajax, Centurion, Erin, Orion, Monarch, Conqueror, Thunderer*; the First Cruiser Squadron of *Defence, Warrior, Duke of Edinburgh* and *Black Prince*. In addition Jerram's force was screened by eleven M-Class destroyers.

110. SWRI, 'Nigg', p. 25.

111. Jellicoe, *Grand Fleet*, p. 80.

112. For the history of liquor control see I. Donnachie, 'World War I and the Drink Question: State Control of the drink trade', *Scottish Labour History Society Journal*, vol. 17 (1982), pp. 19–26. Carter, *Control of the Drink Trade*, pp. 63, 175–8, gives details of the arrangements around the Cromarty Firth. Between 1916 and 1918 a total of 39 licensed premises were acquired and nineteen suppressed as redundant. In Invergordon there were two hotels with public bars, two public houses and three licensed grocers, in Cromarty there were two hotels with public bars, three public houses and one licensed grocer. 'Off' sales were concentrated at one licensed premise in each town. With the establishment of the American base at Dalmore in 1918 the system was extended to Alness and its surrounding settlements; and by the summer of that year it was extended again to include Dingwall and the remainder of the coastline of the Cromarty Firth.

113. 'Griff', *Surrendered*, pp. 172–3.

114. The following discussion of the American minelaying base and its activities is based on 'Griff', *Surrendered*, pp. 177–83 and 'Minelaying bases at Grangemouth, Dalmore and Glen-Albyn', *Technical History of the Great War*, vol. 6, Part 45, London, 1920.

115. The American flotilla included the *San Francisco, Baltimore, Roanoke, Canadaigua, Caronicus, Housatonic, Quinnegang, Saranac, Shawmut, Arostook*.

8

'The war was a very peculiar thing'

> The war was a very peculiar thing. People talked about it a great deal, and always in phrases like 'because of the war' and 'to, with, by and from the war' and in a sighing way of 'before the war' and in a sad way of 'at or in the war'. The war did hundreds of dreadful things . . . it was a thing even more mysterious than the tide that swung the big ships round in the Firth on their buoys . . . But even the moon, which controlled the tides, and the sun, which could ripen the corn, could do nothing about the war apparently.[1]

That child's eye view of the effect of the Great War around the Cromarty Firth, from Jane Duncan's novel *My Friends the Miss Boyds*, catches the all-pervasive influence of the conflict on the local population who, in a sense, experienced two wars. The first was the 'public' war, connected with the navy and army on their doorstep, the second was the 'private' war of change and personal loss.

Many local people worked in the dockyard or in other naval establishments around the Firth or were engaged in reserved agricultural work. Volunteers helped run canteens and social clubs for the thousands of servicemen who thronged the countryside. There were regular concerts and collections to raise money for war charities. Local girls were in great demand for dances and outings. All these personal contacts created a highly efficient bush telegraph that kept local people well informed of naval events including ones supposed to be top-secret, such as the return of the fleet from Jutland. The people saw the great ships come and go, and took pride and had compassion in their exploits (Fig. 55).

Many of the events of these years have become part of the folklore of the Cromarty Firth. Memories of the *Natal*, the bombardment of Jemimaville, and the arrival of the German crews from the ships scuttled at Scapa Flow in 1919 are still current as are stories of the day in 1917 when a group of Russian soldiers passed through Invergordon on their way to the Western Front. Stories of Russians marching through the streets of Britain in the Great War were common; what is unusual about Invergordon's Russian story is that it is true. The main contingent disembarked with their French officers from *The City of Marseilles*, and marched past large and curious crowds to the railway station to music provided by the Cameron Highlanders' Band. Part of the contingent, however, was quarantined in war workers' huts behind the church, where they became an object of curiosity for the small boys of the town who hoped for souvenirs of buttons and insignia. Some Russian soldiers made friends with local girls and maintained contact by military post cards after they had reached the Western Front.[2]

55. The fleet in the Cromarty Firth.

There was not a single aspect of local life that was not touched by the war. Local houses, church halls and schools were taken over as hospitals, canteens, social clubs and offices. Within five weeks at the end of 1914 a camp with over one hundred buildings and space for 3,000 officers and men was built at Nigg; others were built at Invergordon and Cromarty.[3] In addition, huts and houses for war workers, such as Admiralty Cottages, and the row of officers' houses along Shore Road were built. It was said that during the war the population of the town and its neighbourhood swelled to 20,000.[4] The thousands of war workers who flooded into the region brought profound changes.

The war opened the region to the wider world. It is difficult to appreciate now how cut off the Cromarty Firth was in the early decades of this century. The seaboard villages were dependent for their war news on a newspaper taken by a single shopkeeper; in Invergordon many people received their news from bulletins posted in shop windows. In 1914 this isolation ended. London policemen guarded the dockyard. A Welsh male voice choir made up of dockyard workers used Invergordon church hall for their rehearsals until it was taken over in 1916 as an emergency hospital during the diphtheria and scarlet fever epidemic. By that year, too, women construction workers had been brought in and the *Ross-shire Journal* remarked with some surprise: 'Women War Workers are engaged as builders' labourers at Invergordon, and are doing what, in other days, would have been deemed heavy work with remarkable ease and ability.' One of the projects on which they worked was the Admiralty Hospital (Fig. 56), where builders had an eighty hour week including something previously inconceivable, Sunday work. It was, in fact, traditional religion that suffered most from the changes brought by war and the war workers. The Ross-shire War Food Production Committee held heated discussions about the morality of Sunday work but had to allow it.[5] Local people were deeply offended by the use of the Invergordon naval sports grounds on Sundays but the practice continued. The last Gaelic service in Invergordon Church took place in 1917 and in the same year an organ was introduced for evening services at Nigg Free Church to make them more attractive to soldiers from the nearby camps.

The war also changed the physical appearance of the countryside. Woods planted in the eighteenth and nineteenth centuries at places such as Novar and the Hill of Nigg and nurtured over the decades were cut down in the space of a few years as part of the war effort.

Trees could be replaced but the soldiers and sailors of the Cromarty Firth who died in the Great War were gone forever. The death of a generation of young men was the central fact of that other, 'private', war experienced by the people of the Cromarty Firth. Something of what this war meant can be glimpsed in the diary Miss Rosa Williamson Ross of Pitcalnie began to keep in the frost-bound early days of 1918. By March the 'Big Push' had begun on the Western Front and she wrote of:

> The dreadful casualty lists that are coming out each day. At the end of last week the death was in the paper of Ian Mackenzie, the Town Clerk's son. They had not been quite certain about him, but they must have heard for certain now. He must have been in that first awful rush of the enemy out of the smoke when our 51st Division met them and the Seaforths returned eight times to the attack.[6]

Death in battle was no respecter of rank: it took the son of the Town Clerk of Tain, the ploughman and the aristocrat. It was said that by 1918 not one direct male heir was left on any estate between Beauly and Invergordon; in the closing weeks of the war the young heir to Foulis was killed.

Many of the men of the seaboard villages were in the Royal Naval Volunteers and served at sea, but the majority of local men joined the army. The local territorial unit was the 4th Battalion of the Seaforth Highlanders, the descendant of the First Company of the Ross Rifle Volunteers, begun in 1860, with companies raised in Invergordon, Tain, Dingwall, Avoch, Knockbain, Alness and Evanton, which in 1887 became the First (Ross Highland) Volunteer Battalion of the Seaforth Highlanders.[7] Early in the following century these volunteer companies became part of the newly-formed Territorial Force and were reorganised into companies raised from Tain (with Fearn and Edderton), Invergordon (with Kildary) and Alness (with Evanton). Both the local Seaforths and the Lovat Scouts (Fig. 57), which had been reformed after the Boer War and whose recruitment area extended to the Cromarty Firth, had just returned from summer training at Aviemore when

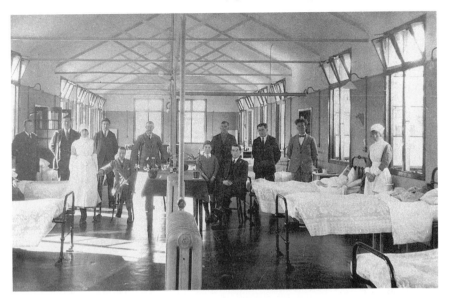

56. The Admiralty Hospital, Invergordon.

the telegram ordering the Seaforths' mobilisation arrived at the headquarters in Dingwall at 6.30 p.m. on Tuesday 4 August 1914. In response to bugle calls of 'Assemble' and 'Fall In' played throughout the town, men began to gather at the drill hall while quiet, anxious crowds filled the streets. There was little of the euphoria which had greeted the outbreak of the South African War. Detachments of Seaforths and Camerons were ordered to garrison the Sutors immediately and by the afternoon of the following day five hundred men of the 4th Battalion were hard at work digging entrenchments at Nigg. They were recalled a few days later for an impressive Sunday church parade at Dingwall before the entire battalion was sent south to Bedford for training. There they were joined for the first time with the 51st Highland Division.

By the first week of November their training was over and the battalion was on its way to France; it was one of the first Territorial units to arrive on the Western Front. The local Seaforths were heavily engaged at Neuve Chapelle, Loos and the Somme, where they captured and held Beaumont Hamel. Losses were heavy and by the end of the war the entire regiment had lost 8,000 men.[8]

The initial excitement at the news of peace in November 1918 was followed by a feeling of relief and a desire to return to normal life as quickly as possible although there were delays. Early in January 1919 seven hundred men of the Third Reserve Battalion of the Seaforth Highlanders protested against their continued training and the slowness of demobilisation by marching into Cromarty from their camp.[9] The following June a contingent of Gordons, encamped at Invergordon, became alarmed by rumours that they were to be

57. Lovat Scouts at Alness station.

drafted to India for two years instead of being demobilised. With the support of the townspeople and dockworkers they marched to the Town Hall and, despite promises that their grievances would be looked into, two hundred and fifty-four men set off to march to their headquarters at Aberdeen. When they arrived in Dingwall they were met by police patrols and curious crowds filled the streets to watch the men march through to a bivouac outside the town. After further appeals from their officers, and much discussion amongst themselves, the soldiers decided to march back to Invergordon where they were eventually demobilised.[10]

These first 'Invergordon mutinies' took place against the beginning of the slow dismantling of the naval presence around the Cromarty Firth. By April 1919 a certain amount of demobilisation had taken place, including that of the fishing vessels requisitioned for patrol duty in the Moray Firth. By July 1919 a decision had been taken about the fortifications on the Sutors. The guns and mountings were to remain in place, with the guns disabled, and the sites looked after on a care and maintenance basis.[11]

That was a relatively straightforward matter: elsewhere the rights and obligations of the Admiralty and the civilian authorities had become completely intermixed. For example, the cost of Invergordon's water supply had been shared by the local authority and the Admiralty. Who would run it in peacetime? And how would rights and responsibility be divided? For some of the buildings and facilities there were neat and satisfactory solutions: the Naval Hospital in Invergordon, with its two hundred and fifty beds and all its equipment, was sold to the new local Health Board for £30,000 in 1921 and became a hospital for infectious diseases.[12] The real problems clustered around the future of the dockyard facilities and the use of the piers and harbours of the Firth.

A few weeks after war began in 1914 the Admiralty and the Cromarty Harbour Trustees had agreed that the harbour was to have new landing stages, a crane and adequate lighting for the use of the navy. These improvements were to be paid for and maintained by the Harbour Trustees.[13] At the end of the war it was relatively easy to return control of Cromarty Harbour to the Trustees who, officially at least, had never ceased to be responsible for it. There was, however, little left for them to administer. The local fishing industry had been finally killed by the naval boom and the mining of the Moray Firth; only inshore line fishing from sailing boats survived. In May 1920 it was claimed that the only ship permanently anchored in the harbour was the lifeboat.[14]

The Trustees never recovered from the wartime cost of improving and maintaining Cromarty Harbour. By 1930 the condition of the harbour works had deteriorated so badly (the bridge was so dangerous that it could not be used) that the local branch of the National Farmers' Union summoned a meeting to see if the debts could not be remitted and some kind of unemployment grant be given to improve the quays; but little was done over the next few years and Cromarty Harbour deteriorated even further.[15]

At Invergordon the problem was larger and a good deal more complex. Invergordon was retained as a Fleet repairing base after the Armistice[16] but soon the Select Committee on National Expenditure was suggesting that high wages and excessive overtime at the dockyard had led to a loss of efficiency and that the work could be as well done in the south.[17] On the whole this idea was resisted, but it did find a firm supporter in the Easter Ross Farmers' Club, whose members complained early in the following year that demobilised servicemen were working at the Invergordon dockyard rather than returning to the land. That was not surprising when the average wage for a week's work on a farm was twenty-one shillings, eight shillings less than could be earned at the dockyard.[18]

Nevertheless, the number of naval employees in Invergordon began to drop. At the end of the war there were four and a half thousand people working for the Admiralty in the town but over the following year this number was cut by two thousand.[19] Admiralty Cottages emptied and some were converted into storehouses. By the autumn of 1919 charges of profiteering and profligacy against the Invergordon dockyard were being made in London papers such as the *Evening Standard* and wild rumours were circulating in Invergordon about the future of the installation.[20] It was said that the floating docks would soon be sent south. On 26 September the *Ross-shire Journal* commented that if the dockyard went, 'Invergordon would return to its earlier state of soporific dreariness, when for hours on end one might wander up and down the main street without meeting half a dozen of his kind.'

In the following month the axe fell. The two hundred oil tanks were to be retained for use as a fuelling base along with necessary plant and machinery. The rest was to go. The yard was to be shut by the end of the year. Hundreds of men were given their notices and began to be paid off. The Admiralty was said to be seeking a civilian buyer to take over the base as a going concern. This devastating announcement was compounded by the arrival of the great influenza epidemic of 1919.

In some ways the atmosphere of these days following the announcement of the closure of the dockyard resembled the emotional and industrial roller coaster ride experienced by Invergordon in the 1970s and '80s. A memorial was sent by the people of the town to the Admiralty urging that a private buyer be allowed to take over the dock to provide a replacement industry for the region and stop the drift of the Highland population south.[21] There were, in fact, discussions about setting up a ship-breaking yard and it was claimed that a Scottish engineering works had offered £4,500,000 for the dockyard although Admiralty records show that the offer was £1,500,000, which was later raised by a further £100,000.[22] More rumours began to sweep the town, born more of desperation than fact. It was said that Lord Leverhulme, then involved in his Lewis schemes, was thinking of doing something similar at Invergordon.[23]

When the offer for the dockyard was turned down by the Admiralty, the base was put in the hands of the Surplus Government Property Disposal Board and the fixtures, including machinery, generators, locomotives and rails, were sold piecemeal.[24] The floating docks left the Firth: one returned to her Dutch owners in Rotterdam, the others to Portsmouth. A good deal of surplus material was sold locally and many families benefitted. Pipes, doors, windows, sinks and baths from redundant camps and huts were bought and used along with corrugated iron and flooring to improve local houses.

But the biggest sale of all, of Invergordon Harbour itself, had already taken place. Although the Admiralty had effectively taken over the harbour at the beginning of the war, the situation was not regularised until a month before the Armistice, when MacLeod of Cadboll sold the harbour and Balblair Ferry to the Admiralty for £16,000, with a further £1,000 paid to the Cadboll Trustees for use before that date.[25]

Within weeks of the end of the war the Easter Ross Farmers' Club and Invergordon Town Council were pressing for the restoration of civilian facilities at Invergordon harbour. Not only had the war cut off nearly all civil shipping into the Firth but it was also claimed that the revival of seaborne trade was being prevented by the high charges made by the Admiralty. The situation was eventually sorted out by the passage of the Invergordon Harbour

58. The High Street, Invergordon.

(Transfer) Bill by Parliament in June 1920.[26] Essentially, this bill legitimated the statutory rights conveyed in the sale to the Admiralty in 1918 and allowed the naval authorities to return to civilian management the control of certain parts of the harbour in which they had no further interest, such as Balblair Ferry.

While allowing civilian use of the harbour, the navy remained in overall control, a situation that continued until the creation of the Cromarty Firth Port Authority in 1974. The dockyard may have gone but Invergordon remained very much a naval town (Fig. 58). The Fleet still came in during its annual spring and autumn exercises and by the early 1920s the Royal Air Force presence in the Firth began to be built up. The Royal Naval Air Service amalgamated with the Royal Flying Corps in April 1918 and was renamed the Royal Air Force with the naval branch of the new force known as the Fleet Air Arm from the early 1920s. At the time the Invergordon Harbour Bill was passing through Parliament the *Ross-shire Journal* reported that seven aeroplanes attached to H.M.S. *Argus* were at Delny airfield. Two years later 'Newton of Novar Aerodrome' (later called Evanton or Novar) was opened as the shore station for the Fleet Air Arm of the Royal Air Force although for some years the station consisted only of a cluster of tents on a corner of the twenty acre site.[27]

The other major installation to be returned to civilian ownership was Dalmore Distillery. Part of the complex had been destroyed by fire in February 1919 and the premises were handed back only in June 1920. It took over a year for the buildings to be restored and malting to resume, by which time the owner, Andrew Mackenzie, and the Admiralty were locked in contention over compensation. Eventually, the case went to the House of Lords in 1925.[28]

But the return to normality was not an easy process; indeed it was impossible, since the whole basis of society has shifted and changed. In *My Friends the Miss Boyds* Jane Duncan reflects one such change: the breaking up of many of the large estates which had provided the framework for so much of the agricultural and social life of the region. At the beginning of the novel the 'Laird of Poyntdale' is still performing his traditional role as a father figure to his tenants and estate workers. It is the laird who charters the puffers to bring tenants' coal and it is he who oversees the seasonal life of the estate which reaches its climax in the harvest-home. By the end of the novel 'Poyntdale' has been forced to sell all but the home farm and to let many of his servants go, including the grieve who is the heroine's father.

This fictional picture was paralleled in real life around the Firth. Some estates changed hands as early as the closing years of the nineteenth century but the process accelerated after the war. Matheson of Ardross was scarcely an old family but it was an important one. The estate was sold by Sir Alexander Matheson's grandson in 1898 to C. W. Dyson Perrins, the sauce manufacturer, director of the Royal Worcester Porcelain Factory, art collector and philanthropist. A few years later Perrins also bought the neighbouring estates of Glencalvie and Dibiedale.[29] The Perrins family came north in the summer for sport but they also continued Matheson's tradition of interest and help for people on the estate and in the local community. In 1904 they gave a public hall and library to Alness and later provided a golf course, and their annual children's parties are still recalled with affection. Mr Perrins also introduced electricity, decades before it was supplied to other rural areas, to the estate and its neighbourhood, with Mrs Perrins switching on the Alness supply in 1924. On the estate itself new roads were built and more land reclaimed. In 1908 Perrins established a model croft at Balrishallich, under the direction of Mr Esslemont; it was later run by the North of Scotland Agricultural College as a demonstration centre for farming techniques suitable for smallholdings. The croft became especially important as a poultry station for the whole north east of Scotland.[30]

Ardross, however, was unusual not just because of the size of the estate but also because of the amount of money the new owners were able to put into local development. The Perrins' fortune protected Ardross against some very harsh winds that blew away other large estates completely and even at Ardross a number of farms were sold in the early 1920s before the estate itself was broken up and sold in the 1930s.

In 1919 MacLeod of Cadboll began to sell his estates between Evanton and Tain.[31] Invergordon Castle with its forty-eight bedrooms was bought, initially by a Larbert timber merchant then by Sir William Martineau, a sugar manufacturer, who lived there until the castle was demolished in 1928.[32] Many of the Cadboll tenants were able to buy their farms as did tenants on the

59. Balnagown Castle.

estates of Findon and Newhall, which were being broken up in the early 1920s. This huge change in land tenure produced the characteristic pattern of large owner-occupied farms that ring much of the Cromarty Firth to the present day.[33]

One exception to this general rule of decline was the estate of Lockhart Ross of Balnagown (Figs. 59–62). In the late nineteenth century the estate had been in financial difficulties, largely due to the ineptitude of the then laird, Charles William. He was a fine sportsman but not an administrator and is chiefly remembered for his eccentricities which included the habit of perching in a favourite oak tree near the castle leaving only when his wife sent a piper to calm him down. Perhaps not surprisingly he became known as 'The Jackdaw', a nickname which survived until recently as the name of a local hotel.

The last laird of Balnagown succeeded his demented father in 1883 when he was eleven years old. Sir Charles was indulged from childhood from the proceeds of the estate: he was sent to Eton with his own piper, footman, gamekeeper and two personal servants. At Cambridge University he excelled in sport and his studies of law, classics and engineering.

His return to his estate began its transformation and also produced the first indication of the excesses and dangerous quirks of character which were to mark the rest of Sir Charles's extraordinary life. He blamed his mother for the poor condition of Balnagown's half million acres and eventually drove her

60. Repairs to Balnagown Castle.

from the castle by dint of boarding her up in her apartments for three weeks and, when that failed, by setting fire to her hair. Once she had retreated to the dower house at Scotsburn Sir Charles instituted proceedings against her for the mismanagement of Balnagown. This was the beginning of a long and colourful litigious career which included litigation with wives, factors, the

61. Sir Charles Lockhart Ross.

Inland Revenue, companies, banks, neighbouring landowners, the American and Canadian governments, insurance companies, lawyers and friends. Where his ancestors used fire and sword, Sir Charles used the law and his own irascible and wayward character to get his way.

Sir Charles was a gifted engineer and determined to revive the fortunes of Balnagown but on his own terms, like so many improvers of the eighteenth century. The estate was reformed using money earned in business ventures elsewhere, in this case from the Ross military and sporting rifles which were his invention. In 1901 the Canadian government decided to have its own military rifle after accepting Sir Charles's offer to manufacture rifles in a factory built at his own expense. At Balnagown Sir Charles built a workshop, and manufactured equipment for use on the estate, land was reclaimed and modern farming techniques, such as feeding silage to cattle, were introduced. Sir Charles oversaw every detail.

By the end of the First World War the Inland Revenue sought to tax his profits. The laird ignored their claims and eventually the Inland Revenue attempted to seize Balnagown itself. The laird retaliated by having Balnagown declared a ward of the Delaware Court thus making it in effect United States' territory. In response the British government declared Sir Charles an outlaw, the last time this ancient practice was invoked. Sir Charles took up residence in the United States and ran his estate from there apart from furtive and

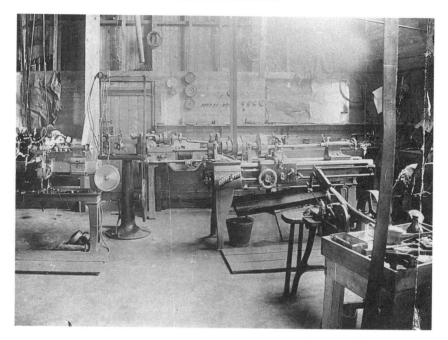

62. The machine shop at Balnagown Castle.

speedy visits to Easter Ross when the American flag was flown from the castle. When it was requisitioned in World War II the laird claimed that British troops were occupying American soil and demanded that these 'foreign troops' should be withdrawn immediately.

Sir Charles Ross died in exile in 1942 but not before he had wired Churchill demanding to be made Minister of Agriculture 'so that when the British, without my advice, are blown to bits they will at least go with full bellies.' If Sir Charles failed in his attempt to be the only genuine outlaw to sit in the British Cabinet, his wilful, larger than life character formed a fitting end to a line which had been major landowners in Easter Ross for centuries.

At the other end of the agricultural scale was the growth of post-war smallholdings. This development had a long pedigree, stretching back to the 'Home Emigration' movement in the 1860s and the Crofters Act. The Small Landowners Act of 1911 extended the protection of the Crofters Act to all holdings in Scotland valued at £50 or less, or an area of less than fifty acres whatever the value.

At the end of the war there was a move throughout the Highlands to provide land for returning servicemen, to create a 'land fit for heroes'. In 1919 the Land Settlement (Scotland) Act extended the powers of the Scottish Board of Agriculture and Fisheries to buy farms and divide them into smallholdings. When it seemed that the implementation of this Act was being delayed in some areas, local men took matters into their own hands and began to occupy land. Most of these land raids took place in the western Highlands and Islands, but the farm of Pitcalnie at Nigg, which had been used as a military camp during the war, was also entered by raiders, encouraged by the local schoolmaster, and a petition was sent to the Board of Agriculture asking for the creation of smallholdings there.[34] In the same year Sir Hector Munro of Foulis placed the farm of Ardullie at the disposal of the Board for the settlement of ex-servicemen, although nothing seems to have come of this offer.[35]

The first place around the Cromarty Firth to be converted into small-holdings was Arabella, bought by the Board of Agriculture a week after the war ended in 1918. There were originally twenty crofts at Arabella and when the Home Farm was later divided eight further smallholdings were created ranging in size from fifty acres down to ten. Because there was no common grazing at Arabella most of the smallholdings concentrated on poultry and pig raising. The Ross and Cromarty Agricultural Committee visited the new smallholdings in the summer of 1920 and although they were impressed by the amenities in the specially built houses, such as hot and cold water and baths, they felt that the houses were flimsily built and also doubted the viability of such small lots.[36]

Although all but one of the legal Arabella smallholdings have now disappeared, many of the 'flimsy' buildings that so concerned the Ross and Cromarty Agricultural Committee survive today at Arabella crossroads, small, square houses built to standard plans provided by the Board of Agriculture, each with its corrugated iron barn. Other local smallholdings were created at Kinbeachie in 1923, where similar Board of Agriculture houses survive, as well as at Tomich and Broomhill (1926), Kinkell and Balnabeen (1929), Cornton (1935) and Culcairn (1938).

The state was active in encouraging forestry as well. The experience of the war had shown the importance of woods and forestry organised on a national scale. The Acland Report of 1918 led in the following year to the parliamentary act establishing the Forestry Commission. After 1926 the Forestry Commission was especially active in the Black Isle, where its activities provided useful paid employment for local crofters as well as a number of St Kildans after their island was evacuated in 1930. Ironically, it was the old commonty of The Mulbuie, the focus of so much feeling amongst the crofters of the 1880s, that began to be transformed, in part by crofters' labour, into the Mulbuie Forest. By the 1930s there was a jetty at Balblair for exporting Black Isle timber.[37]

It was jobs, such as those provided by the Forestry Commission, that allowed the survival of crofting on the Black Isle well into the 1960s.[38] There used to be a large number of crofts in the glens at the back of Alness and Evanton and the crofters held their own annual agricultural show at Evanton but there are none there today. Aside from some holdings at Strathpeffer, crofting has virtually disappeared over the last fifty years from the northern shores of the Cromarty Firth.[39]

The years immediately following the end of the First World War brought some other positive changes, including the beginnings of the welfare state. Old age pensions were introduced as was a local health system. But none of these reforms could solve the intractable problems of the Highlands where the population continued to fall. In part this was due to late marriages and a low birth rate, but the major reason was emigration. Local papers regularly carried steamship notices and articles about local emigrants bound for Canada, Australia, New Zealand and South Africa. Only the patterns of emigration changed as people now took trains to the ports of Glasgow, Liverpool and London. Yet the problem was as bad as ever, or perhaps even worse. Highland emigration may even have been accelerated by the new social services since the introduction of old-age pensions meant that young people no longer had to stay at home to look after elderly parents. In the 1920s emigration levels soared throughout the Highlands and even the relatively favoured area around the Cromarty Firth was not spared. It was estimated that between 1911 and 1926 the population of the Black Isle fell by nearly four thousand.[40] A good deal of this fall took place in Cromarty itself, where the cessation of fishing meant that the population of the burgh fell from nearly 2,000 on the eve of war to 1,126 in 1921 and to 837 ten years later.

The land fit for heroes to live in failed to materialise and the 1920s were a time of deepening crisis throughout Britain. Because of its distant and rural location the Cromarty Firth region was shielded from the more obvious manifestations; the General Strike of 1926, for example, left little mark on the area beyond the fact that the trains did not run and southern newspapers were held up for a week of Sabbath-like quiet. Yet, appearances were deceptive for poverty was poverty wherever it was found. As the *Ross-shire Journal* remarked truthfully in 1935, 'Cromarty is as depressed as any area of Scotland.'[41]

The rundown of the dockyard had left agriculture as the main local employer, along with associated industries such as the bone mill in Invergordon, although throughout the 1920s British agriculture declined. The local situation was exacerbated by a serious outbreak of 'grass sickness' in horses in the 1930s which led to an unusually quick changeover to power-driven farm machinery although horses went on being used on some farms until the mid 1950s and even longer in forestry work.[42] By 1937 the official unemployment rate for Ross and Cromarty was 40.6% of all insured persons, which did not cover agricultural workers, although the *Ross-shire Journal* suspected that the figure was slightly lower at about 33%.

Out of this decline there came another groundswell of alienation and anger which was expressed in a growing demand for a radical restructuring of society. Ross and Cromarty had long been a Liberal stronghold, but in 1924 a local branch of the Independent Labour Party was founded just two years after the first ILP Members of Parliament had been elected from 'Red

Clydeside'. The roots of the new party went back to the land agitation of the 1880s. The ILP's local founder was the minister of Fodderty, who was also the organiser of the Scottish Farm Servants' Union, begun in 1892 as a Ploughmen's Union in the wake of the success of the crofters' agitation. The new party's inaugural meeting was held at Alness, that old centre of the Highland Land League, and it grew rapidly.[43] In the 1929 election which brought Ramsay MacDonald to power the Labour candidate, Hugh Macintosh, came near to unseating the Liberal. The *Ross-shire Journal* remarked of the result, prophetically as it turned out, that there was now 'a deep cleavage in the political faith of this constituency.'

It was Ramsay MacDonald's National Government that was to bring about the event for which the Cromarty Firth is best known in the outside world: the Invergordon Mutiny of 1931. Ironically, it was an event which could have taken place anywhere, and had in fact little to do with the town from which it took its name although there is some evidence that the political lessons of the mutiny had local repercussions.[44]

By the early 1930s Britain, in common with the rest of the industrialised world, was in severe economic difficulties. On 10 October 1931 Philip Snowden, Chancellor of the Exchequer, rose in the House of Commons to announce a series of tax increases, cuts in state benefits and in the salaries of government employees of between ten and twenty per cent. The corresponding naval cuts were announced at the same time by Sir Austen Chamberlain, First Lord of the Admiralty. The rates were variable, but the cuts fell most heavily below decks, amounting in the case of an able seaman to twenty five per cent of his total pay.

Although there had been rumours of cuts before the Atlantic Fleet left its home ports for its autumn manoeuvres based at Invergordon, the details of the cuts were announced in Parliament while the Fleet was at sea. Word of the parliamentary statement was picked up on ships' radios from BBC broadcasts and rumours began to spread throughout the Fleet. The ships arrived in the Cromarty Firth in the afternoon of Friday 11 September, when at last the official Admiralty letter detailing the cuts reached Rear Admiral Tomkinson's flagship, H.M.S. *Hood*, where it was pigeonholed for future distribution. (In fact, copies were not provided for all the Fleet until Tuesday morning). Rumours continued to circulate and the first real confirmation of the proposed cuts came from newspapers purchased in Invergordon on Saturday morning.

The arrival of the Fleet on its autumn cruise was always marked by the Invergordon Highland Games at the Naval Playing fields. This Saturday, in addition, there was a Fleet Cup football final between teams from the *Nelson* and the *Dorsetshire*. That evening, as the ratings gathered in the naval canteens, anger against the cuts began to grow into something more concentrated and serious. Not only were the cuts devastating in themselves, so serious that some men feared their wives might be forced into prostitution to survive, but they were also due to come into effect on 11 October, long before the men could return home and sort out the consequences of such things as hire-purchase agreements.

The men returned to the ships on Saturday evening but there were unusually large church shore parties on the following morning when the Sunday papers contained fuller details of the cuts. Throughout the day increasingly heated meetings of ratings were held throughout Invergordon. At one o'clock it was proposed to commandeer a train to go to London to put the men's case to the Admiralty. By the evening, in the shore canteen, excitement reached fever pitch. Len Wincott of H.M.S. *Norfolk* leapt onto a table to address the men. He called for the men to return to their ships and begin a strike: 'Men, go aboard. It'll be passive resistance and no bloodshed'.[45] The meeting ended on a note of euphoria and groups of singing men went back through the streets of the town to the pier where there were more impromptu speeches before the liberty boats departed for the ships anchored in the Firth.

Rear Admiral Tomkinson had great sympathy for the men and was later to argue that the normal channels of complaint 'were in this case valueless, and . . . the men had no other course than the one they took . . .'[46] He had considered cancelling shore leave on Sunday but in the end decided to allow the men ashore. On Monday Tomkinson wired the Admiralty to report the Sunday night meetings in the canteen, claiming to 'attach no importance to the incident from a general disciplinary point of view . . .' but warning against press exaggeration.[47] The Admiralty did not reply.

On Monday afternoon another football match was scheduled and it became the vehicle for another meeting. Unusually, large numbers of sailors took shore leave that day. When permission to use the Naval Canteen for a meeting was refused about seven hundred men gathered at the sports grounds. Pickets were posted to keep out civilians and the newspaper reporters who had begun to arrive at Invergordon. It was determined to continue with the policy of passive resistance; no ships would sail from the Cromarty Firth on exercises. The men returned to their ships, singing popular songs. And that was the end of Invergordon's connection with the mutiny. All leave was cancelled and all communication with the shore cut off. The men remained on board and on most of the vessels they continued to perform normal shipboard duties while refusing to allow the ships to sail. Songs and messages were shouted from ship to ship, and it was this noise of hundreds of voices calling across water that remains an abiding memory of the Invergordon Mutiny amongst local people.

It was a strange sort of mutiny. The participants themselves called it a 'strike' or 'passive resistance'. There was no doubt what the grievance was and how the men had responded to it but no officers were captured and no ships taken over. The crew of the *Rodney* were the most radical but, despite claims by some that the whole affair was a preconcerted Bolshevik plot, there is little evidence for this; the 'Red Flag' was certainly played and sung and yet, as the flag was lowered on Tuesday evening, the bands played 'God Save the

King' and the men of the fleet cheered. The movement seemed oddly leaderless. It was only on the *Norfolk* that something like a single spokesman emerged: Len Wincott. In response to a request from an officer for a statement of grievances he dictated the following to a typist friend but it is scarcely a revolutionary manifesto:

> We, the loyal subjects of H.M. the King, do hereby present my Lord Commissioners of the Admiralty, our representatives to implore them to amend the drastic cuts in pay that have been inflicted on the lowest paid men on the lower deck. It is evident to all concerned that this cut is the forerunner of tragedy, misery and immorality amongst the families of the lower deck . . .
> The men are quite willing to accept a cut which they, the men, consider in reason.

It was said later that George Hill, Wincott's typist, added the compromising final sentence.[48] A copy of this declaration was smuggled to the *Daily Herald* and was a major factor in spreading word of the 'mutiny' throughout Britain and the world in the course of Tuesday.

For the men on board the ships in the Cromarty Firth there was a growing fear and uncertainty as the hours of Wednesday passed without a response to their protest. In London the Admiralty at last acted to stop the growing rumours of the revolt. There was a genuine fear that the protest might spread to the other armed services. At one point it was proposed to bombard the Fleet from the hills around the Cromarty Firth. On Monday afternoon this idea was abandoned in favour of the more sensible course of ordering the Fleet to return to its home bases in the south. At least one ship had to be taken to sea by her officers, but by late on Wednesday night the Fleet was slowly leaving the Firth.

As the men had waited on board the ships during Wednesday, a run began on the government's gold reserves: the unprecedented sum of five million pounds was withdrawn. On Thursday, as the Fleet sailed south, the Prime Minister attempted to reassure the country, and stop the financial panic, by announcing that there would be no courts martial or victimisation as a result of the events at Invergordon. Everything would return to normal. But the run on gold continued, rising to eighteen million pounds on Friday. By the time the Atlantic Fleet arrived home, it was clear that Britain must go off the gold standard. Within days the value of the pound sterling fell from $4.86 to $3.49.

That, at least, was the one obvious and clear-cut result of the 'Invergordon Mutiny'. For the rest, controversy about the event continues to the present day. Was it a preconcerted plot or a spontaneous outbreak? Was it even a mutiny? Aside from finally forcing Britain off the gold standard what did it achieve? In the short term, the naval cuts were reviewed and reduced, and from this time too there was a growing awareness that the Royal Navy must take greater care of the welfare and conditions of service of its men. In the years immediately after the mutiny the navy made a successful effort to reorganise itself and to do away with the class divisions and failure of communication, especially on board ship, that had caused so many of the problems at Invergordon in 1931. Despite Ramsay MacDonald's promise of no victimisation, however, the ring-leaders were dismissed following the General Election of October 1931 that swept MacDonald's National Government from power. The careers of a number of naval officers were blighted by the mutiny.

The result of the mutiny on the town and townspeople of Invergordon was immediate. The Fleet with its 12,000 men had been expected to stay seven or eight weeks but was ordered home after only five days. The economic consequences of this change of plans were devastating and there were justified fears that because of what had happened the Fleet might never return to Invergordon. Certainly, when the Fleet sailed north again in mid-October it went to Rosyth, and in 1932 the navy's exercises at Invergordon were severely curtailed.

Suddenly, it seemed as though it all might end. It was not just the loss of money that was frightening to the local community, although that was bad enough. Not only were the big supply contracts threatened, along with the business of the small specialist shops that sold everything from ices to jewellery to the sailors, so too were the smaller more irregular commercial transactions, such as the country people who would cycle down to the dockyard with eggs or a brace of rabbits on their handlebars, hoping to supplement their income by selling them to the officers' mess. Navy wives took rooms in local hotels and lodging houses for the duration of the stay. Cromarty was especially popular with officers' wives since it was quieter and more genteel. These long-term visitors represented a considerable portion of the local economy.

There were also less tangible consequences such as the loss of colour and excitement brought by the Fleet. To this day, many local people can recite like a litany the dispositions of the ships as they lay in the Firth in the 1920s and '30s from the admiral's flagship (usually the *Nelson*), the smaller craft, such as destroyers and submarines, and their attendant ships anchored off Invergordon and Balblair, with flying boats further up the Firth, to the larger battle cruisers, including the 42,000 tons *Hood*, the biggest warship afloat, usually anchored off Cromarty. Relations with the ships were close and affectionate. There was scarcely a house on Cromarty that did not contain photographs of the *Hood* and her crew; it was 'our ship' and it was unthinkable that the mutiny could mean that she would never come into the Firth again. The arrival of the great ships in the Firth brought the place alive with noise, colour and movement, 'just like a highway, only on water.'[49]

The streets of the towns were equally busy. Each day the Royal Marine bands marched through the streets of Invergordon to the playing fields with the men following behind. In addition to the annual Highland Games, there were dances, sometimes as many as four on a Saturday night, and a myriad of other events from Masonic meetings to whist drives. The streets of Cromarty and Invergordon were thronged with incomers. Naval outfitters came north and opened their shops for the duration of the stay. There were travelling shows and fairs, with steam organs, rides and stalls featuring coconut shies and shooting galleries. While special trains brought hundreds of visitors into Invergordon to see the Fleet and its attendant entertainments, the most dependable arrivals were the prostitutes, some from as far away as London, although local talent came as well. Their annual migration could be guaranteed: 'They'll be here, even on crutches'.

The Cromarty Firth did not just depend on the money the navy brought for relations between the two had passed beyond the purely functional and economic to something like a long and successful marriage. The people of the area both needed and enjoyed what the Fleet brought and the sailors knew it. As one rating said to a local, 'What do you do here in the winter, Jock?' For years after 1931 there were strong local feelings of resentment and embarrassment that the mutiny should ever have taken place or, to be more precise, should have taken place in Invergordon. On the other hand there is some evidence that the example of the sailors was not lost on one group of local workers. In 1933, when a 10% reduction in agricultural wages was announced, many of the younger agricultural workers refused to accept the new rates and military recruitment soared.[50]

Within two years of the mutiny, however, it appeared that all was forgiven, if not forgotten. In 1933 the largest Fleet ever seen in the Cromarty Firth arrived with over 20,000 men and its exercises set the pattern for the remaining years of peace. Yet, despite this apparent return to normality, there were still fears that history might repeat itself. That year Admiral Sir William James had relieved Tomkinson and as part of his programme to build up crew morale on the *Hood* he devised a shore exercise known as 'The pirates of Cromarty'. It involved seamen and marines from the *Hood* being landed near Nigg Golf Course. Half the complement were pirates, the other half sent out to capture and bring them in: 'It was a good drill and great fun. One of the signals received was: Have captured a pirate but can get nothing out of him except that his handicap is plus two'.[51] Within a week, however, news that men had been seen being chased about the Hill of Nigg and ferried backwards and forwards to the *Hood* had produced stories in the press of further unrest aboard the ship.

Despite these small setbacks, during the rest of the 1930s the Cromarty Firth resumed its position as an important centre for naval exercises, especially target practice. A target depot was established at the dockyard. Throughout the 1930s four grey-painted wood and cork target ships (Fig. 63) and the remote controlled H.M.S. *Centurion* were stationed in the Firth, and would be hauled out to target areas at Nigg Sands and Udale Bay or the outer Moray Firth during Fleet manoeuvres. There were also a number of yellow-painted biplanes called *Queen Bees* used for aerial bombing practice. The 1933 manoeuvres had included seaplanes and aeroplanes from the aircraft carriers

Furious and *Courageous* and Novar aerodrome. In the following year the Admiralty announced plans for the construction of more oil tanks. The buildup to war had begun again although this naval revival did not have the dramatic effect on the local economy of the buildup to the Great War since the ships and planes that now came into the Cromarty Firth were much more self-sufficient and not so dependent on local farmers and businesses for their supplies.

By the mid-1930s the economy of the Highlands had become so depressed that a special committee was set up by Sir Godfrey Collins, Secretary of State for Scotland, and the Scottish Economic Committee, chaired by Major E. L. Hilleary, to make recommendations about the future of the region. 'The Highlands Economic Report' appeared at the end of 1938. Beginning from the premise that the position of the Highlands was so extreme that only a special authority could deal with it, the Committee suggested the creation of a special Development Commission for the Highlands, along with a central marketing agency to buy cheap bulk agricultural supplies. In addition, roads and transport were to be improved and harbours enlarged.[52]

Any chance that the recommendations of the report would be acted upon were swept away by the approach of war and it would be nearly thirty years before the Highland Report's central idea of a Highland Development Commission became a reality with the creation of the Highlands and Islands Development Board. Yet, at the same time as the Report, a number of changes were taking place which would lead to the transformation of the Highlands after 1945.

In 1925 plans had been drawn up for a hydro-electric scheme at Lochluichart to provide power for a wide area of Easter Ross. A one hundred foot dam was to be built with a turbine house and generator. The electricity was to be carried by overhead lines as far as Tain.[53] The system was in operation by the mid-1930s although many rural areas around the Cromarty Firth were not connected to the electricity supply until the 1940s and '50s.

Beginning in the 1930s, too, increasing numbers of tourists began to come to the area encouraged after 1938 by the beginning of paid holiday time. The beaches of the region were the big attraction along with the well-run state managed hotels. Invergordon, with its cinemas, annual regatta, and specially built sea-bathing pool (the only swimming pool in the north of Scotland) was the centre for the growing tourist industry of the Cromarty Firth Region. From the town visitors could tour the countryside by private car or public transport and there were also popular sailings to Nigg, Cromarty, Nairn and Inverness on Captain Albert Watson's pleasure steamer, the *Ailsa*.[54]

By the late thirties it was clear, and not just from the increased naval presence in the Firth, that war was coming. As early as 1937 air-raid precautions were being discussed by the County Council along with plans for a county-wide fire service. In the following year the navy again took over the hospital at Invergordon and construction was begun on the underground oil

63. A gunnery target, pre-1939.

tanks at Inchindoun, three miles north of Invergordon, although they were not completed until 1944.

The coming war, so far as the Cromarty Firth was concerned, was not to be a maritime one for the safe waters of the Cromarty Firth which had protected the Fleet during the Great War had now become a trap for ships. The buildup of the Firth's land bases and defences in the late 1930s, therefore, concentrated on the demands of aerial warfare with new defences built with anti-aircraft guns on the Sutors covering the narrow entrance and the Moray Firth beyond.

Evanton aerodrome had begun to be expanded in 1937, as the Admiralty again assumed separate responsibility for naval aviation and it became a flight and bombing training school and repair base. Evanton continued to be shared with the Royal Air Force and although the two services worked together they maintained their separate traditions. Naval personnel worked to ship's bells and piped signals and were administratively under the mother ship of H.M.S. *Merlin* at Donibristle in Fife. There was even a fenced-off naval area within the aerodrome, extending down to the Firth, so that the ratings could receive their duty-free tobacco and rum tots.[55] By 1943 the RAF site at Evanton was used for Coastal Command maintenance and in October the following year the Fleet Air Arm section of the field became a Royal Navy Aircraft Maintenance yard with a maximum capacity of two hundred and fifty aircraft.

In 1938 a Sunderland flying boat training base was established at Alness and by 1939 there were three flying boat squadrons stationed at Invergordon, patrolling as far as Shetland and the southern Norwegian coast.[56] Invergordon became the local main base for the joint Fleet Air Arm–Royal Air Force Coastal Command in the Cromarty Firth during the war. The craft were serviced at the west pier in Invergordon until 1943. It was from Alness that the Duke of Kent, the King's youngest brother, was to leave on his last, ill-fated flight in August 1942.

While the aerodromes at Evanton, Alness and Tain were being enlarged, regular Fleet visits continued and manoeuvres became increasingly elaborate, with a heavy emphasis on target practice involving ships and aeroplanes. In May 1938 the Fleet that arrived in the Firth included the aircraft carrier, *Courageous*. As usual the Provost of Invergordon went aboard the flagship, this time it was the *Ramilllies*, to welcome the Fleet. Shore leave was granted over the weekend and the town and countryside filled with sailors and visitors. A special feature of this visit was the four-day open house held at Evanton Aerodrome for Empire Air Day. By now the base had a garrison of two hundred and fifty officers and men living in wooden huts. There was also a hospital, hangar and recreation facilities. On Monday the exercises began with target practice on stationary targets set up within the Firth and much flying between Evanton and the new station near Tain.[57] It was, in fact, business as usual — but not for much longer. The local territorial army units also began to prepare for war. Then there were the Lovat Scouts. By the mid-1930s the War Office had determined that the Lovat Scouts were to have a new role as a fully mobile scouting and observer corps. In 1939 the Scouts held their last peace-time encampment at Strathpeffer.[58]

In the weeks and months before the outbreak of war on Sunday 3 September 1939, the pace of preparations accelerated. Plans were drawn up for local civilian defence, including a system for air raid signalling and first aid posts around the Firth. Gas masks were assembled in Invergordon for distribution throughout the county. About the only thing Ross and Cromarty did not have to contend with were plans to take in evacuees since all of Scotland north of the Great Glen was a restricted area for which permits were required for travel beyond Inverness, while all mail going in and out of the area was subject to censorship. By Saturday night, 2 September, the local Territorial units had been called up, and the area was tense.[59] The Fleet was in the Firth again, having arrived in mid August in brilliant summer weather to a welcome by unusually large and enthusiastic crowds. In the last few hours of peace signals arrived ordering the Fleet to leave the Firth. It was a warm, still evening and the sound of anchor chains carried across the water to the land as, one by one, the ships sailed quietly out through the Sutors to the safety of the wider seas beyond. The ships would not return for six years and when they did both the Fleet and the Cromarty Firth would be vastly different.

Immediately, however, all the local and military planning of the past few years came into play. Lighting restrictions for homes and cars were announced; local units of the Home Guard were set up and began drilling in village halls on both sides of the Firth. Military restrictions increased. For example, local people were forbidden to come near the forts on the Sutors and with good reason for by 1940 the fortifications there included an early and most secret radar installation.

Within weeks of the outbreak of war the aircraft carrier *Courageous* was sunk by a U-boat while on submarine patrol, the first such loss of a ship that had long been a familiar sight within the Firth. The sinking of the *Royal Oak* in Scapa Flow a few weeks later was another blow since there were a number of local men serving on her. Perhaps as many as forty men from the Cromarty fisherfolk community who were RNVR volunteers were killed on active service between 1939 and 1945 and there were other losses from the seaboard villages.

But much of this was in the future. Unlike the rest of Britain where little seemed to happen during the 'phoney war', from September 1939 to April 1940, the Cromarty Firth was transformed during this period. Hundreds of military and naval personnel flooded the area with many being billeted with local families or in commandeered buildings. Novar House, for example, became a Wren billet and the lower floor of the old hemp factory in Cromarty housed Gordon Highlanders. Once again small villages of huts appeared at Cromarty, Nigg, Invergordon and elsewhere around the Firth and Women's Land Army hostels were quickly constructed at Nigg and Cromarty.

The war brought the world to the Cromarty Firth. After the fall of Poland a Polish liner entered the Firth with refugees, and after the conquest of Denmark, in early April 1940, a small flotilla of Danish fishing boats arrived.[60] Later, there would be refugees and servicemen from occupied Europe, Czechs, Poles, and Norwegians. The exiled King Haakon visited Cromarty and stayed at Achandunie House. Canadian and Newfoundland lumberjacks came to cut down the woods of the Black Isle and along the north shore of the Firth.

During the early months of the war local defences were strengthened. There was no boom at the entrance to the Firth but the Sutors and the waters of the outer Moray Firth were guarded by converted seine netters equipped with ASDIC and carrying depth charges. These ships were stationed at Cromarty. The mine laying base at Nigg was involved in the mining of the outer Moray Firth early in 1940 although the field was so far out that a large area of open sea was left between the minefield and the entrance to the Cromarty Firth and a number of ships were sunk here.[61] Later, barrage balloons would be added to the defences of the Firth.

By the time the Moray Firth minefield was being laid, the shooting war had begun. Denmark, Norway and the Low Countries were over-run. Now it was France's turn. The local battalions of the Seaforths, as part of the 51st Highland Division, were under French command when the general retreat of the British Expeditionary Force began in the late spring of 1940. After failing

to link up with the British troops at Dunkirk the Highland Division was taken
to the Somme to fight with General de Gaulle's Armoured Division but again
had to retreat with heavy losses until eventually surrounded and forced to
surrender at St Valéry en Caux on 12 June 1940. Many local soldiers spent the
rest of the war in German prisoner of war camps; others would join the
reconstituted Highland Division and fight in North Africa, Sicily and Normandy.

In the immediate aftermath of the fall of France, Churchill made his
famous speech promising to fight on the beaches and on the landing places, a
promise that was given a local dimension when personnel were drafted from
local air stations to do guard duty in the lower reaches of the Firth. For one
such guard Nigg Sands became a frightening place:

> with all the squelches and bird noises when the tide was out . . . every squelch was
> a jackboot being pulled out of the ooze and daylight was most welcome with the
> arrival of the 'Tea Boat' with bacon sandwiches.[62]

This was very nearly as close as the Germans ever got to the Cromarty
Firth, with one exception. Late on the morning of 17 February 1941 a lone
German bomber managed to fly into the Firth under the guns on the Sutors
and scored a direct hit on number thirteen tank in Seabank Tank Farm at the
back of Invergordon (Fig. 64). The bomb exploded inside the tank rupturing
its sides. The top of the tank fell down intact. Oil spilled down into the railway
cutting and into the sea.[63]

The fall of France also meant that all Atlantic shipping from east coast
ports was diverted from routes around the south coast of Ireland to the
passages between Orkney and Shetland. Loch Ewe in Wester Ross became a
major convoy gathering base. In the North Sea, however, mining by both the
British and the Germans forced shipping into constricted areas and this was
exploited by German E boats and aircraft able to attack allied shipping forced
into close-packed convoy lanes. In August 1940 the German Navy's Air Arm
attacked Convoy O.A. in the Moray Firth, sinking two ships and damaging
another.[64]

Fighting ships came into the Firth only rarely, often under cover of darkness,
and did not linger. One such rushed trip took place early in the war when, on
6 October 1939, the Provost of Invergordon received a message to go to the
pier to greet an 'important visitor'. It was King George VI, who had arrived to
be taken on board H.M.S. *Glasgow*.[65]

If visits by fighting ships were unusual, supply ships, however, were regular
visitors. One at least, the *Hirondelle*, was sunk just outside the Sutors and the
salvaging of her cargo of food and supplies provided a local version of *Whisky
Galore* when sacks of pease and meal, tins of food and even blankets were
washed up on shore after the wreck. Some water-damaged stores were resold
as salvage by Scottish Agricultural Industries in Invergordon but other flotsam
from this and other wrecks quietly found its way into local homes.[66]

Aside from such rare excitements the war around the Cromarty Firth soon

64. Naval tank farms in 1941. The fuelling facility dominated Invergordon then as today.

settled into a kind of pattern. Invergordon was a base for the transhipment of troops to Shetland and Faroe. Each week thousands of personnel would arrive on the 'Jellicoe Trains', stay overnight in the nissen huts set up in the castle grounds at Invergordon, then march through the streets to the middle pier and the waiting ferries, the *Prague* and the *Amsterdam* (both converted Channel ferries), or the *Ben Machree* and the *Lady of Man*, former Isle of Man ferries.

The flying boats and seaplanes came and went from the west pier at Invergordon. Another airfield was built at Fearn in 1940 as a satellite to RAF Tain, a Coastal Command base charged with anti-submarine patrol work, and opened in the following year as a training base for torpedo, fighter and night flying. There were, inevitably, occasional accidents. One well-remembered occasion was when a Sunderland hit a house at Allerton near Cromarty and a child was killed. Eventually, the situation was improved somewhat by the positioning of landing lights around the Firth, but to this day the seabed of the Cromarty Firth is littered with wrecked Sunderlands and Catalinas. The new war cemetery at Rosskeen began to receive burials, men from the Royal Air Force and the Royal Air Forces of New Zealand, Australia and Canada.

On the whole relations between the services and the local population were good but in ways that were different from the Great War and the years between the wars. It was not just that the flying fields were mostly well away from the towns, whereas the navy presence had been concentrated on Cromarty and Invergordon, and that personal links with the navy had been forged largely during short periods of shore leave and at social events such as the Invergordon Highland Games. The huge wartime influx meant that the local population was permanently outnumbered. Soldiers and sailors came to dominated local life by sheer force of numbers. For example, in Evanton the 'Novar Arms' was completely taken over every evening by servicemen and women. There was no where else in that area.[67]

There was, in addition, a certain amount of cross-cultural misunderstanding. Service men often only had Sunday off and they could not understand the strict sabbatarianism of Easter Ross. Consequently, RAF and Navy personnel tended to make their own entertainment, sporting events (sometimes against local teams), walks in the countryside and other excursions. In addition many of the bases had regular ENSA entertainments; for example, stars from London appeared at Evanton where there were shows six nights out of seven. When leave came after long periods of concentrated work service men and women wanted a complete change away from the Cromarty Firth although getting away was not easy:

> We were allowed weekend leave once a month but no one was really able to take advantage of it, the only place to go was Inverness. The train through about 2 pm on Saturdays was packed with servicemen from Tain, Fearn, Invergordon, Alness having all boarded prior to reaching Evanton . . . the last train back Saturdays was 11.30 pm. You can imagine what that was like, and with no trains at all on Sundays . . . it meant that unless you were prepared to cycle back sometime on Sunday a weekend pass was of no more use than an 'evening' ashore . . .[68]

Local landladies took in visiting service families but in retrospect most of the remembered contacts between service personnel and the local population seem to centre on food, a subject for increasing preoccupation as wartime restrictions began to bite. It was still possible to get something like a pre-war tea at some local inns and pubs. Some local farmers and estate owners arranged shoots or fishing parties for officers and the results provided a welcome supplement to mess food. On the other hand, local farmers were plagued with requests for eggs and chickens to take home on leave.[69]

On the whole local people kept themselves to themselves not out of dislike of the incomers but because of the time-consuming demands of wartime civilian life. There was the blackout and food and coal rationing. Virtually all private transport disappeared off the roads to be replaced by fleets of buses. Living in a restricted zone everyone had to carry passes. On the farms most of the labour had been called up and their places were taken by German and Italian prisoners of war from Brahan and Kildary Camps. Some were billeted on the farms, like the Italian soldier in Jessie Kesson's Black Isle novel, *Another Time, Another Place*, but the majority were brought by lorries each day. Usually, relationships with the prisoners were good although some gibbed at being fed porridge.[70] The scarcity of farm labour during the war produced a shift away from arable towards dairy herds; between 1939 and 1945 fifteen new herds were created in the Cromarty Firth region but by the early 1950s most of these herds had disappeared.[71]

Local volunteers ran a number of canteens and clubs for service people including the highly popular Church of Scotland canteens at Evanton and elsewhere. There were regular flag days and collections for war charities, 'weapons weeks' and 'warship weeks'. In May 1942 the minesweeper H.M.S. *Cromarty*, built with the help of local collections, was 'launched', with the help of a model of the ship, by Lady Marjory Mackenzie of Gairloch in front of the Town House in Dingwall at almost the same time as the actual ship was taking part in the capture of the Vichy fortress of Diego Guarez in Madagascar.[72] The county took great pride in this ship. In some measure it helped to compensate, at least for the people of the town of Cromarty, for the loss of the *Hood* almost exactly a year before, blown up by an unlucky hit on her magazine while in pursuit of the *Bismarck* and *Prinz Eugen*. Of the ship's crew of 1,500 only three survived. The blow was a terrible one in the town that regarded the *Hood* as 'our ship'. Then *Cromarty* itself was sunk in November 1943; the county again raised money to launch the second *Cromarty* in 1944.[73]

By this time it was clear to many local people that something very unusual was going on in the Tarbat peninsula. The entire population had been moved out late in 1943 with only six weeks notice, many of them staying with friends and relations in the area. Their cattle and smaller livestock were sold up at the Dingwall auctions or to local butchers although the sale could not be advertised for security reasons. Horses were taken to neighbouring farms outside the restricted area, which included all of the peninsula from north of Hilton to west of Inver (excluding Portmahomack). Evacuees were allowed to return at stipulated intervals, and some necessary workers, such as a local school teacher who travelled daily from Hilton to Portmahomack, were allowed to cross the military zone at set times. Large numbers of soldiers and WRENS appeared in Easter Ross and the sound of shelling was heard in the Tarbat peninsula. It was clear that extensive military exercises were taking place and that something was afoot. In May the activity ceased and the service men went away. It was only on 6 June 1944, when news came of the Normandy landings, that the mystery of the Tarbat evacuations was solved;

the area had been used for exercises in preparation for D-Day.[74]

V-E Day was marked by rapidly-organised celebrations and church services around the Firth. Bunting appeared on houses and public buildings as soon as the news arrived. At Saltburn there was a children's party with entertainment supplied by the RAF band from Invergordon. On the following Saturday there was a sports meeting and childrens' treat at the naval playing fields in Invergordon when each child was given a shilling and a poke of sweets upon leaving the ground.[75] But perhaps best of all, local prisoners of war began to return home from Germany.

In the following year there were more formal celebrations of peace, on Friday and Saturday 7–8 June 1946. These 'Victory Days' put the emphasis on youth; every child was given a specially minted shilling. On Friday night there were parades, parties and bonfires all around the Cromarty Firth. Most local shops shut on Saturday afternoon for the real celebrations to begin. Cromarty and Invergordon both had fancy-dress parades and sports events for the children. A feature of the Invergordon sports days was the entertainment provided by 'Cheerful Charlie Hercher' and the Polish Army Orchestra. At Logie Easter there were sports and games in the grounds of Arabella House, while at Evanton the sports day included an epic tug-of-war between the Navy and the Women's Rural Institute which was won by the ladies. A ball in Alness Town Hall on Saturday evening was attended by five hundred. The celebrations were climaxed by a fireworks display at Cromarty which was seen all over the Firth.[76]

In the months after the end of the war the camps and bases slowly emptied. Some local girls had married British, Canadian, Norwegian and Polish servicemen and left the area; and some of the foreign servicemen and prisoners of war elected to stay on in the district. Fearn Airfield was closed down in 1946. By the late summer of that year a number of local homeless families were squatting in abandoned nissen huts, an early sign of one of the problems that would have to be dealt with in peacetime.

At the end of the Great War in 1918 there had been great optimism and wild talk of a greatly expanded town of Invergordon, extending from Alness to Tain. Nothing came of this idea because of the economic problems of the period. The end of the Second World War brought another surge of optimism but tinged with a good deal more realism than in 1918. This time society was to be rebuilt along more rational lines with national and regional planning as the key to the future. Ross and Cromarty County Council's planning consultant, H. A. Rendal Govan, issued a series of working papers in November 1946 dealing with the future development of the county. His plans were a follow-on from the Highland Economic Report of 1938 and the act of 1946. A core feature of this brave new Britain was the 'new town' provided for by the New Towns Act of 1946. The proposals included a new town of between thirty and fifty thousand in order to arrest depopulation and provide an alternative of agriculture as virtually the sole local industry: 'Only as we accept the fact that the maintenance of a well distributed population busy on work of many kinds is the true way to national prosperity shall we be truly economic.'[77]

The new town was to stretch from Evanton to Rosskeen, the site having been chosen because there was land on which to build and because the Firth provided scope for the development of an international port, the centre of a trade nexus stretching from Canada to Scandinavia, the Continent and England. It was proposed to spend £230,000 on this new harbour. In addition Rendal Govan's proposed new town was to have specially built industrial and social facilities that would provide a local outlet for the hydro-electric projects then being set up by the North of Scotland Hydro-Electric Board, created in 1943. Amongst the industries which were thought to be suitable for this new centre were metals, including light alloys such as aluminium, wood and paper products, and trade.

Rendal Govan's proposals formed the basis of a report published by the County Council in the following year, 'A Highland County Plan', which argued for an integral approach to development:

> The Highlands have had too much emergency treatment in the past, designed to alleviate this or that symptom of general trouble. Such treatment but tends to aggravate the major trouble.[78]

In this report the proposed new town in Easter Ross achieved a more definite form; it was to stretch from Evanton to Rosskeen, to link up with Invergordon. For a time there was a private company interested in developing the Invergordon site but in the autumn of 1947 it withdrew from the project.[79]

This was a difficult time. The severe winter of 1946-7 and continuing acute shortages led to an energy crisis in 1947. The autumn cruise of the Home Fleet was cancelled in order to save fuel and Evanton air base was temporarily shut down as an economy measure.[80]

Despite its title, 'A Highland County Plan' had ended up with a plea for government help, recognising that the rates of a large and sparsely populated county could not deal with the problems outlined in the report. In January 1947 the Secretary of State for Scotland had set up the Highlands and Islands Advisory panel, but, as its name implied, it had no executive powers and this fact attracted criticism. In *Scottish Prospect* (1948) John Gollan proposed the abolition of the Advisory Panel and its replacement by a 'Highlands and Islands Planning and Development Board' with executive powers and a full-time chairman.[81] In Gollan's plan Invergordon new town was to be the centre of heavy industry (plastics, aluminium and other smelting) but there was also to be:

> private industry in small industrial estates or individual factories provided the Board of Trade could establish light industries associated with these basic industries . . .[82]

Twenty years later something of these grand schemes would begin to emerge in circumstances that could scarcely have been foreseen by Govan and Gollan. In the meantime, however, a number of the more basic changes proposed in 'A Highland County Plan' began to be implemented as the crisis of 1946–7 receded. In 1949 the district between Inverness and Tain was declared a development area, 'because of its suitability as a local centre of industrial development for the Highlands as a whole.'[83] Work began on improving the county's 'wispy' road system, a process that was crucial not only in encouraging trade and industry but also to the growth of the tourist industry which began to take off in the early 1950s. A good deal of work was also done to provide public services, such as an adequate public water supply. In 1953 Jemimaville finally obtained piped water; before that the seventy villagers obtained their supplies from two hand-worked pumps in the street. By the early 1950s, too, virtually all the parishes around the Cromarty Firth had electricity.[84]

Most industrial development was small-scale, except for forestry. Once again, the woods of the Cromarty Firth region had been swept away by war. The 1945 Forestry Act placed the Forestry Commission in Scotland under the control of the Secretary of State. Half a million acres were marked for planting in Scotland, a good deal of it around the Firth. The Forestry Commission became an important local employer. In the parish of Resolis, for example, the Forestry Commission gave employment to twenty families which counted as large scale industry in such a sparsely settled area. On the north shore of the Cromarty Firth the Forestry Commission began planting on Ben Wyvis and in Strathrusdale. There was extensive private reafforestation work as well, especially after the gales of January 1952. But this large-scale forestry was the exception to the rule. The small and tenuous 'industrial' situation in Cromarty in 1953 was much more typical of the region. In Cromarty parish, aside from a nursery garden run by Colonel Ross at Cromarty House and hopes of a knitwear factory, there were no industries, apart from agriculture.

Only Dingwall and the area around Invergordon showed any industrial diversification and this was obviously at the expense of the other Cromarty Firth parishes. Dingwall, in addition to being the county town, was then the northern headquarters of the North of Scotland Hydro-Electric Board and the local centre for the Milk Marketing Board. By the early 1950s the main industries in the Invergordon-Alness area were Scottish Agricultural Industries, the naval dockyard and the airbase at Evanton. Alone amongst all the towns and parishes of the Cromarty Firth, Dingwall and Invergordon had increased their populations but still tended to lose their young people through emigration. Some found employment labouring on hydro-electric schemes but these were not life-time jobs. It was clear that even in this relatively favoured area of the Highlands the industrial base was too small and too precarious.

In the autumn of 1952 the Town Council of Invergordon met to discuss the future of their 'dying town.'[85] The *Ross-shire Journal* put the position in a nutshell:

> [The] naval and air force establishments . . . were good substitutes for what the County so seriously lacks in industrial concerns. What the position would be had not hydro-electric schemes got under way can best be imagined.[86]

Hydro-electricity had not turned out to be the panacea for all the region's economic problems. The Town Council was concerned about Invergordon's narrow industrial base. Therefore the town was put on the Scottish Council of Industry's list of towns with room for industrial development. But what sort of development could there be? Amongst the ideas considered was the development of light industry such as a knitwear factory and the milling of locally produced grain and other products. One councillor added hopefully 'They could perhaps can rabbits . . .' The terms of the discussion show a marked decline in the optimism of 1945–6 and, indeed, there is almost a sense of desperation in the Council's proposals. At the back of everyone's mind must have been the question: 'What happens if the armed forces again leave Invergordon as they did after the First World War?'

The Navy, in fact, had undertaken a certain amount of improvement work in the early 1950s. New NAAFI stores were constructed on the quayside and in 1952–3 the Admiralty Pier was rebuilt.[87] The Fleets still called into the Firth but they were not the same as before. The war had rung the knell of the large battleship and the future belonged to smaller, lighter craft, and to submarines and aeroplanes. Moreover, Britannia no longer ruled the waves. The Cromarty Firth base was increasingly visited by fleets of other NATO navies. Nevertheless, the Fleet visits were still spectacular and popular occasions. In 1955, for example, the Home Fleet arrived at the end of May. It consisted of the cruiser *Bermuda*, the destroyer *Delight*, two aircraft carriers, seven destroyers and three frigates, in addition to the usual satellite vessels such as oil and water tankers and the NAAFI stores vessel.[88]

By this time a 'New Deal' for the services was being worked out by the Admiralty, involving a general tightening up of resources and a review of future requirements. The First Sea Lord who was behind this review was Lord Louis Mountbatten, who came himself to the Cromarty Firth in May 1956. It was symbolic of this new post-war Navy that he did not arrive by sea as his father had done in 1913, when the Invergordon base was being established; instead he was landed on the Naval Recreation Grounds by helicopter, before going on board the flagship, H.M.S. *Tyne*.[89]

Mountbatten had come to see for himself what future the base at Invergordon could have. Within weeks of his visit the local implications of the naval 'New Deal' were becoming clear. Fearn airfield, which for some years had been used for storage, was to be sold; Evanton was scheduled for closure in 1961. In August 1956, just as the Suez crisis was beginning, it was announced in Parliament that the naval bases at Scapa Flow and Invergordon were to be put on a care and maintenance basis. By the end of the year the details of the closure had become more clear. There was to be a gradual run-down of everything except the oil fuel depot and that, too, might be reduced depending on future naval requirements. The only workers to be retained at Invergordon were those necessary to maintain the fuel depots and run the harbour, along with the groundsman at the recreation fields.[90] About sixty five of the one hundred and seventy workers at the base would lose their jobs and another sixty-five were offered employment elsewhere. The general feeling was that the situation was 'bad enough but it might have been worse'.[91]

In May 1957 the royal yacht *Britannia* sailed into the Cromarty Firth at the head of the Home Fleet. Thousands lined the shores and hillsides to see this sight, one they knew they probably would never see again. The cheers and car horns that greeted the fleet were not just expressions of loyalty but a kind of farewell. In the evening the ships were floodlit and the following day the Queen and Prince Philip visited ships of the Fleet. Over the weekend there were parties, receptions and band concerts.[92]

And then it was over. The ships left the Firth and a century of naval history was at an end. The Fleet review was a grand and public occasion but perhaps the event which more than any other symbolised what the Navy had meant to Invergordon, and Invergordon had meant to the Navy, had taken place in the previous year and was a much more private occasion. For thirty-six years the Naval Recreation Grounds had been looked after by one man, James Chapman, who had come to Invergordon after twenty-two years' service in the Royal Marines. Like so many other naval personnel he had settled down in Invergordon and raised a family. The Grounds were his pride and joy and he was known as 'Groundy' throughout the Fleet and was the terror of local children caught trespassing on his beloved playing fields. Just as the cuts were announced James Chapman was killed in a road accident. In response to his own wishes, 'Groundy's' ashes were scattered on the Recreation Grounds that had been his life.[93] The grounds are now used as the school playing fields.

Feelings about the long connection with the Royal Navy are still strong since for many people of the Cromarty Firth the Navy days were the 'great days'.

NOTES

1. J. Duncan, *My Friends the Miss Boyds*, p. 24.

2. This account of the Russians in Invergordon comes from pictures and letters sent to the *Ross-shire Journal* in response to a letter of Hugh MacLeod Taylor (28 November 1969) denying claims in Otta Swire's *The Highlands and their Legends* (Edinburgh, 1963) that the story was imaginary. A post card from a Russian soldier

sent to a local girl is still in the possession of Mrs Peggy Gourgey, Invergordon Community Council. Ironically some of the Russian stories may have been due to Gaelic speaking soldiers; certainly members of the local 4th Battalion of the Seaforths had been mistaken for Russians when they went south to England for training. When asked by the ladies at southern railway stations where they came from they replied, 'Ross-shire'. Their Gaelic accents turned this into 'Russia' in the ears of the Sassenachs. See M. L. Melville, *The Story of the Lovat Scouts, 1900–1980*, Edinburgh, 1981.

3. *RJ*, 4 December 1914, p. 7.

4. D. Fraser, *The story of Invergordon Church*, p. 82.

5. *RJ*, 23 March 1917, p. 7.

6. SRO GD 199/310.

7. Much of the following discussion is based on Melville, *Lovat Scouts*, and M. M. Haldane, *A History of the 4th Battalion of the Seaforth Highlanders*, London, 1928.

8. *RJ*, 26 November 1920.

9. *IC*, 10 January 1919.

10. *Ibid.*, 20 June 1919, p. 5; *RJ*, 22 October 1976, p. 4.

11. PRO, ADM 2073 (A) 'Future of Cromarty and Invergordon 1919–20'.

12. *RJ*, 11 March 1921, p. 2.

13. 'Minute of Agreement between The Admiralty and the Cromarty Harbour Trustees, 1914 (O.N. 8953/14) 29 September 1914 (typescript) in Queen's Harbour-master's Office, Invergordon.

14. *RJ*, 28 May 1920, p. 2.

15. *Ibid.*, 21 March 1930, p. 2.

16. PRO, ADM 116 2073 (A).

17. *RJ*, 22 November 1918, p. 2.

18. *IC*, 2 May 1919, p. 6.

19. *Ibid.*, 28 November 1919, p. 6.

20. *RJ*, 12 September 1919, p. 2.

21. *Ibid.*, 16 January 1920.

22. *Ibid.*, 16 January 1920; PRO, ADM 116 2073 (B).

23. *RJ*, 21 November 1919, p. 2.

24. PRO, ADM 116 2073 (B).

25. *IC*, 21 May 1920, p. 3.

26. PRO, ADM 116 2073 (B).

27. *RJ*, 20 May 1938, p. 5.

28. *Ibid.*, 22 May 1925, p. 6.

29. Much of the following discussion is based on R. A. Pelik, *C. W. Dyson Perrins, A Brief Account of his Life, his Achievements, his Collections and Benefactions*, Worcester, 1983.

30. *RJ*, 21 August 1908, p. 4; 22 February 1924, p. 2.

31. See 'Articles of Roup of the Tain, Fearn and Tarbat properties of the Cadboll estate, 1918', Mackenzie and Black WS, 28 Castle Street, Edinburgh (copy in possession of Mrs Jane Durham, Scotsburn).

32. Interview, Col. Torquil MacLeod, 5 June 1987.

33. As part of the break-up of the Cadboll Estates the famous Cadboll stone, that had been moved in the late nineteenth century to the 'American Garden' at Invergordon Castle from its original site at Hilton, was sent off to the British Museum.

This move provoked an outcry, not only in the region but throughout Scotland, and the stone was eventually returned to the National Museum of Antiquities in Edinburgh (now the Royal Museum of Scotland) where it still is.

34. Gordon, 'Nigg' Farming II and interview with W. W. Munro, Clashnabuiac, 9 November 1986. Pitcalnie eventually remained in private hands but was broken up into four Board of Agriculture 'Part Two' smallholdings that were too small to support a family; see *TSA*, p. 202. For the petition, see *IC*, 18 May 1920.

35. *Ibid.*, 13 August 1920.

36. The detail for this discussion of the Cromarty Firth smallholdings is based on Department of Agriculture, Land Settlement Files, held at Chesser House, Edinburgh. I am most grateful to the Department of Agriculture and Fisheries for allowing me to see these files.

37. J. B. Cruikshank, 'The Black Isle, Ross-shire: a land-use study', *SGM*, vol. 77 (1961), p. 12. For information about the Balblair jetty (which closed before the outbreak of war) I am indebted Somerled Macdonald, Easter Sheep Park, interview 27 January 1988.

38. Much of this discussion of modern crofting around the Cromarty Firth is based on J. Tivy, 'Easter Ross; a residual crofting area', *SS*, vol. 9 (1965). Although the position described in that article no longer obtains, the trend towards amalgamation has continued and subsequent reforms of crofting law have allowed 'de-crofting' and purchase of crofts. Many of the Black Isle crofts have been amalgamated and some of them, particularly at the western end of The Mulbuie, became in effect substantial farms.

39. Interview with W. W. Munro, Clashnabuiac, 9 November 1986.

40. *RJ*, 21 May 1926, p. 4.

41. *Ibid.*, 3 May 1935, p. 4.

42. Interviews with W. W. Munro, Clashnabuiac, 9 November 1986 and Mrs Bright Gordon, Rosefarm, Cromarty, 28 November 1987.

43. *RJ*, 29 February 1924, p. 3; 7 March 1914, p. 2.

44. The following account of the Invergordon Mutiny is based on D. Divine, *Mutiny at Invergordon*, London, 1970, A. Ereira, *The Invergordon Mutiny*, London, 1981, L. Wincott, *Invergordon Mutineer*, London, 1974 and the accounts carried in the *Ross-shire Journal*, 18, 25 September 1931, 27 November 1931.

45. Ereira, p. 56.

46. *Ibid.*, p. 61.

47. Divine, p. 131.

48. Ereira, p. 103.

49. Much of the following description of Fleet visits in the 1920s and '30s is based on interviews with F. Cross, Invergordon, 25 January 1988 and B. Dalgarno, Invergordon, 26 January 1988.

50. *RJ*, 2 June 1933.

51. Letter, Bob Hector, 9 March 1988.

52. The report's full title was 'The Highlands and Islands of Scotland: a review of the economic conditions and recommendations for improvement' (Scottish Economic Committee Publication, 1938); see also *RJ*, 1 December 1938, p. 4.

53. *Ibid.*, 26 June 1925, p. 4.

54. *Ibid.*, 7 June 1935, p. 6.

55. Much of this description of Evanton in wartime is based on letters from R. H. Shelton, C.P.O., R.N. (Retd), 13 February 1988 and Charles F. Lamdin, 20 February 1988.

56. S. Roskill, *The War at Sea*, vol. 1, London, 1954, p. 36.

57. *RJ*, 20 May 1938, p. 5.

58. Melville, *Lovat Scouts*, pp. 48–9, 57–62.

59. Much of this discussion is based on accounts from the *Ross-Shire Journal*, 1, 8 September 1939.

60. Interview, Douglas and Donald Matheson, Robert Hogg, Cromarty, 27 January 1988.

61. Roskill, *The War at Sea*, vol. 1, p. 36.

62. Letter, R. H. Shelton, C.P.O., R.N. (Retd), 13 February 1988.

63. Interview, F. Cross, Invergordon, 25 January 1988.

64. Roskill, *The War at Sea*, vol. 1, pp. 263, 326.

65. *RJ*, 15 February 1952.

66. Interviews, F. Cross and B. Dalgarno.

67. Letter, C. F. Lamdin, 7 March 1988.

68. Letter, C. F. Lamdin, 20 February 1988.

69. Letter C. F. Lamdin, 8 March 1988; Interview, W. W. Munro, Clashnabuiac, 30 January 1988.

70. Interview, W. W. Munro, Clashnabuiac, 30 January 1988.

71. 'Contrasting economic interests in Ross-shire', *Glasgow Herald*, 8 November 1946.

72. *RJ*, 8 May 1942, p. 5.

73. *Ibid.*, 19 November 1943, p. 5; 5 May 1944, p. 4.

74. Interviews, W. W. Munro, B. Dalgarno, Mrs M. Willis and in the *RJ*, 10, 17, 24 December 1987; 14, 21 January 1988.

75. *RJ*, 16 May 1945, p. 4.

76. *Ibid.*, 14 June 1946.

77. 'Potential development of the Cromarty Firth area', November 1946, p. 2, typescript in the possession of Dr Macdonald, Leeds; the report was covered in *RJ*, 29 November 1946. Amongst Govan's informants was Captain D. J. Munro who had fortified the Sutors in 1913.

78. Ross and Cromarty Council, 'A Highland County Plan' (1947), p. 13.

79. *RJ*, 12 September 1947, p. 6.

80. *Ibid.*, 3, 34 October 1947, p. 4 (*bis*).

81. J. Gollan, *Scottish prospect: an economic, administrative and social survey*, Glasgow, 1948, p. 193.

82. *Ibid.*, p. 194.

83. *RJ*, 21 September 1950, p. 6.

84. Much of the following discussion of the changes brought to the region by the early 1950s is based on the parish accounts in *TSA*.

85. *RJ*, 5 September 1952.

86. *Ibid.*, 10 October 1956, p. 4.

87. *Ibid.*, 27 April 1951, p. 5; Interview with Commander D. Kempsell, Q.H.M. Invergordon, 27 November 1987.

88. *RJ*, 27 May 1955.

89. *Ibid.*, 25 May 1956.

90. A. Cecil Hampshire, *The Royal Navy Since 1945*, London, 1975, pp. 34ff; *RJ*, 3 and 10 August 1956.

91. *Ibid.*, 15 February 1957.

92. *Ibid.*, 31 May 1957.

93. Letter (and cuttings), C. C. Chapman, 22 February 1988.

9

'A kind o' perpetual Hogmanay'

In the immediate aftermath of the dockyard closure the industrial future of the Cromarty Firth region again became the focus of intense local discussion. The *Ross-shire Journal* put the problem in a nutshell:

> Naval and Air Force establishments were good substitutes for what the County so seriously lacks in industrial concerns. What the position would be had not hydro-electric schemes got under way can best be imagined.[1]

What kinds of industries could take the place of the dockyard and the flying field at Evanton? It was suggested that the central pier at Invergordon should be handed back to the local authority in order to stimulate trade. Tourism was a possible solution: Invergordon, it was claimed, 'could become the holiday centre of the Highlands, given the "Butlin" touch and the right kind of publicity'.[2]

Despite its fine harbour (Fig. 65) and good communications there seemed to be few options for local development around the Cromarty Firth, largely because of two factors: the high costs of transport and the lack of specialist local labour. In order to build up a local workforce with basic industrial skills the County Council flirted briefly with the idea of an overspill agreement with Glasgow,[3] but with local unemployment figures standing at 12.5% for men and over 19% for women by the middle of 1959 the scheme was soon abandoned.

In the late 1950s both the County Council and local authorities in Invergordon made a number of attempts to attract new industries to the region including ship-breaking and building, and wooden door-making. Late in 1958 it was agreed that the Admiralty Pier would be available to commercial traffic (except in time of emergency) but the Admiralty refused to repair the centre pier, which it claimed was adequate for the civilian traffic using it. Initially, much of this traffic was connected with the Strathfarrar hydroelectric scheme, which provided local jobs until 1962, but with high school-leaving figures it could be foreseen that by the time the project ended there would be a crisis in local employment.

In the event the industrial regeneration of the Cromarty Firth began not with a new industry but an old one — whisky making. In April 1959 it was announced that a grain distillery was to be built in Invergordon, partially on the site of the former Naval Links Camp at Saltburn.[4] Plans for the distillery went back to the mid-fifties and were the brainchild of Provost James Grigor of Inverness who, to help make the scheme a reality, brought in a young accountant from Dingwall. His name was Frank Thomson.[5]

65. Invergordon, *c*.1965.

Financial problems soon forced Grigor to sever his connection with the project and Thomson acquired title to the distillery and it was he who brought in Max Rayne's London Merchant Securities with the necessary rescue capital. When Invergordon Distillery went public Frank Thomson became the managing director.[6] Construction began in August 1960. As the first of the large-scale developments which were to take place around the Cromarty Firth in the 1960s, its progress was watched with interest throughout Scotland and inspired the folksinger Ian Campbell to write:

> In Invergordon by the sea
> They've built a new distillery
> And all the gulls are on the spree
> That live in Invergordon;
> The mash that's flowing from the still
> They gobble doon wi' right good will
> And every gull can haud his gill
> That lives in Invergordon.

The distillery came onstream on 21 July 1961 and within a few years had become the largest grain distillery in Europe. At its peak in the early 1960s Invergordon Distillery provided about four hundred jobs within the plant plus local jobs in haulage and agriculture. A new sense of local optimism, almost euphoria, began to grow.

> Now when we die some people say
> We come back in some other way
> Oh how I'd like to come and stay
> As a gull in Invergordon;
> Durrum ado adum aday,
> Reincarnation wad be gay
> A kind o' perpetual Hogmanay
> Wi' the gulls o' Invergordon.

The impact of the distillery on the local community was a small foretaste of what was to happen in the late 1960s and early '70s, with the coming of the aluminium smelter and North Sea oil. In 1960 the Local Employment Act marked a major shift in government policy; the whole of the Highlands and Islands were designated a Development District although there was little initial improvement to show for this change. On the other hand, there was a growing realisation that in order for problems to be solved, and the benefits conferred by Development District status to be exploited, it was necessary first to identify the region's problems. The first steps were, in fact, taken in the town of Cromarty.

While Invergordon Distillery was coming into production the situation on the southern shores of the Firth was, if anything, deteriorating. Aside from agriculture and forestry there was no industrial base in the Black Isle at all; it was perhaps a sign of how bad things were that late in 1959 it was seriously suggested that the depleted mussel scalps at Nigg might be developed.[7] The barometer of this decline was the town of Cromarty itself. Its population was already imbalanced with a high proportion of women and the elderly. Between 1950 and 1962 Cromarty's population fell from 734 to 572.[8] There was little industry aside from agriculture and forestry. The town had one small-scale ship-building business and there was a certain amount of inshore fishing for the local market. There was also a short, two-month tourist season. Many houses, especially in the fishertown, were substandard and the decline in population was reflected in the demolition of dwellings, leaving ugly gap-sites in the fine ranges of eighteenth and nineteenth century vernacular and classical buildings. Communications were also declining; the Nigg passenger ferry closed in the early 1960s although there were discussions about a car ferry to take its place and encourage tourist traffic.

In 1962 the Town Council of Cromarty decided to commission a report to be carried out by students of town and country planning at Edinburgh College of Art. Their proposals for the development and regeneration of Cromarty came down heavily for the development of the town's tourist potential. Indeed, the students were by no means the first to see that Cromarty's isolation and its wealth of fine buildings could be positive attractions. Amongst other things they recommended the removal of unsightly overhead telephone wires and the rehabilitation of the burgh's historic buildings. Cromarty House was to become a hotel, the Old Brewery a Youth Hostel, and there was to be a Tourist Recreation Centre (including a rifle range) in the Ropeworks. While not all of the proposals came to pass many of the general ideas in the Edinburgh College report were accepted. The population of the burgh began to grow slowly although much of this growth has been due to economic developments on the north shore of the Firth rather than in Cromarty itself.

Many of these early developments were connected with the name of Frank Thomson, who became a flamboyant and controversial figure in local life and throughout Scotland.[9] Until he quit as director during the slump of 1966 the reputation of Thomson and Invergordon Distillery marched together along with Thomson's other local interest, the Ross and Cromarty Football Club. Thomson was chairman of the Invergordon Development Corporation and in the mid-1960s became increasingly involved in a number of projects related to the industrial regeneration of the region. His rise as an entrepreneur was fuelled by the fight to save the region's railroads. In 1960 twenty stations north of Inverness were closed, including Foulis, Evanton, Alness, Delny, Kildary and Nigg. Worse was to follow in 1963 with Dr Beeching's proposed withdrawal of all rail services north of Inverness. There was an immediate and violent reaction to the proposals in the Highlands. Ross and Cromarty County Council threatened to resign *en masse* if the closures went ahead; similar threats were made by the town councils of Invergordon, Dingwall and Tain. But it was the group that Thomson helped to found, 'The Scottish Vigilantes', which mounted the 'MacPuff' anti-closure propaganda campaign and captured the public imagination.

Early in 1964 it seemed clear that the closures might not take effect; the momentum of the 'Scottish Vigilantes' was continuing and the Transport Users' Consultative Committee held a statutory inquiry into Highland transport in Inverness and produced a report on the future development of the Highlands. *Highland Opportunity* was published in Invergordon in August 1964. It envisaged integrated development in the Highlands based on local resources such as agriculture and fishing, animal and vegetable by-products, tourism, minerals and chemicals, timber, construction, textiles and engineering.[10]

The recommendations of this report were the starting point for much of the industrial development which took place, or was planned to take place, around the Cromarty Firth over the next few years although a major factor in the changes to come was totally unforeseen: in 1964 the government granted the first licences for off-shore oil exploration in the British North Sea Sector.

Using *Highland Opportunity* as a starting point Thomson himself went ahead and commissioned a detailed £55,000 feasibility study, funded by Invergordon Distillery, for the establishment of a petrochemical plant on the north shore of the Cromarty Firth. This was, in fact, a natural consequence of his interest in by-products from the distillery.[11]

The final element in the beginning of industrial development around the Cromarty Firth was the Labour victory in the general election of October 1964, although Ross and Cromarty returned to its former Liberal allegiance, largely as a reaction to Beeching. The policies of Harold Wilson's government were to be crucial factors in the development of the Moray Firth region over the next few years. Not only was Labour committed to government help and intervention in development areas such as the Highlands, it also believed in the efficacy of industrial and social planning to restructure British society. This was the age of the 'white heat of the technological revolution'. The phrase may ring hollow today but its potency in the mid-1960s cannot be underestimated.

In August 1965 Frank Thomson announced plans for an oil refinery with an annual capacity of two million tons, an ammonia plant (of 3,300,000 tons capacity), a fertiliser unit (of 750,000 tons capacity) plus a plastics factory. These industries were to provide at least 1,500 jobs and have an annual turnover of £20 million. The sponsoring company, Invergordon Chemical Enterprises, was registered by Thomson in November 1965 (with paid up capital shares of just over one hundred pounds), and approaches were made to Armand Hammer's Occidental Oil to help finance the £30 million project which was to be sited at Delny. Occidental, in turn, commissioned a $400,000 report by M. W. Kellogg into the proposed petrochemical developments,[12] and made it clear that it expected a substantial government investment in the project before it would commit itself. It was claimed that 30% of the funding would come from British interests, 30% from America and the rest from the government (local development grants of up to 40% were available). This project, and others, was fostered by the newly-formed Highlands and Islands Development Board, set up by the Labour government late in 1965 with wide-ranging executive and financial powers. Frank Thomson became a member in March 1966. Planning was the key to Highland development and a favoured concept was the creation of 'growth points', large industries, which would attract numerous satellite and service industries. This 'growth point' concept had first been enunciated in the 1942 report by the Committee on Hydro-Electric Development in Scotland. The centrepiece of the thinking of the new Highland Board was the siting of major, primary industrial complexes around Invergordon.

The year 1966 was in a real sense the honeymoon period of the Highland Board. There was a genuine optimism and hope abroad that at last the long decline of the Highlands would be reversed, given careful planning and government help allied to local initiative. It was, however, somewhat ironic that the focus for these changes was to be the least Highland part of the entire region, that is the Moray Firth. In its first year of existence the Board commissioned a series of confidential planning papers (the *Proplan Reports*) which looked at future developments around the Cromarty Firth and became the basis for Board strategy in the area:

> By the end of 1967 the most advanced concept of the growth area policy in Britain had been pronounced. Never before had such a close inter-relation of industrial processes, development planning, and fiscal incentives been proposed . . . certainly not in such a detailed way.[13]

When he joined the Highland Board Thomson took with him the plans for the proposed petrochemical complex and it became the centrepiece of the Board's planning for the Cromarty Firth. According to the first *Proplan Report* the complex was to be supplied by natural gas and crude oil 'imported initially, but later taken from the Moray Firth if drilling is successful.'[14] Amongst the other industrial developments which the report foresaw were food and mineral processing and the manufacture of timber products. Around this core of primary industries would be a cluster of service industries including power (hydro-electricity and steam), handling, transport and waste disposal. The report also suggested that a local development corporation should be set up to acquire land to lease to companies or to take equity shares in any new venture likely to improve the local economy. Agricultural land taken for industrial development could be replaced by building dams and reclaiming tidal areas in the upper Dornoch, Moray and Inverness Firths as well as at Nigg Sands within the Cromarty Firth. The key to this industrial development was cheap electrical power; the report suggested that the Highland Board should sponsor the creation of a power company to set up a station at Invergordon to supply electricity to local companies.

The first *Proplan Report* envisaged an ultimate population for the Moray Firth of about 250,000 (necessitating the construction of over 40,000 new houses) dispersed in existing communities and new 'garden towns' to be built above the five hundred foot contour to avoid using productive farming land.

All of this was to take place over twenty years. After initial parliamentary approval was obtained, detailed reports would be drawn up and construction begun; the first five years would see 'spectacular action (a controlled explosion of development)'[15], with substantial industries coming in and starting production. Housing and road construction would be at full output. After this initial burst the next period of development would see the filling in of the industrial areas with more enterprises, the completion of land reclamation for agricultural purposes and the building of five new towns.

In November 1966 there was a further *Proplan Report* by the Highland Board setting out the development required for the Port of Invergordon to accommodate all these proposals.[16] It was estimated that £10 million would need to be spent on upgrading the port if Occidental Oil was to go ahead with its plans for the petrochemical plant.[17] The old harbour facilities were left out of the scheme, although they would continue to be used by the Navy and for recreational purposes, and a new complex of docks for bulk carriers of oil, chemicals and other bulk cargoes was planned to the east and west of the existing harbour area. Separate, long jetties were to be built for dangerous cargoes such as vinyl chloride and chlorine. A number of large, new piers with numerous moorings capable of taking tankers of 250,000 tons were to be built including a 4,000 foot oil jetty and a 2,000 foot long dry cargo pier. It was envisaged that there would be between 1,100 and 1,400 berthings per year for about twenty million tons of cargo. Crude oil, rock phosphate, potash, alumina, chrome and manganese, coke and iron ore were to be imported. Exports from this huge new port complex would include refined petroleum products, fertilisers, polymers, chlorine and other chemicals in addition to cement clinker. Invergordon was to become '"the" container port for the north.'[18]

The two *Proplan Reports* were worked out in detail in the report which the Highland Board commissioned in January 1967 from the Jack Holmes Group of Glasgow and which, after its publication in March 1968, became the basis of planning policy for the Highland Board and Ross and Cromarty County Council.[19] Invergordon was to be the centre of major capital intensive industry for the whole of the Moray Firth region with outlying industrial areas at Evanton, Muir of Ord, Kirkhill, Inverness, Dalcross and Tore. The Holmes Report foresaw a population of between 250,000 and 300,000 living in what was essentially a linear city from Tain to Dingwall, Inverness and Dalcross. Alness, Evanton and Muir of Ord were to be expanded to take populations of between sixteen and twenty-two thousand, while Dingwall, Maryburgh/Conon Bridge, Tain, Beauly, Kirkhill, Aultfearn and Belladrum were to be expanded by between three and seven thousand. In addition there were to be new towns at Fearn (17,000), Brahan (16,000) and Balloch (20,000). This complex of new and old towns was to be linked by a major motorway from Inverness to north of Invergordon with loop roads taking in communities along the way.

From the time of the 1966 *Proplan Reports* the Black Isle had been perceived as the 'green centre' in this crescent of development (the Tarbat peninsula was also excluded from development because of its high potential for agriculture). Elsewhere, it was becoming clear, there would need to be considerable rezoning of agricultural land on which to build the industrial centres.[20]

The terms of the *Proplan Reports* were confidential, but rumours of their details soon began to circulate fanning claims that the Highland Board was over-secretive. Secrecy bred rumour, local fear and distrust. Early in 1967, for example, there were rumours that the village of Saltburn might be cleared for industrial development. When details of the *Proplan Reports* did leak out in March 1967 the stage was set for the beginning of years of controversy over the industrial development of the Cromarty Firth. No one doubted that industrial development was necessary and suitable, given the Cromarty Firth's natural advantages; the questions were 'What kind of development?' and 'Where is it to go?'

Meanwhile other local industries were in difficulties. In February 1966 the Evanton timber factory closed with a loss of seventy-five jobs. Whisky sales were in steep decline and by the autumn there were layoffs and short-time working at Invergordon Distillery. Amongst those to leave was Frank Thomson. Clearly a replacement industry was necessary; the petrochemical scheme was beginning to look increasingly doubtful. Aluminium smelting seemed to be the answer and this was given added force by Harold Wilson's speech at the Labour Party Conference in October 1967, when he announced the government's plans to build two smelters by 1974 to improve Britain's balance of payments and to strengthen the government's application to join the European Economic Community.[21]

By this time three companies were in competition to build the proposed Invergordon smelter: the Canadian company Alcan, Rio Tinto Zinc and British Aluminium. By mid-1967 Alcan and British Aluminium were active in putting forward their claims to the local community. Alcan published a slick booklet, *Invergordon and Aluminium*, stressing its huge global interests and the local benefits in jobs, housing, education and improved standards of living. British Aluminium made much of its long history of production in the Highlands and mounted a large public relations campaign, including a travelling exhibition for Easter Ross, and public meetings backed by a letter to every local resident describing its plans.

By the end of the year planning was going ahead for the necessary infrastructure. The farms of Ord and Inverbreakie were rezoned for industrial use and in November 1967 planning permission was granted for the building of five hundred council houses in Alness. There were numerous objections to the plans for the smelter. Norway intervened to claim that the plans for a subsidised smelter were a violation of the European Free Trade Area (EFTA) agreement and, as a result, the production capacity of the proposed smelter had to be reduced to 100,000 tons per annum. There were also local objections, mostly on the grounds that the plant would be built on prime agricultural land. A fifteen day public enquiry into the proposed rezoning opened in Dingwall on 28 February 1968. Local feeling became increasingly fragmented. There were marches in favour of the development and the jobs it would bring; there were claims that the objectors to the smelter were anti-industry at all costs. In fact, there were all shades of feeling and opinion about the smelter and industrial development, although as the pace of development accelerated feelings became increasingly polarised. It was the beginning of a long period of conflict over the development of the region which divided families and communities.

A crucial question in the claims and plans of all the competing companies was the source and the cost of the energy that was to power the furnaces. At a news conference during the Labour Party Conference in October 1967 the

Energy Secretary, Peter Shore, gave the impression that the smelter would be nuclear powered.[22] Early in 1968 Alcan announced that it had negotiated a deal with the National Coal Board for cheap coal and that, if they were granted permission to build at Invergordon, they would construct their own coal-fired electricity generating station. Harold Wilson was said to be furious since the agreement went against his government's commitment to nuclear power.[23]

By June, however, Alcan had decided to site their smelter in the north eastern coal field at Blyth in Northumberland. At the end of July Anthony Crosland, President of the Board of Trade, announced in the House of Commons that British Aluminium had been chosen to build the Invergordon smelter. The plant was to be powered by electricity produced by the nuclear-powered Hunterston Electricity Generating Station in Ayrshire. William Ross, Secretary of State for Scotland, put the official view succinctly: 'This is really the touchstone. We are now beginning to rebuild and regenerate the Highlands'. For most local people the coming of the smelter was seen in more human and individual terms. The smelter meant guaranteed jobs and even the possibility of a return home for natives who had been forced to leave the area in search of employment.

From the outset, however, there were serious doubts about the viability of the smelter. Not only was its operation contingent on preferential tariffs for electrical power, it was also widely felt that decisions about its development were often made for political as much as for economic reasons. The Industrial Correspondent of *The Scotsman* claimed that Alcan had had the strongest commercial claim but that 'all three main contenders . . . have been anxious at the way political considerations have tended to dominate commercial factors throughout.'[24]

But, as the details of the proposed smelter became clearer, those of the long-promised petrochemical complex became less and less specific. Details of the project were constantly changing. Originally it was said that 2,000 acres would be required; this was later reduced to 1,000, then 300. The original American backer had pulled out in 1966 and by the following year Occidental Petroleum was said to be maintaining a silence about their intentions 'that would have done credit to a Trappist monastery.'[25] Essentially, the arguments over the viability of the petrochemical works polarised, as to a certain extent they did over the smelter, 'between those who regard the plan as economically unjustified and those who think it politically attractive . . .'[26]

The fullest and fiercest attack came in an article by Bill Williams in the *Glasgow Herald* of 14 July 1967:

> In the eighteen months of its life to date the board has shown an alarming disregard for 'local conditions' and 'local needs' . . . Critics of Invergordon have been branded anti-Highland and are assumed to be in league with the wicked landlords. By the same token the supporters of the scheme are cast in the role of

Highland heroes, and saviours of the forgotten land. These emotional attitudes and the unreasonable absence of hard facts have made dispassionate discussion of the Invergordon project almost impossible. In the cold light of economic day the Invergordon scheme as we know it at present fails to convince. And it is no excuse to plead special economic treatment because Invergordon happens to be situated in the Highlands . . . An ice-cream factory on the summit of Ben Nevis could be made viable by a government who were prepared to find the money to make it . . . In its projected form each job created by the Invergordon development would cost £6,000. By any reasonable standard this is too much to pay to give a man a job anywhere in Britain.

By the summer of 1967 it was clear that Occidental was not going ahead with Frank Thomson's scheme. Early in 1968, however, the idea of a petrochemical plant on the Cromarty Firth was revived by the Scottish businessman, Eoin Cameron Mekie, who floated another £100 company, Grampian Chemicals, with proposals to build a £50 million plant at Invergordon, producing petrochemicals and feedstocks, and employing one thousand workers.[27] Early in 1969 Grampian Chemicals presented a detailed proposal to the County Council for a petrochemical plant to be built at Pollo and Delny and an oil tank farm and pumping station at Nigg Ferry and Castle Craig. In addition to a two mile long pier to accommodate supertankers, there was to be a pipeline built from Nigg Bay to Delny. Five hundred houses would have to be built for the plant's workers.[28] The County Council voted to amend their development plan and rezone the land for industrial use; there were thirty-four objectors to the rezoning of Pollo and Delny but not Nigg. In December 1968 another public enquiry began into the rezoning required for Grampian Chemicals. This time the Enquiry Reporter found in favour of the objectors, ostensibly because the plant at Pollo would be built on some of the best farming land in the area. A major factor in the Reporter's decision, however, was Grampian Chemicals' lack of experience and the company's refusal to name buyers or associates. Once again, estimated needs, capacities and costs were constantly changed. As time passed, for example, the one thousand workers dropped to three hundred and ten, while the estimated output and construction costs doubled.

The Public Enquiry recommendations were overturned by the Secretary of State for Scotland, William Ross, a decision later reinforced on appeal to the Court of Session. Labour support in Scotland was slipping away to the Scottish National Party; once again local developments hinged to a large extent on political needs. On 1 August 1969, in a blaze of publicity, bulldozers appeared at Delny: work was about to begin. The next day, however, the bulldozers failed to reappear and it was later claimed that the day's work was merely soil sampling. The plant was never built.

The failure of Grampian Chemicals' proposals was due to undercapitalisation. The rezoned land at Delny lay unused for several years, providing Easter Ross with its first home-grown example of planning blight. The

Grampian Chemicals enquiry and its consequences (or lack of them) led to a growing cynicism amongst many people around the Cromarty Firth: what good was a public enquiry if its decision was overturned, or if the successful applicant was unable to fulfill its plans and the land was left in a kind of limbo?

But at the same time as it was becoming increasingly clear that, once again, a petrochemical complex was not going to materialise, the smelter began to grow. Nearly two thousand workers were required for its construction and, for the first time perhaps since the agricultural boom of the Napoleonic Wars, Easter Ross enjoyed full employment; indeed, extra workers had to be drafted in from other areas and live in caravan parks and construction camps in order to complete the smelter on schedule. This experience was a foretaste of things to come. The smelter brought relative prosperity, and the beginning of industrial problems which would become more pronounced with the oil related developments, with the differing attitudes between locals and incomers to their work: 'Whilst the locals were pleased to have a job, the immigrants knew how to make the best of it . . .'[29] To the incomers the smelter was a job, no more; to the locals the smelter was a symbol of new hope for the Highlands. There was a good deal of local idealism and pride involved in the early years of the smelter's construction and work.

Soon after British Aluminium was given the go-ahead, the Invergordon Steering Group was set up with representatives of the local authorities, the company, the HIDB and the Scottish Development Department. This body co-ordinated construction of the smelter and housing, and arranged water supply, sewage and port facilities. British Aluminium held a public meeting to explain its plans and begin the long process of recruiting workers. In December 1968 G. Gordon Drummond was named manager-designate of the smelter and a construction consortium, Taywood Wrightson, was appointed the main contractor. By the late spring of the following year the three-quarters mile long smelter pier began to push out into the waters of the Firth. In May 1970, after a long, well-organised local and national recruitment campaign, the first production workers were appointed and in January 1971 the first delivery of raw alumina took place at the newly completed pier (Fig. 66). Five months later the first metal was smelted, although a slump in world prices for aluminium meant that full production was not reached until the first half of 1973. The growth of the smelter itself was backed by an extensive local public relations campaign designed to consolidate the company's position in the local community. There were a number of well-publicised events, such as the presentation of an aluminium flagpole to the Invergordon Highland Games, and the gift of an aluminium bardic crown donated to the National Mod in 1969, which captured local and national attention. The smelter was the start of a bold new experiment with ramifications extending beyond Britain. Invergordon was the 'boom town of the north, and all eyes were upon it.'[30]

Four years after the creation of the Highlands and Islands Development

66. The Invergordon smelter nearing completion in 1971.

Board it looked as though the great master plan envisaged in the *Proplan* and Holmes Reports was beginning to take shape despite worries about the non-appearance of the petrochemical plant. A key 'growth point' was being built at Invergordon, along with some of the hundreds of houses required for the workers. The only element lacking in the plan was something which had always militated against local development — good land transport. Existing plans had called for the upgrading of the A9 via Beauly and Dingwall. In October 1969 a pamphlet was published recommending the upgrading of the A9 between Perth and Inverness, and the building of bridges across the Inverness, Cromarty and Dornoch Firths to service the coming developments.

> Here in the future will be the deep water harbour serving aluminium smelting and possibly oil refining and other industries . . . The most vital planning question in the whole of the Northern part of Scotland today is, therefore, the line that the new fast road will take.[31]

In January 1971 the County Council opted for this plan, with a bridge to be built over the Cromarty Firth at Ardullie and the construction of the Dingwall

258

by-pass, a project which had been 'temporarily' shelved at the outbreak of war in 1939.[32] The bridge over the Cromarty Firth opened in April 1979 and the Kessock Bridge two years later. The road and bridge network to Invergordon was completed in 1987.[33] Construction of the Dornoch Road Bridge was begun in 1988.

The completion of the Cromarty Firth Bridge sounded the death knell of the Invergordon-Balblair Ferry. It had had a rather chequered career from the time it was taken over from the Admiralty by a local committee of management in 1920. There were a number of lessees in the interwar period and more after the war. All had had to be subsidised. In 1970 it was closed but it was given a new lease of life after a strenuous campaign by the Resolis Community Association. Early in 1971 Somerled Macdonald of Easter Sheep Park took it over with daily runs scheduled to allow local workers to arrive in time for the day shift at the smelter. The ferry continued to run until shortly after the opening of the Cromarty Firth Bridge, when it was killed off by better communications and the beginning of the oil boom: amongst other changes, prosperity brought increased car ownership.[34]

But for North Sea oil the ferry might still be running and these new roads and bridges unbuilt. The industrial history of the region since the early 1960s has been full of ambiguities, of which the greatest is the fact that as soon as the long-planned industrial developments did begin they were overtaken by the unforeseen discovery of North Sea oil. From famine, the Cromarty Firth region moved to feast — indeed, to satiation. The juxtaposition of planned development and what has been called the 'happy accident' of oil has not made life around the Cromarty Firth easy.

As with so much else in the history of the Cromarty Firth the story of oil begins with Hugh Miller. In his *Letters on the herring fishery* he described how the favourite haunt of the fish, the Guillam Bank:

> Is covered by a black adhesive mud in which no shell-fish can live; and the fishermen remark, that though at the depth of thirty fathoms from the surface it emits when brought above water a more disagreeable stench in warm than in temperate seasons.[35]

Future historians of the Cromarty Firth region will, almost certainly, see the first few years of the 1970s as a major turning-point. Oil had been discovered in the North Sea and in the winter of 1971–2 a spate of applications began for oil-related developments around the Firth. One result of this was that, at long last, steps were taken to regularise the position of the port of Invergordon, which had effectively been left in the hands of the Admiralty (after 1964 part of a unified Ministry of Defence) since the end of the Great War. The decline of civil shipping in the 1930s and '40s had allowed arrangements at the port of Invergordon to continue virtually unaltered into the 1970s. The harbour dues had been fixed in 1933 and when the new Authority increased them in 1975 they went up by between 600 and 1,000%. A shadow port authority was set up by the County Council in 1970 in order to secure the necessary legislation to create an independent port authority for the Cromarty Firth. This parliamentary act received the Royal Assent on 18 July 1973 and came into effect on 1 January 1974.[36] The Cromarty Firth Port Authority was given overall control and management of seaborne traffic in the Cromarty Firth and its approaches, as well as the general conservation of the port. In the first year of operation there was discussion about building a new pier between the British Aluminium and navy jetties, but this idea was soon abandoned in favour of development west of the existing harbour.

In addition, the Port Authority was made responsible for virtually all that happens within the Firth below high water, navigation channels, buoys and markers. The new Authority was also required to exercise a development function in and around the Firth and was given sole power of reclamation in two areas of one thousand acres each at Balintraid and Nigg Bay.

In its first year the Cromarty Firth Port Authority was mainly serviced by County Council officials on an agency basis and had its headquarters in the County Buildings in Dingwall until full-time staff, a typist, Secretary and Port Manager, were appointed. Upon the appointment of Captain A. S. Black as manager, the Port Authority moved to a Ministry of Defence hut in the Admiralty compound at Invergordon which was later extended to a linked complex of Portakabins which were moved to the recently purchased site on Shore Road in the spring of 1979. In the early 1980s a specially designed headquarters was built and officially opened in September 1983.

The growth and development of the Cromarty Firth Port Authority marched with local oil-related developments. British Petroleum had found oil in the deep waters of the Forties Field but its extraction demanded new technology of unprecedented size and complexity. Brown and Root of Houston, Texas (part of the Halliburton group of companies, the largest oilfield supply company in the world) had the answer: four huge steel platforms, standing five hundred feet high and weighing fifty-seven thousand tons, linked by a pipeline to Cruden Bay. It was necessary to build these platforms as close to the Forties Field as possible. In the summer of 1971 Brown and Root formed a new company, in conjunction with the British-based George Wimpey, to be called Highlands Fabricators (Hifab), and revealed initial plans for a platform construction yard at Nigg (Fig. 67). It was the opening of the floodgates.

In January 1972 plans were approved for an oilfield supply base at Nigg which was, in fact, never built. In May approval was given for another platform construction yard at Evanton and M. K. Shand were given permission to build a pipe coating works at Saltburn. In June Taylor-Woodrow announced their interest in building a concrete platform construction yard at Alness and Lithgow shipbuilders made public their plans for an oil based industrial estate at Evanton. In the following month Scottish Technopark, soon to be renamed the Cromarty Firth Development Company, expressed interest in taking over Fearn aerodrome as an airport and oil service base and bought the land at

67. An early contract underway by Highlands Fabricators, 1974.

Delny and Nigg owned by Grampian Chemicals. Plans were announced for a six hundred acre industrial estate there, with a pier giving deepwater access. Over the next two years, until their activities were curtailed by spiralling interest rates, the Cromarty Firth Development Company would spend nearly four million pounds in acquiring land around the Firth: by the end of 1972 there were plans for oil-related developments along virtually all of the north shore from Nigg to Evanton.[37]

The scale and rate of change was, almost literally, overwhelming. By the autumn of 1971 Highlands Fabricators had completed purchase of the land they needed at Nigg and announced their plans for building a graving dock there ('Europe's largest man-made hole') with associated workshops and quay. Construction work began early in the following year. In just under two years (Fig. 68) the workforce at Nigg rose from zero to two thousand.[38] The building and staffing of Highlands Fabricators' yard meant that, at long last, Ross and Cromarty had full employment — indeed, the local labour force was

261

inadequate. Workers had to be imported, and there was not enough housing for them. Some lived in caravans and later one enterprising Hifab worker was to convert a pillbox on the North Sutor. For a time some of this massive influx of construction workers were housed in two converted cruise ships, the *Highland Queens*, anchored at Nigg pier.

Aside from the naval dockyard and the war years the people of the Cromarty Firth region had no experience of large-scale industrial work; until the early 1970s most local employment was small-scale and individually-based. The smelter had given local people their first taste of large scale industrial work with genuine attempts by British Aluminium to involve workers in the project and explain developments to the local community. The effect of these new industries was also soon felt on local businesses. Both British Aluminium and Hifab made efforts to use local subcontractors, thus forcing local firms to mechanise and rationalise their operations to meet the needs of these new industries.

> The sheer size and technical complexity of the plant was without local precedent. The rig building yard at Nigg was even more alien . . . the largest dry dock in Europe and unique working conditions (welding in cramped pipe interiors, or at an altitude of two hundred feet or more). The scale and scope at Nigg was beyond anything imagined when recent industrial development commenced . . .[39]

The arrival of Shand and Hifab triggered large scale movements within the local workforce. Many of the Invergordon smelter employees were siphoned off to these new firms, especially Hifab, attracted by the large salaries. Thirty-five per cent of Hifab's construction work force had previously worked for British Aluminium and at M. K. Shand the figure was seventeen per cent.[40] The dichotomy between a 'job for life' (offered by the smelter) and the well-paid but often short-term or 'hire and fire' work patterns of these oil-related industries created further strains for local people.

The arrival of outside workers to fill the vacancies at British Aluminium or to work for Shand and Hifab put all aspects of local life under further pressure — schools, amenity, recreation, health and, especially, housing. It was agreed to build houses for these new workers but there was virtually no local work force left to construct them.

Population increases had been foreseen in the *Proplan* and Holmes Reports; what could not have possibly been foreseen was the speed at which population growth would take place. Its most spectacular manifestation was at Alness, which had originally been conceived of as the dormitory town for smelter workers. Now it was taking in Hifab and other workers as well, and between 1970 and 1973 the town's population doubled, from 1,680 to 3,253.[41] In those same three years the locally-born element in that population dropped by seven per cent to 62%. The number of Alness residents born in the central belt of Scotland rose by 157% and incomers from the rest of Great Britain by 138%. It was a young population; by 1973 67% of the inhabitants was under

68. A North Sea production jacket nearing completion at Nigg, 1974.

thirty-five. One result of the growth of Alness was the reopening of the railway station early in 1973.

It was not just local workers, and local communities, that had been overwhelmed by the coming of oil; so too was the local authority. Ross and Cromarty County Council became a District Council (covering a somewhat reduced area) within the Highland Region as a result of local government reform in 1975. All the careful planning of the previous years had to be amended, changed, and speeded up to deal with the situation as it was, not as it was planned to be. The Tenth Amendment of the County Development Plan brought forward in March 1973 was an attempt to regain control of the situation. Land was rezoned for heavy industry at Nigg and other land set aside for housing: 1,200 acres were marked out for the first phase of Lamington New Town, with a planned population of between fifty and one hundred thousand. In addition, parts of the Cromarty Firth, such as Nigg and Udale Bays, were designated nature conservancy areas. The proposed changes produced acrimonious local debate and this time the objectors who had tended to be from substantial, long established families were joined by people who had moved into the area with the smelter and who 'had seen the ravages of development elsewhere.'[42] An aspect of protest this time was the growing sense that developments had moved beyond local or even national control:

> The great backwater of the Cromarty Firth had moved into the centre of a massive economic and industrial game which was being controlled in Houston, London, Paris and Milan.[43]

The plans for Lamington were soon dropped, but the provision for industrial development in Amendment Ten to the County Plan became the matrix for the events that led to the third local planning enquiry in the region in six years, the proposals for a huge oil refinery and tanker terminal at Nigg point.[44]

At the end of August 1973 another £100 paper company, Cromarty Petroleum, bought two hundred and thirty six acres at Nigg Point from the Cromarty Firth Development Company. Cromarty Petroleum was in fact part of National Bulk Carriers, owned by the mysterious and reclusive American, Daniel K. Ludwig, possibly the richest man in the world. In December the company applied for permission to build an oil refinery at Nigg Point with huge underground storage tanks and a one thousand foot jetty capable of receiving crude oil cargoes from tankers of up to 450,000 tons. Onshore the crude oil would be cracked and turned into various petroleum products such as naphtha, benzine, kerosene and petroleum. Construction of the complex would employ 2,000 men and just over three hundred skilled workers would be required to run the completed works: 'The Ludwig project dropped like a depth charge into the already troubled waters of the Cromarty Firth area . . .'[45]

Although the controversy over the oil refinery was essentially about whether more development was, or was not, a good thing, behind this was the added (and unprecedented) question of whether Ross and Cromarty, hitherto depressed and underdeveloped, needed or could accommodate another large scale project. The county had full employment, thanks to the Howard Doris yard at Kishorn and Hifab at Nigg. The Aberdeen *Press and Journal* neatly described it as 'the county that has jam on both sides'. Over the months, too, questions about conservation and the environment became increasingly important. What would be the effect of a spillage of crude oil from one of these huge tankers within the Cromarty Firth? What if there was an accident at the plant itself? It was said that many people in Cromarty were preparing to leave if the project, just across a very narrow stretch of water, went ahead.[46]

The proposal was initially turned down by the Ross and Cromarty Planning

Committee but, following widespread protests, this decision was reversed. Thereafter, opinion polarised around two groups: the anti refinery CROW (Cromarty Refinery Opposition Workers) and SCOT (Support the Cromarty Oil Terminal). Objectors to the scheme eventually demanded a public enquiry, which opened in Dingwall early in 1975 and ran for ten weeks. The Reporter recommended the rejection of the proposals but this was again overturned by the Secretary of State for Scotland, William Ross. If the political arguments for the Labour government to allow development had been strong the last time this happened they were even more compelling now:

> At the beginning of 1975 the Labour Party's fortunes were at a low ebb. Party organisation was poor, morale was crumbling, many young activists had drifted away, and some had gone to form their own Scottish Labour Party . . . Running on a platform of 'It's Scotland's Oil' the SNP had almost wiped out the Conservative Party in Scotland, had taken 30 per cent of the Scottish vote, and were now challenging Labour strongly.[47]

Despite this decision, however, there were further delays. Michael Nightingale of Cromarty refused to sell a portion of the foreshore at Nigg offering instead a ninety-nine year lease. The Cromarty Petroleum Order Confirmation Bill, designed to force the sale of the land, became bogged down in Parliament and was abandoned. The Nigg foreshore land was eventually sold to Cromarty Petroleum in November 1976 with the proceeds of the sale going into a trust fund for local development. By this time, however, there were growing concerns about how serious Cromarty Petroleum was about proceeding with the planned complex. Some details remained vague. It was said that the company was refusing to say where it would obtain its supplies of crude oil or where it would sell its refined products. Finally, in June 1978 the company put a moratorium on its original project for an oil refinery and began instead to talk of a massive petrochemical complex; neither has, so far, been built.

The long saga of the Ludwig refinery had a number of side effects. It hampered the work of the Port Authority in laying navigation channels within the Firth. In 1977, however, an £80,000 workboat, mv *Udale* was built in Hampshire and brought to the Firth, to be used for hydrographic surveys, servicing small navigation buoys, towing small craft and assisting with anti-pollution measures.

The Nigg refinery was not the only project that failed to materialise. Another was the proposed Taylor-Woodrow concrete platform construction yard at Alness. Then in 1974 there were proposals by a company called Marine Oil Industries Repairs (MOIRA) to use a refitted naval repair ship moored between Balblair and Cromarty as a floating rig repair base. The ship arrived in the Firth in March 1975 but by September the company was in liquidation. Nevertheless, MOIRA was a portent of the future use of the Cromarty Firth as a major rig-repairing centre.

The Ludwig controversy also diverted attention from other developments around the Firth which, as it turned out, were to be of much greater long-term significance. Amongst these was the conversion of the old Evanton airfield to Highland Deephaven in 1974. The land, lying between the sea and road and rail communications, was ideally suited for industrial development aimed at North Sea oil. In 1977 Cromarty Firth Engineering built a £160,000 fabrication plant there.

In June 1975 the Minister for Energy, Tony Benn, officially turned on the flow of North Sea oil and over the next few years the industrial history of the Cromarty Firth underwent further change. Platforms and their components would still be built there but increasingly the emphasis would turn to servicing existing oil installations. A sign of this change was the proposed £4 million oil supply base, announced late in 1979, to be built on a five acre reclaimed site next to the Invergordon Harbour by the British National Oil Corporation (BNOC). The base was to have berthing facilities for two supply ships and one tug, with storage for diesel fuel, water and chemicals.

By this time an oil field was being developed by Mesa Oil, run by the colourful Texas oilman, T. Boone Pickens, close inshore to the north-east of the Cromarty Firth. Early in 1977 Pickens named the field 'Beatrice' after his wife. In 1978 British National Oil took up an option to acquire up to 51% of the production of Beatrice, which was to start to flow in 1980. Initially, it was planned that oil from this field (an estimated 100,000 barrels a day) would be taken direct from the production platforms by tanker. The plan was resisted by Highland Regional Council and eventually vetoed by the Department of Energy; instead Mesa invited funding for a back-up base in the Cromarty Firth. Early in 1978 plans for a jetty at Highland Deephaven to service the Beatrice Field were announced and in June the Cromarty Firth Port Authority, in conjunction with Wimpey and Brown and Root, announced plans for a fifty million pound storage complex at Nigg to take oil from the Beatrice Field to be piped ashore at Shandwick. Work started at Shandwick almost exactly a year later and the terminal began construction in November. The first Beatrice oil reached the base at the end of September 1981.

But, even as preparations were made to receive the first oil, there were signs that the peak of development had been reached — and passed. In the second half of 1975 a report published by Aberdeen University, 'Prospects for the Moray Firth Subregion', claimed that oil-related development had reached a plateau and could only decline. The author, Tony Mackay, predicted that after 1981 both Shand and Hifab would be in intermittent operation and went on to claim that even for the old established industry of distilling the likely future was takeover by larger consortiums rather than the creation of new plants. In most respects the terms of this report have been fulfilled. The peaks and troughs of employment at Hifab have become increasingly pronounced and Shand, following its takeover by British Pipecoaters, has effectively closed. Teaninich distillery, once the most modern in the region, is no longer in continuous operation.

The buccaneering days were, however, not yet quite over. Between 1978 and 1980 oil prices nearly doubled. The possibility of creating onshore facilities was fuelled by this bonanza and led to further extraordinary happenings. There was, for example, the saga of the Nigg sandbank, sold early in 1976 for £50,000 to an interlocking and secretive group of offshore companies. As this land was in the area designated as suitable for reclamation by the Port Authority the question of ultimate ownership was crucial and almost impossible to determine. In March 1977 the sandbank again changed hands for £600,000 and early in 1980 the American Company, Dow Chemicals, bought the sandbank for £1.3 million as the site of an ethylene plant using North Sea gas.

By now a new factor had appeared on the local energy scene, the proposed North Sea pipe line, planned to gather gas from as many as twelve oil fields and pipe it ashore for processing. One of the sites being considered for the pipeline's landfall was the Cromarty Firth. On the basis of these plans three companies began planning gas fractionation plants in the area, including Dow Chemicals, British Gas and Highland Hydrocarbons, a new company which appeared in 1980 backed by a group of local businessmen. It had plans to build a £750 million plant on reclaimed land at Nigg Bay. Sir Kenneth Alexander of the Highland Board predicted that the Cromarty Firth would become a major gas processing centre. In 1980 it was claimed that the £2,700 million gas line project was on schedule for completion in 1985. By the following year, however, it was clear that there were deep divisions within the Conservative government over the cost of a project which might force up public sector borrowing. In September 1981 the project was abandoned. Thatcher's Britain was a different place from the idealistic and expansive days of the mid-1960s. In June 1982 the Highland Regional Council refused to allow further planning extension to Cromarty Petroleum/Dow Chemicals, which had merged the month before. As one councillor said: 'A great big gas plant with all the trimmings is dead.'[48]

It was clear at the time that the abandonment of the gas gathering pipe line was a major blow to the Cromarty Firth region. What was worse was that it came as part of a package of changes and reverses in the second half of 1981 which showed that the great days were over. In June 1981 James Nott, Minister of Defence, announced that the naval refuelling base at Invergordon would close in 1984. The base had recently undergone modernisation. The job losses involved in the shut-down were few, about three dozen, but the psychological effect of the closure was enormous. It was the last break in the link with the Royal Navy which went back over two centuries. But history can sometimes play tricks: in 1914 ships had sailed from Invergordon to the South Atlantic and victory in the Battle of the Falklands. In 1983 Britain went to war with Argentina in these same islands and Invergordon's oil tanks were suddenly needed again. The base was reprieved, at least until the 1990s.

Then in late September 1981, a few weeks after the naval announcement,

69. The *Deep Sea Saga* undergoing a six month conversion to a floating production system and later named *Deep Sea Pioneer*, 1984.

BNOC announced that they were reconsidering the operation of their Invergordon base. But the greatest blow of all was yet to come. On Hogmanay 1981 the British Aluminium smelter shut.

Although warnings of cutbacks and rumours of closure had been circulating, no one was prepared for the suddenness and completeness of the end. All through the oil bonanza the smelter had been there as a promise of continuous, guaranteed work. Now it was gone. Men who had left the night shift woke up in mid-afternoon to find that they were unemployed. The loss of 900 jobs in so small a population was devastating: local unemployment jumped to twenty per cent. It was nothing less than a disaster of monumental proportions and a communal trauma. Most local people can remember with clarity exactly where they were, what they did and said when they heard the news. The ostensible cause was the cost of energy, but there were other factors.

After the immediate incredulity there was the inevitable reaction. A workers' committee was formed and the plant was occupied. Delegations went to Edinburgh and London but to no avail. As *The Times* wrote in an editorial on 8 January 1981: 'Invergordon's problems illustrate the weakness of bringing

70. The *Sedco 700*, the first drilling rig to berth alongside Invergordon.

large scale industry to remote areas'. The days of the 'growth point' were dead.

In the past when industries, such as the Great War dockyard, closed the workers left the Cromarty Firth. After the smelter closure, however, most of them stayed. Unemployment was rising throughout Britain; no other part of the country could take up the slack. A year after the smelter closed over half of those who had lost their jobs were still unemployed and the local unemployment rate stood at nineteen per cent.

By 1982, however, the use of the Cromarty Firth as a major floating oil rig repairing centre began to grow (Fig. 69). The Cromarty Firth Port Authority agreed in June 1982 to take over the BNOC oil service base and in October the Port Authority formed a new division, Moray Firth Service Company, to operate the base. In December 1983 the Port Authority joined with the Aberdeen Wood Group and Caledonian Towage to form a new company to lease and operate the oil base from 1 January 1984.

Rig repair was, however, not a replacement industry for the long-term employment offered at the smelter. The work is highly skilled and based on short periods of intense labour. For example, in mid-August 1983 seven

71. KCA *Sandpiper*, the one hundredth rig in the Cromarty Firth and the first jack-up to berth alongside the Queen's Dock, nearing completion in the background.

hundred men were working twelve hour shifts on the SEDCO 700 (Fig. 70). About 60% of this force was recruited locally; when the rig went out to sea again the work ended.

By the autumn of 1983 there were six rigs in the Firth for servicing and the Port Manager, Captain Black, quipped, 'I think they are breeding.' But this boom period for oil rig repair ended with the drastic fall in the price of oil in 1985; then the Cromarty Firth became, in effect, a parking lot of unemployed rigs.

By the end of 1982 some steps were being taken to replace at least some of the long-term jobs lost when the smelter closed. In some senses there was a return to some of the ideas of the Martech report. Industrial development was to be small scale and based on local resources. The government promised to invest thirty-five million pounds on the local infrastructure to boost prospects; part of this was to go towards the creation of the Invergordon Enterprise Zone with estates at Invergordon and Alness which became effective in September 1983. Integrated action and planning were the keys to the future. What was large-scale now was the way this growing complex of industries and services presented themselves to the outside world. A year after the smelter

72. A successful float out from the Cromarty Firth.

closure the Cromarty Industries Group was set up, comprising representatives of statutory bodies such as the HIDB and the Port Authority as well as local businesses.

Although oil has continued to dominate local life in the 1980s, it has been largely through the use of the existing infrastructure. With one exception, all major projects mooted since 1981 have not materialised. In 1984 Highland Hydrocarbons submitted plans for an eight million pound plant on the foreshore at Nigg to produce a chemical substitute for lead in petrol. A few months later a twenty million pound project was announced at Alness Point to build a dry dock facility for rigs. Neither was built. In 1985 the Cromarty Firth Port Authority announced plans for a wet dock to be built west of the oil service base at Invergordon (Fig. 71). This facility was opened by the Queen in 1987.

The past quarter of a century has brought great changes to the Cromarty Firth region. In some senses, those since 1965 were the most fundamental, important and far-reaching since the introduction of bronze-working four thousand years before. These modern developments were the result of decades, if not centuries, of planning and dreaming of how the natural advantages of the Cromarty Firth region could be used to create work and prosperity for the area's inhabitants (Fig. 72).

The rate and scope of change around the Cromarty Firth in the last quarter century has almost certainly been unique in Britain for regions of comparable size and population. The people of the Cromarty Firth have witnessed and experienced more change than falls to the lot of most populations in several lifetimes. And it is not over yet.

NOTES

1. *RJ*, 19 August 1956.

2. *Ibid.*, 8 February 1957.

3. *Ibid.*, 26 December 1958.

4. *Ibid.*, 15 April 1959.

5. Much of the following discussion of the growth and development of Invergordon Distillery is based on an interview with, and information supplied by, Mr W. Scott, Distillery Manager.

6. *The Scotsman*, 17 March 1967; *The Sunday Times*, 19 March 1967.

7. *RJ*, 25 December 1959.

8. These details of Cromarty in the early 1960s are based on 'The burgh of Cromarty Report', compiled by the School of Town and Country Planning, Edinburgh College of Art, 3 vols, 1962, in the Hugh Miller Institute at Cromarty.

9. Much of the following discussion of Thomson is based on profiles in the *Scotsman* 17 March 1967 and *The Sunday Times* 19 April 1967.

10. Martech Consultants, Ltd., 'A Report: Highland Opportunity', Scottish Vigilantes Association, Invergordon, August, 1964.

11. Much of the discussion of the Board's early activities around the Cromarty Firth, and Thomson's role in them is based on an article, 'How the Highland Board was railroaded', in *The Sunday Times* 19 March 1967.

12. *RJ*, 3 September, 19 November 1965; *Scotsman*, 17 March 1967.

13. A. Varwell, 'The social impact of large scale industry: a study of the British Aluminium plant in Invergordon', HIDB unpublished report, November 1975, p. 19.

14. Proplan (HIDB) 'Invergordon Chemical Complex, development in the Moray Firth Area, credibility study', two parts, August 1966.

15. *Ibid.*, pp. 34ff.

16. Proplan (HIDB) 'Port of Invergordon, study of facilities required for handling traffic generated by proposed industrial development at Invergordon', November 1966.

17. *The Times*, 10 March 1967.

18. *Proplan Report*, November 1966, p. 65.

19. Jack Holmes Planning Group, *The Moray Firth: a plan for growth in a sub-region of the Scottish Highlands*, March 1968; 'North 7, Special Issue', [1967], The Highlands and Islands Board Newspaper (special Holmes Report edition).

20. The following discussion of the coming of the aluminium smelter at Invergordon is based on the following sources: Interview with G. Gordon Drummond, 21 March

1988; Alcan, 'Invergordon and Aluminium', and 'Invergordon, Aluminium and Chemical Industries, 1965–73' (cuttings book), Edinburgh Central Library, Scottish Room, G. Gordon Drummond, *The Invergordon Smelter; a case study in management*, London, 1977 and G. A. Mackay, *A study of the economic impact of the Invergordon Smelter*, HIDB Special Report 15, Inverness, 1978 and Varwell, 'Social Impact'.

21. *Ibid.*, pp. 20ff.

22. *Ibid.*, p. 24; *Glasgow Herald*, 26 December 1957 (Edinburgh cuttings book).

23. *Scottish Daily Express*, 23 January 1968 (Edinburgh cuttings book).

24. Chris Baur, the *Scotsman*, 25 July 1967 (Edinburgh cuttings book).

25. *Ibid.*, 1 July 1987.

26. *Ibid.*

27. Much of the following discussion is based on James Poole's article 'Dead end of £100 million Highland Fling?' *The Sunday Times*, 15 March 1970, and *RJ*, 29 March 1968.

28. *RJ*, 3 January, 14 March 1969.

29. Varwell, op. cit., p. 37.

30. *Ibid.*

31. R. D. G. Clarke, J. Hunter Gordon, J. S. Smith, 'The Crossing of the Three Firths', Glasgow [1969], p. 4.

32. *RJ*, 29 January 1971, p. 6.

33. R. W. Munro, 'New Ways and Old in Ferindonald', *Clan Munro Magazine*, vol. 15 (1979), p. 18.

34. *RJ*, 6 November 1970, p. 6; 27 November 1970, p. 7; 12 March 1971, p. 6 and interview with Somerled Macdonald, Easter Sheep Park, 27 January 1988.

35. H. Miller, *Tales and Sketches*, p. 174.

36. This discussion of the early history of the Cromarty Firth Port Authority is based on an MSC interview with its first chairman, Vice Admiral Sir John Hayes, along with extracts from his first report (*RJ*, 12 April 1974) and notes supplied by W. Easson, the Authority's first Secretary.

37. A more detailed account of these early oil-developments can be found in G. Rosie, *Cromarty: the scramble for oil*, Edinburgh, 1974.

38. Much of the following discussion of Highland Fabricators is based on an interview with Bill Shannon, 1 February 1988 and the company newsletter, *Hi Fab News*, March 1973.

39. Varwell, 'Social Impact', p. 146.

40. *Ibid.*, p. 62.

41. These statistics about Alness' growth are from *Ibid.*, pp. 56–62.

42. *Ibid.*, p. 201.

43. Rosie, *Cromarty*, p. 13.

44. The story has been fully told in G. Rosie, *The Ludwig Initiative: a cautionary tale of North Sea Oil*, Edinburgh, 1978. The following description is based on this book plus a background article in the *Financial Times*, 13 September 1976.

45. Rosie, p. 51.

46. *Highland News*, 10 October 1974.

47. Rosie, p. 89; The SNP would come within a few hundred votes of capturing Ross and Cromarty in the 1975 General Election.

48. *Press and Journal*, Aberdeen, 17 June 1982.

Bibliography

I. BACKGROUND

Adams, I. H., *Descriptive list of plans in the Scottish Record Office*, 3 vols, Edinburgh, 1966–74.
Dictionary of National Biography.
Scottish Record Office, Source List 1: National record sources for local history (typescript).
Scottish Record Office, Source List 2: National record sources for economic history (typescript).
Scottish Record Office, Source List 5: Source list of material on communications in Scottish Record Office (typescript).
Scottish Record Office, Source List 25: Official records and local history (typescript).
Scottish Record Office, Source List 26: The Highlands and Islands (typescript).

II. MANUSCRIPTS AND OTHER MATERIAL IN PUBLIC COLLECTIONS

A. National Library of Scotland

Calder, Rev. John of Rosskeen, Diary 1775–1782, MS 14279.
Gordon, A., 'Nigg, a changing parish' (2 vols, typescript), 1977.
Gordon, Sir John, Pocket Book, MS 108.

B. Scottish Record Office

1. Church Records

Synod of Ross Minutes, 1750–1876: CH2/312/4-6.
Kilmuir Easter Kirk Session Minutes 1771–1840: CH2/429/1.
Kiltearn Kirk Session Minutes 1770–97; 1817–1847: CH2/569/3.
Tarbat Kirk Session Minutes: CH2/350/1-2.
SPCK Register of Society's Schools, GD95/9/1.

2. Estate papers

Cromartie: GD305.
Dundas of Arniston: GD235/1-13.
Gordon of Invergordon: GD235/7.
Munro of Allan: GD71.

Munro of Foulis: GD93.
Rarichy farm rent book, 1783–1834: GD1/519.
Robertson of Kindeace: GD146.
Ross of Balnagown: GD129; GD297.
Ross of Cromarty: GD1/481; GD159.
Ross of Pitcalnie: GD199.

3. *Exchequer records*

Forfeited estates papers: E700–E788.
Highlands roads and bridges papers: E330, E416.

4. *Industrial records*

Accompts of linen cloth stamped in Scotland: NG1/15/1-2.
Board of Trustees for Fisheries, Manufactures and Improvements in Scotland,
Minutes: NG1/1/11-39; NG1/2/13.

5. *Plans*

Cromarty Estates and Architectural Plans, including Tarbat Castle and House,
c. 1777–1914 (ex GD305), RHP 45173–233.
County and Estate plans in Ross and Cromarty, 1833–1956; roads, railways,
harbours etc; Inverness and adjacent counties, 1836–1956 (ex Sc. 29), RHP
46254–462.

6. *Sheriff Court records*

Cromarty, SC24.
Dingwall, SC25.

C. Signet Library, Edinburgh

Session Papers, vols 139–40 (1765–68).
Cases Decided in the Court of Sessions, Third Series Vol. 16.

D. Public Record Office, London

Admiralty Papers: ADM
War Office Papers: WO

E. Department of Agriculture and Fisheries (Scotland), Edinburgh

Land Settlement Files

F. Reports of Parliamentary Boards, Committees and Select Committees

Administration:

Report upon the boundaries of the several cities, burghs and towns in Scotland in respect to the election of members to serve in parliament (PP 1831–2 XLII).
Commissioners appointed to inquire into the state of municipal corporations in Scotland, General Report and local reports (PP 1835 XXIX; 1836 XXIII, XXIX, XXXIII).

Agriculture:

Select Committee appointed to inquire into the state of agriculture, Third Report (PP 1836 VIII).
Documents relative to the dearth and famine in Scotland in the year 1783, in consequence of the late harvest and loss of the potato crop (PP 1846 XXXVII).
Highland and Agricultural Society of Scotland, Report . . . to the Board of Trade on the agricultural statistics of Scotland for the year 1854 (PP 1854–5 XLVII).

Communications:

Telford, Thomas. A survey and report of the coasts and central Highlands of Scotland (PP 1802–3 III).
Committee on the survey of the coasts etc., of Scotland, Second and Fourth Reports (PP 1802–3 IV).
Commissioners for making roads and building bridges in the Highlands of Scotland, Reports, etc. (PP 1803–4 V; 1805 III; 1807 III; 1809 IV; 1810–11 IV; 1812–13 V; 1813–14 III; 1814–15 III; 1817 IX; 1821 X, XVI; 1824 IX; 1825 XV; 1826 XI; 1826–7 VII; 1828 IX; 1829 V; 1830 XV; 1830–1 IV; 1831–2 XXIII; 1833 XVII; 1834 XL; 1835 XXXVI; 1836 XXXVI; 1837 XXXIII; 1837–8 XXXV; 1839 XV; 1840 XXVIII; 1841 XII; 1842 XXV; 1843 XXIX; 1844 XXXI; 1845 XXVI; 1846 XXIII; 1847 XXXIII; 1847–8 XXXVII; 1849 XXVII.
A return of the rents of all turnpike gates in each county in Scotland for the last three years preceding Whitsunday 1835 (PP 1836 XLVII).

Distilling:

Committee appointed to examine the matters contained in several papers which were presented to the House on the 21st of February last, relative to the distilleries in Scotland, etc., Report, 11th June, 1798 (PP 1803 XI).
Committee appointed to consider the laws relative to the distilleries in Scotland, Report 12th July 1799 (PP 1803 XI).
Stills licensed and revenue collected, 1813–18 (PP 1819 XV).
Accounts relating to the distilleries in Scotland, 1815–1818 (PP 1818 XVI).

Education:

An account showing the state of the establishment for parochial education in Scotland (PP 1826 XVII).
Education enquiry, Scotland, Abstract of the answers and returns 1834 (PP 1837–8 VII).
Select Committee appointed to inquire into the state of education in Scotland, Report 1838 (PP 1837–8 VII).
Select Committee appointed to inquire into the state of education in Scotland, Answers made by schoolmasters in Scotland to queries circulated in 1838 (PP 1841 XIX).
Parochial schoolmasters (Scotland), return to an address of the House of Commons (PP 1854 LIX).

Emigration:

Select Committee on emigration, Scotland, First and Second Reports (PP 1841 VI).

Fisheries:

Committee appointed to enquire into the state of the British Fisheries and into the most effectual means for their improvement and extension, First, Second, Third and Fourth Reports, 1786 (PP 1803 X).
Commissioners for the Herring Fishery, Reports 1822–3 (PP 1824; 1825 XV).

Poor Law:

Select Committee on the Poor Laws, Third Report (PP 1818 V).
Select Committee to inquire into the education of the poor. Digest of parochial returns (PP 1819 IX).
Church of Scotland, General Assembly, Committee on the management of the poor in Scotland, Report (PP 1839 XX).
Commission for inquiring into the administration and practical operation of the poor laws in Scotland, Report (PP 1844 XX–XXI; XXIII–XXVI).
Board of Supervision for the relief of the poor in Scotland, First, Second, Third and Fourth Annual Reports (PP 1847 XXVIII; 1847–8 XXXIII; 1849 XXV; 1850 XXVII).

Society:

Census Returns 1801–1881.
Commission of inquiry into the condition of the crofters and cottars in the Highlands and Islands of Scotland, Report (PP 1884 XXXII–XXXVI).

G. Newspapers

The Cromarty News, 1891–2.
Invergordon Times and General Advertiser, 1856–1915

The Inverness Courier
The Northern Chronicle
The Ross-shire Journal, 1875ff.

H. Miscellaneous unpublished material and MSS

1. Mr Alasdair Cameron, Well House, Muir of Ord
   Minute Book of Mulbuie Highland Land League 1883–9.
2. Cromarty Firth Port Authority, Invergordon
   Cutting books.
   Minute books.
3. Mr and Mrs P. Durham, Scotsburn, Kildary
   Cutting book.
   Teaninich Farm diary, 1848–50.
4. Mrs M. Gill, Rosskeen, Invergordon
   Culcairn Farm, Nov. 1829–October 1831.
   Arabella, December 1831–24 November 1832.
   Labour Book of Tarlogie, Morangie and Culcairn, May–Nov. 1829.
5. Groam House Museum
   Black Isle Poorhouse Book and Record Books.
6. Mr J. Hoseasons, Belleport
   Letters of Captain James Hall and Family.
7. Dr. W. S. Macdonald, Leeds
   Gorran, H. A. R., 'Potential Development of the Cromarty Firth Area,
   November 1946' (typescript).
8. Mrs Rosemary Mackenzie, Tain
   Ross and Cromarty Valuation Rolls, 1868–9, 1898, 1919.
   Voters rolls, 1832, 1836.
   Ross of Balnagown: cuttings, family history (typescript).
   Cutting scrapbook: Ross-shire folk as I knew them by W. T. Munro.
   Valuation of Cromarty-shire in 1698 and 1775.
   Valuation Book of the County of Ross, the parishes alphabetically
   arranged, 1826.
9. Captain Patrick and Mrs Munro of Foulis, Foulis Castle, Evanton
   Memoirs of woods etc on Foulis, 1833.
   Account of meal taken into the storehouse at Foulis, 1789.
   Note of the barley and oat meal given in to the storehouse, 1795.
   Discharge to tenants, 1794.
   Agreement by Donald Cameron . . . for repairing old county road, 1830.
   Miscellaneous MSS relating to ferry and foreshore at Foulis and Ardully,
   1835–1988.
10. Mr and Mrs Arthur Munro Ferguson of Novar, Novar, Evanton
   Estate map by David Aitkin, 1777.
   Map of Mains of Novar, 1788.

11. Mrs Isobel Rhynd, Pollo House, Invergordon

Minute Book of the nursing association, 1935–1954 and nurses' reports, 1938.

Strike News.

Teachers' Roll Book, Invergordon, 1911, 1916 etc.

Pierrot Troop Memorabilia, 1920s.

Miscellaneous: Fly leafs etc: World War II passes.

Small Lett's diary kept by Invergordon schoolgirl, 1916.

12. Mr and Mrs John Shaw of Tordarroch, Newhall

Estate maps:

(a) 'A plan of the Mains of Newhall and of part of the estate, 1788'.

(b) 'The plan of the Mains of Newhall, William Matheson, 1799'.

(c) 'Plan of the Mains of Braelangwell and the plantations of William Matheson (probably same date as b).

(d) 'Plan of the estate of Newhall and of part of the estate of Braelangwell . . . surveyed in the year 1813 by James Chapman'.

(e) 'Plan of the Estate of Newhall' by C. Campbell Smith, Banff, 1849.

I. Interviews and Personal Communications

(MSC indicates an interview carried out by the Manpower Services Team based in Invergordon, 1986–7).

Mrs M. Chamier, Achindunie, 28 January 1988.

A. Chappel, H.M. Customs and Excise, Invergordon, 28 January 1988.

R. Corbett, Invergordon, undated [1986], (MSC).

F. Cross, Invergordon, 25 January 1988.

B. Dalgarno, Invergordon, 26 January 1988.

G. Gordon Drummond, Inverness, 21 March 1988.

Mrs J. Durham, Scotsburn, Kildary, 13 December 1986.

Mrs B. Gordon, Rosefarm, Cromarty, 28 November 1987.

Mrs P. Gourgey, Invergordon, 28 January 1988.

Vice Admiral Sir John Hayes, Arabella, 28 October 1986 (MSC).

R. Hogg, Cromarty, 27 January 1988.

J. Kelman, Milton, 23 May 1986 (MSC).

Lt. Commander Kempsell, R.N., Invergordon, 27 November 1987.

The Rev. A. G. MacAlpin, pers. com.

A. McCreevy, Invergordon, 23 March 1988.

Mrs J. MacDonald, Balintore, 22 March 1988.

S. MacDonald, Easter Sheep Park, Black Isle, 27 January 1988.

Dr W. S. Macdonald, Leeds, pers. com.

Mrs R. Mackenzie, Tain, 21 March 1988.

Mr and Mrs MacLean, Easter Ardross, 16 July 1986 (MSC).

Miss M. MacLeod, Dalmore Eventide Home, Alness, June 1986 (MSC).

Col. Torquil MacLeod, 5 June 1987 and 5 June 1986 (MSC).

A. Macrae, Dingwall, 26 January 1988.
R. Main, Invergordon, 26 January 1988.
Donald Matheson, Cromarty, 27 January 1988.
Douglas Matheson, Cromarty, 27 January 1988.
W. W. Munro, Clashnabuiac, Alness, 9 November 1986, 14 December 1986, 30 January 1988 and personal communications (also MSC).
Mrs M. R. Patterson, Alness, 27 July 1986 (MSC).
Mr and Mrs William Rae, Nonikiln, 19 August 1986 (MSC).
Mrs I. Rhynd, Pollo, Invergordon, 28 November 1987.
J. Robb, Alness, 25 May 1986 (MSC).
Mr and Mrs Ross, King Street, Invergordon, 21 August 1986 (MSC).
D. C. Ross, Cromarty, 13 December 1986.
W. G. Scott, Invergordon Distillers, Invergordon, 25 January 1988.
W. Shannon, Highlands Fabricators, Nigg, 1 February 1988.
Mrs Nan Sutherland, Barbaraville, 9 November 1986.
C. Watson, Nairn, 31 January 1988.

III. BOOKS AND ARTICLES

A. General histories and collections

Anderson, A. O., *Early Sources of Scottish History*, Edinburgh, 1922.
Bain, R., *History of the Ancient Province of Ross, the County Palatine of Scotland, From the Earliest to the Present Time*, Dingwall, 1899.
Baldwin, J. R. (ed.), *Firthlands of Ross and Sutherland*, Edinburgh, 1986.
Barron, J., *The Northern Highlands in the Nineteenth Century*: Newspaper index and Annals 3 vols, Inverness, 1903–13.
Barrow, G. W. S. (ed.), *Regesta Regum Scottorum*, Edinburgh, 1971.
Beaton, A. J., *Historical and Traditional Notes on Cromarty*, Dingwall, 1894.
Cromartie, Earl of, *A Highland History*, Berkhampstead, 1979.
Dalyell, J. G., *The Darker Superstitions of Scotland*, Edinburgh, 1835.
Dickinson, W. C. and Donaldson, G., *A Source Book of Scottish History*, 2nd revised edn., London, 1961.
Duncan, A., *The Making of the Kingdom*, Edinburgh, 1975.
Exchequer Rolls of Scotland, ed. J. Stuart *et al*, Edinburgh, 1878–1908.
Laing, D. (ed.), *The Orygynale Cronykil of Scotland*, Edinburgh, 1872.
Macdonald, D. F., *Scotland's Shifting Population, 1770–1850*, Glasgow, 1937.
Macgill, W., *Old Ross-Shire and Scotland as seen in the Tain and Balnagown Documents*, 2 vols, Inverness, 1909.
MacKenzie, W., *Ross and Cromarty in Prose, Verse and Music*, Dingwall, 1907.
MacLean, A. C., 'Ross-shire in Dream and Drama', *Scottish Notes and Queries*, 3rd series, iii, 12 et seq, Aberdeen, 1926.
McPherson, J. M., *Primitive Beliefs in North East Scotland*, London, 1929.

Mowat, I., *Easter Ross, 1750–1850: The Double Frontier*, Edinburgh, 1981.

Omand, D. (ed.), *The Ross and Cromarty Book*, Golspie, 1984.

Phillipson, N. T., and Mitchison, R., eds., *Scotland in the Age of Improvement*, Edinburgh, 1970.

Richards, E. and Clough, M., *Cromartie: Highland Life 1650–1914*, Aberdeen, 1989.

Smith, A., *The Jacobite Estates of the Forty-Five*, Edinburgh, 1982.

Smout, T. C., *A History of the Scottish People 1560–1830*, London, 1969.

Smout, T. C., *A Century of the Scottish People 1830–1950*, London, 1986.

Turnock, D., *Patterns of Highland Development*, London, 1970.

B. Topography, travel and archaeology

An Account of the Present State of Religion Throughout the Highlands of Scotland, Edinburgh, 1827.

Anderson, G. and P., *Guide to the Highlands and Islands of Scotland*, London, 1834 (2nd edn, Edinburgh, 1842; 3rd edn, Edinburgh, 1850).

Brown, P. H., *Early Travellers in Scotland*, Edinburgh, 1891.

Brown, P. H., *Early Descriptions of Scotland*, Edinburgh, 1893.

Brown, W. L. W., 'Alness in the eighteenth century', *Transactions of the Inverness Scientific Society and Field Club* 6 (1899–1906), pp. 18–25.

Burt, E., *Letters from a gentleman in the North of Scotland to his friend in London, containing the description of a capitol town in the northern country . . . likewise an account of the Highlands with the customs and manners of the Highlanders*, 2 vols, 2nd edn, London, 1759 [reprinted Edinburgh, 1974].

Campbell, J., *A Full Particular Description of the Highlands of Scotland . . .*, London, 1752.

Carruthers, R., *The Highland Notebook; or Sketches and Anecdotes*, Edinburgh, 1843; new edition 1887.

Chambers, R., *The Pictures of Scotland*, Edinburgh, 1827.

Cooke, G. A., *A Topographical Description of the Northern Division of Scotland*, London [1810].

Cordiner, C., *Antiquities and Scenery of the North of Scotland*, London, 1780.

Cruikshank, J. B., 'The Black Isle, Ross-shire', *Scottish Geographical Magazine*, 77 (1961), pp. 3–14.

Defoe, D., *A Tour through the Whole Island of Great Britain*, London, 1971 edn.

Duns, J., 'Notes on Easter Ross', *PSAS*, 21 (1887), pp. 165–9.

'Excursion to Alness and Strathrory', *Transactions of the Inverness Scientific Society and Field Club*, 2 (1880–3), pp. 317–23.

'Excursion to the Black Isle', *Transactions of the Inverness Scientific Society and Field Club*, 4 (1888–95), pp. 268–74.

Forsyth, R., *The Beauties of Scotland*, 5 vols, Edinburgh, 1805–8.

Franck, R., *Northern Memoirs Calculated for the Meridian of Scotland to which is added the Contemplative and Practical Angler, Writ in the Year 1658*, new edn. with an introduction by Walter Scott, Edinburgh, 1821.

Fraser, H. C., *The Land Statistics of the Shires of Inverness, Ross and Cromarty in the Year 1871*, Inverness [Advertiser Office], 1972.

Geddes, A., 'Scotland: Statistical Accounts of Parish, County and Nation 1790–1825 and 1835–1845', *Scottish Studies*, 3 (1959), pp. 17–29.

Gray, M., *The Highland Economy, 1750–1850*, Edinburgh, 1957.

Gray, M., 'Settlement in the Highlands, 1750–1950: the documentary and the written record', *Scottish Studies*, 6 (1962), pp. 145–54.

Haldane, J., *et al., Journal of a Tour through the Northern Counties of Scotland . . . in Autumn 1797*, 2nd edn, Edinburgh, 1798.

Hall, James, *Travels in Scotland*, 2 vols, London, 1807.

Heron, R., *Scotland Described*, Edinburgh, 1797, 3rd edn, Edinburgh, 1806.

The Highlands of Scotland in 1750, Edinburgh, 1989.

Home, John, *The County of Caithness*, Wick, 1907.

Johnston, W. and A. K., *Gazeteer of Scotland*, Edinburgh, 1937.

Jackson, A., *The Symbol Stones of Scotland*, Stromness, 1984.

Knox, J., *A Tour through the Highlands of Scotland and the Hebride Isles in 1786*, London, 1787.

Knox, J., *A View of the British Empire, more especially Scotland*, London, 1784, 3rd edn, 2 vols, London, 1785.

Lettice, J., *Letters on a Tour through Various Parts of Scotland in the Year 1792*, London, 1794.

Loch, D., *A Tour through Most of the Trading Towns and Villages of Scotland*, Edinburgh, 1778.

Macdonald, D., and Polson, A., *The Book of Ross; and Sutherland and Caithness*, Dingwall, 1931.

Macfarlane's Geographical Collections, 3 vols, Scottish History Society, Edinburgh, 1906ff.

Maclean, R., 'Notes on the parish of Alness', *Transactions of the Gaelic Society of Inverness*, 14 (1887–8), pp. 217–32.

Maclean, R., 'Notes on the parish of Kiltearn', *ibid*., 15 (1888–9), pp. 302–10.

Maclean, R., 'The parish of Rosskeen', *ibid*., 12 (1885–6), pp. 324–39.

Maclennan, F., *Ferindonald Papers*, Ross and Cromarty Heritage Society, Evanton, n.d.

Macrae, N., *The Romance of a Royal Burgh; Dingwall's story of a thousand years*, Dingwall, 1923.

Meldrum, H. M., *Kilmuir Easter. The history of a Highland parish*, Inverness, 1935.

Meldrum, E., *The Black Isle* (Local History and Archaeology Guidebook No. 3), Inverness, 1984.

Miller, H., *Scenes and Legends of the North of Scotland*, Edinburgh, 1885.

Mitchell, J., *Reminiscences of my Life in the Highlands*, 2 vols, reprint, Newton Abbot, 1971.

The New Picture of Scotland, Perth, 1807.

The New Statistical Account of Scotland, 15 vols, Edinburgh and London, 1845.

Nigg Women's Rural Institute, *The Parish of Nigg*, Aberdeen [1967].

The Old Statistical Account of Scotland, 21 volumes, Edinburgh, 1791–9.

Patch, Peter and Co., *Sayings and Doings in the Counties of Ross and Cromarty and District of Ferintosh*, Inverness, 1824.

Pennant, T., *A Tour in Scotland 1769*, 5th edn, London, 1790.

Pigot and Co., *New Commercial Directory of Scotland*, 1825, 1837.

Playfair, J., *Geographical and Statistical Description of Scotland*, 2 vols, Edinburgh, 1819.

Pococke, R., *Tours in Scotland 1747, 1750, 1760*, Scottish History Society, no. 1 Edinburgh, 1887.

Polson, A., *Easter Ross*, Tain, 1914.

Richmond, I. A. (ed.), *Roman and Native in North Britain*, Edinburgh, 1958.

Robertson, A. G. R., *The Lowland Highlanders*, Tain, 1972.

Rylands, T. G., *The Geography of Ptolemy Elucidated*, Dublin, 1893.

Scotland Delineated, or a Geographical Description of every Shire in Scotland, Edinburgh, 1791.

Scottish Development Department, Lists of Buildings of Architectural or Historic Interest, Ross and Cromarty, 1965–8.

Society of Antiquaries of Scotland, *The Archaeological Sites and Monuments of Scotland*, (6) Easter Ross, Ross and Cromarty District, Highland Region, Edinburgh, 1979.

Society of Antiquaries of Scotland, *The Archaeological Sites and Monuments of Scotland*, (9) The Black Isle, Ross and Cromarty District, Highland Region, Edinburgh, 1979.

Sinclair, Catherine, *Scotland and the Scotch*, Edinburgh, 1840.

Southey, R., *Journal of a Tour in Scotland in 1819*, London, 1929 edn.

Spence, E. I., *Letters from the North Highlands, During the Summer 1816*, London, 1817.

Stewart, D., *Sketches of the Character, Manners and Present State of the Highlanders of Scotland*, 2 vols, Edinburgh, 1822 [reprinted 1977].

Stoddart, John, *Remarks on Local Scenery and Manners in Scotland During the Years 1799 and 1800*, 2 vols, London, 1801.

Sutherland, A., *A Summer Ramble in the North Highlands*, Edinburgh, 1825.

Teignmouth, C. J. S., 2nd Baron, *Sketches of the Coasts and Islands of Scotland*, 2 vols, London, 1836.

The Traveller's Guide through Scotland, 3rd edn, Edinburgh, 1806.

Walker, G. S. M., *The Parish of Resolis*, Resolis, 1958.

Watson, W. J., *Place Names of Ross and Cromarty*, Inverness, 1904.

Willis, D., *Discovering the Black Isle*, Edinburgh, 1989.

Wilson, D., *Archaeology and Prehistoric Annals of Scotland*, Edinburgh, 1851.

Young, W. G., *The Parish of Urquhart and Logie Wester*, n.d.

C. Transport and communications

Act of the Justices of Peace and Commissioners of Supply of the county of Ross, Met at Dingwall, on the 22nd May 1793 . . . respecting roads, bridges and ferries, Edinburgh, 1793.

Beaton, A. J., *Illustrated Guide to the Black Isle Railway*, Dingwall, 1894.

Bracegirdle, B., and Miles, P. H., *Thomas Telford*, Newton Abbot, 1973.

Clew, K. R., *The Dingwall Canal*, Tadworth, 1975.

Gardiner, L., *Stage Coach to John o' Groats*, London, 1961.

Haldane, A. R. B., *The Drove Roads of Scotland*, Edinburgh, 1952.

Haldane, A. R. B., *New Ways through the Glens*, Edinburgh, 1962.

Haldane, A. R. B., *Three Centuries of Scottish Posts*, Edinburgh, 1971.

Inglis, H. R. G., 'Roads and Bridges in the early history of Scotland', *PSAS*, 47 (1912–13), pp. 313–33.

The Life Boat, 4 (1858–9); 21 (1910–12); 28 (1930–2).

Lindsay, J., *The Canals of Scotland*, Newton Abbot, 1968.

Macdonald, J., 'Smuggling in the Highlands', *Transactions of the Gaelic Society of Inverness*, 12, pp. 264ff.

Mackenzie, Sir K. S., 'Military roads in the Highlands', *Transactions of the Inverness Scientific Society and Field Club*, 5 (1895–9), pp. 364–84.

Moir, D. G., 'Statute labour roads: the first phase', *Scottish Geographical Magazine*, 73 (1957), pp. 101–10, 167–75.

Morris, R. and F., *Scottish Harbours*, Everton, 1983.

Munro, J., *Recollections of a Bygone Age*, Thurso, 1974.

Munro, R. W., 'New Ways and Old in Ferindonald', *Clan Munro Magazine*, 15, 1979.

Observations on the manner in which the liberal offer of government to assist the county of Ross in building bridges and making roads has been received by certain individuals of that county, Inverness, 1804.

Report of the Commissioners of Tidal harbours, PP, 32, 1847.

Ross, Alexander, 'Old Highland roads', *Transactions of the Gaelic Society of Inverness*, 14 (1887–8), pp. 172–93.

A Ross-shire farmer, 'On the assessment for roads in Ross-shire', *Farmers' Magazine*, 15 (1814), pp. 300–4.

A Ross-shire Heritor, 'On the assessment for roads in Ross-shire', *Farmers' Magazine*, 15 (1814), pp. 155–9.

Skelton, R. A., 'The military survey of Scotland, 1747–55', *Scottish Geographical Magazine* 83, 1967, pp. 5–16.

Smout, T. C., *Scottish Trade on the Eve of Union*, Edinburgh, 1963.

Taylor, G., and Skinner, A., *Taylor and Skinner's Survey and Maps of the Roads of North Britain or Scotland*, London, 1776.

Telford, T., *Life of Thomas Telford, Civil Engineer, written by himself* [with a folio atlas], 2 vols, London, 1838.

Travellers Directory through Scotland; being lists of all the direct and principal cross roads of Scotland, Edinburgh, c. 1792.

Vallance, H. A., *The Highland Railway*, Newton Abbot, 1969.

Webb, W., *Coastguard! An Official History of H.M. Coastguard*, London, 1976.

Wills, V., *Reports on the Annexed Estates*, Edinburgh, 1973.

D. Agricultural

'Agricultural Intelligence Scotland. Ross-shire quarterly reports', *Farmers' Magazine*, 1 (1800) – 26 (1825).

Anderson, J., 'Essay on the present state of the Highlands and Islands of Scotland', *Prize Essays and Transactions of the Highland Society of Scotland* 8 (1831), pp. 16–62.

Anderson, M. L., *A History of Scottish Forestry*, 2 vols., Edinburgh, 1967.

Bailey, F. *et al.*, *Woods of the Novar Estate: plan or scheme of management for twenty three years from 1899-1900 to 1923-4*, Edinburgh, The Royal Scottish Agricultural Society, 1900.

Board of Agriculture. Agricultural state of the kingdom in February, March, April 1816, being the substance of the replies to a circular letter, London, 1816.

Boutcher, W., *A Treatise on Forest Trees*, Edinburgh, 1775.

Bowley, A. L., 'Agricultural wages in Scotland', *Journal of the Royal Statistical Society*, 62 (1899), pp. 140–51.

Clericus, 'On farm houses in Ross-shire', *Farmers' Magazine*, 7 (1806), p. 217.

Clough, M., 'Making the most of one's resources: Lord Tarbat's development of Cromarty Firth', *Country Life*, 162 (1977), pp. 856–8.

'A directory of landownership in Scotland c. 1770', ed. L. R. Temperley, *Scottish Record Society*, new series 5, Edinburgh, 1976.

Donaldson, J., *Modern Agriculture; or the Present State of Husbandry in Great Britain*, 4 vols, Edinburgh, 1795–6.

Douglas, C. L., 'Cattle King of Texas: Mackenzie of the Matador', *The Cattleman*, 23 (1937).

Fenton, A., *Scottish Country Life*, Edinburgh, 1976.

Forbes, D., 'Report of improvement of waste ground', *Transactions of the*

Highland and Agricultural Society of Scotland, New Series, (1853–5), pp. 99–110.

Gray, M., 'The abolition of runrig in the Highlands of Scotland', *Economic History Review*, New Series 5 (1952), pp. 47–63.

Gray, M., 'The Highland potato famine of the late 1840s', *Economic History Review*, 2nd series 7 (1954–5), pp. 357–68.

Grigor, R., 'Report on publications of Pinus Sylvestris, forming part of the Forest of Balnagown, the property of Sir Charles Ross, Bart', *Transactions of the Highland and Agricultural Society of Scotland*, New Series, 1845–7, pp. 120–34.

Handley, J. E., *The Agricultural Revolution in Scotland*, Glasgow, 1963.

Handley, J. E., *Scottish Farming in the Eighteenth Century*, London, 1953.

Houston, G., 'Agricultural statistics in Scotland before 1866', *Agricultural Review*, 9 (1961), pp. 93–7.

Houston, G., 'Farm Labour in Scotland', 1800–50, *Bulletin of the Society for the Study of Labour History*, 11 (1965), pp. 10–13.

Houston, G., 'Farm Labour in Scotland, 1800–50', *Bulletin of the Society for Agricultural History Review*, 6 (1958), pp. 27–41.

Macdonald, J., 'On the agriculture of the counties of Ross and Cromarty', *Transactions of the Highland and Agricultural Society of Scotland*, 4th series, vol. 9 (1877), pp. 67–209.

Mackenzie, Sir Francis, *Hints for the Use of Highland Tenants and Cottagers*, Inverness, 1838 (in Gaelic and English).

Mackenzie, Sir George Steuart (of Coul), *A General View of the Agriculture of the Counties of Ross and Cromarty*, London, 1810.

Mackenzie, Sir George Steuart (of Coul), 'Letter . . . concerning the price of labour', *Farmers' Magazine*, 5 (1804), p. 45.

Mackenzie, Sir George Steuart (of Coul), Letter to the proprietors of land in Ross-shire, Inverness, 1803.

Mackenzie, Sir Kenneth S., 'Changes in the ownership of land in Ross-shire 1756–1853', *Transactions of the Gaelic Society of Inverness*, 12 (1885–6), pp. 293–324.

Mackenzie, W., 'Report of improvements at Ardross', *Transactions of the Highland and Agricultural Society of Scotland*, new series (1857–9), pp. 137–8.

Marwick, J. D., *List of Markets and Fairs Now and Formerly Held in Scotland*, London, 1890.

Mason, J., 'Conditions in the Highlands after the '45', *Scottish Historical Review*, 26 (1947), pp. 134–46.

Millar, A. H. (ed.), *A Selection of Scottish Forfeited Estate Papers,* Edinburgh, 1909.

Morgan, V., 'Agricultural wage rates in later 18th century Scotland', *Economic History Review*, 2nd series 24 (1971), pp. 181–200.

Neill, P., *On Scottish Gardens and Orchards*, n.p., n.d.

Pearce, W. M., *The Matador Land and Cattle Company*, Norman, Oklahoma, 1964.

'Plantations', *Prize Essays and Transactions of the Highland and Agricultural Society of Scotland*, 6 (1824), pp. 258–60.

Political observations occasioned by the state of agriculture in the north of Scotland, n.p., 1756.

Ramsay, A., *History of the Highland and Agricultural Society of Scotland*, Edinburgh, 1879.

'Report on the depressed state of the agriculture of the United Kingdom', *Farmers' Magazine*, 22 (1821), pp. 325–44.

'Review of a general survey of the counties of Ross and Cromarty', *Farmers' Magazine*, 11 (1810), pp. 217–52.

Sinclair, Sir John, *An Account of the Systems of Husbandry adopted in the more Improved Districts of Scotland*, 2nd edn, 2 vols, Edinburgh, 1813.

Sinclair, Sir John, *General View of the Agriculture of the Northern Counties and Islands of Scotland*, London, 1795.

Symon, J. A., *Scottish Farming, Past and Present*, Edinburgh, 1959.

Tivy, J., 'Easter Ross: a residual crofting area', *Scottish Studies*, 9 (1965), pp. 64–84.

Turnock, D., 'Small Farmers in North Scotland: An Exploration in Historical Geography', *Scottish Geographical Magazine* 91 (1975), pp. 164–81.

Ure, J., 'Of 144 acres 2 roods 23 poles on the farm of Easter and Wester Corntown, County of Cromarty', *Prize Essays and Transactions of the Highland and Agricultural Society of Scotland*, 13 (1841), pp. 516–19.

Walker, J., *An Economical History of the Hebrides and Highlands of Scotland*, 2 vols, Edinburgh, 1808.

Whyte, I. D., *Agriculture and Society in Seventeenth Century Scotland*, Edinburgh, 1979.

Whyte, I. D., 'The growth of periodic market centres in Scotland 1600–1707', *Scottish Geographical Magazine* 95 (1979), pp. 13–26.

Wight, A., *Present State of Husbandry in Scotland*. Extracted from reports made to the commissioners of the annexed estates, 4 vols, Edinburgh, 1778–84.

Youngson, A. J., *After the Forty-Five*, Edinburgh, 1973.

E. Fishing and kelp

Anson, P., *Fishing Boats and Fisher Folk on the East Coast of Scotland*, London, 1971.

Anson, P., *Scots Fisherfolk*, Edinburgh, 1950.

Anson, P., *Fisher Folk Lore*, London, 1965.

Coull, J. R., 'Fisheries in the North East of Scotland before 1800', *Scottish Studies*, 13 pt. 1 (1969), pp. 17–32.

Dempster, G., *A Discourse, containing the Proceedings for the Society for extending Fisheries and improving the Sea Coasts of Great Britain, and Thoughts on the Present Emigration from the Highlands*, London, 1789.

Duff, R. W., *Herring Fisheries of Scotland.*

Gray, M., *The fishing industries of Scotland, 1790–1914: a study in regional adaptation*, Oxford, 1978.

Gray, M., 'The Organisation and Growth of the East coast Herring Fishing, 1800–1855', in Payne, P. L., ed., *Studies in Scottish Business History*, London, 1967, pp. 187–216.

Knox, J., *Observations on the Northern Fisheries*, London, 1786.

McCulloch, L., *Observations on the Herring Fisheries upon the North and East Coasts of Scotland*, London, 1788.

Macdonald, J. and Gordon, A., *Down to the Sea*, Aberdeen, 1971.

Munro, J., [Jean Dunlop], *The British Fisheries Society, 1786–1893*, Edinburgh, 1978.

Muir, H. F., *The Scottish East Coast Herring Fishing*, International Fisheries Exhibition publication, 1883.

Ross, A., 'Social Life among the Easter Ross fishermen', *The Highland Monthly*, 1889–90, pp. 157–66.

Rymer, L., 'The Scottish kelp industry', *Scottish Geographical Magazine*, 90 (1974), pp. 142–52.

Stewart, J. I., 'The Scottish herring fishing industry', *Scottish Geographical Magazine*, vol. 47 (1931).

Thompson, P., Wailey, T. and Lummis, T., *Living the Fishing*, London, 1983.

Thomson, J., *The Value and Importance of the Scotch Fisheries*, London, 1849.

Young, A., *Harbour Accommodation on the East and North East of Scotland*, n.d.

F. Towns and politics

Brown, W. L. W., 'Alness in the eighteenth century', *Transactions of the Inverness Scientific Society and Field Club*, 6 (1899–1906), pp. 18–25.

Ferguson, W., 'Dingwall burgh politics and the parliamentary franchise in the 19th century', *Scottish Historical Review*, 38 (1959), pp. 89–108.

Fergusson, J., '"Making interest" in Scottish County Elections', *Scottish Historical Review*, 26 (1947), pp. 119–22.

Houston, J. M., 'Village planning in Scotland — 1845', *The Advancement of Science*, 5 (1948), pp. 129–32.

Mackenzie, W. M., 'The Royal Burgh of Cromarty and the Breaking of the Burgh', Cromarty Literary Society (1924).

Mackenzie, W. M., 'The royal burgh of Cromarty and the breaking of the burgh', *Transactions of the Gaelic Society of Inverness*, 31 (1927), pp. 289–325.

Macrae, N., *The Romance of a Royal Burgh (Dingwall)*, 1923; reprinted 1972.

Munro, R. W. and J., *Tain Through the Centuries*, Tain, 1966.

Nightingale, J., 'The threat to Cromarty', *Country Life*, 157 (1977), pp. 338–40.

Pryde, G., *The Burghs of Scotland, a Critical List*, London, 1965.

Pryde, G., *The Scottish Burghs of Barony in Decline, 1707–1908*, Glasgow, 1949.

G. Manufactures and trade

Cooper, A. S., *Linen in the Highlands, 1753–1762*, Edinburgh, 1969.

Dean, I., *Scottish Spinning Schools*, London, 1930.

Durie, A. J., 'Linen spinning in the north of Scotland', *Northern Scotland*, 2 (1974–7), pp. 13–36.

Durie, A. J., *The Scottish Linen Industry in the Eighteenth Century*, Edinburgh, 1979.

Home, H. (Lord Kames), *Progress of Flax Husbandry in Scotland*, Edinburgh, 1766.

Knox, J., *Curious and Entertaining Letters concerning the Trade and Manufactures of Scotland*, 3rd edn, Edinburgh, 1754.

Knox, J., *Essays on the Trade, Commerce, Manufactures and Fisheries of Scotland*, Edinburgh, 1775.

Mill, J., 'On the spinning of linen yarn in Ross, Caithness, etc.', *Prize Essays and Transactions of the Highland Society of Scotland I*, 2nd edn, 1811, pp. 62–79.

Richards, E., 'Structural change in a regional economy: Sutherland and the Industrial Revolution 1780–1830', *Economic History Review*, 26, 2nd series (1973), pp. 63–76.

H. Distilling, brewing, and the drink trade

Barbars, A., *The Whisky Distilleries of the United Kingdom* [reprint], Newton Abbot, 1969.

Carter, H., *The Control of the Drink Trade*, London, 1919.

Devine, T. M., 'The rise and fall of illicit whisky making in northern Scotland, 1780–1840', *Scottish Historical Review*, 54 (1975), pp. 155–77.

Donnachie, I., *A History of the Brewing Industry in Scotland*, Edinburgh, 1979.

Donnachie, I., 'World War I and the Drink Question: State Control of the Drink Trade', *Scottish Labour History Society Journal*, 17 (1982).

Mackenzie, Sir G. S., 'On the distilleries of the Lowlands and Highlands', *Farmers' Magazine*, 8 (1807), pp. 375–9.

Ross, W., *The Present State of the Distillery of Scotland*, Edinburgh, 1786.

A Ross-shire farmer, 'Remarks on the Ross-shire resolutions concerning the Distillery Laws', *Farmers' Magazine*, 8 (1807), pp. 174–80.

I. Clearances, land reform, poverty

Adam, M. I., 'Eighteenth century Highland landlords and the poverty problem', *Scottish Historical Review*, 19 (1921–2), pp. 1–20.

Blackie, J. S., *The Scottish Highlanders and the Land Laws*, London, 1885.

Cameron, A. D., *Go Listen to the Crofters*, Stornoway, 1986.

Central Board for the Relief of Destitution in the Highlands and Islands of Scotland, Edinburgh Section, Third Report, Edinburgh, 1848.

Gibson, R., *Crofter Power in Easter Ross: The Land League at Work 1884–8*, [Highland Heritage Educational Trust], Dingwall, 1986.

Grimble, A., *The Deer Forests of Scotland*, London, 1896.

Hunter, J., 'The emergence of the crofting community, 1798–1843: the religious contribution', *Scottish Studies*, 18 (1974), pp. 95–116.

Hunter, J., *The Making of the Crofting Community*, Edinburgh, 1976.

Leneman, L., *Fit for Heroes? Land Settlement in Scotland after World War I*, Aberdeen, 1989.

Logue, K., *Popular Disturbances in Scotland, 1780–1815*, Edinburgh, 1979.

Mackenzie, A., *The Highland Clearances*, Inverness, 1883.

Macleod, H. D., *The Results of the Operation of the Poor House System in Easter Ross*, Inverness, 1851.

Mitchison, R., 'The making of the old Scottish poor law', *Past and Present*, 63 (1974), pp. 58–93.

Orr, W., *Deer Forests, Landlords and Crofters*, Edinburgh, 1982.

Pelik, R. A., *C. W. Dyson Perrins, A Brief Account of His Life, His Achievements, His Collections and Benefactions*, Worcester, 1983.

Richards, E., *A History of the Highlands Clearances*: volume 1, *Agrarian Transformations and the Evictions, 1746–1886*, London, 1982; volume 2, *Emigration, Protests, Reasons*, London, 1985.

Richards, E., 'How Tame were the Highlanders during the Clearances?', *Scottish Studies*, 17 pt. 1 (1973), pp. 35–50.

Richards, E., 'The last Scottish food riot', *Past and Present*, Supplement 3, London, 1981.

Richards, E., *The Leviathan of Wealth*, London, 1973.

Richards, E., 'Patterns of Highland discontent', in Quinault, R., and Stevenson, J., (eds), *Popular Protest and Public Order: Six Studies in British History 1790–1920*, London, 1973, pp. 75–114.

Ryder, M. L., 'Sheep and clearance in the Scottish Highlands', *Agricultural History Review*, 16 (1968), pp. 155–8.

Whitehead, G. K., *The Deer Stalking Grounds of Great Britain and Ireland*, London, 1960.

J. Church

Brown, T., *Annals of the Disruption*, new edition, Edinburgh, 1893.

'The Cambuslang and Kilsyth Revivals, 1742: a bibliography', *Records of the Scottish Church History Society*, 1 (1926).

Cowan, I. B. and Easson, D. E., *Medieval Religious Houses: Scotland*, 2nd edn., London, 1976.

Cowan, I. B., *The Scottish Covenanters, 1660–1688*, London, 1976.

Cowan, I. B., *The Scottish Reformation*, London, 1982.

Cromarty East Church (guide), 1981.

Dilworth, M., 'The Commendator System in Scotland', *Innes Review*, 37, no. 2 (1986).

Disruption Worthies in the Highlands, enlarged edn., Edinburgh, 1886.

Drummond, A. L. and Bulloch, J., *The Scottish Church: 1688–1843*, Edinburgh, 1973.

Ewing, W., *Annals of the Free Church of Scotland, 1843–1900*, 2 vols, Edinburgh, 1914.

Fasti Ecclesiae Scoticanae; Synod of Ross, Presbyteries of Tain and Dingwall, volume VII, new edn., Edinburgh, 1928.

Fawcett, A., *The Cambuslang Revival: The Scottish Revival of the Eighteenth Century*, London, 1971.

'Fearn Abbey, Ross-shire', *Scots Magazine*, 23 (1899), pp. 98–100.

Fleming, J. R. A., *History of the Church in Scotland, 1875–1929*, Edinburgh, 1933.

Forbes, R., *Journals of the Episcopal Visitation of the Rt Rev Robert Forbes M.A. of the Diocese of Ross and Caithness . . . with a History of the Episcopal Church in the Diocese of Ross . . . and a Memoir of Bishop R. Forbes*, edited and compiled by the Rev. J. B. Craven, 2nd edn, London, 1923.

Fraser, D., *The Story of Invergordon Church*, Inverness, 1946.

Goldie, F., *A Short History of the Episcopal Church in Scotland*, London, 1951.

Hay, G., *The Architecture of Scottish Post-Reformation Churches, 1560–1843*, Oxford, 1957.

Hunter, H., *A Brief History of the Society in Scotland for Propagating Christian Knowledge in the Highlands and Islands and of the Correspondent Board in London*, London, 1795.

Kennedy, J., *The Days of the Fathers in Ross-shire*, revised edn., Edinburgh, 1895.

Kilmuir and Logie Easter Magazine, nos. 1–11 (1983ff.): Articles on the history of the parish and its ministers by the Rev. A. G. MacAlpin.

Kirk, J., 'The Kirk and the Highlands at the Reformation', *Northern Scotland*, 7, no. 1 (1986), pp. 6–22.

Lochead, M. C., *Episcopal Scotland in the Nineteenth Century*, London, 1966.

Macdonald, M., *The Covenanters of Moray and Ross*, Inverness, 1892.

Macdonald, R., 'Catholics in the Highlands in the 1760s', *Innes Review*, 16 (1965), pp. 218–20.

Macfarlane, L., *Bishop Elphinstone and the Kingdom of Scotland, 1431–1514*, Aberdeen, 1985.

MacInnes, J., *The Evangelical Movement in the Highlands of Scotland, 1688–1800*, Aberdeen, 1951.

Mackelvie, W., *Annals of the United Presbyterian Church*, Edinburgh, 1873.

Mackenzie, W. M., *Cromarty: its Old Chapels and Parish Church*, Scottish Ecclesiological Society, Edinburgh, 1905.

Maclean, D., *Beaton of Rosskeen (1678–1754), a Famous Son of Skye*, Dingwall, 1926.

Maclean, D., 'The presbytery of Ross and Sutherland, 1693–1700', *Records of the Scottish Church History Society*, 5 (1935), pp. 251–61.

Macnaughton, C., *Church Life in Ross and Sutherland from the Revolution, 1688, to the Present Time . . .* , Inverness, 1915.

Macrae, A., *The Life of Gustavus Aird*, Stirling, n.d.

Macrae, D., 'The Kalendar of Fearn', *Transactions of the Inverness Scientific Society and Field Club*, 9 (1918–25), pp. 138–53.

Martin, J. R., *The Church Chronicles of Nigg* [n.p., 1967].

Mechie, S., *The Church and Scottish Social Development, 1780–1879*, London, 1960.

Noble, J., *Religious Life in Ross*, Edinburgh and Inverness, 1909.

Origines Parochiales Scotiae, 2 vols, Edinburgh, 1850–55.

Phillips, A., *My Uncle George*, Glasgow, 1984.

Records of the Presbyteries of Inverness and Dingwall, Scottish History Society, 1896.

Robertson, A. G. R., *The Story of Old St Duthus Church*, Tain, n.d.

Sage, D., *Memorabilia Domestica*, Wick, 1889.

Scott, A. B., 'The Celtic monastery and Roman abbey of Fearn', *Transactions of the Gaelic Society of Inverness*, 28 (1912–14), pp. 391–410.

The Society in Scotland for Propagating Christian Knowledge, *A summary account of the rise and progress of the Society in Scotland for Propagating Christian Knowledge*, Edinburgh, 1783.

The Society in Scotland for Propagating Christian Knowledge, *An account of the funds, expenditure and general management of the affairs of the Society*, Edinburgh, 1796.

Thoyts, G., 'Notes on some Ross-shire churches', *Transactions of the Aberdeen Ecclesiological Society*, 1888.

Watson, W. J., 'The Celtic Church in Ross', *Transactions of the Inverness Scientific Society and Field Club*, 6 (1899–1906), pp. 1–14.

Watt, D. E. R., *Fasti Ecclesiae Scoticanae Medii Aevi*, 2nd edn., St Andrews, 1969.

K. Education

Church of Scotland, General Assembly, Committee on Education, Educational statistics of the Highlands and Islands of Scotland, Edinburgh, 1833.

Mackay, W., 'Education in the Highlands in the olden times', *Celtic Monthly*, 14 (1905–6), pp. 131–4, 155–6, 173–5, 182–5.

Mackinnon, K. M., 'The school in Gaelic Scotland', *Transactions of the Gaelic Society of Inverness*, 47 (1971–2), pp. 374–91.

Marwick, W. H., *Mechanics Institutes in Scotland*, London, 1934.

Mason, J., 'Scottish Charity Schools of the eighteenth century', *Scottish Historical Review*, 33 (1954), pp. 1–13.

Withrington, D. J., 'The SPCK and Highland Schools in Mid-Eighteenth Century', *Scottish Historical Review* 41 (1962), pp. 89–99.

L. Naval and military

Annand, A. McK., 'Major General Lord MacLeod . . . 73rd MacLeod's Highlanders', *Journal of the Society for Army Historical Research*, 37 (1959), pp. 21–7.

Army and Navy Gazette, 1914.

Chalmers, W. S., *Life and Letters of David, Earl Beatty*, London, 1915.

Clower, W. L., ed., *The Royal Navy, a history from earliest times to the present* (1897–1903), reprinted 1971.

Divine, D., *Mutiny at Invergordon*, London, 1970.

Ereira, A., *The Invergordon Mutiny*, London, 1981.

Gibson, J., *Ships of the Forty-Five*, London, 1967.

'Griff' (A.S.G.), *Surrendered: Some Naval War Secrets*, Twickenham, n.d.

Haldane, M. M., *A History of the 4th Battalion of the Seaforth Highlanders*, London, 1928.

Hampshire, A. C., *The Royal Navy Since 1945*, London, 1975.

Hampshire, A. C., *They Called It Accident*, London, 1961.

Hildesley, A. C., *The press gang*, London, 1925.

Hough, R., *The Great War at Sea, 1914–1918*, Oxford, 1983.

Inverkeithing High School, *The Story of Rosyth*, revised edn., n.p., 1982.

Jellicoe, J., *The Grand Fleet, 1914–16*, London, 1919.

Knox, W., 'The Latest Comedy in Home Defence', *The Nineteenth Century*, 19 (1914).

Marcus, G. J. A., *A Naval History of England*, vol. 2, *The age of Nelson*, London, 1971.

Marder, A. J. (ed.), *Fear God and Dread Nought: The Correspondence of*

Admiral of the Fleet, Lord Fisher of Kilverstone, 1904–1914, London, 1956.

Marder, A. J., *From Dreadnought to Scapa Flow: The Road to War, 1904–14*, Oxford, 1961.

May, W. E., 'The *Shark* and the '45', *Mariner's Mirror*, 53 (1967).

Melville, M. L., *The Story of the Lovat Scouts*, 1900–1980, Edinburgh, 1981.

Monro, R., *Monro his expedition with the worthy Scots regiment (called Mac-Keyes Regiment) levied in August 1626 . . . collected and gathered together at spare houres*, London, 1637.

Munro, D. J., *Scapa Flow: a Naval Retrospect*, London, 1932.

Prebble, J., *Mutiny: Highland Regiments in Revolt, 1743–1803*, Harmondsworth, 1977.

Roskill, S., *The War at Sea*, London, 1954.

Roskill, S., *Admiral of the Fleet: Earl Beatty, the Last Naval Hero*, London, 1980.

Schofield, B., *British Sea Power: Naval Policy in the Twentieth Century*, London, 1967.

The Sphere (Special Naval Section), 19 April, 1913.

The Technical History of the Great War (Minelaying bases at Grangemouth, Dalmore and Glenalbyn), 6, pt. 45, London, 1920.

Webb, W., *Coastguard! an official history of H.M. Coastguard*, London, 1976.

Wincott, L., *Invergordon Mutineer*, London, 1974.

M. Local Families and biographies

Ane breve cronicle of the Earlis of Ross, including notices of the Abbots of Fearn, Edinburgh, 1850, *and of the family of Ross of Balnagown*.

Society, vol. VII, Pt VII, New Series.

'Articles of Roup of the Tain, Fearn and Tarbat properties of the Cadboll estate, 1918' Mackenzie and Black, WS, 28 Castle Street, Edinburgh.

Bateman, John, *The Great Landowners of Great Britain and Ireland*, London, 1878.

Bulloch, J. M., *The Families of Gordon of Invergordon, Newhall, also Ardoch, Ross-shire and Carroll, Sutherland*, Dingwall, 1906.

'Calendar of Writs of Munro of Foulis, 1299–1823', *Scottish Record Society*, no. 71, Edinburgh, 1940.

Dunlop, Jean, *The Clan MacKenzie*, Edinburgh and London, 1953.

F.N.R., 'McCullochs of Plaids, Kindeace and Glastulloch', *Scottish Antiquary*, 5 (1891), pp. 58–66.

Ferguson, W., 'The Urquharts of Cromarty', *Scottish Genealogist*, 6, nos. 2 and 3 (1959).

Forbes, D., *Some Kindeace Letters*, Dingwall, 1896.

The Fowlis Case [bound book of printed depositions and other legal documents relating to the succession to the estate of Foulis, 1831–5: in the possession of Mr R. W. Munro, Edinburgh].

Fraser, C. I., *The Clan Munro*, Edinburgh and London, 1954.

Fraser, Sir William, *The Earls of Cromartie: Their Kindred, Country and Correspondence*, 2 vols, Edinburgh, 1876.

Genealogy of the Families of Douglas of Mulderg and Robertson of Kindeace with their Descendants, Dingwall, 1895.

Highlander, The present conduct of the chieftains and proprietors of lands in the Highlands of Scotland, towards their clans and people, considered impartially, n.p. 1773.

Lang, A., *Sir George Mackenzie*, London, 1909.

Macfarlane's Genealogical Collections, 2 vols, Scottish History Society, 1900.

Maciver, E., *Memoirs of a Highland Gentleman*, Edinburgh, 1905.

Mackenzie, A., *History of the Mackenzies*, Inverness, 1894.

Mackenzie, A., *History of the Munros of Foulis*, Edinburgh, 1898.

Mackenzie, A., 'The late Duncan Davidson of Tulloch', *Celtic Magazine*, 6 (1880), pp. 486–7.

Mackenzie, A., 'Sir Kenneth Mackenzie of Gairloch, Bart.', *Celtic Magazine*, 6 (1880), pp. 26–34.

Mackenzie, A. and Macbain, A., *History of the Mathesons*, Stirling and London, 1900.

Mackenzie, Sir George, *Memoirs of the Affairs of Scotland*, Edinburgh, 1821.

Reminiscences of a Dingwall Centenarian, Miss Mackenzie, Inchvanie, by a friend, Inverness, 1908.

Mackinnon, D., *The Clan Ross*, Edinburgh, 1957.

Mackintosh, C. F., *Antiquarian Notes: A Series of Papers regarding Families and Places in the Highlands*, Inverness, 1865.

Mackintosh, C. F., *Letters of Two Centuries*, Inverness, 1890.

Munro, Robert [Lord Alness], *Looking Back*, London, 1930.

Munro, R. W. (ed.), *The Munro Tree (1734)*, Edinburgh, 1978.

Munro, R. W. (ed.), *Monro's Western Isles of Scotland*, Edinburgh, 1961.

Reid, F. N., *The Earls of Ross and their Descendants*, Edinburgh, 1894.

Review of H. Taylor, 'History of the Family of Urquhart', *Scottish Historical Review*, 26 (1947), pp. 168–78.

Ross, A., 'The Munros of Culcairn', *Celtic Magazine*, vol. 10, number 120 (1885), pp. 495–506, 559–66.

Ross, A., 'The Munros of Milntown', *Celtic Magazine*, 10 (1885), pp. 49–56; 103–12; 151–8; 230–7.

Ross, A., 'Sir Robert Munro', *Transactions of the Gaelic Society of Inverness*, vol. 11 (1885), pp. 199–209.

Ross, A. M., *History of the Clan Ross*, Dingwall, 1932.

Ross, J. R., *The Great Clan Ross*, 2nd edn. [Canada], 1972.

Seed, G., 'A British Spy in Philadelphia: 1775–77', *The Pennsylvania Magazine of History and Biography*, 85, no. 1, 1961.

Shaw of Tordarroch, C.J., *A History of Clan Shaw*, Chichester, 1983.
Taylor, H., *History of the Family of Urquhart*, Aberdeen, 1946.

N. Culture and language

Larner, C., Lee, C. H., and McLachlan, H., *A Source Book of Scottish Witchcraft*, Glasgow, 1977.
Mackenzie, A., *Prophecies of the Brahan Seer*, Inverness, 1877.
Mackenzie, D. A., 'Cromarty dialects and folk lore', *Transactions of the Rymour Club*, 3 (1928), pp. 75–82.
Maclean, D., 'Highland Libraries in the eighteenth century', *Transactions of the Gaelic Society of Inverness*, 31 (1922–4), pp. 69–79.
Maxwell, S., 'Highland dress and tartan in the Ross of Pitcalnie papers', *Costume*, 10 (1976), pp. 49–52.
Mowat, I. R. M. 'Literacy, libraries and literature in 18th and 19th century Easter Ross', *Library History*, 5 (1979), pp. 1–10.
Sutherland, E., *Ravens and Black Rain: The Story of Highland Second Sight*, London, 1985.
Swire, O., *The Highlands and their Legends*, Edinburgh, 1963.
Withers, C. W. J., '"The Shifting Frontier": The Gaelic-English Boundary in the Black Isle, 1698–1881', *Northern Scotland*, 6, no. 2 (1985), pp. 133–55.

O. Literature

1. Sir George Mackenzie of Rosehaugh:
   Aretina, London, 1661.
   Institutions of the Law of Scotland, Edinburgh, 1684.
   Jus regium, Edinburgh, 1684.
   A Moral Essay, London, 1685.
2. Sir Thomas Urquhart of Cromarty:
   The works of Sir Thomas Urquhart of Cromarty . . . reprinted from the original edition (Maitland Club, 30), Edinburgh, 1834.
   The jewel, ed. R. D. S. Jack and R. J. Lyall, Edinburgh, 1983.
   A Challenge from Sir Thomas Urquhart of Cromartie (Luttrell reprint, 4), Oxford, 1948.
   The life and death of the Admirable Crichtoun, New York, 1927 edn.
   Logopandecteision, London, 1653.
   Tracts of Sir Thomas Urquhart, Edinburgh, 1774.
   Selections from Sir Thomas Urquhart of Cromarty, ed. J. Purves, Edinburgh, 1942.
3. Hugh Miller:
   Scenes and Legends of the North of Scotland; or the traditional history of Cromarty, Edinburgh, 1835.
   Memoir of William Forsyth, Esq.; a Scotch Merchant of the eighteenth century, London, 1839.
   The Old Red Sandstone, Edinburgh, 1841.

My schools and schoolmasters, or, the story of my education, Edinburgh, 1854.

Tales and sketches, ed. with a preface by Mrs Miller, Edinburgh, 1869.

Mackenzie, W. M., *Selections from the Writings of Hugh Miller*, Paisley, 1908.

Bayne, P., *Life and Letters of Hugh Miller*, 2 vols, London, 1871.

Brown, T. N., *Labour and Triumph: the life and times of Hugh Miller*, London, 1858.

Leask, W. K., *Hugh Miller*, Edinburgh, 1896.

Mackenzie, W. M., *Hugh Miller: a critical study*, London, 1905.

Rosie, G., *Hugh Miller: outrage and order. A biography and selected writings*, Edinburgh, 1981.

4. Duncan (Sandison), J., *My Friends the Miss Boyds*, London, 1959.

Duncan (Sandison), J., *Letters from Reachfar*, London, 1975.

5. Dunnett, D., *King Hereafter*, London, 1982.

Kesson, J., *Another Time, Another Place*, London, 1983.

Sutherland, E., *The eye of God*, London, 1977.

P. Modern Developments

Aberdeen University Department of Political Economy, *Impacts of individual developments in East Ross*, North Sea Oil Project internal working paper 37, 1975.

Branson, N. and Heineman, M., *Britain in the 1930s*, London, 1971.

Cooper, B., and Gaskill, T. F., *North Sea Oil, the great gamble*, London, 1966.

'Cromarty Firth', Special Lloyd's List, 30 January 1986.

Cromarty Firth Joint Promotion Panel, Oil, gas and petrochemical industry potential on the Cromarty Firth, Highland Regional Council, 1981.

Cruikshank, J. B., 'The Black Isle Ross-shire, a land use study', *Scottish Geographical Magazine*, vol. 77, no. 1 (1961), pp. 3–14.

Currie, A., The Objectives of Highland Development, an Easter Ross Case Study, Lamington (Currie and Associates), 1973.

Drummond, G. G., *The Invergordon Smelter, a case study in management*, London, 1977.

Edinburgh College of Art, School of Town and Country Planning, *The Burgh of Cromarty Report*, 1962.

Fairey Surveys Limited, Final report for the Cromarty Firth project area, report to the Scottish Development Department, 1980.

Gaskin Report, *North Eastern Scotland, a survey of its development potential*, HMSO, 1969.

Gollan, J., *Scottish Prospect: an Economic, Administrative and Social Survey*, Glasgow, 1948.

Grimble, I. and Thomson, D. S., eds, *The future of the Highlands*, London, 1968.

Knox, P. L., and Cottam, M. B., 'North Sea Oil and the quality of life, an attitudinal profile of Evanton, Easter Ross', *International Journal of Sociology and Social Policy*, vol. 1, no. 3 (1981), pp. 70–88.

Knox, P. L., 'Social well-being and North Sea Oil, an application of subjective social indicators', *Regional Studies*, vol. 10, part 4 (1976), pp. 423–32.

Mackay, G. A., A Study of the Economic Impact of the Invergordon Smelter, HIDB Special Report 15, Inverness, 1978.

Martech Consultants Ltd., 'Highland opportunity: a report for the Scottish Vigilantes Association', Invergordon, 1968.

The Moray Firth: a plan for growth in a subregion of the Scottish Highlands (Jack Holmes Planning Group: Report commissioned by the HIDB), March 1968.

Pease, G., 'Towards a planning strategy for the East Ross area of the County', Ross and Cromarty County Council, September 1972.

Philip, G., *et al*, 'Oil related construction workers: travelling and migration', in Recent migration in Northern Scotland, Jones, H. R., ed., Social Science Research Council, 1982, pp. 27–60.

Proplan Reports, HIDB.

Rodger, A., 'British Aluminium's blueprint for integration', *Scotland*, vol. 16, no. 4, 1972; vol. 15, no. 8, pp. 51–5.

Rosie, G., *The Ludwig Initiative, a cautionary tale of North Sea oil*, Edinburgh, 1978.

Rosie, G., *Cromarty: the scramble for oil*, Edinburgh, 1974.

Scottish Economic Planning Department, *Closure of the Invergordon Smelter; impact and action programme*, SEPD and HIDB, 1982.

Smith, J. S., 'Development and rural conservation in Easter Ross', *Scottish Geographical Magazine*, vol. 90, no. 1 (1974), pp. 42–56.

Smith, J. S., Moray Firth Development, Ecological Study, HIDB, 1979.

Varwell, A., 'The social impact of a large scale industry: a study of the British Aluminium plant in Invergordon', 1976 (copy in HIDB Library).

Varwell, A., 'A study of industrial settlements in sparsely populated areas with special reference to the mediation of extra local politics'. [Part 3: Cromarty Firth], Aberdeen University PhD Thesis, 1977.

Index

Abertarff, Lord of, 11
Achnacloich Castle, 83
Achnagarron Free Church, 63, 66
afforestation, 76, 83
agriculture: neolithic, 3; 17th century, 21, 77-84; 18th century, 70-4; improvement, 70-1, 73, 74, 83-5, 106-12; landlord/tenant relationships, 79-80; rents, 79; 19th century, 108-12, 116, 117, 121-2, 130-1, 132; depression in, 116, 132; crofting, 222-4; smallholdings, 222-3; between the wars, 224
air force see Royal Air Force
Aird, Rev. Gustavus, 124
airfields, 217, 231-2, 235
Alcan, 254-5
Alexander II, King of Scots, 11, 14
Alness, 114-15; 18th century, 72-3; aerodrome, 232; oil-related industry, 260, 262-3, 265
aluminium smelter, 254-5, 257, 268-9
Anderson, Hugh, minister of Cromarty, 49-50
Ankerville estate, 90, 111
appropriation, 13
Arabella smallholdings, 223
Ardoch (Poyntzfield), 111
Ardross Castle, 129
Ardross estate, 128-9, 218
Ardullie, bridge at, 258, 259
Ardullie farm, 223
army: World War I, 212-13; World War II, 233-4, see also soldiers
Arthur, Rev. Robert, 74
Avoch, 166

Baird, Thomas, factor, 95
Balblair Ferry, 143, 216, 217, 259
Balfour, Rev. John, 52, 55
Balintore, 156, 162, 163, 167-8, 169
Balintraid, 152, 156
Balliskilly, 8
Balnabeen, 223
Balnabruaich, 156
Balnacraig, 8
Balnagown, 8
Balnagown Castle, 219, 220
Balnagown estate, 71, 84, 98, 219-22
Balnapaling, 156
Balrishallich, model croft, 218
Barbaraville, 156
Barkly, Gilbert, 76
baron courts, 27, 81
Baylie, James, of Migdie, 144

Beatty, Admiral David, 194, 196-7
Beauly, 12
Belleport, 152, 153
Belsches, Thomas, 85
Bissets, Lords of the Aird, 11, 12
Black Isle Farmers' Club, 110
Boniface, 8
boom, naval, 194, 196-7
Braelangwell, 9
Brahan Seer (Coinneach Odhar), 24, 25
bridges, 82, 258-9
British Aluminium, 254, 255, 257, 262
British Fisheries Society, 160-1
British National Oil Corporation (BNOC), 266, 268
British Pipecoaters, 266
brochs, 5
Bronze Age, 3-4
Broomhill, 223
Brude, King of the Northern Picts, 5, 6
burghs: royal, 14; of barony, 37

Cadboll, 9
Cadboll Castle, 22
Cadboll estates, 218
Calder, Rev. John, 53-4
Carment, Rev. David, 55, 56
Carn Mor, 5
Castle Leod, 32
Castledownie, 5
Castlehaven see Portmahomack
Celtic church, sites of, 6-8
Celts, 4-5
chambered tombs, 3
Chanonry castle, 28, 29
Chanonry Point, lighthouse, 155
Chapman, James, 242
Charles I, King, 47
cholera epidemic, 120-1
Christianity: Celtic church, 6-8; coming of, 6, 8
church: Celtic, 6-8; Roman, 8; medieval, 12-14; lands, 27-9; Reformation, 42-6; Gaelic and, 43-4; 17th century, 47-50; 18th century, 51-5; patronage, 53-5; 19th century, 55-9; music, 58; social role, 60-1; buildings, 63-4, see also Christianity; individual branches of church
Church of Scotland, Disruption, 55-7
Churches (Scotland) Act, 1905, 60
Churchill, Winston, 187-8, 191, 192, 194
Civil Wars, 17th century, 29-32, 33-5, 37
Clach a'Mheirlich, 6

clans/clan system, 21, 27, 32-3, 80, 96; clan regiments, 27
clearances, 117, 123-4; church and, 55-6
Cnoc an Duin, 5
coach travel, 116
coal importing, 152
coastal defences, 175, 180, 181, 197, 223; The Sutors, 191-2, 214, 231
coastguard service, 155
common land, 77
communication: ancient tracks, 3; roads and, 115-16, *see also* transport
Conon, bridge across, 115
Cornton, 223
cottars, 71-2
courts of law, 27, 80-1
covenanters, 47, 48-50
Crimean War, naval activity, 179-80
Crofters Act, 1886, 135
Crofters Commission, 135
crofting, 133-5, 223-4
Cromartie, George Mackenzie, 3rd earl, 85, 86-7
Cromartie estate, 37-8, 90; forfeiture, 87, 88
Cromarty: medieval, 14; 17th century, 21, 37; church, 63; school, 63-4; 18th century, 74-5, 147-9; courthouse, 91, 92; new town, 112; 19th century, 113-14; harbour, 148, 150-1, 215; lighthouse, 155; Royal Navy and, 178-9, 180, 192, 194, 199; post-war development, 249
Cromarty, county of, 37
Cromarty, HMS, 237
Cromarty and Dingwall Light Railway, 132
Cromarty Firth Bridge, 258-9
Cromarty Firth Port Authority, 260, 269, 271
Cromarty Industries Group, 271
Cromarty Petroleum, 264-5, 267
crops, 77, 109
Culbokie, 5, 112
Culcairn, 223
Culrain riots, 117, 123, 124
Curitan, 8
customs and excise, 147, 155

Dalmore distillery, 152, 217; mine assembly at, 203-5
David I, King of Scots, 14
Decantae, 5
deer forests, 121
defences, coastal *see* coastal defences
Delny, industrial rezoning, 256
Delny Castle, 83
Delny Muir, 71-2, 77, 88
Denoon, Walter, minister of Golspie, 48
Dibiedale estate, 218

Dingwall, 9, 10; 18th century, 73; church, 51; harbour and canal, 151-2, 153; industry, 240; medieval, 14
Disruption, 55-7
distilleries *see individual distilleries*; whisky industry
docks, floating, 191-2, 199, 216
Dow Chemicals, 267
drainage, 110
Drummond, fermtoun, 114
Dundas, Anne (nee Gordon), 85, 87
duns, 4
Dunskeath Castle, 10, 143

Earnan, 6
Easter Rarichie, 5
Easter Ross Farmers' Club, 110
Eathie Den, 1
economic depression, 116, 132, 224, 230
Edderton, 101
education, 61-3
electoral reform, 118-19
emigration, 75-6, 117, 122-3, 132, 224
enclosure, 70, 71
episcopacy, 49-51
estates: 17th century, 77, 79-80; 18th century, 83; forfeited, 88, 90-1; sporting, 121; effects of World War I, 218-19
evangelism, 52, 55, 58
Evanton, 114; oil-related industry, 260, 266
Evanton (Novar) Aerodrome, 217, 231, 232, 241, 266

famine, 21, 75, 123, 125
farmers' clubs, 110
farming *see* agriculture
Fearn: 18th century, 70; airfield, 235, 238, 241
Fearn Abbey, 12
Ferguson, Munro, of Novar, 134
Ferintosh, 75
Ferintosh privilege, 73-4
ferries, 143, 150
Ferryton, girnel, 56
feudalism, 11
Findon estate, 219
fish: curing, 145, 162, 163, 164, 166, 168; salesmen, 168
Fisher, Admiral Sir John, 183-4, 186-7, 188
fisher lassies, 168
fisherfolk, traditions, 157-9
Fisheries Act, 1868, 165
Fisheries Officer, 162
Fishery Protection Vessels, 163
fishing: industry, 70, 145, 156-7, 160-70; rights, 156; villages, 156-7, 159-60; boats, 160, 164, 165, 166, 167, 168; parliamentary commission, 163-4; bait, 164-5
fishwives, 157

flax spinning, 71, 148
Fleet Air Arm, 217, 231-2
Fleet visits, 181, 182, 184-6
Forbes, Captain —, of Newe, 90
Forestry Commission, 223, 240
Forfeited Estates, Commissioners for, 88, 90-1
Forsyth, James, 147
Forsyth, William, merchant, 75, 145, 147-8
forts, promontory, 4, 5
fossils, marine, 1
Foulis Castle, 83
Foulis Ferry, girnel, 81, 82
Foulis, Katherine Munro, Lady, 23-5
Franck, Richard, 20
Fraser, Alexander, of Balcony, 114
Free Church of Scotland, 56-9
Fyrish Hill, 96
Fyrish Monument, 96

Gaelic language, 8-9, 43-4, 61-2
Gaelic Schools Society, 62
gardens, landscaped, 83
garvie fishing, 165
gas, North Sea, 267
general bands, 22
geology, 1-2
George VI, King, 234
Gillanders, James Falconer, 124
girnels, 37-8, 81
glaciation, 2
Glencalvie, clearances, 124
Glencalvie estate, 218
Gollan, John, 239-40
Gordon family, 84-5
Gordon, Adam, Collector of Customs, 84-5
Gordon, Adam, of Dalpholly, 84
Gordon, Sir Adam, of Kilcalmkill, 84
Gordon, Alexander, 84
Gordon, Anne, 85, 87
Gordon, Charles, 85
Gordon, Henrietta, 91
Gordon, Isabella (Bonny Belle Gordon), 85
Gordon, Sir John, 53, 54, 72, 85-9
Gordon, John, of Straloch, 76
Gordon, Sir William, 72, 84, 85, 87
Gordon Highlanders, 213-14, 233
Gorry, John, 85
Govan, H. A. Rendal, 238-9
grain trade, 81, 145-6
Grampian Chemicals, 256
Grant, Rev. Patrick, 55
Great Awakening, 52

Hall, Captain James, 152-3
Hamilton, Patrick, Commendator of Fearn, 42-3
harbours of refuge, 155

herring fishing, 148, 161-2, 163, 164, 166, 169
Highland and Agricultural Society of Scotland, 109-10
Highland County Plan, 239
Highland Deephaven, 266
Highland Land League, 134
Highland Opportunity, report, 250
Highlands Economic Report, 230
Highlands Fabricators (Hifab), 260, 261-2, 266
Highlands and Islands Advisory panel, 239
Highlands and Islands Development Board, 251-3
Hilton, 156, 162, 167
Hog, Rev. Thomas, 47-8, 49-50
Holmes Report, 253
Honourable Society of Improvers in the Knowledge of Agriculture in Scotland, 85
hydroelectricity, 230, 240, 241
hydroplane station, 192-4

Independent Labour Party, 224-5
industry: 18th century, 145, 148; 19th century, 152; post-war development and plans, 239-41, 247-67, 270-1; recent decline, 267-8, *see also specific industries*
Innes family of Plaids, 21-2
Inver, 156
Inverbreakie *see* Invergordon
Invergordon: planning of, 88; development, 112-13; 19th century, 114, 148-50; meal riots, 126-8; harbour, 143, 150, 181-2, 185, 189, 215-17, 247, 252-3, 259-60; Royal Navy and, 178, 181, 182, 187-9, 199, 203, 215-17, 225-6, 228-9, 230-1, 241-2, 267-8; World War I, 211-12; hospital, 212, 215, 230; RAF, 232; industry, 240-1, 247, 247-9, 251-4, 268-9, 270, 271; aluminium smelter, 254-5, 257, 268-9
Invergordon Castle, 83, 85, 88, 218
Invergordon Chemical Enterprises, 251
Invergordon distillery, 247-9, 254
Invergordon estate, 84-5
Invergordon Mutiny, 225-8
Invergordon Steering Group, 257
Invergordon–Balblair Ferry, 143, 216, 217, 259
Iron Age, Celtic, 4-5

Jacobite Rebellions, 85-7; naval activity, 175-7
James IV, King of Scots, 43
James VI, King of Scots, 22, 25
Jellicoe Trains, 235
Jemimaville, 118, 196, 240
Jutland, Battle of, 201-3

kelp, 148, 159
Kennedy, Rev. John, 59
Killearnan, 6

Kilmuir Easter, 18th century, 71
Kiltearn, church, 47-50
Kinbeachie, 223
King's Ferry, 143
Kinkell, 223
Kinrive Wood, 4
Kirkwood, Rev. James, 62
Kyle, Margaret, 26

Lamington, 264
land: common, 77; tenure, 80, 133-5, 218-19; drainage and reclamation, 110
Land Settlement (Scotland) Act, 1919, 222
landlords: relationship with tenants, 79-80; absentee, 117, 121
landscape: creation of, 2; 17th century, 20, 76, 77
law courts, 27, 80-1
law enforcement, 16th century, 21-2
Leslie, John, bishop of Ross, 28-9, 45-6
levies, military, 33-4
libraries, 62-3
lifeboat stations, 155
lighthouses, 155
lime making, 71
linen industry, 71, 72, 73, 90-1, 145, 148
literacy, 61-3
lobster fishing, 169
Loch na h-Annaid, 6, 8
Lochluichart hydro-electric scheme, 230
Loudon, Lord, 175-6
Lovat Scouts, 212, 232
Ludwig, Daniel K., 264

MacAdam, Rev. Alexander, 55
Macbeth, King of Scots, 9, 10
MacDonald, Rev. John, of Ferintosh, 52
MacDonald, Dr Roderick, 134
McGillivray, William, 24
MacHeth Earls of Ross, 10
Mackenzie family, 31-2, 33
Mackenzie, Sir George, of Rosehaugh (Bloody Mackenzie), 32, 46
Mackenzie, Sir George, of Tarbat, 32, 36-9
Mackenzie, Sir George Steuart, of Coul, 107-9
MacKenzie, Murdo, 132
Mackenzie, Sir Rorie, Tutor of Kintail, 32
McKillican, John, 49
MacLaren, James, 112
MacLeod, −, of Geanies, 115
MacLeod, John Mackenzie, Lord Macleod, 86-7
MacPhail, Rev. Hector, 53
Macrae, John, 133
Macrae, John, episcopalian minister, 51
MacTaggart, Sir Farquhar, earl of Ross, 11, 12
Maddadson, Harald, 10
Maddadson, Thorfinn, 10

maps: John Gordon of Straloch, 76; General Roy, 82
Marine Oil Industries Repairs (MOIRA), 265
markets, 116
Martineau, Sir William, 218
Matheson, Sir Alexander, 128-9, 131
meal riots, 124-7
mealers (mailers), 71-2
Mekie, Eoin Cameron, 256
'Men' of Ross-shire, 48
Mesa Oil, 266
middens, 3
Middleton, George, 108
Middleton, George, of Fearn, 108-9
Middleton, Jonathan, of Clay of Allan, 109
Miller, Hugh, 1, 27, 50
millers, 79-80
Milntoun (Milton), 32, 37-8, 112
Miltown, castle, 20
minefields, naval, 200, 203-5, 233
Moluoc, 6
monasteries, 12
Monro, Donald, minister, 44, 45
Montgomery, John, merchant, 71
Moody (Dwight L.) and Sankey (Ira D.), 58
Moray Firth Service Company, 269
Mormaers of Moray, 9, 10
Mountbatten, Lord Louis, 241
Mowat family, 11
Mowat, James, 144
Mulbuie, 74, 77, 123; crofters, 134-5; forest, 223
Munro family, 11, 29, 33; of Foulis, 16
Munro, −, of Culcain, provost of Dingwall, 118
Munro, Sir Alexander, of Novar, 107
Munro, Andrew, of Milton (Black Andrew of the Seven Castles), 79
Munro, Andrew, of Newmore, 79, 81
Munro, Commander Donald John, King's Harbourmaster, Cromarty, 188, 191, 192, 194, 196-7
Munro, George, of Foulis, 25
Munro, Sir George, of Newmore and Culcairn, 29
Munro, George Gun, 111
Munro, Sir George Gun, 117-18
Munro, Hector, of Foulis, 25
Munro, Sir Hector, of Novar, 72, 91-6, 100
Munro, Captain Hugh, of Teaninich, 107, 114
Munro, John (Caird), 48
Munro, Sir John, of Foulis (the presbyterian mortarpiece), 29
Munro, John, of meal riots, 127, 128
Munro, Katherine, Lady Foulis, 23-5
Munro, Col. Robert, 29
Munro, Robert, of Foulis, MP, 118
Munro, Robert, laird of Foulis, 23, 24, 25, 28, 43

Munro, Robert, younger, of Foulis, 23-5
Munro, Robert Dubh (Black Baron), of
    Foulis, 29
Murdoch, John, 133
mussel beds, 164-5

Napier, Admiral Sir Charles, 179-80
Napier Commission, 134, 166
Napoleonic Wars, 109, 116; naval activity,
    177-8
Natal, HMS, 200-1
National Covenant, 47
naval base, 188, 190, 194; suitability of
    Cromarty Firth, 175, 178-9, 180-1, 182-3, *see
    also* Royal Navy
Navity, 8
navy *see* Royal Navy
Nechtan, Pictish king, 8
Neinan, Janet, of Kiltearn, 35
Neolithic age, 3
New Tarbat, 32, 38
New Tarbat estate, 90-1
New Tarbat House/Castle, 32, 38, 112, 146;
    gardens, 83
new towns: 19th century, 112-13; proposed,
    238-9, 253, 264
Newhall estate, 219; crofts, 123-4
Nichol, Bailie Thomas, 133
Nigg: early church at, 6; patronage case, 55;
    18th century, 70-1; Hill of, 77; plain of, 110;
    oil-related industry, 260, 261-2, 264-5, 266-7;
    sandbank, 267
Nigg Revival, 52
Nigg stone, 6
Nigg-Cromarty ferry, 143
Nightingale, Michael, 265
Norman families, 11
North Sea gas, 267
North Sea oil, 259, 260-7, 269-70
Novar Aerodrome *see* Evanton Aerodrome
Novar estate, 72-3, 92-6, 117
Novar House, 94, 233

Obsdale, attack on suspected witches, 26
oil industry, 259, 260-7; platform construction,
    260, 265; Nigg refinery proposal, 264-5;
    Beatrice field, 266; service industries, 266,
    269-70
Orkney, earls of (Scandinavian), 9, 10
oyster beds, 165-6

parklands, enclosing, 83
patronage, 53-5
Perrins, C. W. Dyson, 218
petrochemical complex, 251, 252, 255-6
Phillips, Alastair, 59

Picts, 5-8
Pitcalnie farm, 223
place names: Gaelic, 8-9; Viking, 9; 19th
    century, 111
ploughing, 77
political reform, 118-19
politics, between the wars, 224-5
Pollo, industrial rezoning, 256
poor relief, 60-1, 121-3
population: 18th century, 75; effect of oil
    industry, 262-3
Port an Ab, 156
Port an righ, 160
Porteous, John, minister, 52
Portleich, 156
Portmahomack (Castlehaven), 37, 38, 146,
    156, 163
ports: 17th century, 81; *see also individual
    ports*
potato famine, 123, 125
Poyntz, Charlotte (Mary), 111-12
Poyntzfield (Ardoch), 111
Proplan reports, 252-3

quarries, Kilmuir Easter, 71

railways, 131-2, 153; closure, 250
Rainy, Principal Robert, 59
Redcastle, 10
Reformation, 27-8, 42-6
religion: fishing communities, 157; effects of
    World War I, 212
religious revivals, 52, 55, 58
Resolis, church, 57
roads: ancient tracks, 3; 18th-19th centuries,
    81-2, 115-16; upgrading, 258-9
Robert I, King of Scots (the Bruce), 14-15
Robertson, Rev. Harry, 73
Rockfield, 156
Rose, Hugh, 111
Ross family/clan, 15-16, 33
Ross, earls of, 10, 14-15
Ross, Alexander, of Balnagown, 21-2, 23, 28
Ross, Sir Charles Lockhart, 219-22
Ross, Charles William Lockhart (The
    Jackdaw), 219
Ross, David, of Balnagown, 31
Ross, George, of Balnagown, 23, 29
Ross, George, laird of Cromarty, 75, 90, 91,
    112, 148
Ross, John, rector of Logie, 23
Ross, John Cockburn, 110-11
Ross, Admiral Sir John Lockhart, 71
Ross, Sir John Lockhart, 98
Ross, Katherine, Lady Foulis *see* Munro,
    Katherine
Ross, Marjory, Lady Balnagown, 23-4
Ross, Nicholas, Abbot, 21, 28, 43

Ross, 'Polander', 90, 111, 144
Ross, Thomas, commendator of Fearn, 22
Ross area, origins, 5
Ross-shire Farmers' Society, 110
Rosskeen: church, 53-4, 57; 18th century, 72
Roy, Agnes, 23
Royal Air Force, 217, 231-2, 235-6
royal burghs, 14
Royal Navy: Jacobite uprisings, 175-7;
   Napoleonic wars, 177-8; Crimean War,
   179-80; Fleet visits, 181, 182, 184-6; early
   20th century, 186-94; World War I, 194-205,
   211-12; Invergordon Mutiny, 225-8; target
   ships, 229-30; World War II, 230-1, 232;
   postwar, 241-2, 267-8

Sage, Rev. Donald, of Resolis, 56
St Columba, 6
St Duthac, 13-14
St Duthus Memorial Church, Tain, 42, 50
St Maelrubha, 8
salmon fishing, 145, 169-70
Saltburn, 113, 260
Sankey, Ira D. *see* Moody and Sankey
schools, 61-3
Scots, 5, 8
Scottish Herring Board, 162
Scottish Society for the Propagation of
   Christian Knowledge (SSPCK), 61-2
Scottish Vigilantes, 250
Seaforth Highlanders, 212-13, 233-4
Shand, M. K., 260, 261, 266
Shandwick, 9, 156, 266
Shandwick estate, 110-11
Shandwick House, 111
sheep farming, introduction of, 96-101, 106,
   124
shell-fishing, 169
shipping, 116, 143, 146-54; 17th century, 81;
   World War II, 234-5, *see also* naval base;
   Royal Navy
shipwrecks, 147, 154, 155, 234
Sigurd, Earl, 9
Sinclair, Henry, bishop of Ross, 28, 45
Sinclair, Sir John, 107
smallholdings, 222-3
smallpox, 75
Smertae, 5
smuggling, 155
soldiers: mercenary, 27; recruitment for
   service, 33-4; quartering, 34; settlement, 91,
   222-3; mutiny, 214, *see also* army
sprat fishing, 165
spy scares, 196
standing stones, 4, 6
steam drifters, 168
steam trawlers, 167, 168
steamers, 19th century, 150, 154

Stittenham, 128
Stone Age, 2-3
Strathconon, clearances, 123
Strathglass Fault, 2
Strathoykel, introduction of sheep farming, 98
Strathrusdale, introduction of sheep farming,
   100
submarines, 184, 196, 199-200
Sutors, The, 1, 2; fortifications, 191-2, 214, 231

tacksmen, 80
Tain, 14, 56; 17th century, 20-1; aerodrome,
   232; church, 57; St Duthus Memorial
   Church, 42, 50
tank farms, naval, 234
Tarbat, 37
Tarbat, Lord, 145, 146
Tarbat Ness: battle at, 9; lighthouse, 155
Tarbat peninsula, evacuation, 1943, 237
Teaninich Distillery, 107, 266
Teaninich estate, 107, 129-31
Telford, Thomas, 115, 143, 152, 178
tenants, 79-80
Thomson, Frank, 247-8, 250-2, 254
Thorfinn, Earl, 9-10
tile making, agricultural, 152
timber trade, 145
Tomich, 223
tourism, 121, 154, 230, 240; Cromarty, 250
towns, new *see* new towns
trade: Bronze Age, 4; 16th–17th centuries, 37,
   81, 143-7; 18th century, 75, 146-8; 19th
   century, 116, 150, 152-4; foreign, 143-4, 145,
   154
transport: road, 79, 81-2, 116, 258-9; sea, 81,
   116, 143, 146-54; rail, 131-2, 153
trawlers, 167, 168
trees: planting, 76, 83-4, 96, *see also* forestry

United Free Church, 59-60
United Presbyterian Church, 58-9
Urquhart (parish), Celtic church at, 8
Urquhart family, 16; of Cromarty, 29-31, 33
Urquhart, Adam, 16
Urquhart, Alexander, 146
Urquhart, Sir Alexander, 31
Urquhart, David of Braelangwell, 91
Urquhart, John, of Craigstoun, 31
Urquhart, Leonard, 87
Urquhart, Sir Thomas, 29-31, 36
Urquhart (parish), 18th century, 73, 75

Victory Days, World War II, 238
Vikings, 9
villages, planned, 112, 114-15

ware gathering, 159
Wars of Independence, 14-15

whisky industry, 152, 247-9, 254; Ferintosh, 73-4
William the Lion, King of Scots, 10
Wincott, Len, 226, 227
witchcraft, 23-7, 43
World War I, 210, 212-14; and fishing industry, 168-9; naval activity, 194-205; spy scares, 196; effects, 210, 211-12; readjustments following, 215, 218, 222-4
World War II, 233-8; preparations, 230-3; post-war plans, 238-40
wrecking, 147